Policy Making and Implementation: Studies from Papua New Guinea

Policy Making and Implementation: Studies from Papua New Guinea

EDITED BY R. J. MAY

State, Society and Governance in Melanesia Program
in association with the National Research Institute, Papua New Guinea

Studies in State and Society in the Pacific, No. 5

ANU
THE AUSTRALIAN NATIONAL UNIVERSITY

E PRESS

ANU
E PRESS

Published by ANU E Press
The Australian National University
Canberra ACT 0200, Australia
Email: anuepress@anu.edu.au
This title is also available online at: http://epress.anu.edu.au/policy_making_citation.html

National Library of Australia
Cataloguing-in-Publication entry

Title:	Policy making and implementation : studies from Papua New Guinea / edited by R. J. May.
ISBN:	9781921536687 (pbk.) 9781921536694 (pdf)
Notes:	Includes index.
Subjects:	Policy sciences. Papua New Guinea--Politics and government.

Other Authors/Contributors:
    May, R. J. (Ronald James), 1939-

Dewey Number: 320.609953

Cover design by ANU E Press

Table of Contents

Acknowledgements

The two workshops with which this project was initiated were supported by AusAID, whose assistance is gratefully acknowledged. The second workshop, in Port Moresby, was held in collaboration with the Papua New Guinea Research Institute. Subsequently, in the process of chasing up authors, and editing and formatting for publication, I have been ably assisted by Allison Ley, Sue Rider and Helen Marshall. Finally, in what has been a long gestation process, I am indebted to the various authors who, while in some cases a little slow to produce, have shown great tolerance and collegiality.

Contributors

Bryant Allen is a Senior Fellow in the Department of Human Geography and Convenor of the Division of Society and Environment, Research School of Pacific and Asian Studies at The Australian National University. He was formerly a senior lecturer at the University of Papua New Guinea.

John Ballard is a Visiting Fellow in the Gender Relations Centre, Research School of Pacific and Asian Studies at The Australian National University. He was formerly Professor of Administrative Studies at the University of Papua New Guinea.

Michael Bourke is an Adjunct Senior Fellow in the Land Management Group, Department of Human Geography, Research School of Pacific and Asian Studies at The Australian National University. He was formerly Principal Horticulturalist in the Department of Primary Industry in Papua New Guinea.

Satish Chand is Associate Professor at the Crawford School of Economics and Government at The Australian National University.

Tim Curtin is a member of the Emeritus Faculty of The Australian National University. He was formerly a World Bank adviser in the Papua New Guinea Treasury.

Anne Dickson-Waiko is a Senior Lecturer in the Department of History at the University of Papua New Guinea.

William Dihm is Director of the National Coordinating Office for Bougainville Affairs, Department of the Prime Minister and National Executive Council. He was formerly Secretary of the Papua New Guinea Department of Foreign Affairs (and Trade).

Sinclair Dinnen is a Senior Fellow in the State, Society and Governance in Melanesia Program, Research School of Pacific and Asian Studies at The Australian National University. He formerly taught in the Law Faculty at the University of Papua New Guinea, and was Head of the Crime Studies Division of the Papua New Guinea National Research Institute and Law and Justice Adviser to the government of Papua New Guinea.

John Duguman is a Senior Lecturer in the Division of Environmental Science at the University of Papua New Guinea.

Colin Filer is Convenor of the Resource Management in Asia-Pacific Program, Research School of Pacific and Asian Studies at The Australian National University. He was formerly Associate Professor in the Department of Anthropology and Sociology at the University of Papua New Guinea and Head of the Social and Environmental Studies Division of the Papua New Guinea National Research Institute.

Martin Golman was, at the time of writing, a Divisional Manager with the Papua New Guinea National Forest Authority.

Richard Guy was, at the time of writing, the Head of the Education Studies Division of the Papua New Guinea National Research Institute.

Hartmut Holzknecht is a Visiting Fellow in the Resource Management in Asia-Pacific Program, Research School of Pacific and Asian Studies at The Australian National University. He was formerly Director of the Morobe Province Research Centre and Provincial Planner in the Morobe Provincial Government.

Ben Imbun is a Senior Lecturer in the School of Management, University of Western Sydney. He was formerly Deputy Executive Dean of the School of Business Administration at the University of Papua New Guinea.

Valentine Kambori was, at the time of writing, Director General of the National Agricultural Research Institute of Papua New Guinea. He has also served as Secretary to the Department of National Planning and Monitoring.

Pascoe Kase is Director, Policy and Planning in the Papua New Guinea Department of Health.

David Kavanamur is a Senior Lecturer in the School of Business Administration at the University of Papua New Guinea.

James Laki was, at the time of writing, a Lieutenant Colonel in the Papua New Guinea Defence Force, on secondment as Head of the Political and Legal Studies Division of the Papua New Guinea National Research Institute. He is currently a private consultant.

Clement Malau was, at the time of writing, Director of the Papua New Guinea National AIDS Council. He later served as Project Director for the Burnet Institute's Pacific Regional HIV/AIDS Project, before being appointed as Secretary to the Papua New Guinea Department of Health.

Ronald May is an Emeritus Fellow of The Australian National University and Senior Associate of the State, Society and Governance in Melanesia Program, Research School of Pacific and Asian Studies at The Australian National University. He was formerly Director of the Institute of Applied Social and Economic Research (now the National Research Institute, to which he is currently an adviser).

Bob McKillop is a Sydney-based consultant. He was formerly an agricultural extension officer in Papua New Guinea and has undertaken consultancies for the Department of Primary Industry.

David Mowbray is Associate Professor of Environmental Science at the University of Papua New Guinea.

Tony Power is Managing Director, Sago Industries Ltd. He was formerly Provincial Planner in the East Sepik Provincial Government.

Jane Thomason is a health policy analyst and consultant, and CEO of JTA International. She has undertaken health policy consultancies in Papua New Guinea.

Oswald Tolopa is Director, Policy Division in the Papua New Guinea Department of Lands and Physical Planning.

Mark Turner is a Professor in the Centre for Research in Public Sector Management, School of Business and Management, University of Canberra. He formerly taught at the Papua New Guinea College of Public Administration.

Edward Wolfers is Professor of Politics at the University of Wollongong. He has served for a number of years as Adviser, Governance and Constitutional, to the Papua New Guinea Department of the Prime Minister and National Executive Council and Consultant to the Department of Foreign Affairs.

Charles Yala was, at the time of writing, Senior Research Fellow in the Economics Division of the Papua New Guinea National Research Institute. He is currently a Visiting Fellow in the Crawford School of Economics and Government at The Australian National University.

Glossary

AIDS	Acquired Immune Deficiency Syndrome
ADB	Asian Development Bank
ANU	The Australian National University
ABG	Autonomous Bougainville Government
BCL	Bougainville Copper Limited
CACC	Central Agencies Coordinating Committee
CSA	Commercial Statutory Authorities
CWO	community women's organizers
CPC	Constitutional Planning Committee
DASF	Department of Agriculture, Stock and Fisheries
DEC	Department of Environment and Conservation
DAL	Department of Livestock
DNPRD	Department of National Planning and Rural Development
DPM	Department of Personnel Management
ESD	ecologically sustainable development
ESNO	El Niño-Southern Oscillation
ECP	Enhanced Co-operation Program
FMA	Forest Management Agreement
FLOJ	Foundation for Law, Order and Justice
GPA	Global Program on AIDS
IMF	International Monetary Fund
INA	Institute of National Affairs
ICPNG	Investment Corporation of Papua New Guinea
JDPBPC	joint district planning and budget priorities committee
JAG	Justice Advisory Group
MTDS	Medium Term Development Strategy
MPPC	Minerals and Petroleum Policy Committee
MUG	minimum unconditional grant
NCD	National Capital District
NCW	National Commission for Women
NEFC	National Economic and Fiscal Commission
NEB	National Education Board
NES	National Education Strategy
NEC	National Executive Council
NLOJC	National Law, Order and Justice Council
NPC	National Premiers Council
NRI	National Research Institute

NWDP	National Women's Development Programme
NGO	Non-Government Organisation
OTML	Ok Tedi Mining Ltd
OLPG	Organic Law on Provincial Government
OLPGLLC	Organic Law on Provincial Governments and Local-level Governments
PNGBC	Papua New Guinea Banking Corporation
PNGDF	Papua New Guinea Defence Force
PDGFA	Papua New Guinea Forest Authority
PNGNES	Papua New Guinea National Emergency Services
PJV	Porgera Joint Venture
PMU	Programme Management Unit
PEA	provincial education advisor
PERR	Public Expenditure Review and Rationalisation program
PSC	Public Services Commission
RMS	Resource Management System
RPNGC	Royal Papua New Guinea Constabulary
RTZ	Rio Tinto Zinc
SFTA	school fee and trust account fee
SFS	school fee subsidy
SOE	State-owned enterprise
UBE	Universal Basic Education
UPNG	University of Papua New Guinea
VAT	value-added tax
WID	Women in Development
WWF	World Wide Fund for Nature

Chapter 1

Introduction

R. J. May

There is a vast literature on the principles of public administration and good governance, and no shortage of theoreticians, practitioners and donors eager to push for public sector reform, especially in less-developed countries. Papua New Guinea has had its share of public sector reforms, frequently under the influence of multinational agencies, notably the World Bank and the Asian Development Bank, and aid donors, including AusAID. Yet there seems to be a general consensus, both within and outside Papua New Guinea, that policy making and implementation have fallen short of expectations, that there has been a failure to achieve 'good governance'. This impression is supported in the indifferent performance of key social indicators in Papua New Guinea.

However, since the early post-independence survey of policy making in Papua New Guinea edited by John Ballard (Ballard 1981), there has been little attempt to study the processes of policy making and implementation across a range of sectors and functions. To provide such an overview, a project was initiated in 2002 within the Australian National University's State, Society and Governance in Melanesia Program, with assistance from AusAID, involving a group of scholars and policy practitioners from Papua New Guinea and Australia with deep experience in specific areas of policy, to examine policy making and implementation since independence, across a range of sectors but within a roughly common framework. Draft papers were presented to workshops in Port Moresby and Canberra, and some further papers subsequently added.

After a lengthy gestation, this volume presents the results of the project. The volume comprises a review of the longer-term and the more recent history of public sector reform in Papua New Guinea, thirteen studies of policy making and implementation in particular sectors — the economy, agriculture, mineral development, health, education, lands, environment, forestry, decentralization, law and order, defence, women and foreign policy — and three studies of government policy responses to particular events or policy issues — the 1997–98 drought, privatization and AIDS. These chapters are not intended to provide an up-to-the-minute account of policies in their respective areas — which are subject to continuous change and evolution — but rather to provide an empirical basis for looking at how policy has been made and implemented over some two and a half to three decades since independence.

The record of policy making and implementation varies significantly between sectors and over time. Thus, for example, to take two critical and sometimes controversial areas of policy, Thomason and Kase argue in chapter 7 that since independence the health system has been in a state of steady decline, while Filer and Imbun suggest that in the area of mineral policy (chapter 6), in comparison with other developing countries 'the government has done a reasonably good job of coping with difficult circumstances and unforeseen events'. Despite the variations, however, several themes emerge from these studies.

One concerns a recurring gap between the diagnosis of weaknesses in the policy process and prescription of remedial action, and effective action to implement changes. In their overview of public sector reform in Papua New Guinea (chapter 2), for example, Turner and Kavanamur note that, in a period of 'creeping crisis in public sector management' between 1985 and 1994:

> There were plenty of policy recommendations and ample policy making. There was also considerable interest and funding from donors. But policy design and implementation were often poor while consistent political support from top decision makers was not forthcoming.

Arguably, as in the case of the Public Service Commission whose demise and subsequent restoration both owed much to the recommendations of World Bank missions, or the statement by a visiting Australian consultant that Papua New Guineans had 'no capacity for problem-solving',[1] there have been misdiagnosed and dubious prescriptions as well as ineffective responses to reform initiatives. Nevertheless, at a number of points in this volume authors refer to instances where potentially useful reforms have not been implemented, either because senior public officials or politicians were unsympathetic to changes proposed or were inhibited by inertia, or because the resources needed to effect change were not provided, or because the proposed changes had not been adequately communicated to personnel down the line of command. In their study of lands policy (chapter 9), Power and Tolopa speak of the need for 'a synergy between active individuals in the bureaucracy and committed politicians who have a shared vision and trust with their bureaucrats' but observe that: 'These conditions do not seem to have existed at the national level in matters related to land management for many years'.

Resistance to change is neither unique to Papua New Guinea nor exclusive to the public sector. Comparative studies of public sector reform provide copious examples of behaviour by public servants and ministers designed to delay, stall or generally undermine proposed changes in established policies and practices. In Papua New Guinea this tendency has probably been exacerbated by the unusually influential role which ministers and senior public officials play in policy implementation. At independence it was often argued that senior public servants, mostly schooled within the Australian colonial tradition, tended to dominate their respective ministers, many of whom had limited education and experience in government. Over the years this has changed, to the extent that ministers frequently dictate to their departmental officials and the appointment of senior officials has tended to become increasingly politicized. Since 1995 this has been true also at the sub-national level, where in some provinces, notwithstanding formal procedures, provincial governors (who are normally national MPs) have selected provincial administrators and even district administrators who can be relied on to carry out their wishes. The high turnover of MPs (50–55 per cent from 1972 to 2002, about 80 per cent in 2002, and just over 60 per cent in 2007), and the even higher turnover of cabinet portfolios, has reinforced this trend. In this environment, it is not uncommon for politicians and even some senior bureaucrats to pursue personal agendas over national policy directives.

A second factor militating against effective policy implementation has been the relatively rapid turnover of governments, ministers and senior bureaucrats. As noted in chapter 14, for example, in the six years between 1997 and 2002, Defence had seven ministers and seven departmental secretaries. Similarly, between 1975 and 2002, Wolfers and Dihm note (chapter 16) that there were twenty-four changes of foreign minister. It is often observed that political parties in Papua New Guinea are not sharply differentiated by ideology or policy platform, and that, as a corollary, changes of government are unlikely to produce major changes in policy direction. Nevertheless, the constant turnover of ministers and senior bureaucrats, and frequent — if often relatively minor — shifts in policies create a lack of stability which makes commitment to a given set of policy actions difficult to maintain. This is particularly so where deficiencies of institutional memory are compounded by poor record keeping, as is so often the case in Papua New Guinea (as noted in chapter 12, for example, in 2004 DPLGA could not locate a copy of the National Development Charter it had negotiated with provinces three years earlier). Even where changes in senior leadership positions have been less pronounced, constant shifts in policy and personnel, as described by Guy in relation to education (chapter 8) and Dickson-Waiko for women's policy (chapter 15), can undermine effective policy delivery.

A third theme which emerges from these studies concerns the issue of policy coordination and planning. Arguably, up till 2001 (and some would say even after 2001) planning and budgetary processes were weak, notwithstanding numerous attempts to strengthen them. Donor-assisted initiatives to improve budgetting often failed because donors overestimated the capacity of departments to maintain fairly sophisticated budgetary procedures once advisers had left. Planned and actual expenditures often had only a loose relation to available revenues (and revenue estimation was sometimes unrealistic); the Defence Department's recurring overrun of its budget during the Bougainville conflict, quoted below, provides an extreme example. National sectoral plans often bore little or no relation to planning and budget priority setting at district and provincial level. Failure of service delivery at local, district and provincial level is often 'explained' in terms of a funding deficiency, but not infrequently the real problem is either that the level of planned expenditures has been unrealistic, or that planned expenditures have not been adequately matched to available resources, or (which is often the same thing) that local-level governments have lacked the capacity to spend money allocated for particular purposes. In recent years the need for better policy coordination has been highlighted in public sector reform, but so far with limited effect on policy outcomes.

A fourth theme relates to the impact of political and administrative decentralization. The issue of decentralization is raised in several papers, particularly that on the health sector (chapter 7), in which Thomason and Kase argue that a key factor [in the steady decline in health services available to rural people] has been the impact of successive decentralization reforms on the organization and management of health services. They quote, critically, a provincial administrator who told a member of a 2001 functional and expenditure review team: 'You may have a National Health Plan and a national policy that says health is a top priority, but that's irrelevant because in our province health is a fourth or fifth priority'. Such attitudes are frustrating for people who see a need for central direction by people with technical knowledge and skills which may not be available at the sub-national level. However Papua New Guinea has opted for a decentralized political system in which some functions are exercised at provincial and local level, and if a national policy does not reflect the differences in priorities of sub-national jurisdictions, then it is simplistic to argue that a 'good' national policy has been undermined by decentralization.

Better coordination of nationally-determined priorities and the priorities of provincial and local-level governments is needed. The 'bottom-up' planning process that is supposed to take place through joint provincial/district planning and budgetary priority committees and national priority setting through the Medium Term Development Strategy do not guarantee consistent priorities at the different levels of government and administration, and some functions have been transferred to provincial and local governments without concomitant funding. However, national policies which attempt to dictate actions to be taken by sub-national authorities are doomed to fail.

One aspect of the decentralization issue is the frequent breakdown of communications, and funding arrangements, between Port Moresby and the provinces. In relation to agricultural policy, McKillop, Bourke and Kambori (chapter 5) refer to 'the constraints of a Port Moresby-based bureaucracy', and in discussions with provincial and district officials one frequently hears complaints that public servants in Port Moresby are out of touch with what is happening at the sub-national level. This is a significant factor in the common failure of service delivery at the local level.

It might also be argued that there is a tendency in Papua New Guinea, when desired policy outputs are not forthcoming, to opt for system changes rather than to address identifiable problems within the existing system; the 'reforms' to provincial and local-level government in 1995 and the more recent calls for the creation of district authorities provide examples. Such a tendency is perhaps exacerbated by external donors who are prone to push new policy initiatives, and promote a proliferation of programs, often without knowledge of past policy experiments or a good understanding of why ongoing policies are not working effectively. Where there is not a strong sense of local ownership of policy initiatives, reforms are unlikely to take root.

More generally, while most of the authors in this volume acknowledge the important role of outside assistance in sustaining government services and achieving reforms — Holzknecht and Golman, for example, observe in chapter 11 that the World Bank and AusAID have been 'critical in moving reform agendas in the forestry and conservation sectors' — several also comment on the downside of a growing reliance on outside assistance, including assistance from NGOs. Thomason and Kase, for example, comment that the escalating level of dependence on donor funds to maintain even the most basic of health services has probably played a role in increasing the disempowerment of senior health officials and suggest that provincial governments have been under-resourcing health services in the expectation that donors will meet the shortfall. They also argue that at the national level, 'The sheer number of donors and their teams to "be serviced" by senior health staff reduces time available for focusing on core business'. With reference to agriculture, McKillop, Bourke and Kambori suggest that a decline in the analytical capacity of the Department of Agriculture and Livestock has resulted in a 'policy vacuum' which has attracted outside consultants and lobby groups. 'Policy making in this environment', they say, 'becomes a disjointed and fragmented process that generates contradictory policies shaped by various interest groups'. Similar comments occur in the studies of forestry, minerals, and environmental policies.

But the issues surrounding external assistance are not always straightforward. In their study of the 1997–98 drought in Papua New Guinea (chapter 17), Allen and Bourke refer to Australia's intervention to provide relief to affected communities, given the clearly inadequate response of the Papua New Guinea government at the time. Australia's intervention, Allen and Bourke argue, saved lives but probably damaged the long-term capability of the Papua New Guinea government to deal with such crises in the future — posing a dilemma: 'do nothing and watch some people die; do almost everything because the Papua

New Guinea government cannot, and destroy local morale and the confidence that a crisis can be met with local resources'.

Since the latter part of the 1980s, much of the effort to improve performance in the public sector has been informed by the dominant paradigm of 'new public management' (NPM), with its emphasis on performance management, privatization, corporatization, and downsizing of the public sector.[2] A broader question relating to external influences on public sector reform concerns the impact of measures introduced within the NPM framework.

An account of privatization in Papua New Guinea is provided by Curtin in chapter 18. It records a saga of discontinuity in policy, dubious transactions and popular opposition which, taken against a background of some spectacular private sector failures in developed Western countries, points to the limitations of privatization in small countries with poorly developed capital markets and weak regulatory regimes. Similarly, attempts to corporatize government operations in selected areas, beginning in 1991 with the Papua New Guinea Forest Authority (a move which had more to do with attempts to curb corruption that than to promote efficiency) and progressing through civil aviation, quarantine, fisheries, marine safety and mineral resources, have had at best mixed results in achieving more efficient use of resources and have sometimes clouded issues of accountability. Downsizing, or 'rightsizing', of the public sector — which has a history dating back to 1990 and an association with World Bank structural adjustment loans — has also been questioned in Papua New Guinea (and elsewhere), especially in view of the fact that, by international standards, Papua New Guinea's ratio of government expenditure to GDP is modest and a large part of the government's wages bill goes to teachers and health workers, such that further downsizing is unlikely to be achievable without placing service delivery in priority areas at even greater risk. The applicability of the NPM model to small developing countries is coming under increasing challenge internationally;[3] Papua New Guinea's experience probably lends weight to such challenge.[4]

The authors of the various studies in this volume were not asked to provide recommendations for policy reform or institutional change, but in the course of their analyses of policy making and implementation a number of issues were identified as weaknesses in the policy process. Many of these will be familiar to students of public administration anywhere, though some have distinctive Papua New Guinea dimensions.

One is an apparent decline in capacity in many parts of the bureaucracy, as training regimes have languished and many of the more capable public servants have migrated across to the private sector. A particular aspect of this is what McKillop, Bourke and Kambori refer to, in relation to agricultural policy, as a 'decline in analytical capacity' and Mowbray and Duguman (chapter 10) identify as a disengagement of policy making from research. The studies contained in this volume leave little doubt that in a number of instances policies have been formulated, and sometimes embodied in legislation, without proper analysis of their feasibility, their likely impact, or the extent of support for or opposition to them.

A second is the generally poor level of coordination between government departments and agencies, both horizontally amongst national departments and agencies, and vertically between Port Moresby and the provinces, districts and local-level governments — though, as noted above, there has probably been some improvement in this area since 2001 and a welcome shift to a 'whole-of-government' approach in several instances.

A third is the frequent lack of commitment to policy directives and institutional mechanisms designed to ensure efficient and equitable service delivery and accountability, from the most senior levels down to local officials. At its worst, this is associated with what many see as a rising level of corruption in both the public and private sectors (Ayius and May 2007). In 1981 Ballard wrote that in most new states 'state penetration of society was limited' (Ballard 1981, 3). A quarter of a century later this is still true of many parts of Papua New Guinea, leaving state institutions and agencies vulnerable to manipulation by bigmen and other personal and local interests.

A fourth concerns Papua New Guinea's capacity to absorb advice and assistance from external donors and NGOs without losing a sense of ownership of policy initiatives.

Under the public sector reform agenda introduced by the Morauta government in 1999 and consolidated and extended under the Somare government of 2002–2007, many of these issues are now being addressed. Although there appears to be some way to go before the reporting and monitoring provisions embodied in the reforms (see chapter 3) come fully into effect, it is to be anticipated that these requirements will eventually provide a clearer picture of how effectively the policies embodied in the government's Medium Term Development Strategy are being carried out and where remedial action needs to be directed. In the meantime, the studies presented in this volume provide some baseline data for the assessment of policy making and implementation in Papua New Guinea since 1975.

References

Ayius, Albert and R. J. May eds. 2007. Corruption in Papua New Guinea: Towards an Understanding of Issues. *The National Research Institute Special Publication No.47*. Port Moresby: The National Research Institute.

Ballard, J. A. ed. 1981. *Policy-Making in a New State: Papua New Guinea 1972–77*. St Lucia: University of Queensland Press.

Barzelay, M. with B. J. Armajani. 1992. *Breaking Through Bureaucracy: A New Vision for Managing Government*. Berkeley: University of California Press.

Batley, R. and G. Larbi. 2004. *The Changing Role of Government: The Reform of Public Services in Developing Countries*. Basingstoke: Palgrave Macmillan.

Curtin, T. 1999. Public sector reform in Papua New Guinea and the 1999 budget. *Labour and Management in Development* (online) 1(14): 39.

Minogue, M. 2000. *Should Flawed Models of Public Management be Exported? Issues and Practices*. Manchester: Institute for Development Policy and Management, University of Manchester.

Osborne, D. and T. Gaebler. 1992. *Reinventing Government*. Reading, MA: Addison-Wesley.

Polidano, C. 1999. *The New Public Management in Developing Countries*. Manchester: Institute for Development Policy and Management, University of Manchester.

Pollitt, C. 1993. *Managerialism and the New Public Services*. Second edition. Oxford: Blackwell.

Schick, A. 1998. Why developing countries should not try New Zealand's reforms. *World Bank Research Observer* 13(1): 123–131.

Turner, M. and D. Hulme. 1997. *Governance, Administration and Development: Making the State Work*. Houndmills: Macmillan.

Whimp, K. forthcoming. New public management and its application in developing countries: the case of Papua New Guinea. In *Management for Nationbuilding*, ed. D. Kavanamur, A. Mellam and H. Moshi. Sydney: InFocus Publishing.

World Bank. 1992. *Governance and Development*. Washington DC: World Bank.

World Bank. 1999. *Papua New Guinea: Improving Governance and Performance*. Washington DC: World Bank

Endnotes

[1] Denis Ives, presentation on Public Sector reform in PNG at the Papua New Guinea update, Sydney, May 2004. See http://peb.anu.au/pdf/PNG%20Update%202004-Ives.pdf.

[2] See, for example, World Bank (1992); Osborne and Gaebler (1992); Barzelay (1992); Pollitt (1993); Turner and Hulme (1997); and in relation to Papua New Guinea, World Bank (1999).

[3] See, for example, Schick (1998); Polidano (1999); Minogue (2000); McCourt and Minogue (2001); Batley and Larbi (2004).

[4] For a review of NPM and its application in Papua New Guinea, see Whimp (forthcoming). Also see Curtin (1999).

Chapter 2

Explaining Public Sector Reform Failure: Papua New Guinea 1975–2001

Mark Turner and David Kavanamur

Reforming the bureaucracies bequeathed by departing colonial powers has been a ubiquitous item on the policy agendas of newly independent countries. The contents of the policies have changed over the years and have varied between countries and political regimes. But the declared commitment to public sector reform has remained constant. By contrast, implementation of the reforms has often remained weak, leading to persistent failures or disappointment with the results (Polidano 2001; Hulme and Polidano 1999; Langseth *et al.* 1995; Kiggundu 1998; Manning 2001).

Papua New Guinea appears to have conformed to this pattern since independence in 1975. A promising start with public sector reform was soon overtaken by policy failure. A succession of reports and publications has traced and lamented declining efficiency and effectiveness in public sector performance (World Bank 1983, 1995, 1999; AusAID 1992, 1994, 1996; Turner 1997; PDP 1997). Conventional explanations blame inadequate bureaucratic capacity or inappropriate donor solutions. Such accounts have validity at one level of analysis, but as one digs deeper another explanation of policy failure is uncovered. That is politics. The hypothesis of this study is that chances of reform failure increase when important sections of the political elite see no direct benefits accruing to themselves or their supporters from public sector reform. While they may wish to control the public sector, they may not wish to pursue reforms which would lead to better performing and more accountable public institutions. Changing reform menus may have little effect in such situations where local political dynamics determine the outcomes of the policy process. For similar reasons, decision-makers may choose to ignore lessons that are known. Building bureaucratic capacity in such circumstances may be a dubious policy, as that capacity may be ignored or misdirected instead of being harnessed to serve the public interest.

1975–1984: tinkering with bureaucracy

Just before independence in 1975, Michael Somare, the prime minister-to-be, expressed concern that 'the public service systems inherited from Colonial

Administration have been unsuitable for a self-governing and eventually independent Papua New Guinea' (Somare 1974, 4). He noted that the public service was an alien apparatus designed for alien purposes. It had an inappropriate modern technology and was too expensive (*ibid.*; Ballard 1981). Reform was undoubtedly needed, said Somare, but incrementally, to avoid undue disruption.

Paradoxically, the period started off with a piece of radical reform. The state was restructured through a devolutionary form of decentralization. Michael Somare had originally dispensed with the Constitutional Planning Committee's recommendation for decentralization, but a secessionist move and other micronationalist movements exerted strong political pressure to follow the devolutionary path. The 1977 Organic Law on Provincial Government gave elected provincial assemblies the responsibility for a range of functions mostly involving service delivery. But the centre still retained some controls. The purse strings were held by the Department of Finance while staff of the new departments of the provinces kept their status as national public servants. Central agencies were often unenthusiastic about decentralization while many public servants were reluctant participants in the process. By 1979, Somare was voicing concern about the implementation of provincial government and in 1985 he wanted a national referendum on its future. Other parliamentarians joined the supporting chorus, possibly through anxiety over the growing power of provincial politicians.

The other leading policies of public sector reform were incremental in nature: localization, public sector growth, training and restructuring. They were non-threatening and elicited widespread support from public servants and politicians.

Localization was the replacement of foreign public sector employees by Papua New Guinean staff. The policy had been instituted before independence. Post-independence localization extended the process upwards and also looked to the total elimination of lower-level foreigners in a short space of time. There is some dispute over the number of expatriates employed in the public service and hence no agreed figure on the rate of localization. Dwivedi (1986) counted 4135 expatriate public servants at independence declining to 2480 in 1985. Another study located 6730 expatriates in 1976 reducing to 3000 in 1985 (Goodman *et al.* 1985). Whatever the numbers, the policy was popular with Papua New Guinean public servants as it opened up numerous promotional opportunities. In financial circles it was applauded because of savings from expensive expatriate salaries. However, one commentator pointed to an 'administrator development lag' (McNamara 1983). He thought the localization process had proceeded too rapidly with the new incumbents of executive positions often lacking the experience and qualifications to undertake their roles effectively.

Public sector growth was another popular policy. The prevailing argument supporting this was enshrined in the Eight Aims which guided Papua New Guinea's national development strategy: 'Government control and involvement in those sectors of the economy where control is necessary to achieve the desired kind of development' (PNG 1976, 15). This justified extending the range of government activities and the numbers of staff engaged in some existing ones. At independence there were approximately 50,000 public servants and another 15–20,000 labourers and employees of statutory authorities (Turner 1991). This represented about 40 per cent of formal employment. By 1981, there were 55,000 public servants. The government began to feel the economic pinch and in 1983 reported that 'Continuing international recession has reduced government revenues…[and] the scale of the adjustment problem is far more serious than previously anticipated' (PNG 1983, 1–2). A retrenchment program was introduced with aim of removing 3,300 funded positions and their 'ineffective' occupants (Turner 1991, 98). The government also justified the policy in terms of the 'very large number of public servants per capita' (PNG 1983, 87), an assertion questioned by some authors (Dwivedi 1986; Bailasi 1990; Turner 1991). The initial experiment with downsizing was not successful in reducing the size of the public service but it did halt expansion.

Training was a major thrust of Papua New Guinea's post-independence strategy to improve its public administration. Training was equated with capacity-building. Knowledge, skills and values were learned by new and existing staff and then put into practice to make for better organizational performance. The Administrative College (Adcol), an arm of the Department of the Public Services Commission, was given major responsibility for the training function. It ran a wide range of pre-service and in-service courses of varying durations covering fields including district administration, public administration, social development, financial management, accounting, general management, local government and librarianship. But concern grew that administrative training had failed to bring about the promised improvements in public sector management. One report concluded that Adcol was characterized by inefficient resource deployment and courses which were no longer appropriate (Turner 1985). However, training was still perceived as a valid strategy for public sector reform, and additional reports recommended better resource management and increased investment in training (Gibson 1983; Creedon 1984).

The final strategy of public sector reform in the immediate post-independence era was restructuring. This involved amputating sections of departments and then reattaching them to other departments or parts of departments. Reshuffling heads of departments and statutory bodies often accompanied this process. What was occurring in Papua New Guinea under the name of restructuring actually left the structural features of organizations largely intact. They did not become less bureaucratic. Indeed, the basic organizational dysfunctions were preserved but were now accompanied by a sense of insecurity and lack of continuity in leadership.

The first decade of independence was characterized by an incremental strategy of public sector reform. The reform and capacity-building activities threatened neither basic organizational forms and practices nor leading officials. Indeed it was a time of great opportunity for officials to get ahead through localization and public sector expansion. However, concerns were being expressed that all was not well with the system of public sector management. The ToRobert Report of 1979 found that Papua New Guinea's administrative system was not responding effectively to national plans and objectives. Capacity problems in public sector management were identified as the culprit and the incremental approach to reform was reaffirmed in the report (PNG 1979). The resulting Administrative Improvement Programme contained various familiar human resource management items on staff development and training, manpower statistics and assessment, job evaluation, documentation of simplification of procedures, staff assessment and appraisal, and career streaming (PNG 1980). There is little record of action and achievement in these or other areas of concern identified in the ToRobert Report. The first World Bank report devoted to public administration in Papua New Guinea reiterated the issues raised in the ToRobert Report but described public administration in Papua New Guinea as a 'generally well-functioning system. In particular, [there were] strong and carefully controlled budget procedures' (World Bank 1983, 1).

1985–1994: the creeping crisis in public sector management

The decade from 1985 can be seen as one of a creeping crisis in public sector management. The term 'creeping crisis' refers to situations 'where a succession of events transforms itself into an acute crisis' (Rosenthal *et al.* 1989, 27). The crisis was not brought about by a lack of policy or interest. There were plenty of policy recommendations and ample policy-making. There was also considerable interest and funding from donors. But policy design and implementation were often poor while consistent political support from top decision-makers was not forthcoming. Concern with accountability faded. The result was a decline in bureaucratic performance, and the public service management that the World Bank had described as 'basically sound' in 1983 became basically unsound by 1995.

Despite its declared general satisfaction with public sector management in Papua New Guinea, the World Bank's 1983 report actually pointed to a number of major problems which required urgent remedial treatment. The public service was too big, over-centralized, hamstrung by excessive proceduralism, lacking incentives for staff, biased against training provincial public servants, and presided over by a Public Services Commission (PSC) which 'could and did ignore the Government of the day' (Cochrane 1986, 58). The response of the Papua New Guinea government was to request assistance from the World Bank to revise the constitution to pave the way for a reduction in PSC powers and then restructure the public service. The request was positively received by the World Bank and in 1984 the Programme Management Unit (PMU) was set up to accomplish these ambitious objectives.

The major casualty of these reforms was the PSC. Since independence it had determined personnel matters and had an autonomy which could lead it to oppose or obstruct government policy. Politicians believed that the PSC was simply too powerful while administrators were frustrated by PSC-induced delays to their projects. Its conversion to an advisory body at the margins of government was not mourned in official circles. The cabinet now became responsible for the broad direction of human resource management (HRM) policy and for appointing heads of departments and agencies. A new 'streamlined' Department of Personnel Management (DPM) was allocated some of the PSC's former general functions and was answerable to cabinet. Many personnel responsibilities were scheduled to be delegated to departmental heads. Efficiency was to be the hallmark of the new HRM system.

Results did not support the theory. The demise of the PSC heralded the increased politicization of the public service. Personal connections started to become more significant determinants of who occupied seats on boards of public authorities or filled the higher departmental positions. The new DPM turned out to be 'a renamed and slightly restructured Department of the PSC with the same staff, the same equipment and the same premises' (Turner 1991, 102). There was no visible improvement in efficiency and no formal monitoring or evaluation. It was somewhat optimistic to expect the Department of the PSC, renowned for red-tape and slowness, to reinvent itself overnight. A succession of projects promised significant improvements in DPM efficiency but there is little evidence of their operations or achievements.

Restructuring was also in the PMU's terms of reference. Detailed diagnoses of organizational pathologies were conducted and remedies suggested for each of the cases. It is doubtful whether the PMU's efforts resulted in improved organizational outcomes. Weak monitoring and evaluation processes meant that, with the demise of the PMU, nobody was examining the implementation of the departmental reform programs.

Another PMU initiative was the Resource Management System (RMS). The RMS had been decreed by cabinet in 1984 but it took the PMU some time to decide what it actually was. The thrust of RMS was to create a new comprehensive planning system which would encompass all the activities of departments and agencies. There would be no divide between recurrent and project budgets. Evaluation would be according to outcomes and outputs and not simply expenditure control. It was to be authentically Papua New Guinean with a strong participative bottom-up approach. The system-wide re-engineering of public sector management would produce accelerated development. This was not to be: there was much objective-writing, timetable-setting and mission-debating, but the RMS did not eventuate as the guiding force of the public sector. There were few supporters outside of the PMU. Many departments did not understand the RMS and saw it as theory devoid of practical relevance. The cabinet appeared to lose interest, absorbed as ever by crisis management and maintaining numbers in parliament. This made it even easier for large central agencies to resist RMS advances. There were also financial constraints greatly exacerbated by a secessionist movement on Bougainville which destroyed the country's largest mine and export earner.

Training was the final component of PMU's broad-ranging activities. The PMU had identified a range of training requirements through its work in organisational analysis. A Central Planning Assistance Team (CPAT) was set up 'to generate training needs and requirements at the provincial level' (PMU n.d., 1). A Transitional Training Unit (TTU) was also formed to conduct management. Like most PMU activities, the TTU initiative started with great enthusiasm but had either disappeared or become entirely marginalized before its declared use-by date. The World Bank now stepped in to assist with the ever-popular non-threatening reform strategy of training. The Bank agreed to fund the government's 1989 National Training Policy. The project was costed at $US23 million and comprised yet another capacity-building effort in DPM, institutional strengthening of the Department of Labour and Employment, support for the new National Training Council, and overseas fellowships. But once again, implementation was not as anticipated in the project plans, and achievements fell well short of targets.

In 1990, budgetary pressures and continuing concerns over the size of the public service led to another downsizing exercise. In common with its predecessors it failed to achieve its objectives (AusAID 1992). While retrenchments were double the 1,250 target, the public service remained the same size because of new hiring. Also, the scheme's generous benefits proved attractive to more competent public servants. In 1992, the government established a Rationalisation Task Force with a familiar brief: 'to examine ways in which the national departments could be restructured and their management practices improved so that the cost of government could be reduced and its efficiency improved' (AusAID 1994, 146). Two years later, an AusAID review of Papua New Guinea noted that the task force's report had been referred to the Policy

Coordination and Monitoring Committee for consideration but that the report was not available for public discussion.

Another familiar theme on the public sector reform agenda was the question of what to do with public enterprises. In 1979, there had been a report by an IMF adviser recommending the government to 'get prices right' (Millett 1993, 6). No action was taken by the government, and in 1982 a study was commissioned by the private sector think-tank, the Institute of National Affairs (INA). This study advised that many public enterprises had performed poorly and needed attention (Trebilcock 1982). Recommendations to improve efficiency and to privatize were provided but not acted upon. In 1983, a public enterprise reform policy was belatedly unveiled based on the 1979 IMF report. It contained various actions to improve the efficiency of public enterprises and by 1987 their performance had improved in absolute terms and in terms of returns on assets (Whitworth 1989). In 1989, privatization was mooted in the Administrative Reform and Improvement Programme in a proposed project to prepare a program of public enterprise sale and to determine what to do with non-performing assets. The structural adjustment loan of 1990 then resulted in the establishment of a national privatization committee. However, progress on privatization was slow and corporatization was only marginally superior. In 1992, the PNG Holdings Corporation was established to develop and implement policy on privatization but little progress was recorded (AusAID 1994). During the period 1985–1994 there was a great deal of policy talk on corporatization and privatization but action was much less apparent. (Policies on privatization are discussed in more detail in chapter 17.) The similarity with downsizing, restructuring and other areas of public sector reform is striking. In all cases there was little implementation.

Meanwhile there was mounting evidence that service delivery was continuing to decline. Mainly in reference to provincial government, May (1999, 123) referred to 'copious documented and anecdotal evidence of lax and inefficient administration, nepotism and outright corruption', noting that he had also witnessed such things in his own fieldwork. As the mid 1990s approached, the World Bank (1995, 12, 16, 19, 22) reported a health system that was 'deteriorating', an education system that 'does not appear to be improving', 'a totally inadequate sum' of government money devoted to agriculture, and 'considerable scope for increasing the effectiveness of infrastructure expenditure'. Everybody agreed that the public was not being served properly and that the situation was getting worse. The creeping crisis in public sector management appeared to have transformed into an acute crisis.

1995–2001: the acute crisis of public sector management

The period 1995–2001 is characterized by recognition of the urgency of the need for public sector reform by government, donors and the long-suffering public.

A steady stream of reports reiterated the need for action to address serious problems in almost every aspect of public sector management (World Bank 1995, 1999; AusAID 1996, 2000; PDP 1997; Turner 1997). The result was a corresponding stream of reform initiatives. These derived both from the external pressures of donors and from domestic initiatives.

One of the first reforms was very much a domestic matter. This was the introduction of major changes to the provincial government system which had been subject to increasing criticism. National politicians and public servants claimed the system was too expensive, lacked financial accountability and was responsible for poor service delivery. Others saw the reforms being about national parliamentarians seeking control over subnational resources and management and not about efforts to improve governance (Filer 2000). There is no systematic evaluation of the 1995 changes but available evidence points to widespread policy failure.[1]

Pre-existing capacity problems in provinces and districts were not fully appreciated by the law's drafters and appear to have been exacerbated. There have been complaints that funds are inadequate to perform decentralized functions. There has been little training. There is weak planning capacity at all levels and infrastructure is in severe decline. The National Monitoring Authority which was established to develop minimum service standards and monitor performance has not been effective. Officials in rural areas complain that the system is complicated and creates confusion among stakeholders. They also report that the bottom-up system of district and provincial planning committees has been characterized by misuse of funds. Many district planning committees exist only in theory while lack of proper accounting records at provincial level facilitates financial mismanagement (see chapter 12).

While central-local relations were being reformed the country was experiencing severe economic difficulties necessitating a World Bank/IMF-sponsored stabilization and structural adjustment program (SAP) in 1994. Thus, in order to secure release of the second tranche of a $US50 million loan from the World Bank in April 1995, the government promised: a public sector wage freeze from April–December 1995; retrenchment for 7.5 per cent of public servants; improvement of personnel management and payroll controls; restructuring of finance and planning functions; privatization; and regrouping, consolidation and corporatization of agencies. The reform agenda was now being set by the multilateral financial institutions, although some of the reform measures were very familiar.

The most familiar measure was downsizing. Under the government's 1995–96 economic reform program, around 3,800 positions were scheduled for abolition (AusAID 2000). Another 700 positions would go later. As usual, the figures were confusing. Some suggest that 2,750 public servants were retrenched (Kavanamur

1998) while others claim that the public service actually increased by 3,183 persons between 1993 and 1997 (Kavanamur and Kinkin 2000). Other reform initiatives to satisfy the multilaterals included a continuation of non-threatening institutional strengthening projects; the normal and ineffectual restructuring of agencies, such as the planning office three times between mid-1995 and 1999; and shuffling of executives (Turner 1997; World Bank 1999). The World Bank was disappointed with progress on conditionalities while the Papua New Guinea government thought the Bank was interfering with the nation's sovereignty (Kavanamur 1998). Relations between the parties deteriorated and the second tranche of $US25 million was released only after the personal intervention of World Bank president, James Wolfensohn.

The government of Prime Minister Bill Skate was next to introduce public sector reforms, not at the behest of the World Bank but on the advice of one of its former Papua New Guinea specialists, Dr Pirouz Hamidian-Rad. While he argued that the World Bank was trying to bully Papua New Guinea to making policy decisions, some of which were unnecessary, he also announced that what Papua New Guinea needed was an aggressive public sector reform program (Wesley-Smith 1999). He believed political manoeuvring in Papua New Guinea would always derail any piecemeal approach. Politicians and bureaucrats would initially agree to reforms only to relent later once loans were released (personal communication, Hamidian-Rad 1998).

Despite the anti World Bank rhetoric, the reform program which emerged in the 1999 budget had strong affiliation with World Bank orthodoxy, except it seemed to be more extreme. The situation was neatly summed up as 'structural adjustment without loans' (Filer 2000). Seven thousand (later 7,500) personnel were to be retrenched. There were no plans indicating who would go, no strategic review of personnel needs. This ambitious policy of across-the-board cuts failed to materialize due to the government's inability to raise the necessary funds to pay for it. Paradoxically, one analyst claimed a net increase of 3,000 public service employees in 1999 (Manning 1999). Privatization returned to the policy agenda with a move to establish a Private Enterprise Ministry to identify which government agencies should be privatized. The 1999 budget also contained provisions to relocate 2,000 personnel to the provinces; the abolition of fifteen statutory authorities and committees; and yet another restructuring for most government departments. Skate's reform effort provoked considerable opposition and his government collapsed in July 1999.

The World Bank breathed a sigh of relief as Sir Mekere Morauta, a technocrat, stepped up to become prime minister. He soon unveiled a reform program which he was anxious to differentiate from previous ones so as to harness local support. Earlier programs, he said, were externally imposed, not understood, and never fully implemented (*Papua New Guinea Post-Courier* 30 November 1999). Thus,

Morauta adopted the label 'Structural Reform Program' (SRP) to distinguish his policy.

But whatever the rhetoric, this new reform initiative embodied ideas favoured by the multilateral financial agencies and had the support of foreign consultants to the Morauta government. His broad goals were to promote good governance and strengthen the institutions of state; to build macroeconomic, financial and budget stability; to introduce public sector reform for improved public sector performance; and to remove obstacles to economic growth. It had obvious kinship with measures proposed in earlier reports for the World Bank (1995, 1999) and AusAID (1996), which called for an urgent adherence to good governance and institutional strengthening.

The Morauta government's wide-ranging reforms also included a new element — political parties and the electoral process, which were seen as being at the heart of bad governance and irrational behaviour by public officials. The quality of the policy process could be improved through political engineering rather than traditional capacity-building initiatives (*The National* 24 April 2001). This new approach led to the Organic Law on the Integrity of Political Parties and Candidates of 2001. Its objective was to limit the numerical dominance of independent MPs and their party-hopping practices as well as to reduce the burgeoning number of political parties. There were additional proposals to reform the electoral system by replacing the current first-past-the-post method with a limited preferential voting (LPV) system to broaden a candidate's representativeness and hence accountability. Under the first-past-the-post system candidates often won seats with small proportions of the total vote, not infrequently under 10 per cent, and then devoted their parliamentary activities to satisfying that narrow constituency (Reilly 2002; Kavanamur 2001; Okole 2001).

Privatization returned to the forefront of reform with the decision of the Morauta government and the Privatisation Commission to sell 75 per cent of the state-owned Papua New Guinea Banking Corporation (PNGBC) to a local private bank (*Papua New Guinea Post-Courier* 24 January 2002). PNGBC was a badly performing asset but opposition to its privatization was strong. In 2001 student-led protests against privatization and land reform resulted in the deaths of three students at the hands of police riot squads, but Morauta pushed on with the privatization.

Morauta also made efforts to restore power to the Public Services Commission (PSC). The objectives were to eliminate the power of politicians to appoint cronies and business associates to senior positions in the public sector; to curb the proliferation of consultancy positions; and to strengthen the PSC's role in appeals on personnel matters. The politicians baulked at the power losses entailed in this legislation and the item was removed from government business.

Morauta halted Skate's policy of downsizing the public service by reinstating suspended officials. But he lined up the Papua New Guinea Defence Force (PNGDF) as a new target of downsizing. Mutiny, disorder and a government-threatening stand-off with troops accompanied this policy initiative. The troops were particularly angry about foreign involvement in determining the downsizing. A new reform package designed internally saved the day but did not prevent a further mutiny in 2002 (see chapter 14). Morauta also responded to multilateral and domestic concerns over the sorry state of the public sector financial system, including widespread corruption.

To pay for these public sector reform initiatives, multilateral assistance was sought. A Governance Promotion Adjustment Loan (GPAL) for $US90 million was provided by the World Bank in 2000 for improving budget management, including debt management, through increased transparency and accountability; delivery of provincial services; forestry management; and the efficiency of financial services, including the privatization of the PNGBC, as well as enhancing the operating environment for business. The Asian Development Bank (ADB) also contributed a $US25.8 million loan in association with AusAID and UNDP in October 1999 for a Financial Management Project (FMP) aimed at improving: planning and budgeting systems; budget execution and accounting systems; information technology systems; the government enterprise network; training and human resources development; and change and program management (ADB 1999). By December 2001, the ADB had approved a further $US70 million loan towards a second public sector reform project known as the Public Service Program (PSP), to be completed in 2003. This program was aimed at supporting policy and institutional reform to build a performance-based public sector and reorient human resources management systems and processes in public sector organizations (ADB 2001). Part of the loan was for short-term structural adjustment costs relating to retrenchments and service improvement plans.

To oversee these and other reforms Morauta established an interdepartmental panel known as the Central Agencies Coordinating Committee (CACC) headed by the chief secretary. The CACC closely liaises with the Public Sector Reform Management Unit (PSRMU), which like the Chief Secretary's office is located within the Department of the Prime Minister and National Executive Council. Parallels with the PMU of a previous decade are obvious. The CACC coordinates implementation of reforms and reports on a monthly basis to the cabinet, the World Bank and other donors such as AusAID.

Conclusion

Public sector reform in Papua New Guinea can be regarded as a case of poor policy practice. There has been no shortage of policy making. Many initiatives can be identified. Where the policies have come to grief has been in implementation. From a technical point of view we can identify a familiar list of problems. There has been little attention to policy analysis, specifically an anticipation of where policies could go wrong. For example, policies are announced when the capacity to implement them is obviously lacking or the financial ramifications are not worked through. Other technical deficiencies include poor definition of processes and responsibilities; inadequate supervision; lack of trained staff; slowness of bureaucratic action; constant turnover of managers; insufficient coordination; and infrastructure shortcomings.

While the technical explanations of policy failure have validity in delineating what the public sector lacks, it is in the political dimension of reform that we find the important root causes. As Caiden (1969, 8) advised, public sector reform is 'transformation against resistance'. In Papua New Guinea the capacity to resist has been extremely strong. Sometimes it may be better described as the capacity to ignore, the exercise of power by doing nothing (Lukes 1974). The technical shortcomings occur because there is no concerted effort by the political elite to ensure that implementation of public sector reform conforms to the policy plans. Despite the numerous consultants' reports and grand statements by prime ministers, there appears to have been remarkably little interest in following through on public sector reform. Leading officials have not monitored reforms, demanded regular updating, enforced accountability and supervised reform initiatives.

There are several reasons for this. In part it stems from the nature of Papua New Guinea politics, in which particularistic concerns of staying in office and of satisfying small groups of supporters have dominated political life. Parties do not have platforms or policies. Thus, Prime Minister Morauta's attempts to engage in political engineering may have a more profound effect on public sector performance than repeated institutional strengthening programs. Secondly, crisis government is typical, and in such circumstances long-term public sector reform is simply not a priority. It is rather dull and does not attract votes. It thus becomes unattractive to own public sector reform. Ownership is sometimes forced upon unwilling political leadership by multilateral financial agencies, but in such circumstances, domestic commitment may be limited.

The third political aspect of public sector reform relates to control of public resources, the public service, and appointments in it. It is significant that the public service reforms that have been pushed through parliament have been of domestic origin and concerned with enhancing the power of the national political elite. They have secured control of appointments and subnational government while simultaneously allowing accountability to go into decline. When looked at from this viewpoint, public sector reform which produces good governance is actually a major threat to the political elite. While the system does not work for the majority of Papua New Guineans it may well work for many in the political elite.

One final and little-used explanation of the unreceptiveness of stakeholders in Papua New Guinea to reform measures concerns the organizational model which they use as a reference. It is a model of bureaucratic organizational structures and practices. This model has inherent dysfunctions such as an input orientation rather than a focus on results. Its colonial origins may also put it at odds with indigenous culture as Michael Somare observed before independence. But in Papua New Guinea the dysfunctionality has been greatly boosted by unplanned changes such as the politicization of appointments, the weak development of public accountability, the absence of evaluation, and low morale. The result is a severely deformed bureaucratic form of organization which bears little if any resemblance to the rationality of the Weberian ideal type. Its members are highly suspicious of change and anyway often lack the capacity to design and implement changes that would lead to performance improvement. The pursuit of political agendas has contributed to the bureaucracy's incremental decay rendering it inappropriate for the tasks it is supposed to perform.

The quest for public sector reform will undoubtedly continue. In 2002 multilateral and bilateral agencies were pouring in money for this purpose and hopes were high. According to the ADB (2001), Papua New Guinea is 'moving to a performance based public sector'. This may prove to have been an optimistic assertion. Previous predictions of reform success have often fallen short of expectation. Some rethinking of policies is essential, as is the capacity to learn the lessons of earlier failures. The learning is not simply a matter for Papua New Guinean officials but also for the international financial agencies which have been and still are so heavily involved in promoting public sector reform. There is also much room for popular involvement, not simply as presenting unrealistic wish lists of projects but in sharing information, participating in planning and assuming some responsibility for accountability. Seeking good practice in Papua New Guinea and how to replicate it is another underutilized strategy, as is good research on management matters. A continuing problem is that we still know very little about how organizations work in Papua New Guinea. But above all else there will need to be changes in the politics of public sector management if reforms are to be successful and the ADB's promised 'performance based public sector' becomes a reality.

References

AusAID. 1992. The *Papua New Guinea Economy: Prospects for Recovery, Reform and Sustained Growth*. Canberra: AusAID.

AusAID. 1994. *Papua New Guinea: The Role of Government in Economic Development*. Canberra: AusAID.

AusAID. 1996. *The Economy of Papua New Guinea*. International Development Issues, No.46. Canberra: AusAID.

AusAID. 2000. *Australia and Papua New Guinea Development Cooperation Program 2000–2003*. Canberra: AusAID.

Asian Development Bank (ADB). 1999. *ADB to strengthen Papua New Guinea's public financial management*. News Release No. 095/99. Manila: Asian Development Bank. http://www.adb.org/Documents/News/1999/.

Asian Development Bank (ADB). 2000. *Financial Management and Governance Issues in Papua New Guinea*. Prepared Under Regional Technical Assistance (RETA) 5877: Strengthening Financial Management and Governance in Selected Developing Member Countries. Manila: Asian Development Bank.

Asian Development Bank (ADB). 2001. *Moving to a performance based public sector in Papua New Guinea*. News Release No.192/01. Manila: Asian Development Bank. http://www.adb.org/Documents/News/2001/.

Bailasi, H. 1990. Public Service Innovations — the Papua New Guinea Experience. Unpublished paper presented to the American Society for Public Administration, Los Angeles.

Ballard, J. 1981. Reforming the bureaucratic heritage. In *Policy-Making in a New State: Papua New Guinea 1972–77,* ed. J. Ballard, 75–94. St Lucia: University of Queensland Press.

Caiden, G. 1969. Development administration and administrative reform. *International Social Science Journal* 21(1): 9–22.

Cochrane, G. 1986. *Reforming National Institutions for Economic Development*. Boulder and London: Westview.

Creedon, D. 1984. *A Training Strategy for Papua New Guinea's Public Service*. Report prepared for the World Bank and Public Services Commission. Port Moresby.

Dwivedi, O. 1986. Growth of the public service in Papua New Guinea. In *The Public Service of Papua New Guinea*, ed. O. Dwivedi and N. Paulias, 72–89. Boroko: Administrative College of Papua New Guinea.

Filer, C. 2000. *The Thin Green Line: World Bank Leverage and Forest Policy Reform in Papua New Guinea*. NRI Monograph 37. Waigani and Canberra: National Research Institute and the Australian National University.

Gibson, R. 1983. *Bilateral Aid Programme to Papua New Guinea: Public Service Management Training. A Training Needs Analysis*. Wellington: State Services Commission.

Goodman, R., C. Lepani and D. Morawetz, D. 1985. *The Economy of Papua New Guinea: An Independent Review*. Canberra: Australian National University, Development Studies Centre.

Hulme, D. and C. Polidano. 1999. Public management reform in developing countries: issues and outcomes. *Public Management* 1(1): 121–32.

Kavanamur, D. 1998. The politics of structural adjustment in Papua New Guinea. In *Governance and Reform in the South Pacific*, ed. P. Larmour. Pacific Policy Paper 23, 99–120. Canberra: Australian National University, National Centre of Development Studies.

Kavanamur, D. 2001. *The interplay between politics and business in Papua New Guinea*. State, Society and Governance in Melanesia Project Working Paper 01/6. State, Society and Governance in Melanesia Project. Canberra: Australian National University. http://rspas.anu.edu.au/melanesia.

Kavanamur, D. and E. Kinkin. 2000. The cost of contract employment, consultancy engagement and office/accommodation rentals in the public service. *Catalyst* 30(2): 114–52.

Kiggundu, M. 1998. Civil service reforms: limping into the twenty-first century. In *Beyond the New Public Management: Changing Ideas and Practices in Government*, ed. M. Minogue, C. Polidano and D. Hulme, 155–71. Cheltenham: Edward Elgar.

Langseth, P., S. Nogxina, D. Prinsloo and R. Sullivan eds. 1995. *Civil Service Reform in Anglophone Africa*. Pretoria: Economic Development Institute, Overseas Development Administration and Government of South Africa.

Lukes, S. 1974. *Power: A Critical View*. London: Macmillan.

McNamara, V. 1983. Learning to operationalise policies: factors in the administrator development lag. *Administration for Development* 20: 19–42.

Manning, M. 1999. Papua New Guinea: Short to Medium Term Scenario. Paper presented at the Centre for Independent Studies, Sydney.

Manning, N. 2001. The legacy of the new public management in developing countries. *International Review of Administrative Sciences* 67(2): 263–71.

May, R. J. 1999. Decentralization in Papua New Guinea: two steps forward, one step back. In *Central-Local Relations in Asia-Pacific: Convergence or Divergence*, ed. M. Turner, 124–45. London: Macmillan.

May, R. J. 2005. *District Level Governance in Papua New Guinea: Preliminary Report of a Pilot Study*. SSGM Report. State, Society and Governance in Melanesia Project, Australian National University.

Millett, J. 1993. *Privatisation in Papua New Guinea: Limited Scope, Slow Progress*. Institute of National Affairs Discussion Paper no. 56. Port Moresby.

Okole, H. 2001. The Fluid Party System of Papua New Guinea: Continuity and Change in a Third Wave Democracy. Unpublished PhD dissertation, University of Northern Illinois.

Papua New Guinea. 1976. *National Development Strategy*. Waigani: Central Planning Office.

Papua New Guinea. 1979. *Report of the Committee on Administrative Improvement in the Public Service* (ToRobert Report). Waigani.

Papua New Guinea. 1980. *The National Public Expenditure Plan 1980–1983*. Waigani: National Planning Office.

Papua New Guinea. 1983. The National Public Expenditure Plan 1983–1986. Waigani: National Planning Office.

Policy Development and Planning Australia Pty. Ltd. 1997. *Review of the Functions of Government: a Framework for Delivering Goods and Services in Papua New Guinea*. Report prepared for the National Planning Office, Government of Papua New Guinea.

Polidano, C. 2001. Why civil service reforms fail. *Public Management Review* 3(3): 345–62.

Programme Management Unit (PMU). 1988. The Resource Management System: an overview. Unpublished discussion paper. Waigani: Programme Management Unit.

Programme Management Unit (PMU). no date. Transitional Training Unit. Unpublished discussion paper. Waigani: Programme Management Unit.

Reilly, B. 2002. Political engineering and party politics in Papua New Guinea. *Party Politics* 8(6): 701–718.

Rosenthal, U., P. t'Hart and M. Charles. 1989. The world of crises and crisis management. In *Coping with Crises: The Management of Disasters, Riots and Terrorism*, ed. U. Rosenthal, P. t'Hart and M. Charles, 3–33. Springfield: Charles P. Thomas.

Somare, M. 1974. The public service — where do we go from here? *Administration for Development* 1: 4–5.

Trebilcock, M. 1982. *Public Enterprises in Papua New Guinea*. Institute of National Affairs Discussion Paper no. 9. Port Moresby: Institute of National Affairs.

Turner, M. 1985. Efficiency and effectiveness in public service training: the case of the Administrative College of Papua New Guinea. *Administration for Development* 25: 1–59.

Turner, M. 1991. Issues and reforms in the Papua New Guinea Public Service since independence. *Journal de la Société des Océanistes* 92–93(1&2): 97–104.

Turner, M. 1997. *Institutional Strengthening Issues in Papua New Guinea*. Study prepared for AusAID. Canberra: AusAID.

Wesley-Smith, T. 1999. Papua New Guinea. *The Contemporary Pacific* 11(2): 438–43.

Whitworth, A. 1989. *Public Enterprise Policy in Papua New Guinea*. Islands/Australia Working Paper no. 89/1. Canberra: Australian National University, National Centre for Development Studies.

World Bank. 1983. *Public Sector Management in Papua New Guinea: An Administrative Overview*. Washington: World Bank.

World Bank. 1995. *Papua New Guinea: Delivering Public Services*. Washington: World Bank.

World Bank. 1999. *Improving Governance and Performance*. Washington: World Bank.

Endnotes

[1] A pilot study of governance in a sample of districts, coordinated by the State, Society and Governance project at the Australian National University in collaboration with Nancy Sullivan, Madang and the National Research Institute, was undertaken in 2004-05. See May (2005).

Chapter 3

Public Sector Reform Since 2001[1]

R. J. May

The later years of the 1990s saw a period of deteriorating governance, economic decline, and rising tensions in relations between the Papua New Guinea government and the World Bank and other donors. This culminated in a vote of no confidence against the prime minister, Bill Skate, and in 1999 Sir Mekere Morauta replaced Skate as prime minister. As documented in Chapter 2, Morauta promptly moved to initiate policies designed to achieve reconstruction and development.

The Morauta government set itself six objectives: to stabilize the economy; to stabilize the budget; to rebuild the institutions of state; to remove impediments to investment and growth; to reach a peaceful political settlement on Bougainville; and to create political stability and integrity. A number of fiscal and broader economic measures were introduced with respect to the first two objectives and a Medium Term Plan of Action for Public Sector Reform was drawn up for the period 2000–2003; steps were taken to safeguard the independence of, and to strengthen, the Bank of Papua New Guinea (see Kamit 2000), the Ombudsman Commission, the auditor general, and the public service; an Organic Law on the Integrity of Political Parties and Candidates was passed and changes made to the electoral system, and a long-running peace process culminated in the *Bougainville Peace Agreement* of 2003. Notwithstanding these reforms, economic and political stability proved hard to achieve.

Following the national elections of 2002 (which were generally conceded to have been marked by greater irregularities and violence than any previous national election), a new coalition government, headed by Sir Michael Somare, came into office. The Somare government quickly made clear its intention to maintain the previous government's commitment to policies of recovery and public sector reform. With respect to the former, and in the context of a substantial deterioration in the fiscal situation, in August 2002 the government announced a Program for Recovery and Development, which identified as its three main objectives, 'good governance; export-driven economic growth; and rural development, poverty reduction and empowerment through human resource development'.[2]

As a framework within which to pursue these objectives, the government presented, after a lengthy process of consultation, a revised Medium Term Development Strategy (MTDS) for 2003–2007, which replaced the previous MTDS for 1997–2002.[3] The MTDS 2003–2007 has subsequently been replaced by the MTDS 2005–2010. With regard to its public sector reform agenda, the Somare government also presented, in November 2003, a *Strategic Plan for Supporting Public Sector Reform in Papua New Guinea 2003–2007*, which superseded the Morauta government's *Medium Term Plan of Action for Public Sector Reform*.

These documents define the broad framework for government policies. Within this framework, however, there has been a proliferation of new systems, programs and initiatives addressing particular aspects of the reform process. For example, in presenting the 2004 budget, the then Minister for Finance and Treasury, Bart Philemon, announced that the government's reform agenda would be supplemented…by a new focus on improving the management of public sector employment and the control of personnel expenditures; restoring the integrity of budget institutions and systems to improve budgetary discipline; and to review the role, functions, and outputs of each spending agency in order to identify ways of improving the allocative and technical efficiencies of public expenditure (Papua New Guinea 2003, 23).

Several new measures were described by the minister, including a Performance Management System for Department Heads, a Medium-term Budget Framework, an Integrated Financial Management System (IFMS), and the creation of a Budget Screening Committee (BSC). (Also see Kua 2006).

The following overview provides a rough guide to recent public sector reforms.

The MTDS 2005–2010

In a foreword to the MTDS, the acting minister for National Planning and Monitoring, Sir Moi Avei, noted that, 'Since independence, successive governments have prepared many worthy development plans and strategies that have promised to realize our national vision', but that, while such plans and strategies 'were often soundly based, they have not been translated into results on the ground' (MTDS, iv). The MTDS 2005–2010, prepared by the Department of National Planning and Rural Development (DNPRD), seeks to reverse this trend.

The role of the MTDS is defined:

First, to articulate an overarching development strategy that will provide the guiding framework for prioritizing the Government's expenditure program.

Second, to identify in broad terms, the wider policy framework that will help strengthen the enabling environment for the Program for Recovery and Development.

Third, to improve fiscal governance by strengthening PNG's Public Expenditure Management (PEM) system (MTDS iii, chapter 1).

The key objectives of the government's development policies, its expenditure priorities, and the principal elements of a 'supporting policy environment' are spelled out in the MTDS (chapters 2, 3), which also lists ten broad 'guiding principles' (i–ii). Also noted are some of the constraints upon, and threats to, development; among these, along with poor infrastructure, HIV/AIDS, high population growth, unplanned urbanization and impediments to land utilization, is listed 'dysfunctional service delivery systems' (see MTDS, 9–10).[4]

The ability of the government to give effect to the MTDS will depend in part upon whether the programs identified are affordable and sustainable. To this end the MTDS is complemented by a Medium Term Resource Framework (MTRF), designed 'to integrate the "top-down" resource envelope with the "bottom-up" sector programs' (MTDS, 52). The '"top-down" resource envelope' is defined by a Medium Term Fiscal Strategy (MTFS) formulated by Treasury for the period 2003–2007.

The implementation of the MTDS also depends on having an effective administrative structure, and the MTDS explicitly recognizes the importance of good governance and credible and stable policies. It devotes some attention to the government's Public Sector Reform (PSR) program, which, in broad terms, seeks to 'reduce the cost of government, abolish waste and non-priority activities, improve service delivery and strengthen accountability and other systems of good governance' (MTDS 2005–2010, v, chapter 5). The PSR program is spelled out in fairly general terms in the *Strategic Plan for Supporting Public Sector Reform in Papua New Guinea 2003–2007*, and addressed in more detail in the Public Expenditure Review and Rationalisation (PERR) program (both of which are discussed below).

In his foreword to the MTDS, Sir Moi Avei commented: '…we can no longer ignore the dysfunctional system of service delivery that has arisen following the 1995 reforms to our system of decentralised government'. Since a large part of governance, including delivery of basic services, is carried out at sub-national level, the performance of government at provincial, district and local level is critical for any program of recovery and development — though it must be observed that problems of service delivery were well in evidence before 1995. With regard to decentralization, the MTDS states: 'Improving the relationship between the three levels of government will be crucial for the effective implementation of the new MTDS', and it notes that a number of activities are in place 'that are designed to identify practical solutions to the functioning of the decentralized system of government' (MTDS 2005–2010, IV, chapter 4). These are discussed below.

A final chapter of the MTDS discusses the issues of monitoring and evaluation. The MTRF, quarterly budget reviews, and the annual budget documents will form part of the financial monitoring process, but in addition, national departments and agencies, provincial and local-level governments, NGOs and community-based organizations, and other stakeholders 'will be required to participate' in monitoring and evaluation. Specific performance indicators (for both the MTDS and the Millennium Development Goals [MDGs] (to which Papua New Guinea is committed as a signatory to the UN Millenium Declaration)[5] were to be prepared by the end of 2005. In a few key sectors (including health and education) performance indicators have already been prepared and incorporated into sectoral plans. Overall responsibility for monitoring and evaluation rests with the DNPRD, which will report through the Central Agencies Coordinating Committee (see below) to the National Executive Council (NEC).

A Strategic Plan for Supporting Public Sector Reform in Papua New Guinea 2003–2007

'Good governance' was listed first amongst the objectives of the Somare government's Program for Recovery and Development. In an address to the National Parliament in August 2002, the prime minister elaborated the goals for good governance:

* Strengthening the democratic process;
* Political stability at all levels of government;
* Efficient and effective delivery of government services;
* A sound regulatory framework; and
* Transparency and accountability.

These were to be achieved through an all-encompassing program of public sector reform (MTDS 2005–2010, 53–57).

A Strategic Plan for Supporting Public Sector Reform in Papua New Guinea 2003–2007 (hereafter Strategic Plan) was presented in November 2003.

In an introductory statement to the Strategic Plan, Prime Minister Somare commented that on taking office in 2002 his government found that progress had been made on many aspects of the reform program initiated by the previous government, but 'felt it was essential to reframe and to more sharply focus what had, by then, proved to be an overly ambitious reform agenda'.

The key objectives of public sector reform for 2003–7 were listed as:

* A public sector with a clear sense of direction;
* Affordable government;

- Improving performance, accountability and compliance; and
- Improving service delivery.

The *Strategic Plan* lists a series of strategies and 'broadly stated' indicators under each of these headings.

The structure for public sector reform

With the introduction of the Medium *Term Plan of Action for Public Sector Reform 2000–2003*, the Morauta government also created a new administrative structure to facilitate and coordinate the reform process. This structure has been broadly maintained by the Somare government.

At the apex of this new structure, a Central Agencies Coordinating Committee (CACC), chaired by the chief secretary to the government, was given overall responsibility for designing and managing the public sector reform program (*Strategic Plan*, 16) The position of the CACC was formalized by provisions of the *Prime Minister and National Executive Council Act*, 2002.

A Public Sector Reform Management Unit (PSRMU) was also created, 'to support public sector reform by providing professional capacity and support to the CACC and government organizations' (*ibid.*). And an independent Public Sector Reform Advisory Group (PSRAG), representative of national, provincial and local-level administrations, the private sector, churches, the public sector union, the National Council of Women, and research organizations, was established to provide stakeholder input.

The *Strategic Plan* (17) outlines the reform implementation process in the following terms:

- The NEC will provide political leadership and direction.
- The CACC will provide strategic oversight of the public sector reform process.
- Departments, agencies and provincial administrations are responsible for implementing public sector reform, with central agency support.
- PSRMU is an expert resource available to assist central and line agencies and provincial administrations.
- PSRAG provides input from external stakeholders to the public sector reform process.

The PSRMU has probably taken a more proactive role than simply 'assisting' agencies, at times putting gentle pressure on them to meet their obligations and commitments.

Though not part of this formal structure, a Consultative Implementation and Monitoring Council (CIMC) provides a private sector input to the policy making process, in part through public national development forums. In 2005 the CIMC was working with government to 'open up the budget process'.

The Public Expenditure Review and Rationalisation (PERR) program

The PERR is a joint initiative of the Papua New Guinea government, World Bank, Asian Development Bank (ADB) and AusAID, initiated in 2002, aimed broadly at improving fiscal management. It is described in the MTDS 2005–2010 (57–58) as 'a key vehicle for generating the savings and cost-efficiencies necessary for the successful implementation of the MTDS'. A PERR Implementing Committee is chaired by Treasury.

In 2003 the PERR produced six discussion papers: 'Road map to fiscal sustainability', 'Civil service size and payroll', 'Restoring the integrity of budget institutions and systems', 'Expenditure adjustment and prioritization', 'Improving health spending', and 'Improving education spending'.

On the subject of fiscal sustainability, the authors of the PERR paper suggested in 2003 that:

> The root causes of PNG's fiscal malaise lie in poor governance in public finance management. Although most of PNG's budget systems are sound, and by some accounts even sophisticated, poor governance over the years has led to an erosion of budgetary discipline, weakening of accountability and proliferation of waste, leakage, irregularities and malpractices across the board....tinkering with budget numbers and mandating ad-hoc expenditure cuts, as the Government has tried in the past, can hardly be expected to be effective in such a flawed system.

Several areas were identified for attention in the subsequent papers.

With regard to civil service size and payroll, it was argued that 'public sector employment in PNG is larger than the country needs or can afford', and that 'the payroll system is flush with waste, leakage and irregularities'. A DPM audit suggested that there were some 2000 unproductive public servants on the unattached list (1200 of them in provincial administrations) in 2002, and 'a large number of ghosts on the payroll'. Departments were said to recruit and make payments with no regard to budget ceilings, and Treasury was accused of 'unrealistic appropriations'.

On the topic of restoring the integrity of budget institutions and systems, it was argued that 'poor governance over the years has allowed [budget systems and processes] to be ignored, neglected, misused and abused' while 'watchdog bodies have been rendered ineffective because of absence of follow-up action on the irregularities they uncover', with cases 'delayed, blocked or even abrogated because of political pressures and vested interests'. There was 'no sense of collective responsibility for the overall budget strategy'. Decentralization was said to have 'led to an erosion of budgetary control'.

In relation to expenditure adjustment and prioritization, the PERR authors proposed an agency-by-agency review of functions (apparently going beyond existing Functional Expenditure Reviews), expenditure patterns and staffing levels, outputs and results, and whether certain functions might be privatized. They also supported the development of a Medium-term Expenditure Framework.

Actions on several of these fronts were detailed by the Minister for Finance and Treasury in his 2004 budget speech. As part of improved management of public sector employment and control of personnel expenditure, measures had been taken to remove ghost names from the payroll, implement a Concept Payroll System, reduce the pool of unattached officers by reassigning them or scheduling their redundancy, reduce the number of casual employees, and improve budget estimates and expenditure controls. In 2003 the *Public Service (Management) Act* was amended to facilitate merit-based appointments at senior levels; this is to be complemented by measures to extend merit-based appointment procedures to statutory authorities, and supported by a system of performance-based contracts (the appointment of senior public servants has, however, remained a point of controversy[6]). A review of government procurement was undertaken in 2001, and subsequently measures have been taken to strengthen the Central Supply and Tenders Board (CSTB), reduce discretionary powers to create lower-level supply and tenders boards, and improve information, reporting and disclosure systems (though not all departments have subscribed to the new measures). A Budget Screening Committee, comprising deputy secretaries of the central agencies, was created in 2003 to evaluate spending programs, assist prioritization of spending, and establish expenditure ceilings in the preparation of the 2004 budget. The government also announced its intention to develop a Medium-term Budget Framework within which to consider adjustments to public expenditure in the light of changes in available funding. And the Financial Management Improvement Program (FMIP), 'an integrated reform program of financial management at all levels of the government', was described as 'the most significant single reform of financial management ever undertaken by the Government'. (Papua New Guinea 2003, 27. Also see FMIP 2003).

Further measures within the context of the PERR have addressed budget stability, budget processes, expenditure controls (including an embargo on out-of-court settlements of claims against the state[7]), payroll processes, salary administration, appointments procedures, expenditure prioritization and adjustment, non-tax revenue, oversight of statutory corporations, and inter-government relations.[8]

'Rightsizing'

Reduction in the size of the public sector has been a recurring theme in reviews of the public sector, particularly reviews by the World Bank, in Papua New Guinea and elsewhere. In 1990 (coinciding with Papua New Guinea's first application for a structural adjustment loan) the World Bank called for a downsizing of the public sector, while at the same time noting the need for improved health and education services (World Bank 2000; also see Curtin 2000). Retrenchment exercises were carried out in 1990, 1994 and 1996, but were generally judged to have had little effect, with retrenched public servants either remaining on unattached lists, being reemployed, and/or being replaced by new recruits. In 1999 the Skate government announced plans to reduce the public service from 60,000 to 52,500, with costs to be met from privatization of public enterprises. But the proposal was not based on any review of functional requirements and substantially underestimated the costs of the retrenchment, with the result that many 'retrenched' personnel remained on the payroll. When the Morauta government came to office, the retrenchment program was suspended, pending further study.[9] As noted, the issue was raised again in the PERR, and is referred to in the MTDS 2005–2010 (54) as a core objective of public sector reform.

In 2005, an independent committee, headed by the late Mike Manning, then director of the Institute of National Affairs, was asked to undertake a study and make recommendations on public sector rightsizing, in the context of a government policy of reducing the public sector by 10 per cent, primarily in 'non-key service areas' (though it does not seem to be clear whether the 10 per cent referred to wage and salary costs or workforce numbers). The committee reported in September 2005. It recommended the abolition or merger of several government departments and agencies (including DPM, DNPRD, DPLGA and the National Research Institute), reduction in the number of ministries and ministerial advisers, closure of several overseas missions, and the outsourcing of some services to public providers (Public Sector Rightsizing Working Group 2005. Also see *Papua New Guinea Post-Courier,* 23, 24, 28 February 2006), but Manning was reported as saying that the committee was unable to achieve the desired reduction of 10 per cent and maintain the essential services of government (*Papua New Guinea Post-Courier,* 24 February 2006). By the end of 2006 few of the committee's recommendations had been implemented.

Separately, retrenchment within the Papua New Guinea Defence Force (PNGDF), as part of a recommended Force restructuring, seeks to reduce troop numbers from around 4200 to less than 2000.[10] But despite external funding for the retrenchment, poor handling of the exercise resulted in early 2001 in a near mutiny, during which soldiers broke into the PNGDF armory. The Morauta government agreed to rescind a cabinet decision on Force size reduction, though in fact numbers continue to decline, primarily through a Voluntary Release Scheme.

The Public Sector Workforce Development Initiative (PSWDI)

The PSWDI was created in 2004 with the aim of providing a 'comprehensive framework...which guides all activities related to public sector workforce development', with emphasis on workforce development rather than 'traditional training', local ownership, use of existing linkages and networks, and incentives to improved performance. It envisages two phases — 2005–2007 focusing on the public service, and 2008–2010 to include the wider public sector — each with a framework and annual implementation plans. The PSWDI is described as a 'cross-agency partnership across the three tiers of government'. It is led by a 'think tank' comprising senior executives of key national institutions, chaired by the deputy secretary of the Department of Personnel Management (DPM). Initially it has identified eight 'action areas': engaging all stakeholders, strengthening lead institutions (listing DPM, CACC, DPLGA, PNG Institute of Public Administration (PNGIPA), and National Training Council (NTC)), executive development, providing the 'new basics', developing the 'next generation', aligning supply with demand, building and sharing knowledge, and coordination and management.[11]

Decentralization

As reflected in comments of the MTDS and *Strategic Plan*, there is a widespread feeling that the reforms embodied in the 1995 Organic Law on Provincial Governments and Local-level Governments (OLPGLLG) have not solved the problems of the decentralized system. In the words of the MTDS (9–10):

> ...in the years since the passage of the Organic Law, service delivery has deteriorated. On the whole service delivery systems are dysfunctional and there remains widespread confusion over functional (who does what) and financial (who pays for what) responsibilities across the three levels of government. As well, institutional capacity to deliver services is best described as grossly inadequate.

These problems, and the policy measures directed at their solution are discussed in Chapter 12 and in somewhat more detail in May forthcoming).

Overview

The post-1999 reforms have given rise to a plethora of 'programs' and 'initiatives', mostly designed to achieve what one might expect to be part of the normal day-to-day activities of departments, agencies and sub-national governments (but which clearly have not been). Inevitably perhaps, much of what is listed in the goals and guiding principles of these programs and initiatives consists of broad, uncontroversial statements of intention; nevertheless experience suggests that it is sometimes useful to spell out what might seem obvious, especially if in spelling out objectives and strategies one can provide a framework within which specific problems may be identified, addressed and monitored. As several people, including Prime Minister Somare, have observed, what has been lacking in public sector reform in Papua New Guinea in the past has been not so much sound policies as a commitment to implement them at all levels of government.

In the proliferation of new initiatives, some of them largely donor-driven, there is a danger that overall coordination becomes more difficult. It is clear that many public servants (and advisers), including some senior officers, have an incomplete knowledge of the range of new activities being introduced. This is exacerbated by the facts that key documents are often almost impossible to obtain,[12] that increasing demands on the time of senior officers means that they frequently delegate or miss attendance at joint committee meetings, and that rapid turnover of staff (not to mention the retrenchment of a generation of middle managers with extensive field experience) shortens collective departmental memories. It is also clear that there is a significant knowledge gap between Waigani and the provincial capitals, district headquarters, and local-level government wards.

References

Barter, Sir Peter. 2004. Blunt Assessment, Hope and Direction. Lower Level Government in Papua New Guinea. Paper for the Public Sector Reform Advisory Group, April 2004. Reprinted in *Governance Challenges for PNG and the Pacific Islands*, ed. Nancy Sullivan, 132–154. Madang: DWU Press.

Curtin, T. 2000. Public sector reform in Papua New Guinea and the 1999 budget. *Labour and Management in Development* (online) 1(14).

Financial Management Improvement Program (FMIP). 2003. Financial Management Improvement Program. The vehicle for financial reforms. In *Papua New Guinea Yearbook 2003,* 10–11. Port Moresby: The National and Cassowary Books.

Kamit, L.Wilson. 2000. Reforms to the *Central Bank Act and the Banks and Financial Institutions Act.* INA Speech Series No. 2. Port Moresby: Institute of National Affairs.

Kua, Bill. 2006. Public Sector Reform in Papua New Guinea. *State, Society and Governance in Melanesia. Public Policy in Papua New Guinea — Discussion Paper* 2006/1. Canberra: The National Research Institute (Papua New Guinea) and the Research School of Pacific and Asian Studies, Australian National University.

Mawuli, A, C. Yala, O. Sanida and F. Kalop. 2005. *Economic Development Planning in Papua New Guinea: The MTDS, 2005, Review and Seminar.* Special Publication 38. Port Moresby: National Research Institute.

May, R. J. 2006. *The public sector reform process in Papua New Guinea.* Public Policy in Papua New Guinea Discussion Paper Series 2006/4. The National Research Institute and the State, Society and Governance in Melanesia Program, Research School of Pacific and Asian Studies, Australian National University.

Papua New Guinea. 2004. *Medium Term Development Strategy 2005–2010. Our Plan for Economic and Social Advancement (MTDS 2005–2010).* Government of Papua New Guinea.

Papua New Guinea. 2003. *2004 Budget. Volume 1. Economic and Development Policies.*

Public Sector Reform Advisory Group (PSRAG). 2005. *Second Report. Improved Decentralisation. Getting People Involved in Democracy, Strong Civil society, Peace and Good Order, and Self-Reliance.* Port Moresby: PSRAG.

Public Sector Rightsizing Working Group. 2005. *Rightsizing the Public Sector. An Initiative of the Government of Papua New Guinea.* Waigani: Report of the Public Sector Rightsizing Working Group.

World Bank. 2000. *Report and Recommendation of the President of the International Bank for Reconstruction and Development to the Executive Directors on Governance Promotion Adjustment Loan in an amount of US$90 million to the Independent State of Papua New Guinea.* Washington DC: World Bank.

Endnotes

[1] This paper draws on material in May (2006). I am grateful to Kathy Whimp for her comments on a draft of that paper.

[2] In the 2004 Budget Speech, these are restated as '(a) promotion of good governance; (b) improving economic management; (c) improving public sector performance; and (d) removing barriers to investment and economic growth' (Papua New Guinea 2003, 23).

[3] Referring back to the MTDS 1997-2002, the MTDS 2005-2010 (pp.5-6) says, 'Although the policies and priorities contained in the MTDS 1997-2002 were soundly based, they were not rigorously applied or followed in practice', partly because there was 'very little ownership of the MTDS, across all levels of government'. Specifically, the earlier MTDS 'was poorly integrated with the policies and programs of the provincial and local level governments'.

[4] For a review of the MTDS 2005-2010, and a summary of its predecessors, see Mawuli *et al.* (2005).

[5] The eight MDGs, to be achieved by 2015, broadly, are: eradicate extreme poverty and hunger; achieve universal primary education for all children ; promote gender equality and empower women; reduce child mortality; improve maternal health; combat HIV/AIDS, TB and other diseases; ensure environmental sustainability; and develop a global partnership for development. Papua New Guinea is currently behind schedule in achieving the targets (see *Millenium Development Goals: Progress Report for Papua New Guinea 2004*, and *The National* 26 September 2005).

[6] See, for example Michael Unage in *The National* 18 August 2005, and Prime Minister Somare's earlier statement to parliament, printed in the *Papua New Guinea Post-Courier* 12 July 2005. Also see the

comments of Chief Secretary Joshua Kalinoe, who accused politicians of bypassing formal procedures required under the *Public Service Management Act* to remove departmental heads who had not 'cooperated' with them (*Papua New Guinea Post-Courier* 30 January 2007, *National* 30 January 2007).

[7] In August 2005 it was reported that successful compensation claims against the state over the past ten years (mostly arising from police actions) had amounted to K500 million (*The National* 16 August 2005); the following month it was further reported that the National Court had ordered the state to pay K266,000 to a victim of a police shooting in 1995 (*The National* 21 September 2005).

[8] Chief Secretary, Joshua Kalinoe, presentation to National Research Institute, 24 September 2005.

[9] Notwithstanding this, in an article in *Papua New Guinea Yearbook 2002*, Morauta stated that retrenchment had cut K27.6 million from the public service wage bill and that in the National Fisheries Agency and the Government Printer alone staff had been reduced by 235 (Morauta 2002, 8-9).

[10] Numbers vary: at the end of 1998 Force size was 4600; in 2000 there was talk of reducing numbers from 4200 to around 3000 at the end of 2000 and 1500 by mid 2001; in January 2001 a Commonwealth Eminent Persons Group recommended a cut from what was then 4150 to 1900 within six months; in June 2001 Force size was quoted as 3340 and the aim was to reduce this to 2000 over three years. At the end of 2006 Force size was around 2300.

[11] See PSWDI, *Framework 2005-2007*, 1 March 2005.

[12] In 2004, incoming Inter-Government Relations minister, Sir Peter Barter commented that the Department of Provincial and Local Government Affairs had been unable to locate a copy of the National Development Charter, which embodied a major policy initiative for the joint funding of programs by the national and provincial and local-level governments (see Barter 2004, 145). Donors are not always innocent on this account: for example, an expenditure tracking exercise for education, undertaken by the National Research Institute for the World Bank in 2003 as part of a Public Expenditure and Service Delivery study, and involving an extensive collection of data, has never been released by the World Bank. The data is now more than five years old.

Part 1. Sectoral studies

Chapter 4

Economic Policy Making[1]

Satish Chand and Charles Yala

The responsibility for economic policy making was transferred from Canberra to Port Moresby and from expatriate Australians to the locals at an accelerating pace from 1951 to 1973. The chief minister and prime minister-in-waiting noted that 'after April 1972 the elected representatives in the House of Assembly felt that they were in reality the government. We began to initiate policy' (Somare 2001, 16). This chapter shows that the period preceding independence and a decade and half after independence saw responsible economic policy making. During this era of hope, policymakers were in control of the fiscal position and on track to see rapid development. This was not to last for long, with the state losing control of its budget, prices, and the exchange rate by the early 1990s. Some of the lost ground was recovered from late 1999 to 2001, but a lot remains to be achieved.

The shift of responsibility for economic policy making from Canberra to Port Moresby was such that by 1972 the Chief Minister's Office, together with the Department of Finance, had close to full autonomy in charting the economic course for the nation. Well before attaining self-government on 1 December 1973, the processes of law making and appropriation of money for public purposes in the Territories were undertaken locally by a legislature, the majority of whose members were elected by the local population. Full independence was acquired on 16 September 1975 when Australia transferred its final responsibilities for defence and external relations (see World Bank 1965; Garnaut 1981).

Australia achieved its goal of a peaceful and amicable transfer of power and responsibility for policymaking to Port Moresby and institutions created at independence achieved the desired objective of ensuring responsible economic policy making. However, the virtuous effects of good governance on responsible economic policy making began to unravel around the early 1990s, and particularly following the Bougainville crisis, leading to repeated economic crises.

Transfer of policy-making responsibilities from Canberra to Port Moresby

The success of the shift of responsibility for economic policy making was due to good planning and methodical implementation by the then colonial administration. The hand-over of power and responsibility for policy making took place on time and in a peaceful, amicable, and orderly fashion (World Bank 1978, 5). In a series of lectures, the options for increased autonomy for the territories were aired by four distinguished academics from the Australian National University (ANU). These lectures, subsequently published as Bettison, Fisk, West and Crawford (1962) provide an excellent account of the thinking that was put into preparing Papua New Guinea for self-rule.[2]

Amongst the several achievements of the early years of self-government, two that stand out in terms of relevance for the current period are the conduct of the 1968 elections and the institutional arrangements put in place for fiscal prudence. On the former, the World Bank (1978, 22) noted that the 1968 election was an 'organizational marvel with voter registration being close to complete with two-thirds registered having voted'. On the latter, pressures for responsible budgeting were created following self-rule by new institutions and procedures established for this very purpose. The outcome was a constant dialogue between the respective ministries and departments. Expenditure requests and program proposals by agency heads were channelled through the Central Planning Office (CPO), which acted as the secretariat to a sub-committee of cabinet, namely the National Planning Committee. These freshly established institutions and procedures, and the accompanying by-product of documents, ensured control over expenditures and hence of the budget. They also served as the mechanism to inform and educate stakeholders about the nation's overall fiscal position and the linkages between programs and the national policy goals of the government.

Other features of the initial conditions included a cadre of well-qualified graduates from the University of Papua New Guinea who took the helm of political leadership during the transfer of responsibility for policy making from Canberra to Port Moresby. The church, together with a significant number of senior expatriate administrative staff, provided much needed support during this transition, though decision making rested fully within the hands of local leaders. These achievements were consistent with West's preferred strategy of preparing Papua New Guinea for independence as announced a decade earlier:

> If, by a change of emphasis in policy, a Papuan elite were to be given every opportunity within the next ten years for education and experience, when the time came for Australia to transfer sovereignty, to hand over power to that Legislative Council the Minister has seen as the sovereign body, I think we would have every reason to be hopeful that an independent state would willingly establish a special relationship,

in terms of defence, economic aid, and diplomatic representation, with
Australia. (Bettison, Fisk, West and Crawford 1962, 58).

In its thirty years of independence Papua New Guinea has maintained a special
(cordial if not always warm) relationship with Australia.

Papua New Guinea achieved the initial successes in economic management
by well considered and responsible action by its leaders, many of whom remain
active some three decades later. Garnaut (1981, 172), for example, notes that:
'The ideas that were important to the evolution of a satisfactory framework for
economic policy making had been around Port Moresby for some time and had
been discussed at length by Chan, Morauta and their advisers'. Mekere Morauta
took office as the first Papua New Guinean secretary of Finance in late 1973 and
played a significant role in seeing that fiscal discipline was maintained during
those early years of self-governance. In these early years, the General Financial
and Economic Policy Division (GFEP) of the Ministry of Finance, headed by a
first assistant secretary (FAS), had a critical role in formulation of economic
policy.[3]   A Budget Priorities Committee (BPC) established systems for
identification and enforcement of long-term budget priorities. According to
Garnaut (1981, 172), by the second half of 1976 the major elements of 'an
internally consistent macro-economic strategy' had fallen into place.

The World Bank (1978, 5) was highly complimentary of Papua New Guinea's
policy making at independence, noting that:

> In the four years after its elections, the Somare government showed an
> impressive ability to deal with the young country's financial, economic,
> and political problems. An effective set of institutions for economic and
> financial management has been created. These include a strong ministry
> of finance that has developed a tight system of budget controls, operating
> through a budget priorities committee; a planning office; and a central
> bank that, with International Monetary Fund assistance, has organized
> a set of international accounts.

The Bank went on to note the successful introduction of the kina, approval of
a set of principles to govern development policy and foreign investment, and
the publishing of investment priorities by the National Investment and
Development Authority (NIDA). These achievements were indeed remarkable,
particularly at the inception of a new nation state and given limited resources.
The Bank qualified its highly favourable assessment by stating that 'no one can
say how sturdy or fragile Papua New Guinea's policy or administration will
prove to be, but the short-run record provides strong grounds for optimism and
few for anxiety' (*ibid.*). At independence, Australian assistance accounted for
between 40 and 45 per cent of the local budget and some 45 to 50 per cent of
the foreign exchange requirements. The World Bank, then, had 'reasonable

grounds' to believe that this dependence on Australian aid 'might end entirely within the next 20 to 25 years' (*ibid.*, 6).

The state of public infrastructure and social service delivery at independence was good, relative to that of recent years and in comparison to the state of the economy at independence. A World Bank mission to Papua New Guinea in 1975, just before independence observed that:

> The strikingly primitive state of much of the economy and society contrasts with the surprisingly well-developed status of the central government and many of its services. Education and health care and some of the country's infrastructure — harbours, electricity supply, telecommunications, and air services — are comparatively advanced (World Bank 1978, 5).

A sharp turnaround in the fiscal position of the state, loss of budgetary control, and widespread allegations of misappropriation of public funds thus give cause for concern; it requires explanation how such good preparatory work leading to an initial phase of responsible policy making could come unstuck over a decade later.[4]

Stated goals for economic policy making

In December 1972, the Somare Government announced its development goals in the form of the Eight Aims of the national government (see Fitzpatrick 1985; World Bank 1978, 66).

The Eight Aims subsequently became the basis for the Five National Goals and Directive Principles included in the preamble to the constitution. These aims and directive principles reflected the government's concerns for equitable and sustainable growth, for the use of natural resources to benefit the wider community, and for protection of the environment. The World Bank in its 1976 economic mission to Papua New Guinea suggested two further goals: to raise the country's fiscal viability,[5] and to achieve a gradual reorientation of the economy to costs and standards that could be sustained within the country's resources. These latter two goals complement those of self-reliance in that they encompass notions of sustainability.

Policies at independence

The third National Goal and Directive Principle of the preamble to the constitution is 'for Papua New Guinea to be politically and economically independent, and our economy basically self-reliant'.

This goal encapsulates themes of localization and national sovereignty. Further, sub-paragraph 4 envisions 'citizens and government bodies to have control of the bulk of economic enterprise and production', while sub-paragraph

5 stipulates strict control of foreign investment. Sub-paragraph 6 mandates 'the state to take effective measures to control and actively participate in the national economy, and in particular to control major enterprises engaged in the exploitation of natural resources'. Sub-paragraph 8 warns against entering agreements on foreign assistance that 'imperil[s] our self-reliance and self-respect' or exposes the nation to dependence on and/or influence of 'any country, investor, lender or donor'.

There was also a clear recognition that resource exploitation would be the core strategy for economic development. The architects of the constitution were cognizant of the policy challenges posed by such a strategy: the fourth national goal and directive principle states:

> We declare our fourth goal to be for Papua New Guinea's natural resources and environment to be conserved and used for the collective benefit of us all, and be replenished for the benefit of future generations.

Sub-paragraph (1) within this goal calls for 'wise use to be made of our natural resources and the environment in and on the land or seabed, in the sea, under the land, and in the air, in the interests of our development and in trust for future generations'. It is difficult to argue that policies implemented since independence have delivered on these goals.

The overriding concerns of the first Somare government were 'Independence, national unity, and politically cohesive national government' (Garnaut 1981, 163). These concerns were addressed with only limited success, and have remained high in the priorities of all subsequent governments. A combination of fiscal, monetary, trade, and incomes policies has been employed in economic management, as considered below.

Changes in economic policy making since independence[6]

Fiscal policy

The period from 1976 to 1990 can be described as one of broad macroeconomic stability with the budget deficit contained within 5 per cent of GDP, the inflation rate low and stable, and nominal interest rates low relative to those of the major trading partners. Fiscal stabilization in the first decade and a half was achieved primarily through the setting of annual expenditures in line with the long-term capacity of the economy to fund such outlays. Revenue relied on the long-term understanding with Australia on aid flows, together with mechanisms in place to stabilize income from commodity exports and judicious use of public sector borrowing. The formative years of economic policy making in Papua New Guinea were exemplary, being characterized by fiscal discipline, stable prices, and responsible governance — a remarkable achievement given limited capacities to achieve any one of the above, and considering the challenges of overcoming barriers to internal trade, seeing a rapid monetization of the economy, containing the emerging social and economic problems from rising urbanization and unemployment, and ensuring greater access to basic services for the broader population. The initial conditions, in terms of macroeconomic fundamentals, institutions, and social infrastructure were favourable for development.

The deterioration in the budget deficit started in 1991 and continued to worsen until 1999, as did other macroeconomic aggregates including inflation, interest rates, government debt and foreign reserves. Mawuli (1999) cites loss of fiscal discipline as the primary reason for the poor growth performance; this hypothesis deserves closer scrutiny in light of quantitative evidence on macroeconomic aggregates.

The hard kina strategy

Until late 1994 the exchange rate, and in particular the use of the so-called 'hard kina policy', formed the principal instrument of monetary policy. The hard currency policy maintained the external value of the kina relative to major world currencies. This policy was used to gain international credibility (including ready convertibility) of the new currency. The same policy was subsequently used to contain the risks of imported inflation, thereby stabilizing domestic prices and real outlays. The kina was launched in April 1975, pegged at par to the Australian dollar. The peg to the $A was rationalized on two counts: first, that Australia was then and likely to continue to be Papua New Guinea's major trading partner; and, secondly, that Australian banks dominated the economy (see World Bank 1978, 115). The kina was revalued by 5 per cent in July 1976 to contain inflationary pressures emanating from rising international commodity prices; this was then possible, given the favourable foreign reserve position. The kina rose an additional 12.5 per cent against the Australian dollar after the devaluation of the latter by 17.5 per cent on 29 November 1976, but fell by 7.2 per cent against other world currencies.

The hard kina policy was only sustainable in the context of mutually consistent fiscal, monetary, and income policies. Garnaut (1981, 171) notes that: 'The art of the hard kina strategy was to establish mutually consistent and sustainable trends in real government expenditure, real wages, and real aid level, and to coordinate changes in money levels of these variables with changes in the exchange rate and price level'. In essence, the hard kina strategy was used to target price stability with the above real variables being the intermediate target.

The simultaneous achievement of three goals of macroeconomic policy — namely, full employment, constituting internal balance; external balance, in terms of a sustainable current account; and price stability, implying low inflation — necessitates use of three independent instruments (Salter 1959). Typically, internal balance is targeted through government spending, external balance is targeted via the nominal exchange rate, while attaining price stability is left to the monetary authority. A hard kina strategy to target price stability was atypical, and therefore the responsibility for attaining external balance rested principally on fiscal policy, given the large share of public expenditure accruing to imports, while price flexibility was used to achieve full employment.

Garnaut (2000, 32) rationalizes that, 'A "hard currency strategy", based on cautious expenditure policies, was designed to achieve low inflation, a convertible currency and financial stability'. According to Garnaut, this strategy was implemented in the immediate post-independence period with tight control over expenditures funded with moderate levels of domestic and foreign borrowing and culminating in real per capita public sector outlays declining over time until the Bouganville crisis of 1989. The hard currency strategy was abandoned with the switch to a floating kina in 1994 in the face of continuing liquidity crises due to the loss of fiscal discipline. The float of the kina provided an opportunity, which was botched, to achieve external balance. The effectiveness of the floating kina in aligning the exchange rate to the fundamentals of the economy was 'hampered by intrusive exchange controls' (Garnaut 2000, 33). As explained later, lack of wage flexibility disallowed achievement of internal balance, thereby making the hard kina policy unsustainable (Duncan *et al.* 1998). The combination of wage indexation together with the hard kina in a climate of subdued productivity growth led to rising unemployment, thereby undermining achievement of internal balance.

Trade policy

Papua New Guinea has traditionally been favourably disposed to international trade. An open-economy policy was pursued at independence with a liberal stance towards the use of exchange controls, foreign investment, imports, and employment of foreign labour. The price incentives provided by the market were allowed to direct resource allocation. Policymakers acknowledged the positive contribution made by international trade and foreign direct investment to development. The policy environment has generally been supportive of foreign investment and the use of necessary expatriate labour. Some activities, however, were reserved for locals in accordance with the stipulation in the constitution, 'particular emphasis in our economic development to be placed on small-scale artisan, service and business activity'.

The early 1980s saw some back-sliding on free trade, as protectionist pressures grew with the political system beginning to respond to lobbying by business interests (see Garnaut 2000). The liquidity problems of the early 1990s increased dependence on import duties for public revenues. Reliance on multilateral agencies, including the World Bank, to rescue the economy from several liquidity crises saw a reversal in the protectionist tendencies of policy making. The introduction of a value-added tax in 1999 reduced the dependence on import tariffs for public revenues, providing further support to liberalization of commodity trade.

The ongoing liberalization of trade can be partly attributed to pressures arising from membership of several multilateral organizations and the signing of trade agreements. The accelerating pace of integration of the Papua New Guinea economy into the global economy may be seen as in conflict with the third national goal and directive principle of the constitution, which cautions against 'dependence on imported skills and resources'. On this count, the constitution is in conflict with current economic thinking that an open trading regime is a critical ingredient for the growth of production (Wacziarg 2002).

Incomes policy

Papua New Guinea pursued an active incomes policy through centralized wage-setting mechanisms. The Minimum Wages Board, together with the labour unions, had a significant role in setting wages until its demise in 1992. Nominal wages were fully indexed until 1992 so that any initial disequilibrium that existed in the market remained until deregulation. As a consequence, real wages in the period 1972 to 1975 were maintained at levels well above those necessary for internal balance. Wages rose rapidly in this period: for example, the minimum weekly wage in Port Moresby rose from K8 ($US9) in 1971 to K25.80 ($US35) by late 1975. Similarly, the national minimum weekly wage rose from K5.30 ($US6) to K8.90 ($US12) for workers in primary industries and to K10.75 ($US15) for other rural workers. The urban minimum wage was raised substantially above the rural minimum, increasing the incentive for rural-to-urban migration. Garnaut and Baxter (1984) estimated that real wages for adult workers in Port Moresby in 1980 would have to fall by as much as 30 per cent to return to the level prevailing in 1971.

The need for growth in employment and the potential for job growth through removal of impediments to the operation of the labour and informal markets were recognized well before independence. In 1973 the Faber Report (Overseas Development Group 1973, 60) warned against the damaging effects of increases in rural wages on employment, and argued strongly for 'a policy of minimum average wage per capita and maximum employment of numbers of wage earners'. The report noted that the informal sector was 'fully indigenous' and argued for 'a liberalization of protective restrictions limiting competition in the urban economy' (*ibid.*, 25) so as to increase opportunities for self-employment. The report also noted that, 'Given that wage employment cannot absorb the growth in the labour force, self-employment must be a major source of indigenous income' (*ibid.*, 25) and saw the informal sector as the springboard for entrepreneurs into the formal sector. Policies implemented from independence to 1992 were basically contradictory to the recommendations in the Faber report.

The labour market was deregulated after unemployment had risen considerably, together with associated social problems of urban squatter settlements and crime. During this period, the general investment climate worsened. High legislated minimum wages for unskilled labour, implying levels above those that would have prevailed under competitive conditions, became entrenched through indexation and fed the growing unemployment problem until 1992. The abolition of the urban minimum wage in 1992 by the Minimum Wages Board was too late in that conditions for investment had deteriorated so badly that wage deregulation on its own was no longer sufficient to reinvigorate private investment. The wage distortion had contributed significantly to urban unemployment and social instability, raising costs of doing business in the country.

Levantis (2000) provides empirical evidence in support of increased formal sector employment after the deregulation. Even though urban real wages fell significantly after the deregulation, this could not be expected to lead to a substantial increase in employment, given the host of other non-wage structural impediments to private sector development that had built up during the period of wage indexation.

State-owned enterprise (SOE) reform

Recent major initiatives on the microeconomic front have included the privatization program, a detailed coverage of which is provided by Curtin in this volume. Here, the broad principles and motivations for the reform are considered. Sub-paragraph 4 of the third national goal and directive principle in the Papua New Guinea constitution calls for 'citizens and governmental bodies to have control of the bulk of economic enterprise and production'. This control was initially exercised by the state engaging in active supply of utilities, transportation and banking services, as well as in manufacturing. This strategy was not sustainable given the poor profitability of SOEs, increasing demands for budgetary support to loss-making enterprises that were funded by debt, and widespread abuse of the proceeds from the SOEs.

By August 1999, the national government of Papua New Guinea had accumulated a debt of K2.2 billion with K1.3 billion of this being owed to the central bank. Debt repayments for 1999 amounted to K300 million, a significant drain on the budget of around K2 billion. Foreign reserves had fallen sharply over the previous six months and the kina was at an all-time low of approximately $US0.27 as of mid 1999. The inflation rate on a year-on-year basis as of December 1998 was 24 per cent, a sharp climb from five per cent for the corresponding period a year earlier. Interest rates were at a record high, with the 180-day treasury bill rate in excess of 25 per cent. These rates were more than four times those prevailing in Australia. The high interest rates constituted a significant drain on the budget, given the high debt levels, and were also suffocating the growth of the private sector. Private sector credit growth was falling while highly-geared firms were facing liquidation. Continuing support to loss-making SOEs in this climate was no longer an option; hence the state had to withdraw from running businesses.

The incoming Morauta government announced a Reconstruction and Development Strategy, of which privatization and corporatization of public enterprises formed the core.[7] A package of policies was announced to deregulate the markets in order to enable the private sector to take the lead role in business activities. The withdrawal of the public sector from commercial enterprise was rationalized as part of a broader strategy to stabilize prices and facilitate sustainable growth. The sale of SOEs was to have a positive (net) revenue impact on the budget that would be used to reduce domestic debt, under the policy announced by the prime minister. It was argued that this in turn would lead to an easing of interest rates, and stabilization of the exchange rate and domestic prices. It was also pointed out that in addition to helping achieve the short-term goal of stabilization, privatization, and more generally the restructuring of the economy, would lead to stable and sustained growth. It was further argued that the withdrawal of the public sector from private commerce would reduce opportunities for waste, thereby enabling more effective use of resources for development.

By early 2002, ownership of one SOE, namely the Papua New Guinea Banking Corporation (PNGBC), had been transferred to the private sector, while several others were in the process of being divested, but the process stalled and as of mid 2005 no other SOE had been sold. By the middle of 2005 the kina had stabilized, the foreign exchange position had recovered to healthy levels, and interest rates on government bonds and inflation had returned to single digits; hence on most counts the announced privatization policy was delivering well ahead of its implementation.

It could be argued that the privatization strategy is not, at least in spirit, consistent with the constitution's stipulation for 'citizens and government bodies to have control of the bulk of economic enterprise and production'. But the economic reality of the situation dictated such a strategy. However, the state may still exert control over all domestic production by performing its tasks as the regulator of commerce; indeed the privatization strategy assigns such a responsibility to the state.

Value-added/goods and services tax

A value-added tax (VAT) was introduced on 1 July 1999 as part of a base-broadening exercise by the government; the VAT (subsequently renamed goods and services tax, GST) was seen as necessary in a climate of trade liberalization where the tariff reductions would erode the revenue base.[8] As part of the rationalization of the tax system, the sales tax imposed by provincial governments was abolished and a mining levy was introduced to offset the loss in tariff revenues from imports by the mineral sector (see Levantis 2001).

The constitution obliges the public to fund development of the nation according to their ability to pay. Clause (g) of the 'Basic Social Obligations' in the preamble to the constitution states this as 'to contribute, as required by law, according to their means to the revenues required for the advancement of the Nation and the purposes of Papua New Guinea'. Given that GST is compulsory on every transaction within the formal sector, this compulsion may be viewed as being contrary to the spirit of the constitution. However, the bulk of the poor avoid GST by remaining in the non-formal economy. Once again, economic pragmatism dictates that the revenue base be broadened, consistent with the global push to liberalize trade.

The remaining policy void

Many of the challenges of development that were highlighted prior to independence remain relevant today. Bettison, for example, noted in 1962 that:

> Along the western border of Papua and New Guinea from Daru in the south to Aitape and Wewak in the north, communication has been difficult, resources poor and the people have remained isolated, difficult to introduce to a cash economy and, in the highlands, undiscovered (Bettison, Fisk, West and Crawford 1962, 22).

The highlands no longer remains undiscovered, but the difficulties in communication, the problems of isolation, and the difficulty of introducing a cash economy remain some forty years later. The fact is that Papua New Guinea is made up of several smaller economies with limited opportunities for trade. The income disparity between regions persists because opportunities for commodity trade are limited by the high costs of transportation. Similarly, opportunities for internal migration, which could reduce the income disparity between regions, are hampered by the lack of secure, long-term access to land. The last also hampers mobilization of credit for investment, and growth of the rural economy.

These problems may be relieved by expansion of infrastructure, entailing expansion of regional road networks, coastal shipping, and the telephone grid. This would facilitate increased internal trade, one of the preconditions for development. Reductions in the monopoly powers of service providers in telecommunications, aviation, shipping, and ports would reduce costs and thereby encourage trade. Access to competitively priced transport and communication services would increase the size of the market, thereby providing the benefits of economies of scale.

Attention has to be given to problems arising from the rapid growth of urban populations. The state must, as a matter of urgency, consider options for expanding water and sewerage systems in Port Moresby and Lae. The burgeoning squatter settlements have to be contained to allow urban planning. The state could assist in facilitating secure long-term access to land for residential and commercial development within the urban centres by acting as intermediary between landowners and tenants. Consideration may be given to expansion and commercialization of the functions of the National Housing Commission[9] to contain growth of squatter settlements. The private sector could be gainfully involved in these areas, with public sector underwriting security of property rights to land and contracts. *Eda Ranu* has made some progress down this path in provision of water in Port Moresby.

More concerted effort has to be given to creating opportunities for productive employment. Expansion of road infrastructure has to remain a long-term objective. Fisk (Bettison, Fisk, West and Crawford 1962, 39) noted, in relation to investments necessary for road infrastructure for access to cost-effective transportation, that the 'sheer magnitude of the investment problem involved in the provision of such an infrastructure is frightening; but it must be faced'. He went on to state that, 'In the absence of an unexpected bonanza, such as the discovery of rich oil fields, *there is no other path to a viable economy*'. In hindsight, even the discovery of rich oil fields has not been sufficient to create a viable economy.

In the immediate short term, better returns may be derived from existing infrastructure by enabling migration to such infrastructure. The state might consider facilitating secure long-term access to land around the major roads by acting as the intermediary between landowners of such land and those wishing to access the lots. The goal would be to move labour to the available infrastructure to create opportunities for gainful employment. This would ameliorate some of the problems arising from fragmented and thin markets, as well as those emanating from high transportation costs that have acted as a drag on internal trade and growth of output. Such developments would need to be taken piecemeal, and be driven by demand, possibly starting on the peripheries of Port Moresby and Lae. The private sector could be encouraged to provide the real estate service, with the state facilitating access to secure property rights and public safety.

It has long been recognized that rapid development of the indigenous agricultural cash economy is crucial for a viable Papua New Guinea. Fisk (Bettison, Fisk, West and Crawford 1962, 25) considered an economy to be viable if it is 'sufficiently independent to be able to refuse aid without catastrophic economic and social consequences if the terms on which the aid is offered are politically unacceptable'. On this definition, Papua New Guinea was not a viable economy during the repeated liquidity crises of the 1990s.

According to Fisk, self-determination and political independence are empty without clear prospects of independence from external aid, at least for recurrent expenditures. Crawford considered political independence separate from economic viability, and argued that external assistance would be necessary for the latter. He asserted that, 'Continued economic progress of New Guinea along modern lines will call for heavy external aid for a long time to come' (Bettison, Fisk, West and Crawford 1962, 61). Crawford saw Papua New Guinea requiring aid for development at least until the early 1980s, and the then Australian leadership showed willingness to provide such support for as long as the people of Papua New Guinea wanted it.[10]

Both West and Crawford, in their lectures some thirteen years before independence, noted that 'the problem of promoting self-government in the Territory as a whole is one of substituting wider loyalties for local village ones' (ibid., 62). The primary challenge for economic policy, according to Crawford was to change the economy from subsistence 'with a fringe of European plantations and urban industries to a modern agricultural and even industrial economy' (ibid., 63). Crawford in 1962 envisaged full self-government in ten to fifteen years, should the process of hand-over be commenced then. Many of the challenges for economic policy making identified by the four distinguished academics in 1962 remain. There was considerable success in addressing several of the initial concerns in the first decade of independence, but many of the problems returned with a vengeance in the 1990s. The solutions for many of the current policy dilemmas lie in the successes of the past; the challenge for now is to rediscover them.

Conclusion

Early policy making in Papua New Guinea placed significant emphasis on equity in income distribution and access to social services, sometimes with full realization of the costs of such interventions to growth. One of the main assertions stated in the preamble to the constitution is ' that our national wealth, won by honest, hard work be equitably shared by all'. The second national goal and directive principle requires that 'every effort to be made to achieve an equitable distribution of incomes and other benefits of development among individuals and throughout the various parts of the country'(clause (3)) while clause (4) calls for 'equalization of service in all parts of the country, and for every citizen to have equal access to legal processes and all services, governmental or otherwise, that are required for the fulfilment of his or her real needs and aspirations'. On these counts, economic policy making has failed. Morauta's (2000, 3) statement, that 'We have not made the most of our resources and our wealth. Our destiny remains unfulfilled' is most telling.

The first minister of Finance, Sir Julius Chan, noted in his 1976/77 budget speech that:

> Without stable revenue, a stable currency and a sound economy the positive work of development would be undermined from the start — a fate, I must add, which has overtaken many developing countries that began with the highest hopes (quoted in Garnaut 1981, 158).

Papua New Guinea has indeed been overtaken in its pursuit of development, and Chan was in the driver's seat during part of this period. Much of policy making in Papua New Guinea has been to the neglect of internal balance. Unemployment has consequently received little attention, and the large and rapidly growing pool of labour in search of work demands urgent attention.

The struggle to stabilize the currency and regain fiscal balance was commenced late in 1999 and continues. But the challenge of policy making for sustainable development in Papua New Guinea is more one of rediscovering what worked in the past than of continually trying new initiatives.

Postscript

The record of policymaking in the new millennium has been more positive than that of the 1990s. This may be due in part to the lessons from the tough times of the late 1990s, but it could equally be the product of healthy terms of trade due to a mineral boom since 2002. Commodity prices, as of late 2008, were once again declining with the potential to hurt the fiscal position of the state, the value of the kina and the general economic health of Papua New Guinea. Policy making in Papua New Guinea may once again be tested during the economic downturn of 2009. This time round, however, the government has the capacity to borrow and thus cushion some of the effects of the downturn.

References

Bettison, D. G., E. K. Fisk, F. J. West and J. G. Crawford. 1962. *The Independence of Papua-New Guinea: Four Lectures Presented under the Auspices of the Public Lectures Committee of the Australian National University*. Sydney: Angus and Roberston.

Duncan, Ronald, Satish Chand, Bryan Graham and Tony Lawson. 1998. *Exchange Rate Policy in Papua New Guinea*. Port Moresby: Institute of National Affairs.

Fitzpatrick, P. 1985. The making and the unmaking of the Eight Aims. In *From Rhetoric to Reality: Papua New Guinea's Eight Point Plan and National Goals after a Decade*, ed. P. King, W. Lee and V. Warakai, 22–31. Waigani: University of Papua New Guinea Press.

Garnaut, Ross.1981. Framework of economic policy making. In *Policy Making in a New State*, ed. J.A. Ballard, 157–211. St. Lucia: University of Queensland Press.

Garnaut, Ross. 2000. The first 25 years of searching for development. *Pacific Economic Bulletin* 15(2) Supplement: 29–36.

Garnaut, Ross and Paul Baxter.1984. Exchange Rate and Macro-Management in Independent Papua New Guinea. *Pacific Research Monograph* No 10. Canberra: The Australian National University.

Levantis, Theo. 2000. *Papua New Guinea: Employment, Wages and Economic Development*. Canberra: Asia Pacific Press.

Levantis, Theo. 2001. *Indirect Tax Reform and VAT in Papua New Guinea: a Critical and Empirical Review*. Institute of National Affairs Discussion Paper No. 18. Port Moresby.

Mawuli, Agogo. 1999. *Economic growth far short of potential*. NRI Searchlight Article (mimeo).

Mawuli, A, C. Yala, O. Sanida and F. Kalop. 2005. *Economic Development Planning in Papua New Guinea: The MTDS, 2005, Review and Seminar*. Special Publication 38. Port Moresby: National Research Institute.

Morauta, Sir Mekere. 2000. Silver Jubilee Address to the Nation. *Pacific Economic Bulletin* 15(2) Supplement: 3–5.

Overseas Development Group, University of East Anglia. 1973. *A Report on Development Strategies for Papua New Guinea* (Faber Report). Port Moresby: Office of the Chief Minister.

Salter, W. E. G. 1959. Internal and external balance: the role of price and expenditure effects. *Economic Record* 35: 226–38.

Somare, Sir Michael. 2001. Reflections on constitution-making. In *Twenty Years of the Papua New Guinea Constitution*, ed. A. J. Regan, O. Jessep, and E. Kwa, 15–18. Sydney: Law Book Company.

Terrell, Deane. 2000. The Australian National University and Papua New Guinea: a special relationship. *Pacific Economic Bulletin* 15(2) Supplement: 1–2.

Wacziarg, Romain. 2002. Measuring dynamic gains from trade. *The World Bank Economic Review* 15(3): 393–430.

World Bank. 1978. *Papua New Guinea: Its Economic Situation and Prospects for Development*. World Bank Country Economic Report. Washington, DC: World Bank.

World Bank. 1965. *The Economic Development of the Territory of Papua New Guinea*. Baltimore: John Hopkins University Press.

Endnotes

[1] Helpful comments from Ron Duncan, Ross Garnaut, Ron May and Peter McCawley are acknowledged with the usual disclaimer.

[2] ANU's active involvement with policy making in Papua New Guinea dates back to 1953 when Oskar Spate, Cyril Belshaw, and Trevor Swan were commissioned by the Australian government 'to investigate the economic structure of the Territory with a view to suggesting gaps in knowledge' (Terrell 2000, 1). Since then a string of ANU academics, including Sir John Crawford, Professor Peter Drysdale, Dr Andrew Elek, Professor E. Fisk, Professor Ross Garnaut and Dr Ron May have been involved in the design and implementation of policy in Papua New Guinea.

[3] Ross Garnaut took up the FAS position in April 1975.

[4] Garnaut (2000, 35) claims that 'by 1999, Papua New Guinea had become a kleptocratic state', a statement highlighting the damning state of governance (and policy making) in the country.

[5] This was to be measured by an increase in self-reliance, the last being defined as the proportion of the government's total budgetary expenditure financed from domestic resources and foreign loans.

[6] This section covers selected policies, up to 2002.

[7] Corporatization had been pursued since the early 1990s; the Morauta regime used the privatization strategy as a means to accelerate and expand the corporatization program.

[8] As of 1998, approximately 25 per cent of total tax revenues of K1.6 billion were from import duties; this share fell to 15 and 7 per cent by 1999 and 2000, respectively.

[9] This would be more akin to Fiji's Native Lands Development Commission (NLDC) than the Housing Authority of Fiji.

[10] See the statement of Minister Paul Hasluck as quoted in Bettison, Fisk, West and Crawford (1962:65).

Chapter 5

Policy Making in Agriculture

Bob McKillop, R. Michael Bourke and Valentine Kambori

Introduction

As successive strategy and policy papers have emphasized, agriculture is the most important economic sub-sector in Papua New Guinea. We are constantly told that agriculture provides the livelihood for about 85 per cent of the economically active population. The agriculture sector covers the activities of the private and public sector in cropping, animal husbandry, management of land and water resources, and post-harvest areas within the continuum of agriculture systems, from small-scale subsistence to intensive, commercial agri-business activities.

The colonial legacy in agriculture was described in an earlier policy-making workshop at the Australian National University, in 1977 (McKillop 1981). It followed a dual policy of encouraging a commercial plantation sector and providing settlers with the 'full benefits of modern agricultural scientific knowledge' on the one hand, and promoting a smallholder peasant proprietorship on the other. Professionals working in the Department of Agriculture, Stock and Fisheries (DASF) provided policy and technical support. DASF was a specialist, technically-orientated department modelled on Australian practice. As such, it stood apart from the generalist administration model generally associated with colonial administration of pre-colonial societies. Well-trained professionals with pride in their achievements staffed the department. Through its research work, particularly at the Lowlands Agricultural Experiment Station (LAES) at Keravat, DASF had established an internationally recognized capability in tropical agriculture. The focus was on export tree crops in which Papua New Guinea had a comparative advantage — primarily coffee, cocoa and coconuts — which reinforced a strong commodity orientation within the Department. The establishment of a palm oil industry in West New Britain in the late 1960s also demonstrated a comparative advantage for Papua New Guinea in this crop and the success of the new industry reinforced the orientation toward export tree crops in agriculture policies.

During the transition through self-government to independence, DASF was able to attract a new wave of dedicated professional personnel in a range of fields. New headquarters sections were established in economic research, training, extension research and planning, while research activities were extended from the station into the village agricultural system. A major survey of subsistence agriculture in 1961–62 had involved practically all DASF field staff in data collection. Field extension staff were required to undertake and write-up a major project on village agriculture as part of their orientation program, while departmental officers and visiting researchers undertook innovative projects to better understand and document village agricultural systems during the 1970s and early 1980s. Much of the basic data pertaining to Papua New Guinea village agriculture was collected in this period and there was a greatly expanded interest in the day-to-day operations, including the strengths and weaknesses, of local farming systems.

An important element of the colonial agricultural administration that was not given prominence in the 1977 workshop was the high level of autonomy due to its Australian heritage. The professionals of DASF reported to generalist administrators in Canberra who had limited capacity to analyze the complexities of Papua New Guinea agriculture, so there was little policy initiative from the centre. Moreover, DASF headquarters officials in Port Moresby were isolated, both physically and culturally, from the day-to-day operations of the district office and research station. Individual field officers therefore had a high degree of latitude in formulating their own policies and programs. It was an opportunity that many exercised to the full.

Papua New Guinea's transition to independence occurred toward the end of the decolonization era. It had become fashionable to blame the focus on export crops for the ills of developing countries, and 'self-reliance' had become the catch-cry for newly independent nations. In Papua New Guinea, visiting experts and local politicians were soon urging more self-reliance in the agricultural sector through increased production of grain crops to replace imports. They made little headway within the technically orientated DASF, which could now draw on empirical data to show that village farmers sought to maximize the returns to labour. This was a matter of considerable frustration to politicians taking up the agriculture portfolio. The flamboyant former minister of Agriculture, Iambakey Okuk, called a meeting of DASF staff in Goroka in early 1973 to express his views that the heavy expenditure that continued to be made in research was irrelevant to the country's needs.

Policies at independence

Policy making at independence was characterized by a plethora of interpretations of how the Eight National Aims for a more equitable, self-reliant nation with Papua New Guineans taking control of the economy might be put into practice. In the agriculture sector, a dominant policy issue was the desire to achieve greater self-sufficiency in food. Politically, urban consumers seeking to reduce the price of fresh food, particularly in Port Moresby, drove the pressure for domestic production of root crops, fruits and vegetables for sale in the urban areas. This pressure led to demonstrations in Port Moresby in 1974. Policies to support this aim therefore had to contend with the inherent conflict of stimulating production while keeping prices down in urban areas.

In keeping with the Australian tradition of local autonomy, the fresh foods 'policy' was generated largely in a series of papers prepared as an individual initiative by a DASF officer appointed as national coordinator for fresh food marketing (McKillop 1981, 245–7). The National Executive, in response to the demonstrations in Port Moresby, hurriedly approved a Fresh Food Project (FFP) in 1974. There was lavish expenditure on marketing and storage facilities and the FFP promoted the concept of centralized warehouses and the establishment of some fifty large-scale farms to supply the fresh food needs of major urban centres. The approach undermined the operations of existing food-marketing organizations that were then emerging in the provinces and drove them out of business. Having achieved this dubious outcome, the FFP then encountered funding problems and the venture folded after incurring high financial losses. The basic policy issues of food production for urban markets remained unresolved. There was no assessment of whether the objective was to encourage urban development through low food prices or rural development by supporting higher prices for producers, while the action of the government in controlling the market and thereby undermining local marketing organizations was simply ignored.

The saga of the FFP provides an example of an ongoing theme in Papua New Guinea policy making. While the rhetoric of politicians might give voice to the claims of rural areas, the actual allocation of resources remains heavily biased toward urban areas.

In terms of food security, the major changes since 1870, and especially after 1940, centred on the introduction of new food crops into Papua New Guinea farming systems. New root crops, banana types, maize and peanuts had extended growing periods and increased land productivity by independence. Enhanced access to cash income, primarily through cash crops, also enabled rural households to improve their food security by purchasing food when local supplies were in short supply. However, the rhetoric of food self-sufficiency also brought political pressure to grow cereal crops, primarily rice, to replace imports. Since the nineteenth century, German, Australian, Japanese and national government administrations had promoted rice to provide an easily stored, easily transported and convenient staple food. Despite large investments and subsidized inputs, these efforts have been unsuccessful as the returns to farmers have not been attractive compared with traditional root crops or introduced cash crops. Despite these failures, the 1975 Food Crops Conference called for investigations into the cost-benefits and acceptability of cereals for human consumption (Willson and

Bourke 1976, 13–17) and heavily subsidized machinery was provided for the remaining rice growers in the Bereina area, west of Port Moresby.

Statements of hope: policy making since independence

Macro-economic framework

The government's macro-economic policies have had a major influence on the agriculture sector. From independence to 1993, the government followed a 'hard kina policy'. This period was characterized by prudent fiscal policies, high kina exchange rates, real wage rigidity, and high import dependency. Protective measures were used to establish several agricultural industries during this period, notably sugar and poultry. Import bans were partially imposed on many imported foods in 1983, and more comprehensively in 1986, then replaced by import tariffs after 1993.

For the agriculture sector as a whole, however, macro-economic policies inhibited new investment and the assets of past investments deteriorated. Cash cropping faced pressure from increasing production efficiencies in other countries that grow the same crops as Papua New Guinea and from high cost structures within Papua New Guinea. Since 1989, the Papua New Guinea macro-economic environment has experienced a series of severe shocks, some of them due to natural disasters, some to external factors, and others as a consequence of internal conflict and policy decisions within Papua New Guinea. Serious drought in 1997 also had an impact. There was a sharp decline in food production in the short-term, but it recovered within 6–18 months, while the production of some cash crops (such as coffee) actually increased in the year following the drought. Nevertheless, the drought helped to highlight the importance of agriculture to the well being of Papua New Guinea and the vulnerability of the food production system to climatic extremes, as well as the paucity of implementable policies on food shortages.

Agriculture policies

Institutionally, much of the policy debate in post-independence Papua New Guinea has reflected nostalgia for the expansive extension services of the colonial era. There has been much criticism of the under-resourced public sector field staff trying to maintain services to communities who were increasingly vocal in their demands for government 'hand-outs'. From this perspective, most agricultural support service delivery is seen to have collapsed following independence. This in turn has generated pressure for improved delivery systems to reach village farmers. Popular 'solutions' include efforts to decentralize government services and to enhance the performance of individual industries through corporatization of marketing and service delivery functions.

Coffee, the dominant cash crop in the Highlands Region, provided the initial impetus for an industry corporation. Rapid expansion of corporate services for the industry occurred to address the threat to the industry's survival as a result of the arrival of coffee leaf rust in 1986. Donor assistance was provided to research the problem and the Coffee Development Agency (CDA) was established to deliver extension packages in response to the crisis. The *Coffee Industry Act* of 1991 formalized the amalgamation of separate organizations responsible for marketing, extension and research in the coffee industry as the Coffee Industry Corporation (CIC). The Department of Livestock (DAL) and provincial divisions of primary industry (DPIs) were to withdraw from these fields.

The apparent early success of the coffee industry model led to a policy to assist the key agriculture industries to corporatize in order to establish a new work ethos for enhanced efficiency and service orientation. The creation of organizations, which would be controlled by, accountable to, and financed by the industries, was a major thrust of these policies. The cocoa and coconut industries, which had maintained their separate marketing boards from the colonial era, formed research and extension organizations under joint-venture arrangements. The Cocoa and Coconut Research Institute (CCRI), established in the mid-1980s, formed the Cocoa and Coconut Extension Agency (CCEA) in 1996 to provide extension services in the cocoa and coconut industries. The CCEA started as a small organization, initially with industry funds used only for top management. Front-line extension staff were to be provided by the provinces. Similarly, the Oil Palm Industry Corporation (OPIC) was established to provide extension services to smallholders as one of its main functions. It is partly funded by levies on production, but has also benefited from STABEX funding as well as government grants. The Livestock Development Corporation (LDC) has a mandate to manage Papua New Guinea abattoirs. It was designed to be self-funding through levies, but has become active in developing horticultural crops in Central Province.

The Medium Term Development Strategy (MTDS) provided the framework for agriculture policy making from 1994. The MTDS sought to redefine the role and institutions of government to give better support to the people in their own efforts to secure a better standard of living. The key priorities of the MTDS were health, education, infrastructure and the private sector. Agriculture was encompassed in the private sector, which was to be the 'engine of growth' for productive enterprise. Government involvement in this sector was to be restricted to facilitating access to credit, research and extension, training services, and monitoring the commercial activities of government.

DAL formulated its own version of a MTDS for the agriculture sector in 1996 (DAL 1996). The DAL paper presented plans for a 'new look' DAL that would serve as a facilitator of growth in the sector. The major strategic initiatives were to be the establishment of the National Agricultural Research Institute (NARI) and the National Agricultural Quarantine Inspection Agency (NAQIA). An Agricultural Credit Guarantee Scheme for smallholders was also to be launched. The strategic objectives were to:

• maintain a macro-economic environment and incentive regimes that do not discriminate against agricultural growth;
• improve the effectiveness of public institutions, programs and expenditure for agriculture;
• foster greater private sector participation in capital investments and in the provision of agricultural support services where it is economically viable;
• promote investments that offer opportunities for new export earnings and efficient import substitutions; and
• address the deficiencies in agricultural production, support services, delivery systems, and in the physical and economic infrastructure.

In 1998, DAL approached the Food and Agricultural Organization (FAO) of the United Nations for technical assistance to reform the country's legal and institutional arrangements for management of the agriculture sector. The intention was to re-establish DAL as the central government body responsible for management of the agriculture sector. The FAO consultants noted that DAL remained in a marginalized and moribund state. While it was no longer appropriate for DAL to implement programs, there was a need to build the capacity of a small office to provide the lead role in policy making for the sector. This would require DAL to significantly enhance its capacity in strategic planning, monitoring and evaluation of programs and projects (FAO 2000, 8). Moreover, these functions should be carried out in close collaboration with other national, provincial, and local government agencies, industry corporations, and the private sector.

In August 2001, DAL launched its agriculture development strategy, Horizon 2002–2012 (DAL 2001). Developed in isolation from other key agencies in the sector, the analysis of the sector given in the strategy paper was supply-driven and it demonstrated little appreciation of factors influencing demand. Horizon 2002–2012 put forward a number of interventions, many of them contradictory, designed to reverse the decentralization and corporatization policies of the post-independence period.

While reiterating the principles of the MTDS and stating support for an efficient private sector as the key force in revitalizing agriculture, it sought to centralize control of the sector through legislative reforms, expanded government spending, and a National Agriculture Development Plan. A 'paradigm shift in land tenure policies' was envisaged, using a cooperative model to mobilize land for big investment projects, but restricting ownership to the members of the clan. On the other hand, the government was 'advised' to secure access to land for private investors. Marketing was to be privatized in the coconut industry, but DAL's marketing role was to be strengthened in the rubber industry. DAL was also to take the lead in forming farmers into marketing cooperatives, apparently drawing on experience from Asian countries. An annual budget of between K102 and K108 million was envisaged for the first five years of the planning period.

Not surprisingly, the launch of the Horizon 2002–2012 strategy paper to industry representatives at a workshop in Lae in late 2001 received a negative response. Those bodies that were invited to the workshop by DAL saw the strategy largely as an attempt by a weak and ineffective department to regain control over all aspects of agriculture policy and production in Papua New Guinea, including the export tree crop sector.

Food security

With the structural changes in the agriculture sector, DAL's policy-making role has been increasingly restricted to food security issues. At the same time, political imperatives have increasingly dominated technical and economic reality.

In 1989, a White Paper on Agriculture recognized that food supplies and the overall levels of nutrition were generally adequate throughout the country and looked to improvements in market access as a means of improving the quantity and quality of domestically produced foods for urban markets (Papua New Guinea 1989). A paper by a DAL agricultural economist in 1992 argued that because rice production in Papua New Guinea was a high risk and high cost activity, the cheapest way for Papua New Guinea to obtain rice was to devote resources to export production (Gibson 1992). The following year, the Papua New Guinea Rice Study showed that the cost of producing rice in Papua New Guinea was more than twice the cost of imported rice (Sloane, Cook and King 1993). It concluded that commercial production of rice was not viable in Papua New Guinea and recommended that rice cultivation be limited to small-scale production for subsistence consumption. Both these conclusions were unpopular in the increasingly politicized culture of DAL, where staff with analytical expertise in the agriculture sector had their contracts terminated and national officers were discouraged from undertaking rigorous assessments of policy issues.

Agriculture policy-making changed significantly as a result of the dramatic impact of the 1997 drought and frosts on food supplies (see chapter 17). There was a total or partial collapse of food supplies in many areas and it was estimated that around 260,000 people were in a life-threatening situation with little or no food other than that collected from the bush. Another 980,000 were estimated to have small and inadequate amounts of food available from gardens, sago palm, coconuts or fish. In response, rice imports increased from a forecasted 170,000 tonnes to 236,000 tonnes in 1997–98 (Bourke 2001). However, following the resumption of normal subsistence food production, food imports declined rapidly to levels well below those pertaining before the drought. As a consequence of the drought experience, food security gained prominence in policy-making circles. The PNG Food and Nutrition 2000 Conference was one of the outcomes of this awareness. The conference proceedings brought together 115 papers on various aspects of food production and food security in the country (Bourke *et al*. 2001). The recommendations from the conference were used as basis for a new policy submission to the National Executive Council (NEC) in late 2001.

Increasingly, official documents have claimed that Papua New Guinea is a food deficit country with poor food security. For instance, the 2000–2010 Food Security Policy concluded that: 'the long-term sustainability of the national food security in PNG is precarious, based on the present trend of over dependence of imported food' (DAL 2000). This argument, based on rhetoric rather than fact, has served as a vehicle for DAL's efforts to regain an implementation role in the sector. For example, in its draft 1993 agriculture strategy, DAL gave priority to establishing the optimum scale and technology for growing rice in Papua New Guinea. This would focus on mechanized rice production in the Bereina area and small-scale upland varieties in the Maprik District of East Sepik Province. A 1998 submission to the NEC proposed investing K36 million over ten years for an intensive program to increase rice production (DAL 1998). It put forward a 39-member DAL-led implementation team, new housing and vehicles for the team, training of the extension team, technicians and farmers, subsidized seed production and distribution, DAL-operated machinery pools, 1000 ha irrigation development and a further 4000 ha of mechanized rice cultivation. The NEC approved the establishment of the Rice and Grain Authority and the allocation of K4 million to the rice programs in 1999. The 2000–2010 Food Security Policy proposed that Papua New Guinea put some 100,000 ha of rain-fed lowland rice into production in order to produce some 150,000–170,000 tons of milled rice per year (DAL 2000). Apparently the figure is derived from the rice import figure, but no analysis is provided as to how this target might be achieved.

Meanwhile in the real world: policy implementation

Policy responses

The dominant features of the protective, self-reliance policies of the immediate post-independence period were the 'hard kina' and import bans of selected food items. One outcome of the protective policies was the establishment of local poultry and sugar industries. Both industries have relatively efficient producers who keep abreast of international trends and performance standards. Ramu Agri-Industries operates a sugar cane estate, an outgrowers' scheme, a sugar factory, a sugar refinery, a distillery, four cattle ranches and a meat processing plant. Sugar production ranges from 30,000 to 44,000 tonnes per annum, with about 7000 tonnes exported in good seasons. About 150 outgrowers produce about 20 per cent of the cane for the mill. Establishment of a technologically advanced industry that provides some employment in the sector has come at the cost of high domestic sugar prices for PNG consumers and degradation of the environment that may affect the long-term sustainability of sugar cane growing (Hartemink 2001, 360–362).

Three major producers, with three large, vertically-integrated operations that control feed milling, breeding, growing, processing and distribution, dominate the poultry industry. They are protected by a 70 per cent tariff on imported poultry products. There are also established poultry farmers servicing the live chicken market in most provinces. Although growers regularly complain of low returns, live chicken prices in many centres are two to three times those of the frozen product from supermarkets. While Papua New Guinea is virtually self-sufficient in poultry meat and eggs, the net foreign exchange saving is reduced by heavy reliance on imported feed. Global changes mean both industries are vulnerable to lower-cost external producers as trade barriers are lowered.

Although these small industries benefited from protection, the overall impact of the 'hard kina' policies on the agriculture sector was negative. While governments have regularly indicated their appreciation that agriculture directly or indirectly sustains the majority of the country's population with food and income, the performance of the sector in terms of productivity and employment generation has sometimes been stagnant since independence. Official figures indicate that agriculture grew at only 1.7 per cent per year during the 1980s, while population growth amounted to 2.3 per cent, but these do not cover subsistence production nor domestically-grown market food. With improved prices for export crops, the agricultural sector grew strongly during the 1990s. The 2004 budget papers indicate that the agriculture, forestry and fishing sector grew at 9.1 per cent in 2000, declined by 5.3 per cent in 2001, grew again by 7.3 per cent in 2002 and was projected to grow at an annual average rate of 2.9 per cent over the five years 2003–2007.

Slow growth in employment is a critical problem in Papua New Guinea. From 1980 to 1990, urban unemployment increased from around 9 per cent to 35 per cent, while rural unemployment rose from 21 to 38 per cent. Lack of employment opportunities has been linked to the rapid increase in crime. High crime rates have generated major costs on business and undermined investor confidence, thereby inhibiting employment-generating activity.

Agriculture previously generated a high proportion of Papua New Guinea's formal employment through a large estate sector. The sector generated 52,000 formal jobs in 1970, but this fell to 45,000 by 1980 due primarily to the decline in the estate sector. Accurate statistics on formal employment by sector are no longer available, but a sector survey in 1998 estimated that the number of formal jobs in agriculture was less than 25,000. Increasingly, non-formal employment in smallholder farming has been seen as a means of keeping the rapidly expanding labour force engaged in gainful activities.

Coffee is the major cash crop industry, generating cash incomes to around two million people, but it has experienced somewhat slower growth over the decade 1991 to 2000. Export volume peaked at 85,000 tonnes in 1989 and again at 83,500 tonnes in 1998. Plantation coffee production has been in decline over recent decades and village-based smallholder producers now account for over 80 per cent of output. High wages and low productivity, together with ambitious localization of ownership/management, deteriorating infrastructure, and the declining security situation, were key factors in the demise of plantations. This in turn has reduced formal employment opportunities. Cocoa production has also stagnated at around 27,000–37,000 tonnes since independence. The industry has been under pressure from a general decline in international cocoa prices, a receding estate sector, natural disasters (particularly the Rabaul volcanic eruption of 1994), and adverse weather conditions. The secessionist rebellion in the cocoa growing province of Bougainville since 1989 resulted in the closure of 15,800 smallholder cocoa blocks and 111 estates (DAL 2001, 22).

After a long period of stagnation, copra production increased for the period 1996–2000 in response to improved prices. Production of other cash crops, such as rubber, tea, pyrethrum and spices, has declined or been stagnant over the past twenty years. The outstanding performer on the export cash-cropping side has been oil palm, where high-yielding genetic material has given Papua New Guinea a comparative advantage over other producers. The industry has expanded to four mills in West New Britain and one each in Oro, New Ireland and Milne Bay provinces. Average palm oil export volumes reached 368,000 tonnes in 2007, compared with an average of 122,400 tonnes per year from 1984 to 1990. The price paid to smallholder growers increased dramatically through the 1990s and again in 2008. The crop is generating considerable wealth in the areas where it is being produced. With a more competitive exchange rate, further investment in industry expansion is occuring given a stable political climate.

The corporatization experiment has yielded mixed results. The Oil Palm Industry Corporation (OPIC), through the PNG Oil Palm Research Association (OPRA), provides a cost-effective and technically well-managed research program for oil palm. While OPIC also has the best-developed management and operating systems of the industry extension services, it has been criticized on the grounds that it is not accountable to industry, which pays a substantial proportion of costs, and that performance criteria are based on area planted, not production. This problem has been addressed in West New Britain, where OPIC extension operations have achieved financial self-sufficiency. In the Hoskins area, the resultant increase in efficiency has seen the extension worker to farmer ratio increase from 1:80 to 1:200.

In the other tree crop industries, the results are less encouraging. Generous aid funding during the 1980s enabled the CIC to rapidly expand its research facilities and extension organization, with the latter employing some 300 staff. When funding to these institutions was sharply reduced in 1997 following the end of donor support and general government budget constraints, a major cutback was required. Politicization has also hindered the effectiveness of CIC operations, which have come under increased scrutiny as the industry faces declining production and quality issues. When the CCEA was established, the rapid and unsustainable expansion of the CIC extension service was identified as a lesson, so the strategy was to mobilize provincial resources. This arrangement was threatened by uncertain managerial responsibility, the unsatisfactory performance of many provincial DPI staff, and the downsizing of DAL and provincial establishments. In order to provide an effective service, CCEA had to recruit its own provincial managers, therefore reducing the financial viability of the service.

The major policy change affecting agriculture in Papua New Guinea has occurred as a consequence of poor economic management. A range of factors has led to the devaluation of the Papua New Guinea currency since September 1994. By the 2007, the kina had declined to a value of K1 = $US0.34, compared with about K1 = $US1 in the early 1990s and K1 = $US0.72 in mid 1997. (It has since recovered somewhat, fluctuating between $US 0.30 and $US 0.36 between January and September 2008).

While the dramatic change in exchange rates has brought hardship for urban consumers and increased the cost of imported farm inputs, it generally has positive outcomes for the agriculture sector. Shifts in exchange rates have helped increase returns to Papua New Guinea primary producers relative to competing imports and make Papua New Guinea's agricultural products more competitive in international markets. To the extent that marketing systems are 'open' and pass on price changes to producers, the big winners are Papua New Guinea farmers who predominantly use local resources (land and capital) to generate their product. These are predominantly small-scale commercial and semi-commercial farmers who use minimal amounts of imported items. In summary, recent economic changes have provided a window of opportunity for agriculture to build on its enhanced comparative advantage to create efficient, sustainable industries that generate income, provide employment, and ensure food security for the majority of the population.

Domestically marketed food production has been one of the success stories in Papua New Guinea agriculture over the past twenty-five years. The available evidence suggests that Papua New Guinea's domestically marketed food production has kept pace with population growth and that it has accelerated rapidly since 1998 following the devaluation of the kina and recovery from the 1997 drought and frosts (Bourke 2001, 6–7). This has occurred despite the constraints of poor governance and an unsatisfactory policy framework. Moreover, the level of food imports into Papua New Guinea is not particularly high. Rural people consume an average of 24 kilograms of rice and seven kilograms of flour per year, while imported foodstuffs account for only one sixth of the calories consumed by rural households (Bourke 2001, 7). Nevertheless, there are significant constraints to the continued supply of quality foodstuffs to urban markets at competitive prices.

The capacity of government to respond to these challenges has been seriously eroded during the post-independence period. Under the above devolution policies, the role of DAL has been dramatically reduced over the past twenty years and especially in the last ten. From being the organization responsible for almost all support services and public capital spending for the sector, DAL has lost responsibility for most projects, general extension, research and quarantine, and for most research, development and extension functions for the coffee, copra, cocoa and oil palm industries.

The supposition was that, when new organizations were formed to take on functions formerly performed by DAL, they would take on most of the resources formerly used by DAL for those functions and that DAL would have cost reductions similar to the cost of the new organizations (Woodward 1998). This expectation was not born out in practice. In common with other areas of institutional change in Papua New Guinea, weak public administration meant that the changes were never implemented as intended. With a strong nostalgia for the past, DAL actively lobbied to retain its staff and budget, despite the transfer of functions out of the department. It had its most dramatic 'success' under the Skate administration, when, in the 1999 budget, the newly established NARI and NAQIA received a zero allocation of funds, while DAL retained substantial funding. In addition, DAL refused to transfer a number of research positions under its establishment to NARI.

By retaining large numbers of staff without useful functions, DAL has become an aimless organization with low staff morale. Motivated, skilled staff have sought opportunities elsewhere, leaving the 'time servers' to fill the numbers. The result has been a decline in analytical capacity and the politicization of policy making. Recent analysis of DAL highlighted the functions of economic research and analysis, strategic planning, market research, and policy advice and coordination as key areas that are not currently being performed (Woodward 1998). Related functions are monitoring and evaluation (M&E), which should generate key data on actual performance across the sector, and training, where

DAL no longer has an implementation function, but for which there is also a policy vacuum.

Functionally, food and food security has been left as the main policy function of DAL. Increasingly, its policy papers have become statements based on narrow arguments that seek increased allocations of funds to politically popular causes, especially rice growing. They lack a sound analysis of the situation and put forward unrealistic hopes.

Farmer participation

In the colonial era, expatriate-dominated bodies, such as the Farmers' and Settlers' Association in the highlands and the Planters' Association in the lowlands, had considerable influence in policy making. The decline of the plantation sector in the post-independence era brought a corresponding reduction in the effectiveness of these bodies. At the same time, grower bodies representing smallholders began to play a more important role as 'watchdogs' for the rural sector and lobbied governments on agricultural issues affecting farmers generally. The former Planters' Association, which changed its name to the Papua New Guinea Growers' Association in 1990, has become an effective lobby group for smallholder farmers in the copra and cocoa industries. Similarly, the Smallholder Coffee Growers Association had emerged as an important player by 1998, representing about 14,000 members across fourteen coffee-growing provinces.

The Papua New Guinea Growers' Association was a prime mover to bring all the farmers and industries bodies of Papua New Guinea together under the Rural Industries Council (RIC) to raise the profile of agriculture in Papua New Guinea and give a stronger voice for policies to support the sector. The RIC has established a representative office in Port Moresby in association with the Institute of National Affairs. Its aim is to establish a powerful advisory body for the agriculture sector with strong private sector involvement.

An important, but neglected, area of policy concerns the role of women in agriculture. The central role of women in agriculture has largely been ignored by farmer bodies and the government institutions servicing the agriculture sector. These institutions interact predominantly with men and, at the operational level, decisions about cash-cropping and the sale of these products are dominated my men. Moreover, there is a strong gender bias against women in the education system and men account for 82 per cent of all formal employment. This pattern in turn reinforces the male bias in access to agricultural services and credit. While DAL established a Women-in-Agriculture Development Programs in 2001, effective strategies to achieve its objectives have not been forthcoming.

The disadvantaged position of women is identified as a key constraint on the further development of the agricultural sector in Papua New Guinea. Not only do women play a significant role in the production of food and other agricultural products, but they are generally the more innovative and reliable operators in the downstream processing and marketing activities of those products. There are many positive cases where women have established successful savings and loans programs or taken the lead in marketing agricultural produce. In the formal sector, most employers find women to be more reliable in handling money and other assets, or in routine tasks requiring high productivity (such as food processing) and give preference to employing women in these areas.

A feature of the Papua New Guinea community response to breakdown of public sector service delivery has been the proliferation of non-government organizations (NGOs) and community-based organizations (CBOs) that seek to help groups meet their development aspirations. These groups comprise the voluntary sector that seeks to initiate local development initiatives. Women's groups have been among the more effective in this movement. Overall, however, NGOs and CBOs demonstrate weaknesses in assessing genuine community needs and identifying, designing, implementing and monitoring projects that actually deliver benefits to the community on a sustainable basis.

In the field of agricultural research, NARI's mandate is to clearly define priority problems deserving research, plan viable research approaches and conduct them in a disciplined manner, and then to ensure that useful results are extended to stakeholders via appropriate channels. It is seeking to tackle the latter task through an outreach and liaison (O and L) program based on different approaches and strategies to those of the past. This seeks to make more efficient use of available resources through strategies that maximize development impact and sustainability.

The challenge has been to focus scarce resources on those target groups that have the potential to respond to opportunities and initiatives. As with other institutions, there is a reluctance to provide a policy framework that supports a performance outcome. Nevertheless, NARI's O and L program has identified four primary target groups: commercial smallholder food producers, at-risk subsistence farmers, alternative cash crop producers, and peri-urban gardeners. These groups provide balance across NARI's areas of responsibility and offer prospects for highly visible and short-term results. NARI's strategy is to build partnerships with a range of extension agencies or facilitators for the effective two-way exchange of information and technology between itself and target groups.

Conclusions

Official 'policy making' has become increasingly irrelevant to farmers and other stakeholders in the agriculture sector. While officials have dithered over impractical proposals, farmers have got on with the job of producing food and cash crops. The evidence is that smallholders are efficient producers of traditional food crops for domestic markets and that they demonstrate strong supply responsiveness to prices. The success of vanilla in the early 2000s is an outstanding example of the latter.

The great majority of smallholders, however, face major constraints in moving to a more commercial form of production that delivers agricultural products that meet market requirements. Social norms, jealousy, factionalism and obligations within the village greatly inhibit the time available for surplus production and the motivation to achieve high incomes to a greater or lesser degree for different groups. Access to adequate areas of good agricultural land, inputs supply, and marketing services are also major factors affecting the response to agricultural opportunities. Taken together, these factors generate a wide range of diversity in the agricultural sector. Some individuals and groups demonstrate a remarkable capacity to respond to new challenges and opportunities; most do not.

Shielded from reality by supply-driven 'solutions', most policy makers have demonstrated limited appreciation of the diverse and dynamic nature of Papua New Guinea's agricultural sector. The result is that policies — and extension effort — have been directed at households that were not responsive to the technology and work obligations being promoted. Nevertheless, since independence, many individuals are overcoming the odds and 'breaking the chains' of social and economic constraints to meet market requirements on a commercial basis. They include migrants who have taken up land near urban centres, individuals who have secured clear title to parcels of customary land, and outreach growers contracted to a central agency providing a tightly managed integrated package of inputs, technical advice, credit/banking, monitoring and transport services.

Unfortunately, neglect and the constraints of a Port Moresby-bound bureaucracy have left policy making bodies, particularly DAL, with little capacity to respond to the reality of the agriculture sector. DAL, in particular, has experienced a decline in analytical capacity and its policy making function has been reduced to political rhetoric. The result is a policy vacuum where documents pertaining to be 'policy' are little more than pleas to 'turn the clock back' to a perceived better past. Not only is this impractical, but the proposals are based on visions of establishing command-based organizations with highly centralized power structures. Such organizations have not worked in Papua New Guinea in the past and they are not likely to do so in future.

In this policy vacuum, outside consultants and technical experts have become highly influential in a piecemeal policy making process. Given the absence of practical policy guidance from government on key issues, industry bodies and lobby groups (including aid donors) have hired consultants and technical experts to formulate recommendations based on the perspective of the particular group. As there is an absence of policy analysis capacity to even examine these documents from a Papua New Guinea national perspective, they inevitably have a stronger influence than they would otherwise have. policy making in this environment therefore becomes a disjointed and fragmented process that generates contradictory policies shaped by various interest groups.

This situation is not helpful to Papua New Guinea agriculture, which needs to become more efficient and competitive in order to meet the challenges ahead. If DAL is to become an effective policy making body, a dramatic turnaround in approach and capacity is a prerequisite. The new DAL will need to revitalize itself as a small organization that works in partnership with key stakeholders to catalyze and facilitate realistic solutions, not a controller. It will also need to build its capacity to understand market systems, collect data, analyze and define problems, and then assemble and/or facilitate the resources of others to address these problems. This implies a new realism in terms of DAL's concept of its role, its performance assessment systems and its reward structures.

The prospects for such an outcome are not bright. DAL has lost the confidence of government and industry as a respectable policy making body. Accordingly, there is limited support for its revitalization. Meanwhile, the agriculture sector limps along. Ironically, its prospects have been significantly enhanced by 'policy failure', in the form of the collapse of the kina, which has greatly enhanced the competitiveness of Papua New Guinea agriculture. The capacity of its agricultural industries to respond to these opportunities will depend primarily on the influence of social factors and security in the main agricultural areas and the market chain that links these producers with consumers. Most likely, agriculture policy makers in Port Moresby will remain irrelevant to this outcome.

Postscript

In 2007 National Department of Agriculture and Livestock prepared a National Agricultural Development Plan for the period 2007 to 2016 (Ministry of Agriculture and Livestock 2007). This was submitted to the National Executive Council which endorsed it and committed significant funds to the NADP of about K1200 million over ten years.

In 2008, K68 million was allocated with a further K100 million in 2009. As with the earlier 2002–2012 strategy prepared by NDAL, the NADP has been viewed poorly by many in the agriculture sector in Papua New Guinea. The comments by the director of the Institute of National Affairs in an article in the *Papua New Guinea Post-Courier* (Barker 2009) are likely to reflect the views of many in the agriculture sector. Barker wrote:

> NADP has largely been a wasted opportunity, so far. Grants have been made to individuals and businesses without clearly applied criteria or quality checks. Why should one group secure a large subsidy and not another, undermining a level playing field, those borrowing, while

encouraging corruption; for example K17 million for 6000 head of cattle indeed, or nearly K3000 per head of unremarkable cattle! We need to be much more prudent with (limited) investment funds.

References

Barker, P. 2009. Economy in good head of steam. *Papua New Guinea Post-Courier*. Focus section. 6 January 2009.

Bourke, R. M. 2001. An Overview of Food Security in PNG. In *Food Security for Papua New Guinea*, ed. R. M. Bourke, M. G. Allen and J. G. Salisbury. Proceedings of the Papua New Guinea Food and Nutrition 2000 Conference, PNG University of Technology, Lae, 26–30 June 2000. ACIAR Proceedings No. 99, 5–14. Canberra: Australian Centre for International Agricultural Research.

Bourke, R. M., Allen, M. G. and Salisbury, J. G. eds. 2001. *Food Security for Papua New Guinea*. Proceedings of the Papua New Guinea Food and Nutrition 2000 Conference, PNG University of Technology, Lae, 26–30 June 2000. ACIAR Proceedings No. 99. Canberra: Australian Centre for International Agricultural Research.

Department of Agriculture and Livestock (DAL). 1996. *Agriculture Sector 5 Years Strategic Development Objectives, 1997–2001*. Port Moresby: Department of Agriculture and Livestock.

Department of Agriculture and Livestock (DAL). 1998. *Increasing Domestic Rice Production as a Component of National Food Security*. Submission to the National Executive Council.

Department of Agriculture and Livestock (DAL). 2000. *Papua New Guinea Food Security Policy 2000–2010*. Port Moresby: Department of Agriculture and Livestock.

Department of Agriculture and Livestock (DAL). 2001. *National Agricultural Development Strategy: Horizon 2002–2012*. Port Moresby.

Food and Agriculture Organization (FAO). 2000. *Assistance in Agriculture Legislation in Support of Food Security*. Report by Legislative Consultant, May 2000.

Gibson, J. 1992. *Rice Self-Sufficiency and the Terms of Trade*. Policy Working Paper No. 2. Port Moresby: Department of Agriculture and Livestock.

Hartemink, A. E. 2001. Sustainable land management at Ramu Sugar Plantation: assessment and requirements. In *Food Security for Papua New Guinea*, ed. R. M. Bourke, M. G. Allen and J. G. Salisbury. ACIAR Proceedings No. 99, 344–364. Canberra: Australian Centre for International Agricultural Research.

McKillop, R. F. 1981. Agriculture policy-making. In *Policy-Making in a New State: Papua New Guinea 1972–77*, ed. J. A. Ballard, 238–256. Brisbane: University of Queensland Press.

Ministry of Agriculture and Livestock. 2007. *National Agricultural Development Plan 2007–2016*. Two volumes. Port Moresby.

Papua New Guinea. 1989. *White Paper on Agriculture: National Policies for the Development of the Agricultural Sub-sector*. Port Moresby.

Sloane, Cook and King. 1993. *Rice Sites Development Studies Volume 1*. Port Moresby: Food Management Branch, Department of Agriculture and Livestock.

Willson, K. and R. M. Bourke eds. 1976. Recommendations. In *1975 Papua New Guinea Food Crops Conference Proceedings*, 13–17. Port Moresby: Department of Primary Industry.

Woodward, K. R. 1998. *Restructuring Plan for the PNG Department of Agriculture and Livestock*. Consultant's Draft Final Report. ADB TA 2898 PNG. Port Moresby: Department of Agriculture and Livestock.

Chapter 6

A Short History of Mineral Development Policies in Papua New Guinea, 1972-2002

Colin Filer and Benedict Imbun

The mineral policy paradox in Papua New Guinea

There was a time, during the 1980s, when Papua New Guinea was an attractive place for mineral exploration and investment, because it was seen to have a stable and user-friendly policy framework by comparison with many other developing countries. This is no longer the case. The circumstances surrounding and following the closure of the Bougainville copper mine in 1989, and the sequence of events which has led BHP Billiton to disengage from operation of the Ok Tedi mine, have both done enormous damage to the country's reputation. To read much of the recent writing on the history of mining and mineral policy in Papua New Guinea, one gets the impression — to use a colourful English phrase — that the Papua New Guinea government could not organize the proverbial piss-up in a brewery, let alone foreign investment in the mining and petroleum industries. And both of these industries have recently been in steep, if not precipitous, decline. However, closer examination of the recent history of mineral policy in Papua New Guinea, when compared with that of many other developing countries, suggests that the government has done a reasonably good job of coping with difficult circumstances and unforeseen events. So it is not at all obvious that disinvestment in either or both of these sectors is a direct consequence of mineral policies which have been poorly designed or implemented.

For the purpose of this paper, we define mineral development as the process of extracting mineral resources from the ground and converting them into mineral commodities which are then traded in a market, thus generating mineral wealth for a variety of national and foreign stakeholders. Mineral resources are understood to include oil and gas, as well as metallic ores, and they count as a form of non-renewable natural capital which can be converted into other forms of capital, but they do not count as mineral wealth so long as they lie buried in the ground. Insofar as public policy is the business of government, the role of government in allocating property rights to mineral resources, and then regulating the distribution of mineral wealth derived from their development, is bound to be a very important element in any mineral policy framework.

Mineral revenues are here defined as the share of mineral wealth which is captured or collected by the government from the development of mineral resources in its territory. Direct revenues are collected directly from the mining industry and its employees, and are specified in the fiscal component of a country's mineral policy framework, while indirect revenues are collected from other industries or individuals whose own incomes are derived from goods and services supplied to the mining industry.

While the government collects two different kinds of revenue from the process of mineral development, the developers themselves incur two different kinds of cost. First, there are the direct or necessary costs which are incurred in the process of discovering, producing and selling mineral commodities with the techniques or technologies which are currently available. Then there are the indirect or surplus costs which are incurred in the payment of taxes to the host government, the mitigation of environmental damage, the management of community affairs, and so forth. But beyond these internal costs which should all appear in a company's balance sheet, there are also external costs or externalities, which are the costs of mineral development borne by other stakeholders, including future generations. These are commonly represented as the negative economic, social and environmental impacts of mineral development whose value exceeds the amount which developers pay to compensate for such damage. The total equation of costs, benefits and impacts is another major point at issue in a country's mineral policy framework. For if developers fail to internalize the full external costs of mineral development, then the simple equation of financial costs and benefits, as registered in corporate and government accounts, will fail to show the extent to which mineral development also counts as sustainable development.

The collection and expenditure of mineral revenues was an essential part of the National Development Strategy at the time of independence, simply because the Bougainville copper mine accounted for 60 per cent of the value of the country's exports. One might suppose that the mineral policy process and framework should be no less essential to the Medium-Term Development Strategy which has since become the government's official planning statement, because Papua New Guinea still has a mineral-dependent economy. Despite the closure of the Bougainville mine, the mining industry currently accounts for about 50 per cent of the country's exports and 20 per cent of its gross domestic product, while the oil industry has been contributing half as much again. As a result, direct mineral revenues have been accounting for about one third, and total mineral revenues for as much as one half, of total government revenues from all domestic sources. Yet the significance of mineral revenues for the government's budget is not reflected in the government's own expenditure plans, because the Department of National Planning has come to regard the mining and oil industries as 'sunset industries' which cannot, by definition, be sustainable, and cannot therefore make a contribution to 'sustainable development'.

There is an element of truth, as well as an element of irony, in this one-eyed vision of the future. During the course of the next decade, government revenues derived from the mining and petroleum sectors are projected to fall to less than 20 per cent of their current levels if no new major projects are developed (Finlayson 2002). The Misima, Porgera and Ok Tedi mines will have closed, and current oil reserves will have been exhausted. Even if the Gas-to-Queensland Project and the Ramu Nickel Project (or another large-scale mining project) begin to operate in the next five years, government revenues from the mining and petroleum sectors are still projected to fall to less than 40 per cent of their current levels by 2012. Some government officials seem to think that these losses can be partly offset by a significant expansion of the oil palm industry, but their optimism is probably unwarranted, and there is certainly no prospect of any major increase in revenues from other domestic sources. So the question of whether and how the country's mineral policy framework relates to the level of foreign investment in the mining and petroleum sectors is hardly one which Planning or Treasury can afford to ignore.

In the same way that large-scale mining and petroleum projects are enclave developments within a national economy which mainly consists of small farmers and gardeners minding their own business, so it can be argued that mineral development policy has become a sort of enclave within the national political landscape. While the construction of mineral policy around the time of independence was closely related to the provisions of the national constitution, the formulation of the National Development Strategy, the passage of the first Organic Law on Provincial Government, and a set of new laws and institutions relating to the use of customary land, the subsequent transformations of mineral policy have been progressively isolated or insulated from changes in other policy domains. Even the second Organic Law on Provincial Governments and Local-level Governments has made a much smaller impact on the mineral policy framework than its designers intended, partly because they failed to grasp some of the basic features of the framework which already existed. The only other policy domain which has retained a dynamic and reciprocal connection with the mineral policy framework throughout the period since independence is that of 'environment and conservation', and that is because the environmental impacts of large-scale mining projects have been the primary focus of policies and laws relating to any form of environmental planning and management.

Our listing of the major landmarks in the development of Papua New Guinea's mineral policy framework (Box 1) is based on the narrow definition of 'policy' as something which is made by governments, even if the policy process engages a wider range of actors. We also take it for granted that mineral policy in Papua New Guinea is something which is made by the national government by virtue of its legal ownership of the nation's mineral resources, even if other actors have sometimes challenged this status. However, we shall not assume that the mineral policy process can be understood entirely by analysis of the design and implementation of successive acts of parliament, such as the *Mining Act* of 1992 or the *Oil and Gas Act* of 1998. Nor shall we assume that policies produced during the lifetime of 'a government' have been part of a distinctive policy agenda pursued by all or any members of the political coalition or parliamentary majority assembled under the leadership of a single prime minister.

Mineral development policy at the moment of independence

The mineral policy framework which prevailed in 1975 was one which took shape during the lifetime of the first and second Somare governments, from February 1972 to March 1980. Its basic features were established in discussion between a few key members of the first Somare government, supported by a team of expatriate advisers, who took the lead in renegotiating the terms of the *Bougainville Copper Agreement* and setting the initial conditions for development of the Ok Tedi project (Jackson 1982, 92). Its further refinement became the responsibility of the Minerals and Petroleum Policy Committee (MPPC) established in 1975, which was chaired jointly by the secretary of Finance and the director of the Office of Minerals and Energy, which made its recommendations to cabinet through their respective ministers,[1] and which continued to function as the voice of the national government in negotiations with foreign investors.

The substance of this policy regime is documented in five of the laws enacted by the Independent State of Papua New Guinea: the *Mineral Resources Stabilisation Fund Act* (Chapter 194) and the *Mining (Bougainville Copper Agreement) Act* (Chapter 196), both of which date back to 1974; the *Mining (Ok Tedi Agreement) Act* of 1976 and the *Mining (Ok Tedi Supplemental Agreement) Act* of 1980, both of which were later subsumed under the *Mining (Ok Tedi) Act* (Chapter 363); and the *Petroleum Act* of 1977 (Chapter 198).[2] Its basic principles were set out in two policy statements produced by the MPPC — a brief statement on *Financial Policy Relating to Major Mining Project* (1975) and a longer statement on *Petroleum Policy and Legislation* (1976). These are both summarized, discussed and endorsed in the report of the World Bank mission which visited Papua New Guinea in 1976 (World Bank 1978). Further endorsement can be found in academic literature published during or immediately after the period in question, some of which came from the pens of those expatriate advisers who played key roles in the policy process (Zorn 1973, 1977; Garnaut and Clunies-Ross 1974, 1975; Zorn and Bayne 1975; Garnaut 1981).

Box 6.1 Major landmarks in the development of Papua New Guinea's mineral policy framework

1974: Renegotiation of *Bougainville Copper Agreement*.

1974: Passage of *Mineral Resources Stabilisation Fund Act* (Chapter 194).

1975: Establishment of Minerals and Petroleum Policy Committee.

1976: Conclusion of original *Ok Tedi Agreement*.

1977: Passage of *Mining Act* (Chapter 195) and *Petroleum Act* (Chapter 198).

1978: Passage of *Environmental Planning Act*.

1980: Conclusion of (first) *Supplementary Ok Tedi Agreement*.

1986: Placer Pacific share float.

1987: Government signs Mining Agreement for development of Misima mine.

1988: Mount Kare gold rush.

1988: Introduction of Development Forum.

1988: Outbreak of Bougainville rebellion.

1989: Conclusion of Porgera Development Forum agreements.

1989: Revision of mineral policy framework by NEC decision 98/89.

1990: Conclusion of Misima and Kutubu Development Forum agreements.

1991: Conclusion of Ok Tedi Development Forum agreements.

1992: Introduction of Infrastructure Tax Credit Scheme.

1992: Passage of new *Mining Act*.

1993: IMF review of fiscal regime.

1993: Government insists on purchase of additional equity in Porgera project.

1995: Revision of fiscal regime by NEC decision 46/95.

1995: Conclusion of Lihir Integrated Benefits Package agreements.

1995: Passage of *Organic Law on Provincial Governments and Local-level Governments*.

1995: Finalisation of natural gas policy statement.

1995: Passage of *Mining (Ok Tedi Restated Eighth Supplemental Agreement) Act*.

> 1996: Passage of *Mineral Resources Development Company Pty Limited (Privatization) Act*.
>
> 1997: Separation of Ministry of Petroleum & Energy from Ministry of Mineral Resources.
>
> 1998: Passage of *Oil and Gas Act*.
>
> 2000: Conclusion of *Ramu Nickel/Cobalt Project Memorandum of Agreement*.
>
> 2000: Independent review of fiscal regimes for mining and hydrocarbons.
>
> 2001: Passage of *Mining (Ok Tedi Mine Continuation Agreement) Act*.

The key question addressed in the construction of this mineral policy framework was a very simple one: how could the national government capture the maximum possible share of the nation's mineral wealth in the form of mineral revenues without alienating foreign investors to an extent which would deter their future investment in the production of more mineral wealth and more mineral revenues? The importance of this question lay in a belief that the revenues derived from two very large and profitable mines, if properly applied to the task of national development, would enable the government and the country to escape their dependence on Australian aid and expertise before those mines had been exhausted. And the credibility of this vision partly depended on the fluctuating price of mineral commodities.

In 1973, the prices of gold and copper climbed to an unprecedented peak. As a result, Bougainville Copper Ltd (BCL) made an enormous windfall profit from the Panguna mine which had been opened in the previous year. Under the terms of the *Bougainville Copper Agreement* of 1967, the government got 20 per cent of the dividends paid by the company, because it held 20 per cent of the shares. But the government's equity stake in the project had been acquired at the cost of granting the company an exemption from corporate income tax for the first three years of production. So the greater part of the windfall profit was destined for the pockets of foreign shareholders.[3] This 'flight of capital' was an affront to the Eight-Point Plan which the Somare government had adopted as the charter for its National Development Strategy. This called for 'a rapid increase … in the proportion of personal and property income that goes to Papua New Guineans' and for 'an increasing capacity for meeting government spending needs from locally raised revenue'.

The Eight-Point Plan also called for 'government control and involvement in those sectors of the economy where control is necessary to achieve the desired kind of development', but the government's policy makers did not regard a mining enclave as a desirable form of development in its own right, expropriation was not a realistic option, and they could see no point in spending more money to purchase a bigger equity stake in BCL if the aim was to apply mineral revenues to the development of other sectors of the national economy. It was the fiscal component of the *Bougainville Copper Agreement* which therefore became the main point at issue in its renegotiation.

The economists on the government side were not content to wind back the various tax concessions granted in the original agreement. They went one step further, by suggesting that the rate of tax on company profits should be adjusted to reflect the total amount of such profits, so that the government, rather than the company's foreign shareholders, would capture the lion's share of any increase due to a surge in mineral commodity prices of the kind which had just occurred (Garnaut and Clunies-Ross 1975, 1983). Aside from the standard rate of corporate income tax, they proposed to levy an additional 'resource rent tax' on any amount of profit which exceeded a 'reasonable rate of return'.[4] CRA and the rest of the mining industry opposed this 'additional profits tax' on the grounds that windfall profits should be their own just reward for the huge risks involved in exploration and investment. But the government's economists maintained that 'resource rents', like royalties, should return to the real owner of the mineral resources from which they were derived. And in this case, the real owner was the nation, as represented by the national government.

This at least was the assumption made in the legislation. But once the national government had settled its accounts with BCL, it still had an account to settle with the Bougainvilleans who were threatening to secede from the Independent State of Papua New Guinea and take away their renegotiated source of revenue. The first price paid for their allegiance to the nation was an agreement to return all mineral royalties to the province from which they originated, and the second price was the organic law which authorized the establishment of provincial governments (Conyers 1976). The House of Assembly had already sought to purchase the political support of the Panguna landowners in 1966, when it agreed to grant them 5 per cent of the royalties from the mine. Now the other 95 per cent would become the main source of revenue for the North Solomons provincial government, whose share in the 'ownership' of mineral resources received additional recognition through the grant of an effective power to veto any further mineral exploration in the province.

Despite the fuss made about the fiscal component of the new policy regime, the more lasting bone of contention would be the set of property relations expressed or implied in the distribution of mineral revenues between the two tiers of government and the 'third estate' of customary landowners. But the principles governing the 'internal' distribution of mineral wealth got no mention in the policy statement of 1975. That is because the policy makers were preoccupied, at that moment, by their failure to persuade Kennecott to develop the Ok Tedi mine on fiscal terms broadly similar to those which BCL had grudgingly accepted in 1974. It took another five years for the Papua New Guinea government (and perhaps also the Australian government) to persuade BHP to take Kennecott's place. During that period, the prices of gold and copper fell to levels which cast considerable doubt on the role assigned to mineral revenues as a catalyst for state-led economic growth (Jackson 1982, 93). But then they hit another peak in 1980, just as the finishing touches were applied to the *Supplementary Ok Tedi Agreement* which, unlike the agreement of 1976, really was an agreement to develop the country's second major mine. And 1980 was the first and only year in which BCL actually paid the additional profits tax. So the key articles of mineral faith in the National Development Strategy appeared to be quite solid after all.

The self-congratulation of the individuals who framed this charter should not lead us to exaggerate the extent of its departure from the principles which had informed the negotiation of the original *Bougainville Copper Agreement* by the Australian colonial administration. Take the question of state equity in mining ventures, for example. The financial policy statement of 1975 declared that the government 'welcomes offers of minority shareholdings in major projects'. It was CRA which had originally made such an offer to the colonial administration, because this would have the highly desirable effect of giving the state a vested interest in the profitability of the mine without yielding effective control over its management (Denoon 2000, 92). At one point in the renegotiation of the agreement, the company offered to sell the government a controlling interest in BCL as a condition for its own acquiescence to the additional profits tax (Garnaut 1981; O'Faircheallaigh 1984). This was an offer which the government's negotiators sensibly declined. But they did not go so far as to question the wisdom of purchasing 20 per cent of the shares in Ok Tedi Mining Ltd, despite their recognition of the risk entailed in this commitment of scarce financial resources, and despite the prospect of a contradiction in the government's role as a shareholder and a regulator.

The tax concessions granted in the original *Bougainville Copper Agreement* owe something to the economic development strategy which the World Bank had recommended to the Australian colonial administration in 1963 (IBRD 1965). The central plank of this strategy was to foster a rapid growth in the export of primary commodities by attracting foreign investment to large-scale forestry and agriculture projects. But once the Panguna orebody had been discovered in 1964, a large-scale mining project was soon added to the shopping list. One way in which the administration sought to encourage CRA's investment in the project was to limit the ratio of output-based taxes to profit-based taxes, regardless of the length of the tax holidays to be granted during the investment recovery period. So the royalty rate was set at 1.25 per cent of the value of mine production, which was very low by the standards of the time. When the tax holidays were renegotiated in 1974, there was no question of raising the proportion of output-based taxes in the total tax package. On the contrary, the new package was a more refined expression of the fiscal principle set down in the original agreement, which is one of the reasons why it found favour with both the World Bank and the Australian government.

What, then, were the implications of the national government's decision to keep a tight lid on the level of mineral royalties, dispatch the whole lot back to their province of origin, and keep a firm central grip on the bulk of the profit-based taxes collected under the new fiscal regime? First, the national government's dependence on forms of mineral revenue that were bound to vary with the fluctuating price of mineral commodities justified the institution of the Mineral Resources Stabilisation Fund, which was meant to stabilize the amounts which found their way into the government's annual budget. Secondly, the national government had an even greater interest in limiting any further additions to the indirect or surplus costs incurred in the production of mineral wealth, which included the cost of managing or mitigating the negative impacts of development, as well as the payment of output-based taxes. Finally, in contrast and opposition to the national government, provincial governments and local landowners had little or no stake in the profitability of mineral development, and would therefore come to regard their output-based share of mineral revenues as a form of compensation for the social and environmental costs which the national government might reasonably want to exclude from the developer's bottom line.

Environmental considerations were not entirely absent from the mineral policy regime established after 1972, but they were not pursued with the degree of diligence that was applied to tax matters. A brief statement of mineral policy in the *Improvement Plan for 1973–1974* included a promise that 'the Government will have power to require the use of the most modern and effective conservation measures'; the value of protecting the natural environment was enshrined in the preamble to the national constitution; and this constitutional imperative informed the passage of the *Environmental Planning Act* in 1978. But the Panguna mine and the Ok Tedi prospect were both exempted from this legislation because the relevant development agreements were signed before it came into force. The *Supplementary Ok Tedi Agreement* of 1980 did mark an advance on the Bougainville agreements in its requirement for construction of a tailings dam, but made no advance on the original *Ok Tedi Agreement* in demanding that serious money be spent on the conduct of environmental impact studies (Jackson 1982, 82ff).

The original *Ok Tedi Agreement* contained a number of clauses which declared that the people of Kiunga and Telefomin sub-provinces (later to be known as districts) should receive preferential treatment in the project's training, employment and business development programs (*ibid.*, 163). This also represented an advance on the Bougainville agreements, because it implied the recognition of a project impact area which was smaller than a province, but larger than the area of land leased from customary landowners for the purpose of mineral development. The significance of this innovation was explored at some length in the socio-economic impact study commissioned by the Department of Minerals and Energy (Jackson *et al.* 1980). That study was also the first of its kind in Papua New Guinea, and it served to underscore the exemption of the Ok Tedi project from the provisions of the *Environmental Planning Act* because it was the government, and not the mining company, which paid for it.

The policy of discriminating in favour of the people who lived in the so-called 'area of preference' was initially justified by reference to the remoteness and backwardness of this area in comparison with other parts of the country. But it also implied the recognition of a series of graduated zones of entitlement to the benefits of mineral development which could be taken as another form of compensation for the social and environmental costs of that development. And, like the 'real' compensation payments due to local landowners, this kind of positive discrimination would seem to internalize some of those costs by adding to the indirect costs of mining itself. However, this should not lead us to suppose that the national government was more generous in its dispensation to provincial and local stakeholders in the Ok Tedi project than it had been in the case of Bougainville. On the contrary, the general feeling in Port Moresby was that the Bougainvillean stakeholders had commanded a premium which should not be allowed to function as a precedent for the distribution of mineral wealth from other projects. So there was no equivalent of the 'Panguna Regional Payment' in the compensation package allocated to the Ok Tedi landowners, Ok Tedi Mining Ltd. (OTML); OTML was not required to pay the 50c per tonne of output which BCL had been obliged to contribute to the 'Non-Renewable Resources Fund' administered by the North Solomons provincial government, and the Fly River Provincial government was not granted an effective power to veto any further mineral exploration in Western Province.

The various charters of the independent state laid great emphasis on the values of 'participation' — the participation of Papua New Guineans in a national economy which was still dominated by foreign companies and expatriate persons, and the participation of those sections of the national population who would nowadays be described as 'stakeholders' in any specific economic venture. In this respect, they were seen to make a clean and decisive break with the economic policies of the colonial administration, including those which had been designed to satisfy the World Bank. But the national constitution also spoke of the need for an 'equitable distribution of incomes' between different parts of the country, and called for the country's natural resources to be wisely used 'for the collective benefit of us all' and to be 'replenished for the benefit of future generations'. This is what we would nowadays call a charter for 'sustainable development'.

The architects of the country's 'new' mineral policy regime thought that state ownership of mineral resources and central government control of mineral revenues were both essential to the cause of sustainable development. If mineral wealth was now to be derived from one of the most remote and backward parts of the country, then the local benefits of mineral development would marginally reduce the spatial inequality of income distribution. But the area around Ok Tedi was only one of many 'less developed areas', and a small number of scattered mining enclaves would still tend to widen the gap between rich regions and poor regions unless the national government could use a significant portion of mineral revenues to achieve the opposite effect. Since non-renewable resources could not exactly be 'replenished' for the benefit of future generations, the wealth derived from their extraction should ideally be invested in another form of development in which a lot more Papua New Guineans would participate for a period which would not simply come to an end with the closure of a mine whose location was an accident of geology. But the local beneficiaries of such an accident could not be expected to make this kind of investment, especially if they had no experience of any other form of development aside from their mineral windfall. So their participation should ideally be limited to a share of mineral wealth which would be just enough to sustain the belief that they had gained more than they had lost from the development of a local resource which was 'really' a national resource (Filer 1997a).

What was this other form of development whose promotion would enable a mineral-dependent state to avoid the perpetuation of a mineral-dependent economy? By most accounts, it was a form of integrated rural development constructed on a solid agricultural foundation. But the government's capacity to realize this vision was undermined by another feature of its own economic policy. This was the so-called 'hard kina' strategy, which had the effect of aggravating that common affliction of mineral-dependent economies which has since come to be known as the 'Dutch disease' (Garnaut and Baxter 1984; Goodman et al. 1985; Duncan et al. 1998; Sugden 2002). The appreciation in the value of the national currency was thought to be a good thing because it lowered the price of the imported goods which were consumed in large quantities by urban wage-earners. But it was not such a good thing for the national producers of agricultural commodities whose prices were artificially inflated (Jarrett and Anderson 1989; Baxter 2001). Since public expenditure and public sector employment accounted for such a large proportion of formal economic activity, it could be argued that the national government's mineral revenues were simply being 'invested' in a widening economic and social division between the urban and bureaucratic elites and the vast majority of rural villagers. If the national government came to be seen as a parasite stuck to the back of the mining industry, then the legitimacy of its claims on the nation's mineral wealth would naturally be called into question.

Transformations of the mineral policy regime under the Namaliu government

The mineral policy framework established during the lifetime of the first and second Somare governments, from 1973 to 1980, began to look a little shaky during the exploration boom of the following decade, but its wholesale reconstruction did not start until 1988. The outbreak of the Bougainville rebellion is commonly cited as the key turning point in this policy process. However, for the better part of 1988, the mineral policy makers in the national capital were less interested in the rumblings of discontent from around the Panguna copper mine than in the problem of securing local consent for the establishment of a new gold mine in the Porgera Valley, at the far western end of Enga Province, while managing the fallout from the Mount Kare gold rush nearby. The sequence of events that led to the closure of the Panguna mine just added to the urgency of a process of policy reform which had already been initiated.

The origin of this process can be traced to the public or populist outcry over the windfall profits harvested by a number of senior politicians and bureaucrats who purchased large bundles of shares in Placer Pacific, the Canadian company which would become the operator of both the Misima and Porgera mines, when the shares were floated on the Sydney stockmarket at the end of 1986. The company's intention was to broaden the base of national support for these two investments by creating a new class of shareholding citizens, but the outcome was a sort of 'mental mineral boom' which not only reflected the actual boom in mineral exploration expenditures, but created a widespread conviction that huge amounts of mineral wealth were on the point of being pocketed by members of a national elite who were themselves living in the pockets of the mining industry, and could no longer be trusted to apply this wealth to the development of the nation as a whole (Filer 1997a, 238). The main target of abuse was the Finance minister, Sir Julius Chan, and the loudest voice in the opposition was that of Father John Momis, the MP for North Solomons Province, whose own campaign for re-election to parliament in 1987 was built around a demand for his constituents to get a better deal from the Panguna mine. Although Paias Wingti's ruling coalition survived that national election, and a Leadership Tribunal eventually cleared Chan of the charges levelled against him, Momis had articulated a new policy agenda for the growing number of 'mineral provinces' and 'project landowners' across the country.

The message was certainly not lost on Ned Laina and Yaungtine Koromba, the premiers of Enga and Southern Highlands, who were instrumental in persuading the National Premiers Council (NPC) to set up a Mining and Petroleum Working Committee to undertake a comprehensive review of the existing mineral policy framework. This body was established in June 1988 and its report was finished in September (National Premiers Council 1988). In the meantime, Wingti's coalition had been toppled in a parliamentary vote of no confidence, Rabbie Namaliu had been elected as the new prime minister, and he had then appointed Patterson Lowa, a member of John Momis's Melanesian Alliance Party, as the new minister for Minerals and Energy. Lowa and Momis immediately set off to Panguna to hear the grievances of the local landowners, and Lowa then ordered his officials to commission a review of the mine's social and environmental impact (AGA 1989). For his part, Namaliu recruited a pair of expatriate economists to advise him on the process of mineral policy reform, and it was their dialogue with officials in the Department of Minerals and Energy which led to the most important innovation in the mineral policy framework since the renegotiation of the *Bougainville Copper Agreement* — the institution of the Development Forum (West 1992). This was the national government's immediate response to the report commissioned by the NPC, and it was made before the outbreak of the Bougainville rebellion revealed the true extent of the local grievances which were still being assessed by the government's team of consultants.

The aim of the NPC was to influence the content of a new *Mining Act* which the Department of Minerals and Energy had begun to design in 1987. This review of the mining legislation was initially a bureaucratic, not a political, initiative, and was primarily intended to rationalize the archaic system of prospecting and mining licences inherited from the colonial era (Dalton 1988; Hunt 1989). Even after this work had begun, the previous minister for Minerals and Energy made a public policy statement which could have been written by the same group of expatriate advisers who had renegotiated the *Bougainville Copper Agreement* (but was actually written by his own officials), citing a 400 per cent increase in exploration expenditures over the previous four years as proof of the 'reasonableness and consistency' of the existing policy framework (Kaputin 1987). However, the Placer Pacific share scandal had created a climate of opinion in which the design of the new act became a hot topic of public debate. The 'general feeling' of the NPC was described on the first page of its own report:

> Here was the National Government about to completely overhaul the Mining Act, the whole legislative framework for the development of the mining industry in this nation, and it hadn't even bothered to see what the views of PGs and the landowners were on this vital issue.

Instead, the Department had been bothering to consult the newly formed Chamber of Mines and Petroleum to ensure the convenience of its legislation for the mining industry (Department of Minerals and Energy 1988).

Most of the provisions of the *Mining Act* that was eventually passed in 1992, in the dog days of the Namaliu government, were in fact the outcome of this earlier round of consultation. The innovation of the Development Forum is confined to the Minister's statutory obligation to convene one 'before the grant of any special mining lease [SML] to consider the views of those persons who the Minister believes will be affected by the grant of that special mining lease', including 'such persons as he thinks will fairly represent the views' of the applicants for the SML, the 'landholders' of the proposed SML and any other land to be leased by the applicants, the national government, and the relevant provincial government.[5] The only provision in the act which reflects the actual outcome of the Porgera Development Forum is the stipulated increase in the proportion of mineral royalties payable to the 'landholders', from 5 per cent to 20 per cent of the total collected by the state.

The text of the *Mining Act* does not reflect the extent of mineral policy reform, nor the intensity of mineral policy debate, during the four years of the Namaliu government. The Porgera Development Forum resulted in three separate agreements between the national government, the Enga Provincial government, and representatives of the Porgeran community which were finally signed in May 1989, and which contained a variety of undertakings that were not reflected in the *Mining Act* (Derkley 1989). The SML landowners (and their children) were to receive a grant equivalent to 13 per cent of the royalties derived from the mine, while another 10 per cent would accrue to a body known as the Porgera Development Authority, which was to be responsible for the delivery of additional public goods and services to the people of Porgera District. The Enga provincial government would be very generously compensated for the diminution of its own share of the royalties by means of a 'special support grant' from the national government, at the rate of one per cent of the value of mine production, for the first decade of the mine's operation.

Arrangements were made for the provincial government and the landowners to acquire 49 per cent of the state's 10 per cent equity stake in the Porgera Joint Venture (PJV), with an option to purchase the remaining 51 per cent after five years.[6] The national government promised to make the mining company phase out the practice of commuter mining and build a mining town at Porgera, because representatives of the local community were determined to gain the development benefits which would flow from the process of urbanization. Even before these agreements were finalized, cabinet had decided that those provisions which related to the distribution of mineral wealth between the three parties to the forum process should henceforth be part of the general policy framework. So these were incorporated into a 'basic mining package' which was used as a template for new benefit-sharing agreements to cover the Ok Tedi and Misima mines, both of which were already in production, and then to cover the development of the Kutubu oilfield, despite the fact that this would not be covered by the provisions of the new *Mining Act*.[7] At the same time, those clauses in the earlier Bougainville and Ok Tedi agreements which obliged the mining companies to implement training and business development programs were now incorporated into a standard mining development contract which was to be used as a template for future agreements between the state and the developers of new mining projects.[8]

While project coordinators in the Department of Minerals and Energy were busily negotiating new 'packages' for landowners and provincial governments in different parts of the country, the managers of the Porgera mine thought they detected a major flaw in the forum agreements to which they had not been a party. It appeared that both levels of government were failing to keep some of their promises to the local community, and community representatives were understandably annoyed. One particular source of annoyance was the national government's apparent failure to do anything about its promise to make Placer Niugini phase out the practice of rotating its 'fly-in/fly-out' workforce through the grey skies of Porgera. The company had good economic reasons for maintaining this practice, and most members of its commuting workforce had no desire to bring their families to Porgera (McGavin, Jones and Imbun 2001). However, the managers also understood the importance of maintaining the political support of the local community for the continued operation of the mine, and the local community now comprised a volatile mix of Porgeran landowners and immigrants from other parts of Enga and the Southern Highlands who were grasping after a share of the mine's economic benefits (Jackson and Banks 2002). So they persuaded Treasury officials to introduce an 'infrastructure tax credit scheme' in the 1992 budget. This entailed an amendment of the *Income Tax Act* which would allow the developers of large-scale mining and petroleum projects to spend up to 0.75 per cent of their gross revenues on the construction of social and economic infrastructure, and to have this counted as corporate income tax already paid to the government. This meant that Placer could use its own engineering capacities to satisfy some of the local community's demands for urban infrastructure, while also doing 'good works' for people in adjoining areas, hence reducing the incentive for them to come and settle in the vicinity of the mine. After all that, they could bill the government for their achievement.

Although this measure would bring about a further transfer of mineral wealth from the national government to mineral provinces, and hence a further dilution of the principles embodied in the previous mineral policy framework, it was actively supported by officials in the Department of Minerals and Energy. This was partly because they understood the economic logic of commuter mining, and had already adopted it as an article of faith when they persuaded cabinet to approve Placer's fly-in/fly-out scheme for the Misima mine in 1987.[9] But more importantly, perhaps, they were painfully aware of their inability to make other national government agencies, let alone provincial governments, honour many of the commitments embodied in Development Forum agreements, even if they thought that these made sense. Even if the Department of Finance and

Planning made timely payments of special support grants to provincial governments, the national government had no way of ensuring that these funds would be used to meet provincial government commitments to project communities. Now at least the Department of Minerals and Energy would have the power to monitor and approve expenditures proposed by developers under the tax credit scheme.[10]

If the institution of the Development Forum and the tax credit scheme were the means by which elements of the national bureaucracy managed to take the heat out of political demands for the redistribution of mineral wealth between different layers of government, or between the state and 'project landowners', this was not the only aspect of the mineral policy framework which came under fire during the lifetime of the Namaliu government. Three other issues became the subject of acrimonious debate. One was the environmental impact or 'external cost' of large-scale mining projects, especially the Panguna and Ok Tedi copper mines. Another was the state's claim to ownership of mineral resources. And a third was the form and extent of national participation in the oil export industry which was about to be established. In all three cases, the same government officials who took credit for inventing the Development Forum were less inclined to tamper with the status quo, but still had a hard time defending it.

The environmental impact of the Panguna mine was one of the issues which aggrieved the local landowners, though the extent of its contribution to the outbreak of the Bougainville rebellion is a matter of some debate (Filer 1992). In April 1989, cabinet tried to close the proverbial stable door on the bolting horse by appointing a committee, under the chairmanship of John Kaputin, the former minister for Minerals and Energy, to investigate the causes of the crisis and devise a strategy for renegotiating the *Bougainville Copper Agreement*. After three years of deliberation, the committee recommended the establishment of a special tribunal to deal with the environmental impact of large-scale resource projects (Kaputin 1992; Wolfers 1992), but no action was taken to implement this recommendation because the government's response to the Bougainville rebellion had by then been detached from the mineral policy process.

The discharge of waste rock and mine tailings into the Ok Tedi River had been an issue ever since the government approved the 'interim tailings scheme' proposed by OTML after a landslide had halted work on the construction of a permanent tailings dam at the beginning of 1984. The end of 1988 was the deadline by which the government required the operating company, BHP, to report on the feasibility of alternative waste retention options under the *Sixth Supplemental Agreement* of 1986. The company worked out that the cost of storing all the waste material would be K1.2 billion (Filer 1997b, 60). Politicians from Western Province, including a former minister for Environment and Conservation, were adamant that a dam should be built or the mine should be closed. The government commissioned two environmental impact studies, one being a study of the other, but by the time the second study had been finished, OTML had announced an operating loss of more than K8 million for the first half of 1989, and BCL had abandoned its efforts to re-open the Panguna mine. The bean counters in the bureaucracy had little trouble in convincing cabinet to ratify the *Seventh Supplemental Agreement* in September 1989, which essentially allowed BHP to continue business as usual. In May 1990, OTML was pleased to report an end-of-year profit of more than K24 million, and was able to portray itself as the saviour of the public purse (*ibid.*, 61).

The public purse had certainly not received any significant share of the estimated K150 million which a small army of amateur miners had extracted from the vicinity of Mount Kare following the accidental discovery of large nuggets of colluvial gold in January 1988 (Ryan 1991; Vail 1995). While the Mount Kare gold rush was a source of some irritation for CRA, which already held a prospecting authority over the area, its impact on mineral policy was not really felt until the party was all but over. In July 1990, parliament passed an amendment to the *Mining Act* which was sponsored by one of the national MPs who had made a handsome personal profit out of the gold rush, and which had the effect of giving customary landowners exclusive rights to any gold which lay within twenty metres of the surface of the ground, regardless of any tenement already held by a mining company. The purpose of this political manoeuvre was to block a plan hatched by officials in the Department of Minerals and Energy to compensate CRA for its costs and losses by issuing a special mining lease to a joint venture which the mining company had formed with a local landowner company which it had helped to establish.

The bureaucrats were able to persuade the prime minister to block gazettal of the amendment while their own scheme was implemented, but this only had the effect of provoking many local 'stakeholders' (including national politicians) whose earlier participation in the gold rush had whetted their appetite for a share of any further profits to be made out of the area. They already had a champion in lawyer and Pangu Party stalwart Peter Donigi, who had been arguing for some time that Section 7 of the *Mining Act* and Section 5 of the *Petroleum Act*, both of which vested mineral rights in the state, were inconsistent with Section 53 of the national constitution, which protects citizens from 'unjust deprivation of property' (Donigi 1994). He orchestrated a series of court actions around the Mount Kare case which helped to delay the passage of the new *Mining Act*, even though they did not validate his argument.[11]

Perhaps his argument was validated in another way, when 'dissident landowners' mounted the first of two armed attacks on CRA's mining camp in March 1991. Later that year, the Minerals and Energy secretary cited the court actions as one of three factors, along with the Bougainville rebellion and the general decline in law and order, which would explain the anticipated decline in exploration spending in both the mining and petroleum sectors.[12] When a second raid took place on the mining camp in January 1992, the government reacted by creating a special police squad, known as the Rapid Deployment Unit, to provide 'round-the-clock security' for major resource projects, and this outfit was deployed to Porgera in June that year (Filer 1998).

The same session of parliament which agreed to amend the *Mining Act* to thwart CRA's designs on Mount Kare declined to amend the *Petroleum Act* in a way that would have thwarted Chevron's plans for development of the Kutubu oilfield. Unlike the amendment to the *Mining Act*, this second amendment had been the subject of intense public debate for several months. Towards the end of 1989, five prominent national capitalists, including the ubiquitous Peter Donigi, proposed that the right to build and own the oil pipeline and other export facilities should not be granted to the Kutubu Joint Venture (KJV) (to which the state would be a party), but should be vested in a separate corporate vehicle, to be known as the Papua New Guinea Pipeline Company, in which Papua New Guinean citizens and national institutions would hold at least 51 per cent, and foreign oil companies no more than 20 per cent, of the shares. Senior bureaucrats were alarmed by the threat thus posed to the profits of the private partners in the KJV, because it meant that they would not be able to depreciate the cost of pipeline construction against their liability to corporate income tax (Brunton 1992). Together with industry representatives, these officials were able to convince a majority of government ministers to oppose the proposal, partly by playing on the fear that the proponents were out to make a profit for themselves, rather than the nation as a whole (Filer 1997a). The petroleum development licence was issued at the end of the year, and the KJV duly built its own pipeline.

However, in January 1992 the prime minister revived the spectre of nationalization when he announced a cabinet decision to establish a 'PNG National Oil and Gas Company' to undertake 'tanker, transport and bunkering operations, marketing and administration, including sale and purchase of oil and gas resources to and from the country, and upstream and downstream development and processing of oil and gas resources' and also to act as a 'tenders and coordination body to ensure equal local participation in the industry' (*Papua New Guinea Post-Courier* 24 January 1992). The Minerals and Energy minister complained that neither he nor his department had been consulted about a proposal which appeared to contradict existing government policy (*Papua New Guinea Post-Courier* 28 January 1992), while the Finance and Planning minister, who also denied any part in the decision, suggested that it might have been based on cabinet's failure to remember the existence of the Mineral Resources Development Company, which had long been established as the vehicle of state participation in the industry (*Papua New Guinea Post-Courier* 18 February 1992).

It soon transpired that the proposal had been contained in a letter from the managing director of a Singaporean company, Quest, to the Foreign Affairs minister, Sir Michael Somare, and the secretary of the prime minister's department, Brown Bai, which one waggish commentator described as a case of 'senior Government officials writing a letter to themselves on a foreign company's letterhead' (*Papua New Guinea Post-Courier* 21 February 1992), because it turned out that Somare and Bai had been nominated as the company's joint owners when its articles and memorandum of association had been submitted to the Registrar of Companies (*Times of PNG* 20 February 1992).

Sir Michael's oil and gas adventure was reminiscent of a deal which he previously tried to make with an American financier to relieve CRA of its equity stake in BCL and thus remove what he believed to be the major obstacle to peace in Bougainville. In both cases, he evidently felt that he was dealing with a multinational corporate cabal which had hijacked the country's mineral policy process and hoodwinked his ministerial colleagues. On the eve of the 1992 national election he announced that he would like to have all existing resource development agreements renegotiated once a new government had been installed, and instantly wiped K200 million off the value of Papua New Guinea resource stocks on the Australian Stock Exchange (*Papua New Guinea Post-Courier* 20 May 1992). Just for good measure, he called for the minister and the secretary of Minerals and Energy to be sacked because they had allowed Chevron to start exporting oil without doing anything about the National Oil and Gas Company (*Papua New Guinea Post-Courier* 22 June 1992). Meanwhile, Namaliu had disowned Somare's remarks, and called instead for all leaders, especially the leader of the opposition, Paias Wingti, to take a strong stand against the 'carpetbaggers, crooks and spivs' who had come to pick the fruits of the mining industry. And he did not mean CRA.

Dilemmas of distribution and disinvestment

After the national election of 1992, Namaliu and Somare found themselves back on the opposition benches, as Wingti had the numbers to secure his second term as prime minister, appointing Julius Chan as his minister for Finance and Masket Iangalio as his minister for Mining and Petroleum. If the officials in Iangalio's department thought they had done a reasonable job of protecting the industry from excessive political interference, they were soon to find that the loss of their 'energy' function was matched by a drastic loss of political influence. Wingti and Iangalio did not have an axe to grind with the oil industry, but did have their sights set on Porgera and Mount Kare. In that context, they took their advice from two of the characters who might have been the object of the previous prime minister's disparagement — Australians Denis Reinhardt and Robert Needham.

Reinhardt's role was to arrange alternative sources of finance to find and develop the rich prize still thought to lurk beneath Mount Kare, while Iangalio and other Engan politicians set about the task of prising CRA from its prospecting authority. This task was accomplished in March 1993, in circumstances which heralded the company's later decision to abandon the whole country (Filer 1998). Needham had been the managing director of Placer Pacific at the time of its famous share float, and he had long since convinced Wingti that Placer had deliberately misled the government over the value of the gold reserves at Porgera in order to discourage the government from exercising the full extent of its option to take up equity in the project. In September 1992, Wingti had him appointed as managing director of the Mineral Resources Development Company, and in the following month, word of the government's intention to renegotiate the *Porgera Development Agreement* reached the pages of the Australian press, from where it inspired a further loss of K450 million in the value of Papua New Guinea resource stocks (*Papua New Guinea Post-Courier* 12, 16 October 1992).

This was indeed a bad month for Porgera, because a member of the Rapid Deployment Unit which had been sent to guard the mine from the forces of darkness allegedly shot and killed a local landowner, thus provoking an armed assault on the company's residential compound which cost about K1 million in repairs and improvements to security installations, and which also frightened a number of staff and workers into tendering their resignations. However, after five months of grumbling about the prospect of 'expropriation', each of the other three partners in the Porgera Joint Venture finally agreed on a price at which to sell the government an additional 5 per cent stake in the project, thus raising the government's share to 25 per cent of the total equity.[13]

Iangalio, Reinhardt and Needham then turned their attention to the Lihir gold prospect, whose development had been delayed by the persistent dithering of Kennecott and its eventual owner, Rio Tinto Zinc. Iangalio caused RTZ to dither even more when he announced that the state would take up its full entitlement to 30 per cent equity in the project and would take another 20 per cent at cost if the company failed to sell that 20 per cent stake to a third party. Reinhardt proposed that a separate company should be formed to develop the project in place of an unincorporated joint venture, while Needham was doing a separate deal with the Malaysian Mining Corporation, whereby it would acquire a 20 per cent stake in the project on the same terms as the government if it managed to arrange finance for the government's own 30 per cent stake. This arrangement was apparently confirmed in talks between Wingti and the Malaysian prime minister, but Iangalio had now decided to support Reinhardt's proposal, and used this as the basis for further talks with RTZ after the company had annoyed the government by selling off part of its equity without prior consultation. Meanwhile, the local landowners had decided that the 'spare' 20 per cent equity stake should belong to them, and made this the sticking point in the first Development Forum convened in November 1993 (Filer 1995).

Wingti moved Iangalio to the Finance ministry in January 1994. The new Mining and Petroleum minister, John Kaputin, decided to suspend talks with RTZ until the company's chairman agreed to come to Papua New Guinea to talk to the prime minister. Needham produced an alternative development plan known as the 'Lihir Mining Study', but would not reveal its contents to other government officials. In April 1994, Iangalio used his own ministerial powers to have Needham fired from his position. Kaputin responded by attacking Reinhardt's role as Iangalio's adviser, but then hired another consultant to review Needham's scheme. This consultant, who was formerly the managing director of OTML, told the minister that RTZ now had the better proposal, and supported Reinhardt's idea of floating a separate company to develop the project. By the end of August, the RTZ chairman, Sir Derek Birkin, had finally agreed to the minister's demand that he should come to Papua New Guinea in person, but before he could meet with the prime minister, parliament had voted to remove Wingti from office.

One of the first public undertakings made by the new prime minister, Sir Julius Chan, was to 'fast-track' the development of the Lihir mine. His interest in the project was partly due to its location in his own constituency, but partly also to his knowledge that the government was virtually bankrupt. [14] The appointment of John Giheno, a Pangu Pati pragmatist, as the new minister for Mining and Petroleum did much to relieve the siege mentality of the Mining Division staff who worked in General Macarthur's wartime headquarters. Giheno was able to reconvene the Lihir Development Forum in February 1995, the Mining Development Contract was signed in March, and in April the leaders of the Lihir community were finally persuaded to accept an 'integrated benefits package' containing all the compensation and benefit-sharing agreements in which they had an interest. [15] In October 1995, amidst great public fanfare, the partners in the Lihir Joint Venture each sold off more than half of their equity in the project through an 'initial public offering' of shares in the new development company, Lihir Gold Ltd, and this provided a large chunk of the finance required for construction of the mine. More to the point, it enabled the state to pay for most of its own share of the development costs, because the price at which it had exercised its option to take a 30 per cent stake in the project was considerably less than the price at which it had now sold part of that stake to the public. [16]

The significance of this point was that the state had still not found the wherewithal to pay for the additional 15 per cent stake in the Porgera mine which it had demanded from the other joint venture partners in March 1993. From the earliest days of the Chan government, those officials who were privy to the scheme to develop the Lihir mine by means of a share float had persuaded their political masters to go one step further, and sell off a proportion of the equity already held by the Mineral Resources Development Company. The 1995 budget contained an undertaking to sell off a fairly modest proportion of the state's equity in the Ok Tedi, Porgera and Kutubu projects, but the *Mineral Resources Development Company Pty Limited (Privatization) Act* of 1996 led to the flotation of another public company, Orogen Minerals Ltd, which was to take over all of the equity previously held by MRDC, except for those assets held in trust for landowners and provincial governments under Development Forum agreements.[17] The state would retain a 51 per cent stake in Orogen, and Orogen would have first option on any equity which the state might choose to acquire in new mining and petroleum projects (if this were not reserved for landowners or provincial governments), but Orogen would not have the power to force the state to exercise its own equity option. By this device, the government was not only relieved of some of its existing debts, but also began to travel the path prescribed by most orthodox economists for more than a decade, which was to recognize that the state equity option was bad for business and bad for the state (see Goodman *et al*. 1985, 138; Tilton *et al*. 1986, 26).[18]

Nevertheless, the government had been obliged to pay a price for insisting that it could not afford to 'carry' the 20 per cent equity stake in the Lihir mine which local community leaders had been demanding since 1993. The landowners were only persuaded to accept a smaller 15 per cent stake (which was then diluted by the flotation of Lihir Gold Ltd) in return for an increase in the royalty rate from 1.25 per cent to 2 per cent of the value of mine production, and hence an increase in the value of the 50 per cent share of these royalties which would return to the landowners or the local government of Lihir under the terms of the integrated benefits package (Filer 1995, 69). This increase in the royalty rate would apply to all mining and petroleum projects, including those already in production, and was included in a policy package unveiled at the Papua New Guinea Mining and Petroleum Investment Conference held in Sydney in March 1995. The other main feature of this package was an undertaking to grant landowners a 'free' 5 per cent equity stake in any major resource projects approved for development after the end of that year, the cost of which would be shared between the state and the developers in proportion to their own stakes in a joint venture.[19]

Both measures would have sounded like very bad news to the investors at the conference if the government had not simultaneously promised to treat the extra royalty as a tax credit and to raise the total amount of expenditure which companies could claim as income tax already paid under the tax credit scheme from 0.75 per cent to two per cent of their gross income. Unfortunately for them, Treasury officials 'forgot' to include this latter measure in the 1996 budget, and although the extension was finally granted in the 1998 budget, this act of belated generosity was offset by the simultaneous requirement for companies to pay the full 2 per cent royalty out of their own pockets, rather than claim 0.75 per cent of it as an additional tax credit.[20]

The looming destabilization of the fiscal regime was compounded by the implications of the Organic Law on Provincial Governments and Local-level Governments which came into effect shortly after the Lihir development agreements had been signed. While this law clearly endorsed and expanded the principle of the Development Forum by requiring all three levels of government to 'liaise fully' with local landowners in the development of any natural resources, the law makers also seem to have decided that the collection and redistribution of government revenues from all natural resource sectors should also be governed by a single set of principles.[21] The organic law therefore proposed that 100 per cent of the royalties derived from any natural resource should henceforth be paid to local landowners, while the developer of any such resource should also pay, 'out of its own cost', an unspecified amount of 'development levies' to the provincial and local-level governments of the province or area hosting the development for the purpose of 'infrastructural development', 'economic development and land use follow-up', and 'community and social development'. Government officials responsible for the mineral policy framework were quick to point out that these provisions were derived from the forest policy framework, that the royalty provision undermined the principle of state ownership of mineral resources, and that the purpose of imposing development levies was already covered by special support grants and the tax credit scheme.[22] Although subsequent amendments diluted the wording of the clause which related to royalties, they left the development levies intact, and even added a requirement for developers to provide all three levels of government with 'expertise and professional advice' about their use (Filer 1997a, 248–9).

Despite the air of additional uncertainty thus imparted to the mineral policy framework, the saving grace of the organic law was that none of the provisions relating to 'benefits derived from natural resources' would affect the substance of existing development agreements, and most could not come into effect until the *Petroleum Act* or the *Mining Act* had been replaced or amended. However, its more immediate effect was to threaten the abolition of the development authorities which had been established at Porgera and Lihir as vehicles for the collection and disbursement of mineral revenues for the benefit of the two local communities. The Porgerans were so incensed by this prospect that they threatened to close down the mine unless the preservation of the Porgera Development Authority was guaranteed by the *Local-level Governments Administration Act* which had to be passed before the new system of local government could be put in place. Their wishes were duly accommodated.[23]

The wishes of the people living near the banks of the Ok Tedi River were not so readily accommodated, despite their longstanding aggravation over the effect of mine wastes on their livelihood. They were not in a position to close down the Ok Tedi mine by force, because their territorial domains do not embrace the mine site or the route through which the mine is supplied and its product is exported. They were not party to a compensation agreement with OTML, they had not participated in the Ok Tedi Development Forum, nor had they seen any noticeable benefit from the swollen revenue streams which had since flowed to the Fly River Provincial government. The new organic law would certainly not make any difference to the other swollen stream which was their daily companion. But they did have the services of an angry anthropologist (Kirsch 2002), and from this modest start, they acquired a larger group of well-heeled foreign sympathizers, including a team of Australian lawyers who acquired a mandate to sue BHP for damages in the Victorian Supreme Court. When news of this action broke out during the final months of the Wingti government, Chris Haiveta, then leader of the opposition, described it as the work of 'foreign spivs, crooks and carpetbaggers' (*Papua New Guinea Post-Courier* 5 May 1994) — a phrase which had now been firmly entrenched in the lexicon of national political debate. With the notable exception of Perry Zeipi, the Western Province MP who had once again become the minister for Environment and Conservation, most politicians on both sides of parliament expressed very similar views throughout the period of more than two years which elapsed before BHP finally agreed to an out-of-court settlement in June 1996.

In April 1995, cabinet approved an *Eighth Supplemental Agreement* in which a new compensation package was offered to those downstream landowners who would agree to dissociate themselves from the Australian court case, and a range of penalties was proposed for those who refused to do so. The Australian judge was not at all amused by the fact that BHP's own lawyers had been party to the drafting of this piece of legislation, and found that this constituted contempt of his own court (Gordon 1997). While the company was greatly embarrassed by this finding, the Papua New Guinea government pressed on with a 'restated' version of the *Eighth Supplemental Agreement*, from which the penalty clauses had been largely removed, and a separate *Compensation (Prohibition of Foreign Legal Proceedings) Act*, which aimed to prohibit any further legal proceedings in foreign courts over claims for compensation against mining or petroleum projects in Papua New Guinea. However, once BHP had agreed to an out-of-court settlement, the government made no attempt to prosecute the former plaintiffs in the case, and allowed that they would still be eligible to receive the compensation offered in the *Restated Agreement*, despite the fact that they had failed to meet the original deadline for acceptance. In its capacity as a partner in OTML, the government also endorsed the *Lower Ok Tedi Agreement* which was concluded in May 1997, granting additional compensation to the people of fifteen villages in the area most seriously affected by the company's waste disposal practices.

Although this process of litigation, legislation and compensation generated a great deal of public debate in PNG, and a good deal of negative publicity around the world, it did not make much immediate impact on the country's wider mineral policy framework, precisely because the legal framework already treated the Ok Tedi project as a special case, and this latest episode simply underlined the government's determination to keep it that way. The passage of the new *Compensation Act* was little more than a way for national politicians and bureaucrats to compensate for what most of them felt to be a serious affront to the sovereign powers of the state. However, the internationalization of the dispute was itself a significant milestone in the mineral policy process, because it showed the extent to which this had ceased to be an exclusive process of negotiation and consultation between the host government and the foreign investor, or even between the parties to the Development Forum, and was now exposed to the intervention of a multitude of 'unofficial stakeholders' (Filer 1997b, 85).

There was at least one corner of the mineral policy domain where official business was still being conducted in the customary manner, with minimal disturbance from the pressures of public political debate. The point at issue here was the need to amend the *Petroleum Act* and the fiscal regime to facilitate development of the very substantial gas reserves associated with the oil which was already being exported from various fields in the Kutubu complex. The technicalities of a national gas policy had been under discussion for several years (see Millett 1992), but this was not the sort of talk that could ignite the public imagination. The government issued a White Paper on the subject in September 1995 (PNG 1995), and that was also the year in which the Petroleum Division began to receive 'technical assistance' to carry the process forward under the terms of a $US11 million loan from the World Bank.[24]

The complexity of the issues at stake was compounded by the appearance of two different proposals for development of the gas reserves. British Petroleum, the operator of the Hides Gas Project which already supplied electrical power to the Porgera mine, was investigating the feasibility of a liquid natural gas project with an onshore liquefaction plant (CIE & NCDS 1997), while Chevron, the operating partner in the Kutubu and Gobe oil projects, was proposing to build a pipeline across the Torres Strait and supply dry gas to industrial customers in Queensland. Discussion of these two proposals was primarily couched in terms of the projected economic costs and benefits to the nation as a whole, but ongoing arguments about the internal distribution of revenues and benefits from the oil industry were seen to constitute an additional political risk for the scale and duration of the investment which either of them would entail.

So the government sought additional technical assistance from the Asian Development Bank to find new ways of dealing with the 'landowner problems' which were specific to the hydrocarbon sector (Taylor and Whimp 1997).

By the time that Bill Skate took over the reins of government after the national election of 1997, a decision had already been taken to split the Ministry and Department of Petroleum and Energy from the Ministry and Department of Mineral Resources. The new policy framework for the hydrocarbon sector was legislated in the *Oil and Gas Act* which replaced the *Petroleum Act* at the end of 1998. The new act, like the *Mining Act* of 1992, was an attempt to square two different circles — one of which was about the promotion and regulation of the industry itself, while the other was about the distribution and consumption of the national share of the wealth which might yet be derived from it. The second of these circles now also had to be squared in a manner that would be consistent with the Organic Law on Provincial Governments and Local-level Governments.

The puzzles contained in this second circle were addressed in a two-day seminar convened by the Department of Petroleum and Energy in January 1998. This led to the creation of a Petroleum Project Benefits Action Team, containing representatives of several government agencies and all the main industry players, which met on numerous occasions throughout the rest of the year. The deliberations of this body may well have constituted the most extensive process of consultation between the government and the private sector over any piece of sectoral legislation in the period since independence, although they did not rate a mention in the national press. By June 1998, the Action Team had come up with drafting instructions for a separate piece of legislation to be known as the *Petroleum (Project Benefits) Act*, but the Department then decided to incorporate some of the recommended measures into the *Oil and Gas Act*, while leaving others to be treated as matters of policy or regulation.

The *Oil and Gas Act* complies with the organic law to the extent of imposing a 2 per cent 'development levy' on the wellhead value of all petroleum products, but neutralizes the fiscal effect of this measure by extending the scope of the tax credit scheme to cover the 2 per cent royalty for which developers are also liable. While this device was designed to protect the industry's bottom line, it also entails a substantial increase in the proportion of mineral wealth which is repatriated from the national coffers to the host province. The act seeks to limit the potential abuse of such revenue flows by regulating the distribution and use of the 'royalty benefits' and 'equity benefits' which the state sees fit to allocate to provincial governments, local-level governments and project area landowners, while apparently conceding that its right to regulate the distribution and use of development levies is constrained by the wording of the organic law.[25] The proportions in which the royalty and equity benefits are distributed between the local landowners, local-level governments and provincial governments 'affected by a project' are themselves to be determined by negotiation between the parties in a Development Forum. However, the act allows the minister to determine the proportions in which the landowner benefits should be subdivided amongst the landowners by reference to the extent of their rights over the land leased to the developers or the extent of the project's impact on their livelihood, and if there is more than one provincial or local-level government 'affected' by a project, the act says that their benefits shall be subdivided in accordance with the number of project area landowners in their respective jurisdictions. Furthermore, the act empowers the minister to decide who counts as a landowner, and who counts for how much of a landowner, on the basis of 'social mapping' and 'landowner identification' studies which have to be carried out before he convenes the Development Forum.

The act goes on to say that the package of royalty and equity benefits distributed through this process must not be worth more than 20 per cent of the 'total net benefit' which the State derives from any given project, and the package must be held in trust for the beneficiaries by a subsidiary of the Mineral Resources Development Company. The act then requires at least 30 per cent of the net income of a trust established on behalf of project area landowners to be spent on the provision of 'social services or community development projects', and at least as much again to be spent for the benefit of 'future generations', which means that landowners cannot access more than 40 per cent of the net income from the trust in the form of cash payments. The act also imposes a parallel form of control over the expenditure of any monetary benefits allocated to a provincial or local-level government, including that made by a developer under the tax credit scheme, by subjecting it to the oversight of an Expenditure Implementation Committee controlled by the national government.[26]

If the *Oil and Gas Act* was meant to construct an appropriate policy framework for development of the country's natural gas resources, it evidently failed to convince the moguls of British Petroleum, who decided to divest themselves of all their assets in Papua New Guinea and focus their attention on development of the Tangguh gas field in West Papua. This decision spelt the end of the proposal for a liquid natural gas project in Papua New Guinea, and thus left Chevron's so-called 'Gas-to-Queensland' project as the only feasible development option on offer to the government. It is hard to assess the extent to which BP's decision was motivated by its assessment of political risk in Papua New Guinea, rather than by wider strategic considerations, but it seems to have reduced the incentive for Chevron and its joint venture partners to expedite their own alternative proposal, while limiting the government's capacity to push them further down the road to development.

The political risks of engaging with the Skate government were certainly not lost on the IMF and the World Bank, whose withdrawal of support was one of the factors which brought about that government's downfall in July 1999. The new prime minister, Mekere Morauta, was seen in Washington as a 'friend of the Bank', just as he was seen in Canberra as a 'friend of Australia'. The Bank was now able to move forward with a structural adjustment program which had the necessary appearance of 'borrower ownership', and under that general umbrella came the design and implementation of two more institutional strengthening projects. The Gas Development and Utilisation Technical Assistance Project was meant to facilitate the implementation of the *Oil and Gas Act*, while the Mining Sector Institutional Strengthening Project was a part of a broader push to reverse the prospect of diminishing returns from a mining industry which showed little interest in the discovery and development of new resources to replace the revenues derived from existing projects. Now, for the first time since independence, the Bank was set to become a key player in the reconstruction of the whole mineral policy framework, and that was because its officials now recognized that the national government and the national economy would sink or swim in the murky waters of mineral dependency.

In the report which accompanied and justified the structural adjustment program agreed at the end of 1999 (World Bank 1999), the Bank put the final nail in the coffin of the Mineral Resources Stabilisation Fund, observing that it had long since failed to prevent the national government from mortgaging its prospective mineral revenues to finance unsustainable levels of public expenditure, and should therefore be replaced by stricter rules for the investment of such revenues.[27] The World Bank also encouraged the government to undertake a thorough review of the fiscal regime in the mining and petroleum sectors, to create additional incentives for investment in these sectors, and to restrict its own right to move the goal posts around the new playing field. The review was funded by the Asian Development Bank (Daniel *et al.* 2000), and some of its key recommendations were incorporated into the 2001 budget, including a promise to reduce and stabilize the effective rates of tax on both industries and to grant investors the right to negotiate fiscal stability clauses into their contracts with the state.[28] The main target of these reforms was the investment climate in the mining sector, but the industry's response was less enthusiastic than it might have been, first because the government had still failed to reduce effective tax rates to levels comparable with those found in many other developing countries, and secondly because these other countries were also given lower risk ratings by the likes of Standard and Poors.

In the absence of any new surge of enthusiasm for mineral exploration, the attention of government policy makers in the mining sector was now firmly focused on the question of how to close mines down rather than how to open them up (Jackson 2002). Although the 'Basic Mining Package' had included a commitment by the national government to fund the production of a 'long-term economic development plan' for the area affected by each major mining operation, this was one of the commitments which had largely been forgotten. Now that the closure of the Misima mine loomed within the government's own five-year planning horizon, officials in the Department of Mining organized a process of consultation which led to the production of a Draft Mine Closure Policy in 2000, followed by the establishment of a Misima Mine Closure Committee in 2001. While the draft policy covered a number of technical issues involved in the rehabilitation of abandoned mine sites, it also called for the incorporation of a long-term 'social and economic development plan' within the mine closure plan to be submitted by the developer as part of the approval process for each major project. This was understood to be a plan to finance the provision and maintenance of benefits for local communities after the point of closure. Although the operator of the Misima mine had already produced its own mine closure plan, had paid for the 'long-term economic development plan' which should have been funded by the national government (Jackson 2001), and was now financing the meetings of the Mine Closure Committee, there was in fact no mechanism to ensure that the people of Misima would continue to receive the benefits to which they had become accustomed under the terms of the mine development agreements. Nor was there any obvious reason why the government or the developer should pay for these people, or the members of other mine-affected communities, to receive such benefits beyond the life of each mining operation if these benefits were in excess of those provided to all other communities in the country and could not be justified as a form of compensation for the legacy of social or environmental damage caused by the mine.

The Ok Tedi mine was one whose legacy of environmental, if not social, damage would indeed be very significant. BHP was now eager to remove this blemish from its own portfolio, and was therefore looking to transfer its majority shareholding in OTML to an institution that would manage this legacy on its own account, without further risk to the Big Australian's global reputation. One of Mekere Morauta's first actions as prime minister was to ask the World Bank to review OTML's own assessment of the risks attached to its 'Mine Waste Management Project'. The Bank recognized that the best option, from an environmental point of view, would be to close the mine down immediately, but the social and economic cost of doing so would be unacceptably high, precisely because there was as yet no clear plan or strategy for managing the closure process (World Bank 2000a). Since Ok Tedi was still regarded as a special case within the mineral policy framework, and BHP's pursuit of an early exit strategy was now serving to underline its unique status, the government was obliged to respond by making further changes to the legislation under which it operated.

The *Mining (Ok Tedi Mine Continuation [Ninth Supplemental] Agreement) Act* of 2001 made provision for BHP Billiton to gift its shareholding to an entity called the 'PNG Sustainable Development Program Company' in return for a government guarantee that it would henceforth be immune to any more 'environmental claims' in respect of the damage caused by the mine. This new company was incorporated in Singapore, with a board comprising one Singaporean member, three representatives of national institutions (the Department of Treasury, the Bank of Papua New Guinea, and the Papua New Guinea Chamber of Commerce), and three people appointed by BHP Billiton.[29] The new company's basic mandate was to invest two thirds of its mining profits in a 'long term fund', and to spend the balance of its income, including the interest on this long-term investment, on the implementation of 'sustainable development projects' in both Western Province and the rest of Papua New Guinea, throughout and beyond the remaining life of the mine (PNGSDPL 2002).

The revenues available to the Program Company would be reduced by a separate clause in the *Ninth Supplemental Agreement*, which required OTML to establish and fund the *Ok Tedi Development Foundation* as a second instrument for the promotion of sustainable development in Western Province. This body would be responsible for spending K180 million on the mine-affected communities over the remaining life of the mine, of which 16 per cent was to be paid in cash to community members, 58 per cent to be provided in the form of development projects, and 26 per cent to be invested in trust for future generations. The 149 'mine-affected communities' were divided into six areas, and community representatives from each area signed up to separate 'community mine continuation agreements' which were attached as schedules to the main agreement. These uniformly state that 'the economic opportunities offered by the Company's Commitments represent to the Communities an acceptable trade off for the environmental impacts of the future operation of the mine', and this is 'the complete, final and binding basis on which they agree to support the continuation of the Mine'. Section 8 of the main agreement states that the 'signature or other execution of a *Community Mine Continuation Agreement* by a person representing or purporting to represent a Community or clan, or that person's delegate, binds all members of that Community or clan' to the agreement, including 'children and persons who are subsequently born into, or who subsequently join, that Community or clan', even if other members or representatives of the group are not party to the agreement.

If this device served to manufacture the appearance of popular consent for the continued operation of the mine, it did nothing to address the lack of government capacity to participate in the planning of mine closure or sustainable development in Western Province. In 2000, when the Fly River provincial government was in one if its periodic states of suspension, OTML was able to persuade the national government to establish a 'Western Province Capacity Building Project' whose staff would be directly accountable to a committee comprising representatives of several national government agencies, as well as OTML and the provincial government. This institution was to be funded through direct transfers of a 25 per cent share of the mining royalties and special support grant that would otherwise have been subsumed in the provincial budget, while its management and technical support costs were also meant to be covered by the government. By 2002, it was already evident that the national government could not or would not meet its own commitments, so the project's funding was limited to the royalty stream which came directly from OTML. The mining company was also covering the project's management and technical support, but was threatening to end this subsidy unless the national government abandoned the practice of placing all of its own contributions in the black hole otherwise known as the Provincial Operating Account (Simpson 2002).

When the World Bank finalized its appraisal of the proposed loan of $US10 million to the Papua New Guinea government for the Mining Sector Institutional Strengthening Project in May 2000 (World Bank 2000b), its primary aim was to strengthen the capacity of national government agencies to attract new foreign investment to the sector, rather than deal with the lack of capacity at lower levels of government or assist in the implementation of agreements already made for existing mines.[30] However, by the end of that year, Bank staff were encouraging the national government to include a 'sustainable development policy' component in the project in order to establish a common planning framework for the local and regional development strategies which had evolved around each of the country's major mine sites. This late addition to the suite of project activities was partly motivated by World Bank president Wolfensohn's decision to commission an independent review of the Bank's involvement in both the mining and petroleum sectors in response to the complaints of 'civil society' (EIR 2003). Although the Bank had not been in any way responsible for the development and impact of the Ok Tedi mine, the global notoriety of this one operation could easily lead the Bank's critics to question the desirability of strengthening the government's capacity to sustain the industry in which it was embedded.

As it happens, the contract to produce the Sustainable Development Policy and Sustainability Planning Framework for Papua New Guinea's mining sector was awarded to a team of consultants headed by the designer of the Western Province Capacity Building Project.[31] During the course of 2002, team members engaged in an extensive process of consultation with national and local stakeholders in the mining industry, wrote eight working papers for the Department of Mining, and consolidated their findings in a Green Paper published by the Department itself (Department of Mining 2003). In the event, the Department of Mining did not have the strength required to complete the policy process initiated by the Green Paper, partly because it lacked the support of other government agencies and partly because the Bank's efforts to strengthen it had only limited success (Mathrani 2003). Most of the Department's functions were transferred to a newly established Mineral Resources Authority which certainly had more resources than its predecessor, but further progress in the reform of mineral policy would have to await the implementation of a second Mining Sector Institutional Strengthening Project whose design had not yet been finalised in 2007.

Evaluation and conclusion

The evaluation of any policy process or policy framework must first confront the question of what counts as success or failure, and yet there is no single yardstick against which this evaluation can be made. For example, policies may be said to have failed because they were inherently faulty or because they were poorly implemented. Design faults may explain the failures of implementation if these failures cannot be explained by other factors which the policy makers had no good reason to anticipate. But policies are rarely made or implemented in a vacuum, so it is also necessary to consider the specific nature of these external constraints on the mineral policy process, and each of these may give rise to its own distinctive form of policy failure. Finally, and perhaps most importantly, the stakeholders who participate in any national policy process do not necessarily share the same goals, and what counts as success for one group may count as failure for another.

Papua New Guinea's condition of 'mineral dependency' (or more broadly 'resource dependency') is one that has lasted throughout the period since independence. The very fact that Papua New Guinea still has a mineral-dependent economy means that the ambitions of the dominant policy makers at the time of independence have not been realized. The country's mineral wealth has not been successfully applied to the creation of a more diversified national economy, nor has it served to reduce the country's dependence on foreign aid. Indeed, for all their problems, the mining and petroleum industries have continued to provide the bulk of the country's exports for the last twenty-five years, yet the overall rate of economic growth has barely kept pace with the rate of population growth. If this is proof of policy failure, it is not the failure of mineral policy per se, but the failure of a broader national development strategy.

For those who believe that large-scale extractive industry has more costs than benefits for a country like Papua New Guinea, the government's ability to foster investment in large-scale mining and petroleum projects would itself count as an instance of policy failure, and any activity which has obstructed this form of investment would count as a positive contribution to sustainable development. From this point of view, the Bougainville rebellion and the Ok Tedi litigation are not only proof of the failure of government policy, but also evidence of the success of other stakeholders within the mineral policy process. Yet this can only be judged as a partial success in light of the history of civil conflict in Bougainville following the closure of the Panguna mine, or the fact that the Ok Tedi mine is still operating at a profit and still causing massive environmental damage. Another kind of policy failure may now be evident in the pessimism of some national government officials who already subscribe to the 'resource curse' thesis, and therefore conclude that there is no point in making new policies for the mining and petroleum sectors or granting additional resources to those government agencies which are responsible for promoting investment in these sectors.

In one version of this argument, the failure of mineral policy has not been in the promotion of all forms of private investment in extractive industry, but in the emphasis placed on 'monster' projects, like Bougainville and Ok Tedi, at the expense of small and medium-scale activities which do not have such major impacts on the physical environment and do not place the same degree of strain on local social and political institutions. This argument applies to the mining sector, rather than the petroleum sector, because Papua New Guinea's oil and gas reserves are not amenable to small and medium-scale forms of extraction. But even in the mining sector, those who say that 'small is beautiful' — or not so ugly — fail to show how a downsized industry can sustain the levels of public expenditure which people are still demanding, and which the government can barely afford to provide with current levels of mineral revenue and foreign debt.

If the measure of good policy is derived from the mission statements of the Departments of Mining and Petroleum, then the overall level of 'responsible' private investment in the mining and petroleum sectors is the ultimate test of policy that works. The decline of exploration spending during the 1990s could thus be taken as evidence of policy failure if elements of the mineral policy framework were responsible for this process of disinvestment. If new investment occurs after recent and current changes to the policy framework have been brought into effect, this might seem to confirm the World Bank's view that good policy is the key which unlocks the process of development. On the other hand, it would also seem to imply that Papua New Guinea still has the capacity to make and implement good policies for the mining and petroleum sectors, even if it can only do so when the Bank is holding its hand. At the time of writing, it is too early to tell which way the barometer will move, but it is also possible that levels of foreign investment have declined, and might yet be restored, for reasons which are either beyond the control of specific government agencies or beyond the reach of the national policy process as a whole. The fickle and cyclical nature of the global markets for different mineral commodities is an external constraint which presents a distinctive challenge for any national policy framework.

The Papua New Guinea Chamber of Mines and Petroleum would sum up the policy failures of the national government under two headings — taxation and security (PNGCMP 2001). From the investor's point of view, the government has failed to understand the connection between these two issues by imposing additional taxes, or constantly changing the fiscal regime, in a political, economic and physical environment whose insecurity already adds to the indirect costs of investment and production. The national government's failure to apply its own share of mineral revenues to a broader national process of economic and social development has only compounded this problem, because it has contributed to the growing demand for a greater share of these revenues to be distributed to the provinces, districts or communities which host the large-scale resource projects from which these revenues are derived. This is often expressed as a demand for local people to be compensated for the social and environmental impact of these mining operations. But if the national share of mineral wealth has so far failed to contribute to a broader national process of social and economic development, there is no obvious reason to believe that a bigger local share of mineral wealth will contribute to a broader local process of economic and social development. If anything, the problem of dependency is more acute at the local level than it is at the national level. The more that local people come to depend on a single mining or petroleum project for their incomes and general welfare, the more they are likely to lose when the process of extraction comes to an end.

By contrast with the forestry sector, we cannot simply say that Papua New Guinea's mineral development policies have failed because developers have failed to comply with them or because the government has lacked the capacity to make them do so. Although the industry has frequently complained about the additional surplus costs which the government has imposed upon it, there has also been a recognition of the need to incur such additional costs, even beyond the level required by national government policy, as the price of securing local political support for its operations. At the same time, the industry has been held accountable for its compliance with government policy through the scrutiny of its own shareholders, by the financial institutions on which it is partially dependent, and by the 'civil societies' of the developed world where it is domiciled (Filer 2002). In these respects, it is quite unlike the logging industry in Papua New Guinea, which is dominated by a small group of family-owned companies domiciled in Malaysia.

Some critics have argued that the Ok Tedi court case and the *Eighth Supplemental Agreement* demonstrated the inability of the national government to regulate an industry in which it had a vested interest, and this contradiction in the role of government was a kind of policy failure in its own right. But if we consider the whole history of debate about the management of Ok Tedi's waste materials, it is clear that the government has kept its own counsel on the merits of the 'trade-off' between economic benefits and environmental costs, and the only obvious evidence of policy failure here would have to be found in a contradiction between the Ok Tedi agreements and the national constitution. And once we look at the bigger picture of relationships between the government and the mining industry, it would be hard to explain the howls of protest with which the industry has greeted many of the government's mineral policy reforms unless the industry is playing a very elaborate double game.

Those critics who find evidence of policy failure in the state's subordination to international capital, or in the contradiction between the government's twin roles as shareholder and regulator in the mining and petroleum sectors, also tend to overlook the deepening divide between the central agencies and the line agencies responsible for various aspects of the mineral policy framework. The Departments of Mining and Petroleum have indeed been driven to defend their respective industries, and to collaborate more closely with the Chamber of Mines and Petroleum, because the rest of the government has either ignored their concerns or made new policy decisions which only add more clouds to a difficult investment climate. In the period from 1974 to 1992, there were policy brokers on both sides of the divide who were able to negotiate a 'whole-of-government' approach to mineral development policy, even while politicians were deviating from the path of righteousness. It may be true that the exploration boom of the 1980s induced a sense of complacency that was rudely interrupted by the outbreak of the Bougainville rebellion, but the simultaneous invention of the Development Forum demonstrated their collective capacity for adaptive management of major policy issues, and has been applauded as a ground-breaking measure by the global policy community (MMSD 2002, 211). What should have followed was a clear articulation of the principles to be applied to the internal distribution and management of the government's mineral revenues, but what happened instead was a lengthy political bunfight over the development of the Lihir gold mine and the parallel design of a new organic law which actually undermined the existing mineral policy framework.

If multinational mining and petroleum companies have their own reasons for implementing national government policy, or being seen to do so, this obviously lightens the load placed on the government's own regulators. But it should not blind us to the real decline in the capacity of the relevant line agencies to accomplish any of their tasks. Like many other government departments, those responsible for promoting and regulating the mining and petroleum industries now operate with budgets whose real value has fallen by more than two thirds in the space of a decade, and whose staffing levels have declined accordingly. Most of the national and expatriate government officials who were involved in the transformation of the mineral policy regime under the Namaliu government or the negotiation of the Lihir project agreements under the Chan government have since defected to the private sector. Their place has been taken by donor-funded consultants who can certainly help to design new policies, but cannot readily create the conditions under which they will be jointly implemented by a number of different government agencies. It is somewhat ironic that the two government agencies which are responsible for promoting the industries that generate as much as half of the government's domestic revenues should now be dependent on loans and grants from donor agencies in order to conduct their business.

References

Applied Geology Associates (AGA). 1989. *Environmental Socio-Economic Public Health Review: Bougainville Copper Mine, Panguna*. A Review Completed for the National Executive Council of Papua New Guinea. Wellington: AGA.

Banks, G. 2002. *Sustainable Development Policy and Sustainability Planning Framework for the Mining Sector in Papua New Guinea*. Working Paper 5: Landowner Equity Case Studies. Port Moresby: PNG Mining Sector Institutional Strengthening Project.

Baxter, M. 2001. Enclaves or Equity: The Rural Crisis and Development Choice in Papua New Guinea. *International Development Issues* 54. Canberra: AusAID.

Brunton, B. D. 1992. *The Struggle for the Oil Pipeline in Papua New Guinea*. Discussion Paper 68. Boroko: National Research Institute.

Brunton, B. D. 1994. *Constitutionality and Resource Development in Papua New Guinea*. Discussion Paper 77. Boroko: National Research Institute.

Centre for International Economics and National Centre for Development Studies (CIE and NCDS). 1997. *Gaining from Gas: The Economic Contribution of the Papua New Guinea LNG Project*. Canberra: Centre for International Economics.

Conyers, D. 1976. *The Provincial Government Debate: Central Control Versus Local Participation in Papua New Guinea*. Monograph 2. Boroko: Institute of Applied Social and Economic Research.

Dalton, D .L. 1988. Papua New Guinea: resources legislation and policy. In *Australian Mining and Petroleum Law Association Yearbook 1988*, 100–124. Melbourne: Australian Mining and Petroleum Law Association Ltd.

Daniel, P., K. Palmer, A. Watson and R. Brown. 2000. *Review of the Fiscal Regimes for Mining and Hydrocarbons*. Port Moresby: Asian Development Bank for PNG Tax Review.

Denoon, D. 2000. *Getting under the Skin: The Bougainville Copper Agreement and the Creation of the Panguna Mine*. Melbourne: Melbourne University Press.

Department of Minerals and Energy. 1988. *Proposals for a New Mining Act: Discussion Paper*. Konedobu: Department of Minerals and Energy.

Department of Mining. 2003. *Sustainable Development Policy and Sustainability Planning Framework for the Mining Sector in Papua New Guinea: Green Paper*. Port Moresby: Department of Mining.

Derkley, H. 1989. *The Porgera Agreements* (Annotated). Wabag: Enga Provincial Government.

Derkley, H. 1999. Indigenous Communities, Major Mineral Projects and the Law: The Porgera Agreements. Hobart: University of Tasmania (unpublished paper).

Donigi, P. D. 1994. *Indigenous or Aboriginal Rights to Property: A Papua New Guinea Perspective*. Utrecht: International Books.

Duncan, R., S. Chand, B. Graham, T. Lawson and R. Duncan. 1998. *Exchange Rate Policy in Papua New Guinea*. Discussion Paper 64. Port Moresby: Institute of National Affairs.

Extractive Industries Review (EIR). 2003. *Striking a Better Balance: The Final Report of the Extractive Industries Review*. Jakarta: EIR.

Filer, C. 1992. The escalation of disintegration and the reinvention of authority. In *The Bougainville Crisis: 1991 Update*, ed. M. Spriggs and D. Denoon, Monograph 16. Canberra: Australian National University, Department of Political and Social Change.

Filer, C. 1995. Participation, governance and social impact: the planning of the Lihir Gold Mine. In *Mining and Mineral Resource Policy Issues in Asia-Pacific: Prospects for the 21st Century*, ed. D. Denoon, C. Ballard, G. Banks and P. Hancock. Canberra: Australian National University, Division of Pacific and Asian History.

Filer, C. 1997a. Resource rents: distribution and sustainability. In Papua New Guinea: A 20/20 Vision. *Pacific Policy Paper* 20, ed. I. Temu. Canberra: Australian National University, National Centre for Development Studies.

Filer, C. 1997b. West Side Story: the state's and other stakes in the Ok Tedi mine. In *The Ok Tedi Settlement: Issues, Outcomes and Implications*. Pacific Policy Paper 27, ed. G. Banks and C. Ballard. Canberra: Australian National University, National Centre for Development Studies.

Filer, C. 1998. The Melanesian Way of menacing mining industry. In *Modern Papua New Guinea*, ed. L. Zimmer-Tamakoshi. Kirksville: Thomas Jefferson University Press.

Filer, C. 2002. Should mining companies 'break new ground' in Papua New Guinea? *Development Bulletin* 58:115–118.

Filer, C., N. K. Dubash and K. Kalit. 2000. *The Thin Green Line: World Bank Leverage and Forest Policy Reform in Papua New Guinea*. Port Moresby and Canberra: National Research Institute and Australian National University.

Finlayson, M. 2002. *Sustainable Development Policy and Sustainability Planning Framework for the Mining Sector in Papua New Guinea*. Working Paper 2: Benefit Stream Analysis. Port Moresby: PNG Mining Sector Institutional Strengthening Project.

Garnaut, R. 1981. The framework of economic policy-making. In *Policy-Making in a New State: Papua New Guinea 1972–1977*, ed. J. A. Ballard. St. Lucia: University of Queensland Press.

Garnaut, R. and P. Baxter. 1984. *Exchange Rate and Macroeconomic Policy in Independent Papua New Guinea*. Canberra: Australian National University, Development Studies Centre.

Garnaut, R. and A. Clunies-Ross. 1974. Using natural resources to achieve national goals. *Yagl-Ambu* 1(1): 54–65.

Garnaut, R. and A. Clunies-Ross. 1975. Uncertainty, risk aversion and the taxing of natural resource projects. *Economic Journal* 85(2): 272–287.

Garnaut, R. and A. Clunies-Ross. 1983. *Taxation of Mineral Rents*. Oxford: Clarendon Press.

Goodman, R., C. Lepani and D. Morawetz. 1985. *The Economy of Papua New Guinea: An Independent Review*. Pacific Policy Paper 1. Canberra: Australian National University, National Centre for Development Studies.

Gordon, J. 1997. The Ok Tedi lawsuit in retrospect. In *The Ok Tedi Settlement: Issues, Outcomes and Implications*. Pacific Policy Paper 27, ed. G. Banks and C. Ballard. Canberra: Australian National University, National Centre for Development Studies.

Hunt, M. 1989. *Planning for the Future: The Legislative Framework for Mining in Papua New Guinea*. Port Moresby: Paper presented to the Papua New Guinea Law Society Conference on The Exploitation of Resources in the Pacific, 6–8 November 1989.

International Bank for Reconstruction and Development (IBRD). 1965. *The Economic Development of the Territory of Papua and New Guinea*. Baltimore: Johns Hopkins Press.

Jackson, R. T. 1982. *Ok Tedi: The Pot of Gold*. Boroko: Word Publishing and the University of Papua New Guinea.

Jackson, R. T. 2001. *Kekeisi Kekeisi: A Long Term Economic Development Plan for the Misima Gold Mine's Impact Area*.

Jackson, R. T. 2002. *Capacity Building in Papua New Guinea for Community Maintenance During and after Mine Closure*. Working Paper 181. London: Mining, Minerals and Sustainable Development Project.

Jackson, R. T. and G. Banks. 2002. *In Search of the Serpent's Skin: The Story of the Porgera Gold Project*. Port Moresby: Placer Niugini Ltd.

Jackson, R. T., C. A. Emerson and R. L. Welsch. 1980. *The Impact of the Ok Tedi Project*. Konedobu: Department of Minerals and Energy.

Jarrett, F. G. and K. Anderson. 1989. *Growth, Structural Change and Economic Policy in Papua New Guinea: Implications for Agriculture*. Pacific Policy Paper 5. Canberra: Australian National University, National Centre for Development Studies.

Kaputin, J. 1987. Government's official policy on minerals development. *Niugini News* 14 November 1987.

Kaputin, J. 1992. *Crisis in the North Solomons Province: Report of the Special Committee Appointed by the National Executive Council*.

Kirsch, S. 2002. Anthropology and advocacy: a case study of the campaign against the Ok Tedi mine. *Critique of Anthropology* 22:175–200.

Law Reform Commission. 1990. *New Directions in Resource Management for Papua New Guinea*. Occasional Paper 20. Boroko: Law Reform Commission.

Mathrani, S. 2003. *Evaluation of the World Bank Group's Activities in the Extractive Industries: Papua New Guinea Country Case Study*. Washington (DC): Report to World Bank Operations Evaluation Department.

McGavin, P. A., L. T. Jones and B. Y. Imbun. 2001. Long-distance commuting and national human resource development: evidence from Papua New Guinea. *Asia Pacific Journal of Human Resources* 39(2): 98–114.

Millett, J. ed. 1992. *Gas Policy Seminar. Discussion Paper* 53. Port Moresby: Institute of National Affairs.

Mining, Minerals and Sustainable Development Project (MMSD). 2002. *Breaking New Ground: Mining, Minerals, and Sustainable Development*. London: Earthscan.

National Premiers Council. 1988. *Report of the Mining and Petroleum Working Committee*. Port Moresby.

O'Faircheallaigh, C. 1984. *Mining and Development: Foreign-Financed Mines in Australia, Ireland, Papua New Guinea and Zambia*. London and Sydney: Croom Helm.

Papua New Guinea, Independent State of (PNG). 1995. *Government Statement on Gas Policy*. Port Moresby.

Papua New Guinea Chamber of Mines and Petroleum (PNGCMP). 2001. *Industry Concerns with the New Mining and Petroleum Taxation Regime Introduced in the 2001 Budget* (Following the Taxation Review). Port Moresby: PNGCMP.

Papua New Guinea Sustainable Development Program Ltd. (PNGSDPL). 2002. *Annual Report 2002.*

Ryan, P. 1991. *Black Bonanza: A Landslide of Gold.* South Yarra: Hyland House.

Simpson, G. 2002. *Sustainable Development Policy and Sustainability Planning Framework for the Mining Sector in Papua New Guinea.* Working Paper 6: Institutional Analysis. Port Moresby: PNG Mining Sector Institutional Strengthening Project.

Sugden, C. 2002. Managing Papua New Guinea's costly economic cycles. *Pacific Economic Bulletin* 17(2): 1–14.

Taylor, M. and K. Whimp. 1997. *Report on Land Issues and Hydrocarbon Framework Study.* Port Moresby: Fuels and Energy Management Group for Department of Petroleum and Energy.

Tilton, J., J. Millett and R. Ward. 1986. *Mineral and Mining Policy in Papua New Guinea.* Discussion Paper 24. Port Moresby: Institute of National Affairs.

Vail, J. 1995. All that glitters: the Mt. Kare gold rush and its aftermath. In *Papuan Borderlands: Huli, Duna, and Ipili Perspectives on the Papua New Guinea Highlands*, ed. A. Biersack. Ann Arbor: University of Michigan Press.

West, R. 1992. *Development Forum and Benefit Package: A Papua New Guinea Initiative.* Working Paper 16. Port Moresby: Institute of National Affairs.

Wolfers, E. P. 1992. Politics, development and resources: reflections on constructs, conflict, and consultants. In *Resources, Development and Politics in the Pacific Islands*, ed. S. Henningham and R. J. May. Bathurst: Crawford House Press.

World Bank. 1978. *Papua New Guinea: Its Economic Situation and Prospects for Development.* Washington: World Bank.

World Bank. 1999. *Papua New Guinea: Improving Governance and Performance.* Washington: World Bank.

World Bank. 2000a. *Ok Tedi Mining Ltd Mine Waste Management Project: Risk Assessment and Supporting Documents.* Washington: World Bank.

World Bank. 2000b. *Project Appraisal Document on a Proposed Loan in the Amount of US$10 Million Equivalent to the Independent State of Papua New Guinea for a Mining Sector Institutional Strengthening Technical Assistance Project.* Washington: World Bank.

Zorn, J. G. and Bayne P. eds. 1975. *Foreign Investment, International Law and National Development*: Papers Presented at the Seventh Waigani Seminar, April-May 1973. Sydney: Butterworths.

Zorn, S. A. 1973. Bougainville: managing the copper industry. *New Guinea* 7(4): 23–40.

Zorn, S. A. 1977. New developments in Third World mining agreements. *Natural Resources Forum* 1(3): 239–250.

Endnotes

[1] A separate Ministry and Department of Minerals and Energy was established after the election of the second Somare government in 1977. In 1975, the director of the Office of Minerals and Energy reported directly to the prime minister in the latter's capacity as minister for Natural Resources.

[2] It is not reflected in the *Mining Act (Amalgamated)* of 1977 (Chapter 195), which recapitulated a much earlier body of colonial legislation and was not applied to the development of the Bougainville or Ok Tedi projects.

[3] The government's share was estimated to be $A29 million out of a total net profit of $A158.4 million (O'Faircheallaigh 1984).

[4] This was defined as the US prime lending rate plus 4 per cent, which then made 15 per cent (Jackson 1982: 64).

[5] In the case of an ordinary mining lease, the minister is only obliged to consult with the host provincial government, but a wider process of consultation has in practice been undertaken for medium-scale projects, such as Tolukuma and Kainantu, which have been developed under this type of lease.

[6] In effect, the national government would 'carry' the cost of the 49 per cent stake, and later recoup this cost out of the profits of mine production (Banks 2002).

[7] The prime minister tried to sell the package to the Bougainvillean rebels in order to save the Panguna mine from permanent closure, but his offer was declined.

[8] The National Premiers Council had wanted provincial governments and landowners to be parties to these development agreements, but national government officials had resisted this demand (Derkley 1999).

[9] Cabinet had initially rejected the proposal in 1986, but changed its mind when it became apparent that the local community was opposed to the development of a town that would accommodate a lot of 'outsiders' (including other Papua New Guineans) on a semi-permanent basis.

[10] It was later relieved of this power by the Department of National Planning.

[11] That is why the *Mining Act* now includes a clause which says that nothing in the clause vesting mineral rights in the state 'shall be construed as an additional acquisition of property in relation to Section 53 of the Constitution beyond that which prevailed' under colonial mining legislation.

[12] The minister subsequently told parliament that he and his secretary had both been subjected to death threats in connection with the Mount Kare case (*Papua New Guinea Post-Courier* 15, 29 August 1991).

[13] This deal was promptly followed by the leakage of an IMF report which strongly advised the government to abandon its policy of taking equity in major resource projects. This caused the Finance minister, who had commissioned the report, to utter dire threats against the government officials who had leaked it to the press.

[14] Future mineral revenues had already been mortgaged to a Swiss bank in return for a commercial loan – much to the annoyance of the World Bank and the IMF.

[15] This package marked a new stage in the development of the Development Forum because it 'integrated' the compensation agreements between the Lihir Management Company and the lease area landowners with the benefit-sharing agreements between the state, the landowners, and the rest of the local community.

[16] The state's option is to take equity at a price which is proportional to its share of the 'sunk costs' of exploration, which is almost bound to be less than the market price of equity in a project under development.

[17] Orogen did not acquire the state's equity in the Ok Tedi project, because that was no longer held by MRDC.

[18] One of the Papua New Guinean members of this economic fraternity, Charles Lepani, was appointed as Orogen's first managing director.

[19] The Finance minister, Chris Haiveta, told the conference that the package was justified by 'a social and moral need … to lock landowners into a real sense of obligation and ownership of projects on their land to reduce or minimise [the] local content of political risk' (*Papua New Guinea Post-Courier* 27 March 1995).

[20] The Department of Mining has since taken the view that the promise of 'free equity' in large-scale mining projects is only an undertaking on the part of the state to 'free carry' the landowning community's share of exploration costs, which does not mean that landowners are exempt from contributing their share of development costs.

[21] This idea had been around for many years, and could even be seen as a sort of constitutional imperative (Law Reform Commission 1990; Brunton 1994), but its main champions had not been active in the drafting of the new organic law, nor was it clearly articulated in the drafting instructions produced in July 1994.

[22] In their haste to assign all royalties to local landowners, the legal draftsmen also seem to have forgotten that 'royalty grants' from the national government to mineral provinces should have been deducted from derivation grants payable to provincial governments.

[23] Part VII of the act as passed in 1997 allows for the national government to establish 'special purposes authorities' to carry out some of the functions which would otherwise be the responsibility of local-level governments.

[24] There could hardly have been a greater contrast between the amount of publicity generated by the World Bank's role in promoting the process of forest policy reform during the years of the Chan government (Filer *et al.* 2000) and the complete absence of public debate about its parallel role in the petroleum sector.

[25] The word 'benefit' is meant to avoid the implication that landowners have an entitlement to royalties or project equity through their claim to customary ownership of subterranean resources.

[26] This body is meant to ensure that the disbursement of all grants (in cash or in kind) made by the national government to provincial or local-level governments, the spending of all funds held in trust for them by a subsidiary of MRDC, and any expenditures by the developer under the Tax Credit Scheme are made 'in accordance with development plans submitted by the relevant Local-level Government or Provincial Government'. Four years after the passage of the act, the Department of Petroleum and Energy was still engaged in the production of guidelines for the operation of such bodies, so none had yet been established.

[27] The Bank argued that since the holdings in the Fund were matched by domestic debt in the form of treasury bills, its abolition would have no monetary consequences provided an equivalent amount of government securities was redeemed. Instead, it recommended that the Bank of Papua New Guinea should manage stabilization issues through the domestic debt market, by tightening monetary policy to safeguard reserves.

[28] The second of these promises was given legal effect with the simultaneous passage of the *Resource Contracts Fiscal Stabilisation Act* (2000).

[29] One of these last three people, who was also appointed as chairman of the board, was Professor Ross Garnaut, the main architect of the original resource rent tax. Professor Garnaut has also been the chairman of Lihir Gold Ltd since that company was established in 1995.

[30] This loan was complemented by a grant of 50 million euros from the European Union under the so-called 'Sysmin' facility, which was partly conditional on the implementation of a proposal to transform the Department of Mining into a Mineral Resources Authority that would be directly funded through a share of the government's mineral revenues. Part of the loan from the World Bank has been used to fund the design of this new entity, but officials in the central government agencies have so far refused to condone its creation.

[31] The principal author of this paper was also a member of the team.

Chapter 7

Policy Making in Health

Jane Thomason and Pascoe Kase

This chapter highlights the current state of affairs in regard to health policy under the decentralization arrangements introduced in 1995. It contrasts the achievements of the health sector during the pre-independence, centralized system with the decentralized systems of governance implemented after independence. It then presents a set of options for policy makers to consider in their endeavour to rectify the declining state of the health services and, most importantly, the state of the people's health.

Papua New Guinea has an accomplished history of sound health policy, and well-articulated health plans. Indeed Papua New Guinea health policies and plans have been widely complemented. Examples of the policies approved and in process for approval include: user fees policy for public hospital and dental services; national drugs policy; national cold chain policy (for pharmaceuticals); hospitals standards policy; partnership policy; health human resources policy; non-government organizations and churches salaries and allowances policy; national health insurance policy; and minimum standards for rural health services policy.

Notwithstanding this strong history of sound health policy, the periods covered by post-independence health plans have witnessed a slow but steady decline in the services available to rural people, and a stalling of improvements in key health indicators.

There are many and complex reasons for this demise. A key factor has been the impact of successive decentralization reforms on the organization and management of health services. Critical flaws are the lack of integration between national health planning and any budgetary planning, and the separation of the policy arm from the implementation arm of the health system.

A health system is a complex and highly technical operation based on scientific principles, and must have a clear vertical link from policy development to its implementation. For a health service to operate effectively there needs to be a single point of budget and management accountability, with direction being provided by people with technical knowledge and skills.

Clearly, these structural and organizational issues cannot be viewed outside of the concurrent social, economic and governance decay in Papua New Guinea.

In the pre-independence time, there was a high level of optimism about the future of Papua New Guinea, the bureaucracy was effective and resource prospects were flourishing. However, since then the effectiveness of Papua New Guinea as an independent state has been questioned and successive governments criticized for mismanagement. The economic climate continues to be extremely fragile, law and order problems remain high on the agenda, corruption is a major problem throughout the country and the capacity of the bureaucracy to deliver basic government services continues to slowly decline. A recent independent review by the Australian Strategic Policy Institute highlights the lack of capacity of the bureaucracy to deliver health services, as one of the key challenges that impact upon the viability of Papua New Guinea as a functioning state. The report suggests that only a generational timeframe is now realistic for arresting the decline (White and Wainwright 2004). Thus, while the structural issues identified here perhaps once could have been addressed by making changes to the Organic Law on Provincial Governments and Local-level Governments, the problems are now too deeply ingrained to be resolved so simply.

Potential for health systems to improve health

There is evidence that the provision of simple, cost-effective interventions can improve health status in Papua New Guinea. Before independence, significant gains were made in the health status of the population. Infant mortality fell from 134 to 72 per 1,000 live births, child mortality fell from 91 to 45 per 1,000, and life expectancy increased from 40 years to 50 years. These improvements have been directly attributed to the provision of health services.

The successes were attributable partially to the pre-independence organization and administration of health services, which was centralized with highly defined vertical public health programs. Well coordinated programs were designed and implemented with emphasis on the district level. Districts, health centres and hospitals became the focal points of service delivery and provincial hospitals provided technical and logistical support whenever required. This highly centralized control ensured more effective management of resources by a functioning bureaucracy that closely supported delivery and management of health services.

At the district level, government services were integrated, even though nationally many programs were vertical. Highly integrated and coordinated support of programs enabled efficient delivery of important priority health services which resulted in marked improvements in the health status indicators of the people. However, these improvements have not continued in the past two decades.

Policy formulation and planning

Decentralization in the 1970s and 1980s

Papua New Guinea first decentralized to nineteen provincial governments in the late 1970s (see chapter 12). Following independence, the government introduced the Organic Law on Provincial Government to decentralize the management and administration of government services, including health. The two main components of health services — rural health and hospitals — which enjoyed a centralized vertical but integrated planning and management approach were now to be under separate authorities. Rural health services became decentralized while hospital services were only delegated to the provinces for planning, management and administration (Thomason, Newbrander and Kolehmainen-Aitken 1991).

For the health system, this presented some significant issues. Appointment of provincial health officers became politicized, mobility of the health workforce declined, and the national Department of Health found it impossible to maintain standards and ensure health policy implementation in the hospitals, which were delegated functions, or in rural health, which was transferred. Functional roles and responsibilities for the two components were poorly defined, leading to much confusion for both national and provincial governments, and consequent uncertainty at both national and provincial government levels. This uncertainty led to poor resource allocation, lack of coordination, and inefficient management of the health services, and thus the deterioration in quantity, quality and coverage of basic health services provided from rural health facilities and hospitals. Gains made under the centralized health system prior to independence were not sustained.

Further decentralization in 1990s

Despite these and a number of other problems which followed the initial decentralization, there was a further decentralization in 1995 through the enactment of the Organic Law on Provincial Governments and Local Level Governments (OLPGLLG), which further decentralized to around three hundred local-level governments.

The present OLPGLLG was adopted with the aim of improving government service delivery, especially health services, to the majority rural population. Where the previous legislation had failed, this new law ambitiously attempted to improvise and enhance the government's ability in service provision by empowering and decentralizing further into the districts the rural health services component. The practical effect of the new OLPGLLG has been to give provincial governments and local-level governments significantly greater discretionary control over spending at the sub-national level, without effective checks and balances to ensure national policies are being implemented.

National public servants in each of the provinces report to a provincial administrator, who is the head of the provincial administration. Each district (corresponding to the area of an open electorate) is under the administration of a district administrator. District health staff report to the district administrator who has limited knowledge of health programs and of what it takes to make the health system perform properly. The hospital CEOs, senior clinical staff and provincial health advisers who have the knowledge and experience to run the health system cannot discipline staff in rural areas, nor direct them or financial and other material resources to where they are needed.

Effective implementation of health policy requires the ability to ensure that resources are directed to the key policy priorities. Under the organic law the sources available for health funding include the national budget (including the District Development Program — see chapter 12) and provincial and local-level government budgets (mostly funded from grants under the OLPGLLG but including some internal revenue). There is no provision at the national level for reviewing the overall sectoral allocation, nor sectoral allocations among provinces or districts within provinces (although the OLPGLLG does provide for joint planning and budgetary priority committees at provincial and district levels). It is currently impossible to even review provincial budget allocations for health, let alone centrally direct or influence them.

There are two key issues in the funding arrangements, which lead to what is essentially an untenable situation. Funding for provincial governments is no longer calculated on the basis of functions they perform, instead the grants are calculated primarily on the basis of population and geography. The funding may not be adequate to carry out all the necessary functions. Grants paid to provincial governments are essentially unconditional, so while the national government can set national policy, it cannot make provincial governments outlay money to implement it.

A further and presumably unintentional anomaly has been the establishment of public hospitals under a separate piece of legislation, the *Public Hospitals Act*. Following the passage of the *Public Hospitals Act*, hospitals have operated as quasi-statutory authorities, responsible to an independent board of management, and through it to the national minister for Health. They are funded from the national budget. This administrative and financial separation of hospitals from rural health services has caused problems in ensuring that hospitals deliver their support services to the rural healthcare system. The lines of direction and control are uncoordinated. Since hospitals are independent of provincial governments, the provincial governments must negotiate the basis on which the services of the two different systems are provided.

The existing situation

The OLPGLLG and the subsequent enabling legislation were meant to further clarify roles and responsibilities between the levels of government and their respective administrations. The organic law was intended to give the role of policy setting to the national government, in order to ensure consistency and unity of national direction. If national health policy is to be carried out, the provincial governments must fund priorities in these areas, and allocate staff into the priority activities. If they do not, however, there is little the national government can do about it. The national government has done very little in the way of establishing mechanisms to ensure that provinces fund important areas of national policy. During the interview process for the 2001 functional and expenditure review of the health sector, one provincial administrator told a member of the review team, 'You may have a National Health Plan and a national policy that says health is a top priority, but that's irrelevant because in our province health is a fourth or fifth priority'.

Even though the intentions of the political and constitutional reforms are commendable, experiences so far in many provinces in fulfilling these intentions are far from convincing. Poor management practices coupled with inadequate allocation of resources, lack of staff capacity, and poor state of facilities and infrastructure at district level are just a few areas that do not support the intention of the reform. The political will may be there, but the public service machinery simply does not have the capacity to deliver.

One of the current underlying issues is that of staff motivation and the required levels of competency. Staff now have to work within a health sector that on the one hand has a clear vision with established prioritized policies but on the other hand is without clear standards, and suffers from eroded and weakened management systems. They have to operate under complex management procedures with weak provincial, district and local health managerial competence. In many cases, their technical skills have not been updated and their technical competence has been allowed to erode during the post-independence period. Disillusioned health workers in many provinces know that provincial governments are choosing not to prioritize health services for resource allocation.

The disillusionment and de-skilling is not confined to provincial health staff. The national Department of Health is also struggling to maintain a cadre of highly skilled and motivated leaders, after a succession of disappointments and continually deteriorating health statistics. Unwittingly, the escalating level of dependence on donor funds to maintain even the most basic of health services has probably played a role in increasing the disempowerment of senior health officials. The sheer numbers of donors and their technical advisers in some areas has probably undermined the leadership and influenced direction of the

Department of Health. The expectations of donors and their teams to 'be serviced' by senior health staff, reduces time available for focusing on core business. An unanticipated consequence of donor interest and support for the health sector, in some provinces, has been the premeditated under-resourcing of health services by provincial governments, in the expectation that donors will fill the gap. This has been consistently reinforced over a number of years.

Policies at independence

Papua New Guinea's health system was developed on two basic principles — that health services should be brought as close to the people as possible, and that the least-trained health worker who is competent to provide such care should deliver all health service activities.

These principles, which address the two basic issues of *access* to and *quality* of health care within the context of a nation with limited resources, are relevant today. A small number of diseases (pneumonia, malaria, diarrhoea, tuberculosis, measles and anaemia) that can be diagnosed and treated at aid posts or outpatient clinics cause 40 per cent or more of deaths of men and women under the age of forty-five years. Another 10 per cent of deaths are attributed to meningitis, typhoid and some of the most important causes of maternal death that could be managed in a health centre ward. The most important preventive services — immunizations and antenatal care — can be provided through mobile and stationary clinics, and do not require a sophisticated service delivery infrastructure. These services can be, and have been in the past, provided to the majority of the population in Papua New Guinea.

Policies adopted at independence remain valid today. Indeed they have been reinforced through the priorities of the *Medium Term Expenditure Framework 2004–2007*, which provides the basis for prioritization for funding and technical support to the following areas: increased coverage of key public health programs, maintenance of essential clinical services for the main causes of morbidity and mortality, and improved sector efficiency and quality. All the activities within the *Medium Term Expenditure Framework* are contained in the overall policy framework set by the *National Health Plan*.

Policy implementation: policy into practice

Despite the sound history of health policy and planning, it has not passed the implementation test. The Department of Health has no control over most of the planning, budgetary and staffing decisions that affect the implementation of national health policies. The Department has made commendable progress to deliver on its obligations under the organic law, and overcome the inherent dysfunction caused by it. A number of important building blocks are in place to facilitate the implementation and monitoring of key health policies within the OLPGLLG. These include:

- A *National Health Administration Act*, which provides a framework for the planning and coordination of provincial health services and the roles and responsibilities of the various levels of government in health;
- A National Health Plan which clearly outlines health policy for the next ten years;
- Minimum standards for district health services, which articulate the health service requirements for districts;
- Partnership agreements which set out the basis of national-provincial funding and performance;
- A performance-monitoring framework, which is the basis for monitoring health system performance; and
- A *Functional Expediture Review of Health Services and Policy Options for Reform.*

The *National Health Administration Act*, passed in late 1997, establishes a framework for health planning and coordination between the Department of Health and provincial and district authorities. The act provides a rational basis for balancing the practical reality of provincial control, with the organic law vision for national policy setting and technical supervision by national line departments. Despite the clarity of the *National Health Administration Act*, there remains a significant blurring of roles and accountability in its implementation.

The *National Health Plan 2001–10* provides the policy basis for the sector. The plan is sound, but its ultimate successful implementation remains in question. The quality of the National Health Plan as a policy framework notwithstanding, the decentralized service delivery and funding structure mandated by the OLPGLLG, coupled with unreliable government transfers, poses a significant challenge to the successful delivery of health services.

A further problem is the disjunction between the sectoral planning systems and the multi-sectoral district-based planning system, which forms the basis for budgeting at both the local and provincial levels. Integrating health planning into these systems represents a major challenge for health staff, particularly because the system of planning at district level is intertwined with political processes. While this will have the benefit of ensuring that plans meet local needs, there is a real capacity deficit at district level in many provinces in terms of planning, management and utilization of information.

Minimum standards for district health services. Under the law, provincial and local-level governments are supposed to ensure that quality health services are planned, resourced, delivered and sustained. In order to form a basis for defining what this means in practice, the Department of Health has developed minimum standards for district health services. These form the basis for service planning, implementation, and evaluation at provincial and district health service levels. The key issues which remain to be tested in relation to the standards are whether, in an aggregate sense, the minimum standards are affordable. A second issue is whether the provisions of the law, in reality, provide an effective basis for the Department of Health to enforce the standards. A third issue is who will enforce the standards, and how will they do so.

Partnership Agreements have been developed between the department and each province. These agreements set out the respective commitments of both parties. The most important requirements for continued participation by provincial government will be a commitment to implement the National Health Plan in the province, and the maintenance of agreed levels of funding by the provincial government for health services and activities. The agreements also define target performance levels for each province.

In 2001, however, not one province allocated the targeted 15 per cent of its discretionary budget to health, and seventeen provinces allocated less than 10 per cent of their discretionary funds to health (*Provincial Health Finance Review 2001*). This has called into question the value of the partnership agreements as a means of leveraging provincial governments to carry out their assigned obligations. Poor health service delivery in one province can impact negatively on other provinces and the nation. Papua New Guinea needs a healthy population and it is not the prerogative of one province to determine not to support a fundamental building block for economic development — a healthy productive population.

A *Performance Monitoring Framework* was designed to operationalize a national system of performance monitoring that can be used as part of the partnership agreements to define agreed levels of performance for provinces.

The 2001 *Functional and Expenditure Review* of the health sector highlighted the incapacity of staff with sufficient skills to manage complex health functions independently at 89 different district locations around the country, as envisaged by the OLPGLLG. The review also noted key issues with the intergovernmental financing arrangements under the OLPGLLG: the funding formulae based on population and area, rather than the actual cost of delivering transferred functions; the lack of ability to address inter-provincial inequity; and the multiple sources of funding for health. The overwhelming conclusion of the review was that the new structure has not worked in the health sector (PSRMU 2001).

Policy options

Since the introduction of the OLPGLLG in 1995, there has been a 'bottleneck' in fully implementing the health reforms. What can be better managed and influenced is the process of implementing health services in an environment where there is full control of resources and focus on a few priorities in order to gain momentum and success. The health system needs to be delivered from a single, coordinated service delivery network, with a single point of management and resource accountability, within each province. The system should be directed and controlled by health professionals and should be responsive to the delivery of national policy and the implementation of the National Health Plan.

In light of these constraints, the government might consider one or more of five options for the recentralization of health services.

Option 1. No change

This policy involves no change but seeks rather to continue to pursue initiatives that are being undertaken by provincial and local-level governments. It is based on the assumption that the implementation of the reforms can be improved and that by modification and improvement of processes, service delivery will improve. It also assumes that resourcing of facilities, especially at the district and local levels, will improve in the not too distant future.

The main attraction of this option is that it requires no further organizational and legislative change. It also has the advantage of providing more time for authorities to take steps to improve the implementation of decentralization. For a few well-performing provinces, like Milne Bay, the 1995 OLPGLLG provided an opportunity for an active and committed province to move well ahead of many others in the delivery of health services, and to access additional funds for health from sources such as the Papua New Guinea Incentive Fund, an AusAID fund that rewards well-performing entities.

However, after more than a decade, the many disadvantages of this option are becoming painfully apparent for most provinces. Many of these have been outlined in this chapter and in most provinces it is a policy that is not working.

Option 2. Recentralize all OLPGLLG health functions to public hospitals

This option seeks to affirm the concept of re-centralization, but rather than taking the concept holistically, it aims to utilize alternative established mechanisms to advance the cause. The option proposes to re-centralize authority from the provinces but rather than fully transferring power and functions to Port Moresby, shifts it to the public hospitals which are physically located in the provinces. The public hospital services are a national function under the *Public Hospitals Act* and could be utilized for this objective. But while they are a national function, as they are located in the provinces they provide a potential mechanism for central coordination and monitoring of priority health programs. Under this option, rural health staff would be transferred to the existing hospital structure, which would establish a division of rural or public health services.

This option is very attractive to many who believe that hospitals can play an influential role in guiding, setting and monitoring clinical, public health and management support standards in the provinces. It would be relatively simple to achieve. Hospitals are large organizations, and are the focal point for the greatest health sector expertise and resources in each province. They could provide a central management and coordination point in each province for health services. The policy of designating all public hospitals as in-service training centres for a province indirectly supports this option. The technical skills and management expertise of hospital staff can be applied to the benefit of rural health services as well as the maintenance of biomedical equipment, and logistic, financial and human resource management skills.

As against this, this policy option has been criticized on the grounds that the main focus of hospitals tends to be curative health provision, and few see them as centres of public health expertise. Many would be fearful that as hospitals are increasingly pressured by their immediate population, they will fail to prioritize public and rural health. The provincial health advisers may not be supportive of this option, as it would mean the loss of their independence from the public hospitals. Provincial administrators may also see this as a loss of control and resources. If the hospitals are accountable for health services, then decisions on the allocation of provincial funds for health services and would be channeled through the hospitals. This is likely to meet with resistance. It may also compromise provincial government funding. Provincial governments are not obliged to allocate a particular proportion of their budgets to health and may not continue to provide funding to health if the responsibility for service delivery is shifted to hospitals.

While CEOs have been chosen for their hospital management skills, these are not necessarily the same skills required to run a public health system. The hospitals may be strained by the additional responsibilities, especially at the district level. Hospital CEOs have not had to cope with the difficulties of administering staff and activities at a distance. A final shortcoming as a national policy is that not all provinces have a provincial hospital, so this option would not be viable in all provinces.

Option 3. Re-centralize all provincial health functions under the provincial health board

This option also seeks to affirm the concept of re-centralization, but recognizes the necessity for coordination, and aims to utilize previously established coordination mechanisms at the provincial health board level. Under this policy option, existing provincial health boards would take over management of the health system in the province.

This is a familiar model and one that most provinces would consider favourably. It retains control of resources and staff at the provincial level, but centralizes coordination and management of resources from the districts. There are several obvious advantages in adopting this option. First, it is the least likely to encounter resistance from provinces. Secondly, it bases its rationale on assisting provinces to be self-reliant, is sustainable in the long run, and would not necessarily need major institutional, administrative, economic or political restructuring and manipulation. Thirdly, it is consistent with the spirit of the 1995 reforms.

As with the other options, however, there are also some disadvantages. Provincial health boards are in varying shapes, with some having only just been established; few have demonstrated their effectiveness on a continuing basis. Unless hospital staff become employees of the provincial health board, this system retains the disadvantage of the hospitals and rural health services being managed separately, and would continue to challenge coordination and integration. It is likely be resisted by district administrators, as it reduces their power and span of control. If hospital staff are directed by the provincial health board, there is a risk that the poor management of hospitals witnessed during the delegated period may reemerge. Gains in hospital management may be lost. Hospital funding may also suffer. Hospitals are funded directly by the national government and because they are statutory authorities they are treated as grant recipients and run their own accounting systems.

Option 4. Re-centralize all health functions under the national Department of Health

This option proposes to re-centralize authority from the provinces through complete transfer of power and functions to Port Moresby. It is likely to encounter most resistance from provinces, is against the spirit of the 1995 reforms, and would be a huge undertaking in terms of planning and resourcing.

For those with memories of the pre-independence system, there may be perceived advantages in re-centralizing services. It yields a single point of accountability and allows for centrally-planned resource allocation and prioritization of key health programs.

Re-centralization would be attractive from a central point of view. However, for one thing, Papua New Guinea has adopted a decentralized political and administrative system and this is now ingrained in the minds of people. Several provincial governments and their administrations have in good faith pursued decentralization, have learnt a lot from the experience, have invested a lot of time, resources and effort in the process, and are making a success of it. For another, recentralization implies unlearning the processes and systems developed, and relearning centralized political and administrative systems. This option poses the question: is full re-centralization of health services a fundamental necessity to improve health service delivery and consequently improve health status indicators for our people? A further question about the 1995 reforms is whether they were always unlikely to improve essential social services such as health and education.

Option 5. Outsource provincial health implementation to competent third parties

This policy would enable provinces which were unable to self-manage their health services to outsource provincial health implementation to competent third parties, including the national Department of Health, private sector entities, and NGOs. This is already partially the case in many provinces, where the churches act as health implementers. It could enable several provinces to form a network which could service their requirements.

This approach would provide for poor performing provinces to opt for outside assistance to manage and coordinate their health services. It could take advantage of economies of scale by consolidating service delivery mechanisms, for example, by more effective use of charter flights and boat travel.

As against this, it would require a funding process agreed between the province and the third party implementers, and regular and complete reporting of the use of provincial funds.

Choosing policy options

A single policy option will not suit all provinces. A province that is already making headway in terms of implementing the 1995 reforms and seeing benefits in health service delivery, would probably wish to continue along this path. One of the drawbacks of the decentralization process was that it disregarded the varying stages of development, economic and political, between provinces and districts. Measures need to be tailored to the specific needs of the different parts of the country.

In considering the policy options, a number of factors need to be considered: first, services should be managed at provincial or district level only if they have the capacity; secondly, no matter which policy option is chosen, funding arrangements need to ensure the timely flow of resources to priority programs; thirdly, some options will require legislative change, enabling line reporting by district staff other than to the district administrator; fourthly, reform of intergovernmental financial arrangements is needed to provide for tying funding to health system performance.

Conclusion

It needs to be recognized that the system of administration prescribed by the OLPGLLG constitutes a major constraint on strengthening the health system. The Department of Health is limited in what it can do to impact on the health of the nation's people, because the power to determine how much is spent on health care, and how health staff are deployed and managed, is in the hands of individual provincial governments.

From a population health point of view, Papua New Guinea has never needed an effective and functioning health system more. Papua New Guinea is on the brink of an AIDS crisis of southern African proportions (see chapter 19). Tuberculosis is reemerging as a major public health problem and is an increased risk with the escalating HIV/AIDS epidemic. Non-communicable or 'lifestyle' diseases are posing a substantial threat to the adult population and threaten to create a chronic burden on the health system which is already incapable of providing basic interventions for the common communicable diseases of pneumonia, malaria and immunizable diseases. Papua New Guinea has long had unacceptably high levels of maternal mortality and these continue unabated. The gravity of the situation, and the consequences of not taking steps to ensure the rebuilding of the system to a level where basic services can be delivered, cannot be over-stated. Papua New Guinea needs to determine its own policy solutions; however, any policy option must incorporate recognition of the depleted state of the health system and its key human resources. Without a strategy for rebuilding systems and human resource capacity to deliver health services, none of the policy options outlined above will succeed.

Postscript

Several important developments have taken place since this paper was written. These include the passing of the Provincial Health Authorities Act (2007), amendments to inter-governmental financial arrangements (2008), the delegation of powers from Department of Personnel Management to line agencies, and the establishment of a Public Private Partnership Taskforce and development of a draft National Public Private Partnership Policy (2008).

The Provincial Health Authorities Act was passed in May 2007. The purpose of the new law is to enable provinces to create provincial health authorities to deliver both public health services and curative services. The initial roll-out will take place in three provinces in 2009. Further work is underway with the Department of Treasury to develop the new financial arrangements necessary to bring together hospital funding from the national government and provincial funds for public and rural health service delivery, and with the Department of Personnel Management to establish management and staffing structures for the provincial health authorities.

In July 2008, the National Parliament approved important changes to the intergovernmental financial arrangements, aimed at strengthening the delivery of basic services by provincial governments. The new system is intended to ensure the flow of funding to key service sectors operating at district level, including health facilities and integrated health patrols. Service delivery priorities are reflected in a set of minimum priority activities approved by an interdepartmental committee responsible for overseeing the implementation of the new system. During 2009, implementation indicators will be developed to enable provincial administrations to monitor and report on both achievements in implementation of programs as well as spending of budgeted funds. The Department of Provincial and Local Government Affairs will be looking at some instances of provincial and local-level funding and service delivery, including specific attention to the funding of rural health centres and aidposts.

In April 2008, the government signed a MoU with the Asian Development Bank (ADB) for Technical Assistance to develop a national public private partnership policy for Papua New Guinea; a draft public-private partnership policy was completed in August 2008. The Department of Health has requested technical assistance from the ADB to develop the capacity to facilitate and monitor public-private partnerships for the health sector.

These developments have the potential to improve implementation of health services to the rural population and to facilitate the development of a differentiated approach to health service delivery in Papua New Guinea on a province-by-province basis. However, whatever the organizational arrangements, sufficient skilled human resources and equipment will still be required to ensure that the Papua New Guinea Minimum Standards for Rural Health Services are provided. This will require the mobilization and organization of resources from national and provincial governments, and donors.

References

Public Sector Reform Management Unit (PSRMU). 2001. Functional and Expenditure Review of Health Services. Interim Report on Rural Health Services. Port Moresby.

Thomason, J. A., W. C. Newbrander and R-L Kolehmainen-Aitken. 1991. *Decentralization in a Developing Economy: The Experience of Papua New Guinea and its Health Services*. Canberra: Australian National University.

White, Hugh and Elsina Wainwright. 2004. *Strengthening Our Neighbour: Australia and the Future of Papua New Guinea*. Canberra: Australian Strategic Policy Institute.

Chapter 8

Formulating and Implementing Education Policy

Richard Guy

Early policies in education

Formal education in Papua New Guinea is of relatively recent origin. Literacy and numeracy programs were first offered to adults in the 1890s in schools established by missionaries to facilitate evangelization. The British administration, at the time, encouraged the establishment of such schools to assist with its policy of 'pacifying the natives'.

By the 1920s there was some concern by the administration with benefiting the natives, rather than white settlers, and emphasis was placed on the transformation of 'the tribe of disappointed warriors into a race of more or less industrious workmen' (Murray 1929, 8). By 1926, technical, industrial and agriculture training in Papua received 95 per cent of the total government education budget. By the 1930s, government policy was more concerned with a blending of cultures in which the best of the old culture was 'vastly enriched and enlarged by contributions from our own' (Williams 1935, 6).

A further shift in education policy took place immediately after the Second World War with greater government involvement in the provision of primary schools. Paul Hasluck, the Australian minister for Territories who then had responsibility for Papua and New Guinea, established a set of definitive policy statements for education (Hasluck 1959). These policies stated that universal primary education would be the focus; all children in controlled areas would be taught in English; church schools would be encouraged and a system of grants established to support these schools; attention would be given to developing local teachers; and manual training would be developed at primary schools. Secondary education was not given any priority and high schools were not introduced on a widespread basis until the 1960s.

Hasluck was criticized for his gradualist policies and not identifying an indigenous elite for future leadership roles. The United Nations (1962) and World Bank (1964) reports insisted that secondary schools be expanded and that planning for a university start immediately to satisfy the impending human resource needs of the country. The University of Papua New Guinea commenced operations in 1966.

Education, prior to independence, was for the few and it was gender specific. The curriculum was academic and strongly oriented to Western forms of knowledge as part of the modernist project for Papua New Guinea. Teaching and learning was carried out in English and the majority of teachers were from overseas; they used Queensland or New South Wales curricula. Teachers were encouraged to adapt the curriculum to the contexts of Papua New Guinea, but few teachers took up the opportunity. The country fell far short of universal primary education despite continuous government rhetoric about attaining universal primary education, embodied in a 1960 government directive and subsequently revised to 1973 (Roscoe 1958).

Policy directions since independence

Policy formulation is best understood by reviewing a number of key documents that established the policy framework for education since independence. Six fundamental issues have consistently underpinned the formulation and implementation of education policy during this time, namely: universal primary education; the nature of the curriculum; language of instruction; financing education; decentralization; and development partners.

The granting of independence was an appropriate occasion to make a substantial break from the past. Alkan Tololo, a Papua New Guinean, chaired a committee (Tololo Committee 1974) that was given the task of reviewing the first five-year education plan from 1969–1973, and to set the parameters for the important education plan for the period 1976–1980. The committee consisted of only Papua New Guineans and outlined several radical policies for education in an independent Papua New Guinea:

• self-reliance as the cornerstone of policy achieved through a community-based education program;
• forms 1 and 2 from high school to be transferred to community schools as Grades 7 and 8, to speed up the process of universal community education;
• teaching for the first three Grades to be in the 'functional language of the community';
• opportunities for education to be expanded to all Papua New Guineans including girls, children from isolated areas, and disadvantaged children; and
• curricula that 'is relevant to the life that students will have to live after school'.

The Committee's recommendations were not adopted. Despite the advent of independence in 1975, the education plan that was formally adopted in 1976 reconfirmed the policy laid down by Hasluck in 1959.

The Education Plan (1976–1980)

The Education Plan (1976–1980) set the direction for education immediately after independence. Policy formulation, curriculum design, inspections and standards, employment of teachers, and pre-service and in-service training for teachers clearly remained the responsibility of the Department of Education. Provinces were responsible for community schools, vocational centres and provincial high schools, and the implementation of policies.

There was some recognition within the Education Plan of the need to expand opportunities, which was done by constructing additional community schools and provincial high schools. Nonetheless, gross enrolment rates show that just 56.6 per cent of the 7–12 year age group was enrolled in Grades 1–6 and just 15.9 per cent of the 13 year age group enrolled in Grade 7 in 1977 (Department of Education 1977).

Significant debates developed at this time as to the relevance of education in Papua New Guinea. The Waigani Seminar report (Brammall and May 1975) presents a range of responses available to education. There is evidence of some innovation at the time, which hinted at the realization that alternative policies were needed. The Secondary Schools Community Extension Project (SSCEP) was introduced in 1978, which connected Grade 10 graduates with a more realistic understanding of the life chances that would be experienced by the majority of those returning to rural environments.

Research at the time indicated that academic results were maintained at the SSCEP schools, and students found employment, or further training, that would not have been available if they had left school at Grade 8 (Crossley and Vulliamey 1986). However, parents rejected this approach, because of the commonly held view that education was an investment in their children, and the return was the securing of formal employment in urban areas and a fortnightly pay cheque. SSCEP was withdrawn from schools as an alternative curriculum model to the academic model by 1986.

National Education Strategy

The National Education Strategy (NES) was formulated in 1978. A committee, chaired by Professor Cyril Rogers of the University of Papua New Guinea, with a mixture of national and expatriate educators, laid the groundwork for the second education plan from 1980–1984. The report provides valuable understanding of the policy framework for education through to the 1990s. Some of its major policy recommendations were:

• English to be the official language of instruction;

- existing general aims of community-based education to continue, but the curriculum systematically tilted in the direction of greater competency in basic subjects such as language, numbers, science, and the social sciences;
- 30 per cent progression of students from Grade 6 to Grade 7; and
- nationally administered examinations to select students for progression to high school.

The NES revisited the goal of universal primary education and optimistically stated that 'the earliest target for universal first level education was 1990... the Committee feels it to be realistic' (IASER 1979, 25).

There was growth in numbers, but the goal of universal primary education was still a long way off. That goal was further compounded by poor participation and retention of males and females in schools. This had been a long-term issue for Papua New Guinea. Some 35 per cent of children in each cohort eligible to enrol in school were unable to do so because schools were not available, the cost of education was too high, or there was little encouragement from (some) parents to participate in schooling. Many of those children who did start school had left by Grade 2 and many others left school at the end of Grade 6 because there were no places available for them in the high schools. Less than 1 per cent of children who enrolled in Grade 1 went on to complete Grade 12 at school by the end of the 1980s.

Matane Report

The influential Ministerial Committee Report on a Philosophy of Education (Department of Education 1986) proposed a radical philosophy of education based on a notion of 'integral human development'. The Report, better known as the 'Matane Report', was officially adopted by the government of the day and states:

> This philosophy is for every person to be dynamically involved in the process of freeing himself or herself from every form of domination and oppression so that each individual will have the opportunity to develop as an integrated person in relationship to others. This means that education must aim for integrating and maximising: socialisation, participation, liberation, equality (Department of Education 1986, 6).

The report was particularly concerned at the loss of relevance of education for the majority of students, and the lack of early childhood education opportunities; it urged that the language of instruction be in the language spoken by the child — that is, one of the over 800 languages that exist in Papua New Guinea. This last point was a daunting challenge, but it was underpinned by a strong maintenance approach to Papua New Guinea cultures and 'ways of doing things'. The report was not fully appreciated at the time of its release, but it forms an important prologue for much of the policy documentation and literature on education in Papua New Guinea today.

Jomtien Agreement

Papua New Guinea was a signatory to the 1990 Jomtien Agreement that endorsed the policy of Education for All (UNESCO 1990). This policy was in effect a continuation of the goal of universal primary education advocated by Papua New Guinea education authorities since the 1950s. The issues and the strategies, which arose from Jomtien, were already evident in the minds of senior educators.

The Education Sector Review

Human resource development has been a high policy priority area of past and present governments in Papua New Guinea. In 1991, consistent with this priority, the government of the time commissioned an education sector review to be carried out by a task force of national and expatriate educators and community representatives. It was to identify, document and develop policies and strategies to rectify problems that had become endemic in the education system during the fifteen years since independence.

The Education Sector Review (Department of Education 1991) confirmed: inordinately high rates of attrition at the primary level, pointing out that universal primary education was unlikely to be achieved in the then policy climate; low transition rates at the post Grade 6 and Grade 10 levels; a largely irrelevant curriculum; weak education management and administration; declining resource allocations combined with high unit costs; and a severe imbalance in the allocation of funding to higher education at the expense of other sectors of education.

The Sector Review suggested that to do more of the same was unlikely to have significant effects and was prohibitively expensive. The review raised the issue of universal primary education and pronounced 'that by 1999 all citizens reaching school age will have the opportunity to obtain at least six years of basic education' (Department of Education 1991, 5).

The sector review ushered in radical policy renewal in education in Papua New Guinea. The reforms advocated at the time of independence by the Tololo Committee, and reinforced in the Matane Report, were finally taken up officially some twenty years after their conception.

Reforming education in Papua New Guinea

The reform of education has initiated major policy shifts in education in Papua New Guinea. The reform commenced in two provinces in 1993 and continues in the current planning cycle, though 'there is still much to be done to reach our targets' (Department of Education 2005, v). The reform set out to improve access, equity, retention and quality at elementary, primary and secondary levels of education and established a lower-cost base at each level of education.

The reform occurred within the context of the *Organic Law on Provincial Government* (1976), the *Education (Amendment) Act*, 1995 (which established the new structure of the education system), the *Teaching Service (Amendment) Act*, 1995, and various major government policies introduced from time to time such as the downsizing of the public service, a user pay policy, and supporting delivery of services at the provincial and district levels.

Although development partners do not engage in direct policy formulation in Papua New Guinea, the policies and forms of assistance provided by development partners have the potential to drive policy formulation. The World Bank, for example, in the mid 1990s, was prepared to support only development projects that targeted universal basic education and would not entertain forms of assistance at the tertiary level of education. Education receives considerable development assistance from the Australian government. AusAID projects account for some K60 million of expenditure each year in addition to the national government budget expenditure. The Curriculum Reform Implementation Project (CRIP), for example, has been criticized on the basis that its technical advisers drive policy decisions and the development of the national curriculum for Papua New Guinea through project activities. The Curriculum Development Division (CDD) of the Department of Education, on the other hand, strongly refutes this criticism and points to the leading role that CDD officers take in designing the curriculum and developing curriculum materials for classroom use.

The new reform structure has been progressively introduced since 1993, and runs parallel with the existing education system in many parts of the country. Thus, one system is expanding, and the other diminishing, until the reform is complete. For the foreseeable future, there will continue to be community schools offering Grades 1 to 6 and provincial high schools offering Grades 7 to 10.

The reorganization of education involved the establishment of a three-year elementary education program, which consists of a preparatory year followed by Elementary Grades 1 and 2. Teaching is conducted in the child's first language, and elementary schools are located in villages to minimize travel by small children, and to acknowledge the local responsibilities for this form of education.

There is a formal connection between elementary schools and the newly designed primary schools, which replace the former community schools. After three years in the elementary school, students are enrolled in Grade 3 at primary school.

Primary schools provide education from Grades 3 to 8. The number of places for students at the upper primary school level has increased significantly as a result of this policy initiative and at a relatively low cost (World Bank 1999). In the past, many students were denied access to Grade 7 because of the shortage of Grade 7 spaces in conventional high schools.

A number of high schools remain as provincial high schools in the new structure and continue to offer Grades 7 to 10 until such time as sufficient primary schools are available to take all Grade 6 graduates. In those places where community schools continue to operate, students will be able to move from Grade 6 at the community school to Grade 7 at a provincial high school.

A number of provincial high schools in each province has been redeveloped as secondary schools to provide upper secondary education from Grades 9 to 12. The original policy regarding secondary schools envisaged the development of one secondary school in those provinces that did not have a national high school (NEB 1995). In effect, this would result in the development of fourteen secondary schools. Politicians, in particular, and provincial education authorities have disregarded the policy and there are sixty-five secondary schools in Papua New Guinea in 2005. As a result, there has been a substantial increase in the number of Grade 12 graduates who are competing for scarce formal employment opportunities and places in a tertiary education sector which has seen little, if any, growth in student places over the past decade. The successful reform of the school system is inconsistent with the lack of reform at the tertiary level. Support for university facilities and programs has a low level of priority within national government circles and also within the concerns of most development partners.

National Education Plan (1995–2004)

The National Education Plan (1995–2004) was released in 1995. It built on the policy directives contained in the Education Sector Review and the education reform agenda. The NEP avoided a timeframe for universal primary education, but indicated that it was an on-going objective: 'The right to education and the right to learn unfortunately still constitute a vision rather than a reality' (Department of Education 1995, 8). The Plan set a number of targets to be achieved by 2004 at the elementary level:

- enrolment in elementary schools to reach 460,000 by 2004;
- some 14,000 elementary teachers needed to cope with the projected elementary school enrolment by 2004;
- the development of an integrated activity-based elementary program with strong community inputs;
- the attainment of initial literacy in the language the child speaks by the end of elementary school;
- equal access opportunities for males and females by the year 2004; and
- 100 per cent transition of children from elementary schools to primary schools.

At the primary level:

- all children to have the opportunity to complete nine years of basic education;
- improvement in the Grades 1 to 6 retention rate; and
- participation and completion rates for females to improve.

The NEP stated that 50 per cent of Grade 8 students from primary schools will progress to Grade 9 at secondary school. Overall, some 30 per cent of students starting elementary school will progress to Grade 12 as these reforms take effect.

So what kind of progress has the reform of education made so far? At the time of writing (2005), the reform appeared to be taking effect. Enrolments had increased by 67 per cent and more children than ever before have the opportunity to enrol in elementary school and continue to Grade 8. There has been a reduction in the gender disparity in schools as well, although more needs to be done in this regard. The national female participation rate in 2000, for example, was 44.9 per cent of the overall primary student population (Department of Education 2002).

The gross enrolment rate was 81 per cent in 2005, a significant increase over the past few years. Nonetheless, 19 per cent of children remain outside the education system without any likelihood of joining education. The progression rate from one year to the next suggests that more students are staying at school, but that a significant number of children attend school for less than six years. A total of 43,245 students, for example, withdrew from Grades 6 to 8 between 1998 and 1999.

One of the major reasons for the high attrition rate (Guy and Paraide 2001) is the high cost of education, which has been brought about by a reduction in the subsidies provided by government relative to the rising costs of education. The national government was unable to increase the size of the subsidies and introduced a 'user pay' policy in 1995, and moved the burden for the payment of school and tertiary fees to students and their parents.

'Free' education policy

The cost of education began to emerge as an issue requiring policy consideration in the 1980s as greater numbers of children had opportunities to enrol in schools and more and more parents sought education for their children. Parents, at the time, were charged two fees: a school fee and trust account (SFTA) fee of K1.50 per year to purchase basic classroom materials, and a board of management (BOM) fee to fund the administration of the school, usually set at K10 per year although it could be as high as K30 in urban areas (Bray 1984).

Mahuru Rarua Rarua moved a motion in parliament in 1981 (Hansard 1981, 1/13/3/1) that reads in part:

> ... that education be made compulsory for all the children of Papua New
> Guinean origin who reach the age of six years at the commencement of

1982 primary or community school year and to continue studies up to Grade 10.

There was a great deal of support for the motion, although there was a lengthy debate over the wording of it. The full motion was eventually passed in 1982, but the word 'compulsory' was replaced by the word 'free'. The policy of free education was born. The fees that were paid by parents would henceforth be the responsibility of provincial governments consistent with their responsibilities as outlined in the Organic Law on Provincial Governments and Local-level Governments, 1995 (LPGLLG).

The provinces were unhappy with this policy direction and the failure of national parliamentarians to consult with them over the matter. Their grievances were resolved by the national government offering provinces funds to cover the cost of fees in 1982 as long as no other provincial fees were charged to parents. Five provinces rejected the offer because they felt that provincial government autonomy was at stake, and because there was no guarantee that the funds would continue after 1982 and provinces would inherit the additional costs.

The disbursement of funds to the provinces, and eventually to schools, was always based on inaccurate enrolment statistics and the majority of provinces were unable to cover all of the cost covered by the SFTA and BOM fees on the basis of the funds that were forwarded to them in 1982.

In June 1982 national elections resulted in a new government, which promptly terminated the free education policy. The government emphasized the important role that parents had in supporting the education of their children. Three policies were put in place by the new government, which allowed schools to charge fees; exempted children from paying school fees on the basis of hardship; and introduced a fee-subsidy scheme in which funds were paid to provinces to support the enrolment of children from low income families at community schools, high schools and students at the College of Distance Education.

Ivarature (1995) points out that this latter policy was flawed in that there was a ministerial statement in 1972 stating that students could be exempted from paying fees on the basis of hardship that had not been withdrawn as a result of the free education policy initiative. He concluded: 'Policy makers and implementers seem to have little or no knowledge of existing policies. Hence, it is probable that policy makers create new policies that are redundant' (*ibid.* 24).

The administration of the subsidies had encountered problems over the years, especially in 'mismanagement and abuse' of the funds. There had been very little impact in terms of quality and physical appearance of many schools. According to a ministerial policy statement (1/2000, 1): 'This has resulted in the general state of school buildings and facilities, curriculum and basic materials and equipment, and the morale of teachers deteriorating to the extent that the implementation of the education reforms is being compromised'.

User Pay Policy

In the lead-up to the national elections in 1992, political parties developed policies aimed at financing the ever increasing cost of education. The incoming government introduced yet another 'free education' policy in 1993. This led to a rapid rise in enrolments and it became clear to government that free education would not be sustainable over the long term. By 1994, a 'user pay' policy was introduced by government and schools were forced to reintroduce school fees and project fees payable by parents. This was unpopular and schools were forced to terminate students because of their inability to meet the high cost of school fees. Many schools, however, allowed students who had not paid fees, or part paid fees, to continue, which in effect meant that full fee-paying students were subsidising non-fee paying students, and the level of school resources and the quality of education deteriorated.

School Fee Subsidy Policy

A school fee subsidy (SFS) policy was reintroduced in 1996 at a total cost of K32 million for all levels of schooling. The national government continued the subsidy in 1997 and 1998 at that level.

The payment of subsidies raised a number of logistical issues and methods of payment varied from one year to the next. Some schools did not have bank accounts and found it difficult to cash cheques for large amounts in rural areas. It was found that very remote schools would spend most of their subsidy on airfares to purchase basic school supplies in urban locations and on freight charges to transport materials back to the school. The amount of subsidy varied by grade and students in upper primary Grades 7 and 8 received a much higher loading than children in lower grades. This encouraged a greater number of students to stay on at school even though they were not coping with the academic requirements of school.

The period from 1999 to 2005 resulted in constant policy changes to the SFS that caused considerable confusion amongst those administering the scheme, and for boards of management and head teachers to whom the funds were directed.

The appropriation from the national government for fees subsidy has remained mostly constant since 1999 at K60 million, of which K40 million is allocated to the Department of Education and K20 million is allocated to the provinces. In effect, real funding per student, as a result, has declined significantly because there has not been any allowance for inflation and enrolments have increased substantially as a result of the reform during this time.

In 1999, the Department of Education was responsible for SFS payments for quarter one and quarter three and the provincial authorities were responsible for subsidy payments for quarter two and quarter four. The national funds were forwarded to provincial education authorities for distribution for first and third quarters. Most schools reported receiving those funds (NRI 2002), but the provincial payments for quarters two and four were often not received by schools, or were paid at a lower rate than that set by the National Education Board. This failure by provinces to pay the full subsidy payment continues.

A number of the recurrent activities of the Department of Education received little or no funding in 1999 and the Department retained a portion of its allocation for subsidies to support its recurrent budget. A total of K5 million from the national component was set aside to support the operational activities of the inspectorate; to pay an 'establishment grant' to community schools that were taking on their first Grade 7s because of the failure of provincial governments to pay this cost under transfer arrangements included in the OLPGLLG; and to meet the cost of the administration of the national Grades 10 and 12 examinations.

In 2000, the government appropriation for SFS continued at the rate of K40 million for the national component and K20 million for the provincial component. A change was introduced in 2000 to overcome the problems that remote schools continued to face in cashing cheques and purchasing basic materials at competitive rates.

A Government Assistance to Quality Education Program (GAQEP) came into existence in 2000. The objective of this program was 'to improve and sustain relevance and quality of teaching materials and their modes of delivery' (Secretary's Circular 12/2000, 1). One of the GAQEP programs was the Curriculum and Basic Material Supply Program which had two elements: the first supported the bulk purchase and direct delivery to the school doorstep of curriculum and basic materials supply for elementary, community and primary schools to a total of K7.6 million; the second component provided direct cash grants totalling K15 million to post-primary institutions.

In 2001, the government appropriation for SFS received a slight increase to K61 million, which consisted of the national component of K40 million and the provincial component of K21 million. The national component of the subsidy was distributed on the basis of the continuation of GAQEP arrangements.

A number of problems were encountered by the Department of Education in tendering the supply of basic materials in 2000 which resulted in the government's reverting to cash grants for basic school supplies, paid to schools in a lump sum through the provincial education offices in 2001. A total of K7.65 million was allocated for the provision of basic school supplies and curriculum materials for elementary and primary schools, and was paid to provincial authorities. Each province was allowed to bulk-buy school materials and distribute them to schools, or to distribute the full cash grants to individual schools, or a combination of these two methods. This policy resulted in considerable 'leakages', mostly at the provincial level, and schools either received less than they were entitled to or did not receive any funds at all from the provincial distribution (NRI 2002).

Free Education Again

In 2002, the national government was elected to office on a 'free education' platform and the SFS increased to K150 million. The entire subsidy was paid direct to the Department of Education as a result of the difficulties encountered in forwarding monies through the provinces in 2001. Parents, according to the announced policy, would not be requested to contribute money to the school because the government would meet the total fee. In reality, a number of schools charged school fees and project fees claiming that they could not operate schools for a full year on the amount of the subsidy paid by government.

This particular subsidy policy was well received by schools and parents in 2002. The majority of head teachers received their subsidy cheques early in each quarter and accessed those funds within two weeks of receiving them.

Financing Education as a Shared Responsibility

The national government decided in 2003 to reduce the level of education subsidies because of the financial burden of the higher SFS in 2002. The subsidy policy reverted to that of 2001 in which the Department of Education and provincial authorities shared the responsibility for quarterly payments. Parents were included as part of an articulated 'shared responsibility policy' and were expected to make significant financial contributions to schools through the payment of school and project fees.

The national component of the subsidy payment for 2003 was intended for use as a 'school infrastructure maintenance grant' (Department of Education 2003, 1). Schools were instructed how this money was to be used in a secretary's circular: it could be spent on activities such as painting, roof renovation, replacing pipes, moving pit latrines, repairing or replacing doors, locks, water tanks and furniture. The cost of purchasing basic materials and supplies for classroom use would come from the payment of school and project fees by parents.

Provinces were not given any guidance in the Circular regarding the area, or areas, of education that the provincial component of the subsidy was meant to support. This decision remained with the province, as well as the schedule of provincial payments to schools. Provinces could, for example, use the subsidy funds to support infrastructure activities, or use it to support the bulk purchase of basic materials for classroom use.

The SFS appropriations for 2004 and 2005 remained at K40 million for the Department of Education and K20 million for provinces. The funds are to be used for infrastructure and maintenance, but schools are allowed to use subsidy funds for the purchase of basic school materials where parental fee payments are insufficient to meet such costs.

The Department of Education continues to use a significant proportion of the subsidy funds for operational costs, such as travel by inspectors to oversight standards, support for national examinations, support for live classroom broadcasts, in-service activities for teachers, audit function support, support for churches, and support for the Literacy and Awareness Secretariat, which cannot be met from the recurrent budget. A total of K12.5 million (32 per cent) of the education subsidy appropriation to the Department of Education was used for these purposes in 2004.

Policy formulation in education

Independence brought with it a rapid process of decentralization and the establishment of nineteen provincial governments and the National Capital District. There were now many more stakeholders than ever before and greater levels of interest in education policy formulation.

Political parties establish policy guidelines and make them known to the electorate. These policies may or may not be adopted. The national government is ultimately responsible for the direction of policy in education and has expressed this in the Medium Term Development Strategy 2005–2010 (MTDS). The National Executive Council (NEC) recommends to the government policy directions that are developed by the Department of Education through a series of internal committees and processes. The annual Conference of Education Ministers' Council is an important layer of policy making and endorsement of policy decisions in education in Papua New Guinea.

Medium Term Development Strategy (2005–2010)

The MTDS provides 'an overarching development strategy that will provide the guiding framework for prioritizing the Government's expenditure program, as expressed in the annual budget' (MTDS, iii).

It continues to highlight the attainment of universal primary education as its major focus:

> A key focus of the MTDS will be to support the continued implementation
> of reforms aimed at achieving the international goal of Universal Primary
> Education (UPE). In Papua New Guinea, this goal is reflected in the
> Government's objective of Universal Basic Education (UBE) by 2015 (*ibid.*
> 38).

The MTDS sets three targets for UBE to achieve by 2015, namely: a gross enrolment rate of 85 per cent at the primary level; a cohort retention rate of 70 per cent at the primary level; and a Youth Literacy rate of 70 per cent. These goals are realistic and are achievable within the timeframe that has been set, as long as adequate funding is provided to support their attainment. The role of the budget process is to ensure that adequate resources are allocated to achieve government policies and targets. Table 8.1 explores the pattern of budget allocations to the Department of Education for 2004 and 2005.

Table 8.1: Percentage Changes in Budget Allocations between 2004 and 2005

	2004 (K,000)	2005 (K,000)	Percentage change
Policy and general admin	49,001.3	52,446.9	7.0
Education standards	9,274.7	6,644.5	-28.4
Primary education	15,704.2	14,978.1	-4.6
Literacy and awareness	474.1	461.6	-2.6
Secondary education	9,711.5	10,612.5	9.3
Vocational education	2,550.5	3,273.4	28.3
Technical education	10,313.7	8,228.7	-20.2
Teacher education	10,826.6	14,768.9	36.4
Library services	969.6	1,087.0	12.1
Govt. records and archives	341.8	382.4	11.9
Total	109,168.0	112,884.0	3.4

Budget priorities are not always consistent with government policies. UBE is the foremost priority of the national government, however the budget appropriation for 2005 was some 4.6 per cent less than expenditure in 2004. The reform has increased access to education, but it is also necessary to ensure that adequate standards of education in classrooms are met. Table 8.1 indicates that there has been a reduction in the appropriated amount for education standards of more than 28 per cent.

The MTDS points out other priority areas such skills acquisition and adult literacy. The Department of Education has made vocational and technical education its second highest priority. Table 8.1 indicates an increase in expenditure on vocational education of some 28.3 per cent, but a decline in expenditure on technical education of 20.2 per cent. The allocation for literacy and awareness activities has also decreased over the period.

National Education Board

The National Education Board (NEB) has a primary role in policy formulation in education. It is chaired by the secretary of Education and has the responsibility, as defined by the *Education Act*, 1995 (S. 17(1) (d)), 'to advise and make recommendations to the Minister on such matters relating to education as he refers to it, and on such other matters relating to education as seem proper'.

The Department of Education is organized on the basis of four divisions, one of which is known as the Policy, Planning, Research and Communications Division (PPRC). One of the objectives of PPRC is 'To advise and assist the Minister in the development of relevant policies in accordance with the legislative requirements and national education objectives' (Department of Education 2001, 38). The activities of the PPRC in relation to policy involve:

• provision of executive services to meetings of NEB, Top Management Team (TMT), and Senior Staff Meetings (SSM);
• provision of executive services to annual Senior Education Officer and Education Ministers Council meetings; and
• co-ordination of policy submissions to NEC and assist in drafting ministerial policy statements, secretary's circulars and ministerial statements to parliament (*ibid.*).

The Division is not a policy think tank as such, but rather a service unit of the department.

How is policy formulated? The Top Management Team (TMT) is the central unit in the policy formulation process. It has steered several major policy initiatives through NEC in recent years, including: TechVoc Corporate Plan (1999–2004); Literacy Policy (2000); National Skills Policy (2000); Self-reliance Policy (2001), and Gender Policy (2002). Ministerial policy statements and secretary's circulars are forwarded to key Education personnel at the national, provincial and district levels and to head teachers of schools and higher education institutions, to advise them of new and revised policy initiatives.

A recent Review of Organisational Capacity (ROC) noted, 'the policy capacity within the PRC Division was not as strong as it had been previously' (ECBP 2005, 24). The ROC review has proposed a separate Policy Development, Review and Co-ordination Branch with the following roles:

• provision of executive support to the key policy and decision making committees in the Department of Education;
• coordination of policy development and policy advice to the Minister, Secretary and NEB when the matter crosses more than one division;
• advice to divisions on the policy development process and establishing a common framework for policy statements;

• monitoring and evaluating the collective policy across all divisions of the department;

• monitoring and evaluating the implementation of policy across the department; and

• provision of an annual report on the status of Department of Education policy to the SSM (*ibid*. 24).

Policy implementation

Education has been one of the most stable national departments since independence. A major reason for this has been the continuity of departmental secretaries. There have been just five secretaries for Education since independence. The continuity and the quality of those secretaries explain much about the progress of education in the thirty years since independence.

The same cannot be said for provincial divisions of education. Not only have they been less stable, but the quality of political leadership and the poor continuity of provincial education advisers (PEAs) in recent times have created difficulties. One province has had eight PEAs between 1985 to 2005, coinciding with the eight provincial administrators appointed during the same period.

Organic Law on Provincial Governments and Local Level Governments (1995)

The OLPGLLG represents a major effort by the national government to redirect focus towards districts and local communities.

National departments are no longer executing agencies for programs at local levels. Rather they are required to concentrate on policies and program frameworks (Rawlinson and Josephs 2001, 7).

The organic law stipulates that the Department of Education is responsible for:

• developing national policies and plans and co-ordinating their implementation in provinces and districts;
• supporting provinces with planning, professional services and standards;
• supporting provinces in research, training and professional development;
• building capacity to implement public investment projects;
• providing extended services in provinces and districts; and
• controlling curriculum at all levels.

On the other hand, provincial offices of education are responsible for:

• the administration of primary, secondary, vocational and technical schools within national policies and plans; and
• provision of support for the activities of the extended services of national departments.

The devolution of functions from central authorities to provincial and local-level governments has changed the role of central departments and increased the scale and level of responsibilities to be undertaken by provincial and district administration and by local-level government. For example, inspectors are placed in provinces and in districts. They are deemed to be national officers and responsible to the Inspections and Guidance Branch of the Department of Education for professional matters, but answerable to the provincial PEA in relation to administrative matters. Officers are unsure of their responsibility and commitment to the province and the district. The Teaching Service Commission (TSC), which is the employing authority for teachers, has delegated its appointment procedures to provincial education boards, and the Department of Education has decentralized some payroll functions to twelve provinces.

In the case of Education, with an existing decentralized structure, there have been fewer major adjustments required than for most other departments. The education reform agenda, and the National Education Plan, have provided a sound platform for provincial and district level initiatives. The changes that are most needed to facilitate the reform are in the areas of planning, resource allocation and management.

There is poor delivery of services at the provincial and district level and the OLPGLLG recognizes the need for capacity building at all levels of government. Provincial education plans are developed, but are often disregarded in preference for ad hoc planning decisions. There is a number of issues in this shift of responsibilities for education as a result of the organic law, for example:

• district planning and budget priority committee members are not fully aware of, or fully understand, the shift in responsibilities;
• officers do not have the required skills to carry out basic planning and budgeting activities;
• Education personal are uncertain as to roles and responsibilities; and
• there is a high turnover of public service staff to administer complex pay and TSC regulations.

Public servants at the provincial, district and local levels must be given ample opportunities to become conscious of, and understand, their responsibilities in terms of education planning, funding, effective decision making and the provision of appropriate services.

Two case studies

Policy implementation at the provincial level

In a study undertaken in 2001, managers of education, such as PEAs, district education administrators, primary and secondary inspectors, and education planners were asked a series of questions relating to policy to do with enrolments, attendance, discipline, language in the classroom, repetition of grades, student food, and appointment and supervision of teachers (Guy *et al*. 2000).

Table 8.2 lists responses to several of the questions. The first column refers to the broad policy area. The second column indicates the official national policy in relation to the broad area. The third column indicates the understanding that the managers of education responding to the survey had of the official policy. The fourth presents a range of reported views from the managers of what happens in reality in their particular province.

There is considerable diversity of views from the managers of education. It appears that policies are initiated not only at the national level, but also at the provincial level, and the individual school level, with some head teachers setting their own policy even where it is clear that a national or provincial policy is in place. In practice, policy decisions undergo a further level of interpretation, commitment and implementation that is not adequately controlled by the Department of Education. There is considerable concern that policy directives that aim to enrol children in schools, and keep them at school, are not understood throughout the teaching service or by provincial and national managers of education. The policy landscape is littered with misunderstood and poorly implemented policies.

There is an additional element of time, which affects the implementation of existing policies. Guy *et al*. (2000) noted that few teachers and inspectors were aware of Secretary's Circulars Nos. 36/89 and 9/90 that encourage flexible timetabling and relevant education practices, at a time when teachers were bemoaning the apparent rigidity of the education system, which they saw as preventing flexibility in timetabling and relevant education approaches.

A good case can be made in these circumstances for a manual of current policies in education to be produced and distributed to key stakeholders in education.

National high schools: selection policy and process

National high schools are national institutions under the *Education Act*, 1995. Six national high schools were established in the 1970s. They were conceived as: national institutions drawing students from all parts of the country; selective institutions enrolling the top five per cent of students based on academic results at the Grade 10 examinations; the sole providers of Grade 11 and 12 education opportunities; and as a mechanism to foster national unity.

Table 8.2: The Interpretation and Practice of Policy by Managers of Education

Policy Area	Official Policy Statement	What is Your Understanding of the Official Policy?	What Happens in Practice?
Attendance	Attendance is compulsory in order to receive school certification	Attendance should be compulsory	Schools turn a blind eye
		Attendance is compulsory	Not all children attend classes
		There is no policy on attendance	Head teachers do their own thing
	The maximum number of days absent is 30 days after this students will be dismissed from school (Sec. Circular and Ministerial Policy Statement No. 2/94)	There is no specific policy on attendance and number of days allowed for absences	Schools use punishment or call parents in for interview
		There is a 30 day rule	It is enforced in this province
		Secretary's Circular 2/94 is clear	PEB overthrows decisions
		No strict policy in primary schools	Students miss classes whenever they feel like it and return at their own discretion
		There is no restriction as to whether attendance is a must	Teachers formulate own rules to counter poor attendance
		A minimum of 10 days absence and truancy rules apply	Policy not well implemented
		Provincial policy is to follow the 30 day national policy	There is a tendency in this province to close schools early each term
Language in the classroom	Bilingual education in primary schools. (Secretary's Circular 38/99)	Schools are instructed to use English as the medium of instruction.	Children are punished if they do not use English
		No policy in place	Encourage children to speak English
		English is the medium of instruction while Motu, Pidgin and vernaculars are used when situation allows	The use of vernacular is breaking through to the schools as part of the reform policy
		Open language policy	Children taught in own language up to Grade 5
		Upper primary and above is English. Lower Grades are mother tongue	Pidgin is commonly used at all levels
		Not very strict	Pidgin is used a lot
		English is official language at secondary school	In reality a lot of Pidgin is spoken
		English is still enforced as the medium of instruction in schools	Children are free to use own language more often
Repetition of Grades	Repetition is not allowed except in special circumstances	No repeating allowed	Children dismissed from school
		There is no policy	Some headmasters allow wantoks to repeat
		PEB can agree to repeating in genuine cases	PEB makes a decision on the merits of each case
		No repeats allowed	Requested by BOM if school is closed or high levels of vandalism
		Secretary's approval is required	No repeat of Grades happens
		Repeats allowed on medical grounds and approved by PEB	A lot of repeats in community schools.
		There really is none in place.	Repeats based on genuine reasons
		There is a policy of no repeats at Grade 6 and 8 but nothing for other Grades.	Schools ensure that no child who sat for a national exam repeats that Grade the following year.
		No repeats at Grade 6 except for very good reasons	Those students performing below expectations are allowed to repeat

The model has been placed under considerable stress over the past ten years as a result of a substantial decrease in the allocation of funds to support national high schools; changes in official policy formulation; an ad hoc approach to the implementation of policy in relation to the management and administration of national high schools; and an unplanned and unbudgeted rapid increase in the number of secondary schools offering Grades 11 and 12 education.

The Australian government's Papua New Guinea Incentive Fund has played a strong financial role in supporting the redevelopment of a number of secondary schools, rather than national high schools, which has helped to shift the balance of public opinion about the relative merits of education in favour of secondary schools.

The *Education Act* clearly states the role of the NEB to establish policy decisions on behalf of the provincial authorities. However, the NEB has adopted several policy decisions in recent times that have resulted in the present set of circumstances that question the role of the national high schools.

Section 17 of the act attributes a number of specific functions relating to the national high schools to the NEB. These include:

f) to allocate quotas of students to national institutions, other than exempt national institutions; and

g) to establish national criteria for the selection of students to attend high schools and national institutions.

The national high school model underwent a significant change in 1994, and the selection criteria for entry into Grade 11 privileged the position of the newly created secondary schools by stating:

2. The selection authority for Grade 11 is currently the National Education Board.

3. Preliminary selection for Grade 11 in 1995 will be done by a committee comprising of the Principals of the National High Schools and the Principals, or provincial representatives, of all Secondary Schools.

6. a) the top 120 students from High Schools in the provinces that have got Secondary Schools will be directed to the School in their respective provinces provided that they have achieved an average of an Upper Pass in each of the four core subjects with an Upper pass, or better, in both English and Mathematics.

b) Once the students above have been identified, students will be selected for the national high Schools ... provided that their provinces have indicated their willingness to accept students from neighbouring provinces.

c) Following this selection, 70% of the eligible students from provinces with National High Schools should be selected for the 'National High School' within these provinces (Secretary's Circular 58/94 of 14/9/94, 1–2).

The selection policy decisions were made on the basis that the new secondary schools needed to establish acceptance in the community that they were capable of achieving academic results comparable to those of the national high schools, and the Department of Education was aware that the cost of transporting students from all parts of the country to the national high schools would become a sizeable burden. The requirement that the top 5 per cent of students based on academic ability be placed in national high schools was thus effectively removed.

The selection policy was revisited in 2004. A submission presented to the NEB in August 2004 outlined three options for selection criteria. It acknowledged that passes at a lower level than those canvassed in the three options would have to be accepted, noting that in 2003 nine provinces 'struggled to find eligible students to fill the secondary schools capacity' (Submission to NEB 17 August 2004, 2).

The submission reiterated that a committee was meeting annually to select Grade 10 students to pursue upper secondary education, but also noted that provincial selection committees had developed and that, 'Normally Principals are not members of these committees, therefore have no say in provincial selection activities' (*ibid.* 3). The main function of the provincial committees is to select students who have missed out because a poor result in one subject deemed them ineligible for selection.

The NEB (Circular 03/2004 of 23/11/04) reiterated that national high schools will select 70 per cent of their students from the host province and 30 per cent from neighbouring provinces, provided they meet the selection criteria. The minimum requirement for selection was upper passes in the four core subjects in the Grade 10 examinations. A selection committee, comprising the principals of those institutions offering Grade 11 education and an officer from the Department of Education, recommends students to the NEB for approval to enter Grade 11. There is no reference to directing the top academic students to any particular institution, and the policy decision of 1994, in which the top academic students would be directed to secondary schools, remained by default. National high schools now accept students with upper passes and, in a few cases, students who have one or two passes at the Grade 10 examinations.

In a recent study (NRI 2005), stakeholders were asked to describe the selection process of students entering secondary schools and national high schools in their province. All claimed that the province followed the national guidelines for the selection of students into Grade 11. In fact, there are several selection systems in place: in one province, the secondary schools and the national high school share the pool of academically strong students equally — which is consistent with national policy; another province has developed a 'feeder system' of Grade 10 students to the upper secondary level, but only after the secondary schools have had the opportunity to retain the best students; several other provinces allow secondary schools to take the strongest academic students, while second and third tier students are sent to the national high schools.

Decisions made by the NEB, such as the 70/30 percentage distribution of students, and allowing secondary principals first choice of Grade 10 students, have unwittingly strengthened the position of the provinces and the secondary schools in the allocation of students to national high schools, and the distribution of Grade 11 and Grade 12 students to the detriment of the national high schools, whose performance and morale has declined correspondingly. The role of the NEB also has been appropriated by the provinces and secondary schools as a result of its 1994 decisions.

Conclusion

The Department of Education has been productive over the years, developing a range of policies directed at overcoming problems that constrain the development and delivery of education services. Some of these policies have been fortuitous, some have been flawed, and others have been forgotten.

The business of education has become much larger and much more complex as a result of the education reform agenda. Good policies that are understandable, can be implemented, and prove to be effective are required if the successful reform of education is to be continued over the next twenty years.

References

Brammall, J. and R. J. May eds. 1975. *Education in Melanesia*. Papers Delivered at the Eighth Waigani Seminar. Canberra: The Research School of Pacific Studies, The Australian National University.

Bray, Mark. 1984. *Educational Planning in a Decentralised System: The Papua New Guinea Experience*. Waigani: University of Papua New Guinea.

Crossley, M. and G. Vulliamey. 1986. *The Policy of SSCEP: Context and Development*. DER Report No. 54. Waigani: National Research Institute.

Department of Education. 1977. *Education Plan (1976–1980)*. Waigani: Department of Education.

Department of Education. 1986. *Ministerial Committee Report on a Philosophy of Education* (Matane Report). Waigani: Department of Education.

Department of Education. 1991. *Education Sector Review*. Waigani: Department of Education.

Department of Education. 1995. *National Education Plan (1995–2004)*. Waigani: Department of Education.

Department of Education. 2001. *Annual Report*. Waigani: Department of Education.

Department of Education. 2002. *Annual Report*. Waigani: Department of Education.

Department of Education. 2003. Secretary's Circular 1/2003. Waigani: Department of Education.

Department of Education. 2005. *Achieving a Better Future: National Education Plan (2005–2014)*. Waigani: Department of Education.

Education Capacity Building Project. 2005. *Review of Organisational Capacity*. Adelaide: SAGRIC.

Government of Papua New Guinea. 2004. *Medium Term Development Strategy 2005–2010*. Waigani: Government Printer.

Guy, R. K. and P. Paraide. 2001. *Mi Lusim Skul: Participation and Retention of Students in Schools in Papua New Guinea*. Waigani: National Research Institute.

Guy, R. K., U. Kombra and W. Bai. 2000. *Enhancing Their Futures: Skills Education in Papua New Guinea: Locating and Understanding the Issues*. Waigani: National Research Institute.

Hasluck, P. 1959. Education in the Territory of Papua New Guinea. Mimeo.

Institute of Applied Social and Economic Research (IASER). 1979. *National Education Strategy: Papua New Guinea Education Plan, Review and Proposals*. Monograph No. 9, Boroko: IASER.

Ivarature, H. 1995. *The Origins of the Free Education Policy in Papua New Guinea: A Case Study in the Formulation and Implementation of Education Policy*. Waigani: National Research Institute.

Murray, J. H. P. 1929. *Native Administration in Papua*. Port Moresby: Government Printer.

National Education Board (NEB). 1995. *Selection Criteria for Grade 11 in 1995*. Waigani: Department of Education.

National Education Board (NEB). 2004. Circular 03/2004. *Selection Criteria for Grade 11 from 2005*. Waigani: Department of Education.

National Research Institute (NRI). 2002. *Public Expenditure and Service Delivery in Education in Papua New Guinea*. Washington: World Bank.

National Research Institute (NRI). 2005. *A Review of the Future of National High Schools in Papua New Guinea*. Waigani: National Research Institute.

Rawlinson, R. and J. Josephs. 2001. *Organic Law and the General Education Sector*. Papua New Guinea Department of Education Institutional Strengthening Project. Waigani: Department of Education.

Roscoe, G. T. 1958. Plan for the Development of Universal Primary Education in the Territory of Papua New Guinea. Mimeo.

Tololo, A. 1974. *Report of the Five Year Education Plan Committee*. Port Moresby: Ministry of Education.

UNESCO. 1990. *Final Report of the World Conference on Education for All: Meeting Basic Learning Needs*. Paris: UNESCO.

United Nations Trusteeship Council. 1962. *Report on Independence for the Trust Territory of Papua New Guinea*. New York: United Nations.

Williams, F. E. 1935. *The Blending of Cultures*. Anthropology Report No. 16. Port Moresby: Government Printer.

World Bank. 1964. *Programmes and Policies for the Economic Development of Papua New Guinea*. Washington: World Bank.

World Bank. 1999. *Resource Allocation and Reallocation Study*. Washington: World Bank.

Chapter 9

Lands Policy

Tony Power and Oswald Tolopa

Defining the field

Policy making may be initiated by politicians, bureaucrats, the private sector, or a combination of these. Policies may evolve through a formal system or be driven by interest groups who bring about changes in administrative practice that become de facto policy. Frequently, actual practice is not enshrined in any defined policy statement; on the other hand intended policies may be restated year after year but never see the light of day. It seems that for policy commitments to be put into practice there must be a synergy between active individuals in the bureaucracy and committed politicians who have a shared vision and trust with their bureaucrats. These conditions do not seem to have existed at the national level in matters related to land management for many years.

Colonial inheritance

In 1952 a Native Land Registration Ordinance was enacted, but it was repealed eleven years later. In 1963–1964 four acts were passed: the *Land Act*, the *Land Titles Commission Ordinance*, the *Land Registration (Communally Owned Land) Ordinance* and the *Land (Tenure Conversion) Ordinance*. In 1969, as a result of a report by S. Rowton Simpson, the 1963 legislation was reviewed and two years later new legislation was presented to the House of Assembly, comprising: the Registered Land Bill, Customary Land Adjudication Bill, Land Control Bill, and Land Titles Commission (Papua New Guinea) Bill:

> There was strong local opposition to an attempt to legislate on such a sensitive subject [land registration], so close to Independence, and the authorities threw in the towel, leaving it to an incoming Papua New Guinea government to handle. So, after self-government, the CILM [Commission of Inquiry into Land Matters] was set up by Somare in 1973, to recommend on land policies across the board (personal communication, J.S. Fingleton 2001).

One can see from the nature of these legislative initiatives, especially registration and tenure conversion, that the main drive in the colonial period was to free up land from customary tenure in order to pursue 'development'. Papua New Guineans resisted this trend.

Policies at independence

The Commission of Inquiry into Land Matters (CILM) established the policies at independence. Its recommendations proposed clear guidelines for management of customary land that should have guided the nation for the next twenty-five years and beyond (see CILM 1973). The government's response to the CILM was stated:

> The Department [of Lands Surveys and Mines] has...created a new Division responsible for Policy and Research to ensure implementation of the recommendations and to review lands policy in the light of changing circumstances. Land tenure systems are important not only in the obvious economic sense but socially in Papua New Guinea. The Department controls all land registration but is trying to replace the existing highly complex and legalistic systems with simplified administrative procedures and to ensure greater decision-making authority at the local level.

> The Department exercises its powers over the granting of land and the sale of land to ensure a greater role for Papua New Guinean people in the economy.... (PNG 1974, 73).

Policy making since independence

Strategies for Nationhood (PNG 1974) and the Papua New Guinea constitution of 1975 summarized Eight Aims and Five Directive Principles for development. Most of these could only come about if there were efficient management of customary land. Dr Jim Fingleton's tenure as an adviser to the Lands Department bridges the gap from pre-independence to post-independence; he recalls:

> My main job from 1974–1978 was to bring forward the CILM's recommendations for government decision-making – the results being the four Acts of 1974 (including the *Land Groups Incorporation Act*; the *Lands Acquisition Act*; the *Land Redistribution Act*; and the *Land Trespass Act*), the *Land Disputes Settlement Act* in 1975, and inputs to the constitution, and the *National Land Registration Act* of 1977. In 1978 we put proposals before Cabinet for reform of all the remaining colonial land legislation – the *Land Act*, the *Land Titles Commission Act, Land (Tenure Conversion) Act*, and new laws for customary land registration. There were four NEC submissions (which I drafted) and a comprehensive set of Drafting Instructions (which Joe Lynch drafted). All proposals were based on the CILM report. There was not, however, any draft legislation

(that is only prepared after policy clearance) (J.S. Fingleton, personal communication 2001).

Differences in cabinet between Prime Minister Somare on the one hand and Iambakey Okuk and Lands Minister Thomas Kavali, on the other, led to the latter two being sacked from cabinet. A series of Lands ministers followed, including Michael Somare, Boyamo Sali and Jack Genia. The initiatives faltered. With the demise of the Kavali/Fingleton combination there was no competent driving force for legislative reform.

Early in the 1980s the Institute of National Affairs (INA), a private sector lobby group, focused attention on the need for land reform for development. Its principal interest was to remove land from customary tenure to facilitate development. In September 1980 INA commissioned consultants Knetsch and Trebilcock to report on land policy for development. Their report (Knetsch and Trebilcock 1981) stressed the need for reform and cautioned that incremental changes were more likely to succeed than grand, unworkable changes; they saw the recommendations of the CILM as being in the latter category. The following year INA organized a public seminar on 'Land Policy and Economic Development in Papua New Guinea'; again, excellent discussions provided grist for government policy makers had they chosen to mill it.

A Land Task Force chaired by Kere Moi delivered a report to the Lands minister, Bebes Korowaro, in April 1983. The Task Force supported the recommendations of the CILM, and made a series of proposals concerning registration of customary land, the formalization of direct dealings in customary land, and the establishment of a Rural Development Agency (see Papua New Guinea 1983).

Specific proposals included: protection against outright alienation; focus on communal title and lack of compulsion; land registration; and use of the *Land Groups Incorporation Act* and the *Land Disputes Settlement Act*. There was recognition that the Lands Department was a total failure in dealing with customary land, and several alternatives were promoted.

In 1983 the Department of Lands prepared drafting instructions for land registration legislation but in January 1985 a World Bank consultant, Raymond Noronha, produced a very critical report on the drafting instructions, which effectively stymied further progress for some time. Noronha's bias against Melanesian customary tenure could not be rebutted by personnel in the Lands Department. Lack of commitment by the Department of Lands, and the failure of the state to provide essential resources, throws doubt on the political support for the mobilization of customary land through registration.

In the following years a massive World Bank-funded program on land mobilization was developed and executed. It began with the Land Evaluation and Demarcation Project (LEAD) and developed into the Land Mobilization Project (LMP). The latter title came from the East Sepik provincial government's initiatives on land registration. Between 1984 and 1987 the East Sepik Province pursued a land registration policy and enacted legislation. During this time there was much interaction between the East Sepik provincial government and the Department of Lands and their World Bank consultants and program managers. The East Sepik provincial government constantly emphasized the fact that customary tenure is a genuine form of tenure and argued that development objectives must be pursued within this context or not at all.

The implementation completion report on the LMP listed indecision on tenurial reform as a major factor limiting the success of the program. The World Bank was apparently not convinced that customary tenure can underpin development: 'The Project envisaged a major breakthrough in transforming the traditional customary land tenure system into a modernized market oriented land tenure system' (Wichramarachchi 1992). It is not clear, however, whether the failure of the Papua New Guinea government to embrace tenurial reform indicated a bias against altering custom or a lack of commitment to doing anything at all.

The World Bank program was ambitious and expensive, and once financial constraints affected the Papua New Guinea government its financial contribution to the program faltered and vital initiatives stalled. The funding of the East Sepik land registration legislation as a pilot project was recommended, but coming at a time when national politicians were trying to reduce the power of provincial governments, it was allowed to lapse.

The INA again made a significant contribution to the ongoing discussion on customary land issues with the visit of Professor Robert Cooter in 1988. An earlier INA consultant, Michael Trebilcock, had interested Cooter in Papua New Guinea when he spent two months in the country, including a month in the East Sepik observing the work being done on customary land registration. Cooter produced a very insightful publication comprising five essays and a series of recommendations on land registration (Cooter 1989). It used a number of case studies from land court hearings to demonstrate a methodology for development of a 'common law' of customary land.

One outcome of the East Sepik initiative was that the World Bank, in conjunction with the Department of Lands and Physical Planning (DLPP), hired the East Sepik land legislation legal draftsman, Jim Fingleton, to advise on national framework legislation for customary land registration. His report discussed the fundamental questions that had been thrashed out in the East Sepik before approval for land registration could take place; these included inalienability of land, group title, use of the *Land Groups Incorporation Act*, systematic project-oriented registration, and lending agencies. Fingleton hailed the *East Sepik Land Registration Act* as 'the only important land registration law to be introduced in the Pacific, since island states began achieving independence in the early 1960's' (Fingleton 1988). Clearly the government did realize that something had to be done about customary land mobilization.

In 1992 Val Haynes was hired to draft a manual on the lease leaseback system, ironically since the inadequacy of this option was one of the considerations which led East Sepik opting for registration legislation.

In 1993, as a result of recommendations by a committee headed by former professor of law at University of Papua New Guinea, Rudi James, the Lands Department produced draft legislation purporting to be framework legislation along the lines that would logically flow from Fingleton's advice. However, the legislation provided a mechanism for land to be individuated and alienated, leading to the very things that the East Sepik legislation and Fingleton's advice sought to avoid. The draft proposed a national act and a model provincial act to be adopted by provincial governments. This initiative seems to have died out without debate.

Two years later, the Department of Lands once again retained a consultant to prepare draft legislation for land registration. Loani Henao came up with a draft act, being an amendment to the *Land Registration Act* (Chapter 191), adding a new section on registration of customary land. Henao stated that:

> In 1988 a report was prepared proposing the national framework legislation. That legislation has been reviewed by the present consultants and the proposals now put forward follow the consultant's recommended changes (Henao 1995).

It was assumed that Henao's reference to 'that legislation' referred to Rudi James's draft. Henao did not review the East Sepik draft, and the provisions for securing the inalienability of land in the East Sepik legislation were lacking. Introductory rhetoric to the contrary, there was no watertight provision to prevent alienation of land.

Henao's draft was released at a time when the Chan government was busy pushing through amendments to the Organic Law on Provincial Government, which amongst other things aimed to severely reduce the legislative powers of the provincial governments, and Henao completely dismissed provincial government's involvement in land registration.

About this time, opponents of the government and the World Bank's Structural Adjustment Programme (SAP) attacked its proposals for land registration, in terms of 'attempts to take over our land'. But students and NGO protests generated more heat than light and failed to generate informed debate. The Department of Lands was equally responsible because it did not sponsor a coherent discussion of Henao's draft legislation. Such a forum could have facilitated a proper assessment of Henao's proposals.

In 1995 Norm Oliver, a very experienced former land titles commissioner, was hired to contribute to 'General Institution Building' for both DLPP and the Attorney General's Department. He gave excellent advice, which, however, does not seem to have had any real impact. Henao re-presented his draft legislation at a seminar on land matters held by Divine Word University in Madang in 2001, but had not taken into account the wise recommendations of Oliver, particularly those concerning outstanding land disputes attributed to lack of manpower and funding resources, and the role of provincial governments. Oliver concluded:

> In order to create a single body incorporating all the functions of the present organizations it will be necessary to amend and repeal the following legislation (i) *Land Dispute Settlement Act*, (ii) *Land Titles Commission Act*, (iii) *National Land Registration Act*, (iv) *Land Tenure Conversion Act*, (v) *Land Act* (Oliver 1995).

In October 2000 Brian Aldrich presented a paper to a Special Parliamentary Committee on Urbanization and Social Development. This paper approached the problems of customary land management from the point of view of someone promoting development for the customary landowners. It suggests that the difficulties were immense, given the almost total lack of governance in the relevant areas (Aldrich 2000).

In 2001 the student body at UPNG once again went on strike and took to the streets, linking a so-called 'Land Mobilization Programme' with the World Bank's Structural Adjustment Programme attached to loans to Papua New Guinea. The prime minister shamelessly denied that the government had a land mobilization program. The crisis was handled badly, and ended up in an armed clash at the university campus, where four activists, three of them university students, were fatally shot by out-of-town mobile squad police.

In June that year the Divine Word University held a conference on land matters, titled 'Culture versus Progress'. This was a further effort to focus political leadership on urgent issues relating to customary land management. Once again Henao presented his draft legislation with a short covering paper (Henao 2001). One contributor commented that the Henao bill had no watertight provision safeguarding clan land from alienation, and that, under the bill 'it certainly becomes possible to dispose of registered customary land' (Irara 2001).

Policy implementation

In relation to land, it seems that Papua New Guinea has had, on the one hand, well-articulated policies that have been reiterated year after year but never activated, and, on the other hand, ongoing practices that have no well-articulated policies. The history of attempts to achieve progress in mobilization of customary land for development over the last twenty-six years demonstrates that there is a wealth of experience and good advice available, and indeed the government and bilateral donors have made some progress in land administration within the DLPP. However, despite expenditure (and borrowing) of millions of kina, virtually no progress has been made in customary land management. Rather, the function of the Register of Title for Incorporated Land Groups has been in total disarray. Programmes have not been brought to a successful conclusion for a variety of reasons, particularly the failure of government to make the necessary financial commitment, and its failure to take the hard policy decisions when faced with a constant stream of advice that customary land tenure is a hindrance for development.

Despite constant demands from the petroleum, forestry, and to a lesser extent mining industries, the government lacks the capability to implement the two most important acts that affect customary land management — the *Land Disputes Settlement Act* and the *Land Groups Incorporation Act*. Although Prime Minister Morauta, in the face of student unrest, said that his government had no land mobilization program, the DLPP in fact retained Henao lawyers to draft a land registration bill — an example of practice without policy.

On the other hand, there has been no articulation by any government (other than the East Sepik provincial government) since the failure of the Kavali-led initiative in 1978, of any clear policy for the management of customary land where customary land tenure is the basis of development and not a barrier to development. This is the case, despite the fact that several officers within DLPP and many other government departments have a clear understanding that development must be based on recognition and management of customary tenure and not tenure conversion.

Why is there such an apparent lack of political will? Essentially, the interests of politicians are elsewhere; they seem to believe that the road to development lies in unmodified Western capitalism, when clearly, after following this model for almost three decades, Papua New Guinea has become less developed and further in debt. Perhaps, in fact, politicians are too busy trying to make capitalism work for themselves personally, to the neglect of the development of the country as a whole. As Power has argued elsewhere:

> In spite of everything to the contrary in the last 25 years, we still have in Papua New Guinea today a situation where land is communally owned by customary groups. Labour is privately owned. All development in Papua New Guinea, no matter how it is ultimately defined, will depend on reconciliation of these two regimes and creatively finding ways to realize their potential for the benefit of all. ...the state of Papua New Guinea has failed to develop legitimacy with its citizens because it has

failed to empower the citizens. It has failed to empower the citizens because it has failed to recognize them as members of landowning groups. For the last 25 years the state has adopted a Western image of itself thereby denying a fundamental Melanesian reality and thereby stifling development (Power 2000).

The problem is systemic, in that there does not seem to be a mechanism to harness the views of many thinking Papua New Guineans on the need to creatively develop customary land management as the basis for a Melanesian capitalism and translate these views into government action.

Conclusion

In 2003 The Department of Lands was dealing with compensation awards, made by the commissioner under the *National Land Registration Act*, which amounted to over K70 million; many more claims have been lodged with the National Lands Commission. An alternative means of dealing with the outstanding claims should be identified. There is a need for broad discussion which takes into account the various proposals already put forward by land experts that highlight the practical aspects of this sensitive issue, including the involvement of (former) landowners.

Norm Oliver provides a critical analysis of the direct role that the Department of Justice must play in facilitating customary land management, suggesting that there must be a cooperative effort by at least two departments to establish mechanisms to serve the land groups which own 97 per cent of the country.

Until some strong individuals are able to articulate a concept of Melanesian capitalism, based on well-managed customary land tenure by empowered incorporated land groups, there will not be the political will to make a change. Without political will in matters of land reform, as De Soto (2000) points out, nothing good will happen. In the meantime, the state legitimacy and good governance are diminished, and orderly development for the rural masses and urban displaced persons becomes more remote.

Political will is required to ensure the availability of the necessary funds for specific functions. A number of recommendations have been accepted over the years, but have not been implemented. The Department of Lands is yet to address the need for a 'customary land unit' to coordinate the implementation of functions relating to customary land, and the unit responsible for registering incorporated land group needs to be rationalized to ensure that it is responsive to the demand for proper registration and management.

Until Papua New Guinea is able to address these problems of customary land management, the downward spiral so evident in recent decades will continue.

References

Aldrich, B. 2000. The Mobilization of Customary Land in the National Capital District. AKT Associates, Submission to Special Parliamentary Committee on Urbanization and Social Development.

Committee of Inquiry into Land Matters (CILM). 1973. *Report of the Committee of Inquiry into Land Matters*. Port Moresby.

Cooter, R. D. 1989. Issues in Customary Land Law. Port Moresby: Institute of National Affairs.

de Soto, H. 2000. *The Mystery of Capital: Why Capitalism Triumphs in the West and Fails Everywhere Else*. Sydney: Random House.

Fingleton, J. S. 1988. *Proposed National Framework Legislation for Customary Land Registration*. World Bank/DLPP.

Papua New Guinea. 1974. *Strategies for Nationhood: Programmes and Performance*. Port Moresby: Central Planning Office.

Papua New Guinea, 1983. *Report of the Task Force on Customary Land Issues*. Port Moresby.

Henao, L. R. 1995. History and Background of Customary Land Registration. Briefing paper for the draft legislation.

Henao, L. R. 2001. Mobilising customary land through customary land registration. In *Culture vs. Progress. The Melanesian Philosophy of Land and Development in Papua New Guinea*, ed. Nancy Sullivan, 136–139. Madang: DWU Press.

Irara, F. 2001. Customary land registration: a demon or a blessing in disguise. In *Culture vs. Progress. The Melanesian Philosophy of Land and Development in Papua New Guinea*, ed. Nancy Sullian, 140–148. Madang: DWU Press.

Knetsch, J. L. and M. Trebilcock. 1981. *Land Policy and Economic Development in Papua New Guinea*. INA Discussion Paper No.6. Pot Moresby: Institute of National Affairs.

Oliver, N. 1995. Review of Land Dispute Settlement Organizations and Mechanisms. T.A. 215. Land Mobilization Programme General Institution Building, Department of Lands and Physical Planning, Port Moresby.

Power, A. P. 2000. Development denied: customary land management neglect and the creeping Balkanization of Papua New Guinea. Paper delivered at Conference on 'Problems and Perspectives on Customary Land Tenure', University of Queensland, Brisbane.

Wichramarachchi, M. S. 1992. *Land Mobilization Project Implementation Completion Report Papua New Guinea*. World Bank/Department of Lands and Physical Planning.

Chapter 10

Environment and Conservation Policy and Implementation

David Mowbray and John Duguman

This chapter provides an overview of environment and conservation policy in Papua New Guinea. It addresses how environment and conservation policy protect the physical, biological and social/cultural environments of Papua New Guinea and looks at how, in a rapidly changing country like Papua New Guinea, human impact is or ought to be managed. Hence the policy areas that are covered include areas of environmental governance that impinge on management of the environment, resource use, and conservation of natural and cultural resources, and, more broadly, policy and planning for sustainable development, The main focus is the role of the Department/Office of Environment and Conservation (DEC). A more comprehensive review would need to discuss the role of the Department of National Planning[1] and the relationships between DEC and all other departments, provincial and local-level governments, the private sector, non-government organizations (NGOs) and the general community.

This review outlines the history of major policies and policy initiatives; discusses some of the challenges to environmental management and their concomitant problems; and finally raises questions and suggests areas in which changes need to be made to render policy, and in particular policy implementation, more effective.

The colonial legacy and the constitution of 1975

Prior to independence in 1975 there was little policy or legislation related to environmental management and conservation, except for some ordinances on fauna protection, the crocodile trade, and national parks and gardens (Unisearch PNG 1992). At independence, Papua New Guinea's founding fathers had the foresight to enshrine environmental and sustainability concerns in the national constitution (*ibid.*). The five National Goals and Directive Principles of Papua New Guinea's constitution reflect a commitment to sustainable development. The fourth is about natural resources and environment:

> Papua New Guinea's natural resources and environment should be conserved and used for the collective benefit of all and should be replenished for future generations, We accordingly call for:

1. Wise use to be made of our natural resources and the environment in and on the land or seabed, in the sea, under the land, and in the air, in the interests of our development and in trust for future generations;

2. the conservation and replenishment, for the benefit of ourselves and posterity, of the environment and its sacred, scenic and historic qualities; and

3. all necessary steps to be taken to give adequate protection to all our valued birds, animals, fish, insects, plants and trees.

The fifth National Goal (*Papua New Guinea Ways*) also emphasized the need to use Papua New Guinean organizational forms, and public participation was stressed in the second National Goal (*Equality and Participation*). The first National Goal is about *Integral Human Development*. These concepts were to be embodied in decision-making.

Environmental policy from 1975 to 1990

At self-government in 1973, a ministry of Lands and Environment was established, but there was no articulated environmental policy. A separate ministry for Environment and Conservation was established in 1974, supported by an Office of Environment and Conservation (OEC); in 1985 this became a full department (Unisearch PNG 1992).

In 1976 a Statement of Environment and Conservation Principles was accepted by the National Parliament (Office of Environment and Conservation 1976). Significant aspects included: the need for ecological, social and culturally suitable forms of development and their consideration in project planning; sustainability; environmental responsibilities; environmental education and awareness; the role of the 'polluter pays' principle; and Papua New Guinea's international role and responsibilities.

By the end of the 1980s there was a plethora of legislation covering areas related directly or indirectly to environment and conservation. These are outlined in Unisearch PNG (1992), Mowbray (2000, 2005) and Yaru and Bulina (2005). Important legislation directly under the ministry and Department of Environment and Conservation included: the *Environmental Planning Act*, 1978; *Environmental Contaminants Act*, 1978; *Conservation Areas Act*, 1978; *Water Resources Act*, 1982; *Fauna (Protection and Control) Act*, 1966; *International Trade (Flora and Fauna) Act*, 1979; and *National Parks Act*, 1982. Other relevant legislation included the *Physical Planning Act*, 1989 and the *Land Act*, 1962, which are significant in Papua New Guinea where only about 5 per cent of land is owned or has been compulsorily acquired by the state.

Together these acts comprised a body of legislation aimed at ensuring the delivery of effective environmental management, affecting the aims of the National Goals.

Since independence a good deal of other legislation has been enacted relating to environmental goals. These include legislation in the forestry, fisheries, mining, energy, health, town planning, water planning, and agriculture sectors (Unisearch PNG 1992, 110). Further, Papua New Guinea has become party to many international conventions and treaties, which in some cases have required enabling legislation which has mostly been enacted (see Unisearch PNG 1992; Mowbray 2000, 2005; Piest and Velasquez 2003; Yaru and Bulina 2005). Two notable recent treaties are the *Kyoto Treaty on Climate Change* of 2000 and the *Persistent Organic Pollutants (POPS) Treaty* signed in Stockholm in 2001.

Rio and after: policy initiatives since 1990

The National Sustainable Development Strategy

Papua New Guinea produced its own national report for the 1992 World Summit on Environment and Development, also called the Rio Earth Summit (Unisearch PNG 1992) and the governor general and the Environment minister led a high-powered delegation from Papua New Guinea to the Summit. Papua New Guinea signed the various Rio instruments, committing itself to the global strategy for sustainable development[2] (Department of Environment and Conservation and Department of Foreign Affairs 1992). In 1993 Papua New Guinea developed its own National Sustainable Development Strategy. The University of Papua New Guinea (UPNG) assisted this process by running the annual Waigani Seminar on the theme, *From Rio to Rai: Environment and Development in Papua New Guinea*. These developments are outlined in various documents: *Stretim Nau Bilong Tumora* (Department of Environmental Science University of Papua New Guinea and Policy Co-ordination and Monitoring Committee of Department of the Prime Minister and NEC 1993); *Yumi Wankain* (United Nations Development Programme (UNDP) 1994); and the Waigani Seminar book series, entitled *From Rio to Rai* (Gladman *et al.* 1996).

This commitment to sustainable development was reiterated when Papua New Guinea's National Executive Council (NEC) endorsed the *National Sustainable Development Strategy* in 1994. The *National Sustainable Development Strategy* was a program of comprehensive capacity building and support for resource and environmental planning, development and management. It was Papua New Guinea's 'Agenda 21', our response to the commitments given by the government at the Rio Earth Summit in 1992 and a reaffirmation of the Five Goals and Directive Principles of the national constitution. It was our commitment to ecologically sustainable development (ESD), the creation of a process for an ecologically and economically sustainable, socially equitable society (Diesendorf 1997).

The activities and recommendations generated by both Rio and by the 1993 Waigani Seminar seem now to have been largely forgotten, or at least given very low priority, though hopefully this is changing. The *National Sustainable Development Strategy* became caught up in a number of ministerial and departmental reshuffles, ending in the Department of National Planning and Implementation. Some of the outcomes are reflected in the 1998 *Papua New Guinea Human Development Report* (Office of National Planning 1999) and the *Papua New Guinea Population Policy* (Department of Planning and Monitoring 1999). In 2000 Papua New Guinea also committed itself to the United Nations Millennium Development Goals (UNDP 2003) and recently published its own *PNG Millennium Development Goals* (Government of Papua New Guinea and United Nations in Papua New Guinea 2005). Through 2005–2006 various workshops have been held in Papua New Guinea involving government departments and including other Pacific nations on 'mainstreaming environment into development planning' (Saulei personal communication 2005; Banga personal communication 2006). In January 2006, through funding from the Global Environment Facility (GEF), the Papua New Guinea government, working with Columbia University and local Papua New Guinea stakeholders/participants, has initiated a strategy to implement Goal 7 of the Millennium Development Goals — 'ensure environmental sustainability' (Melnick *et al.* 2005). Both DEC and UNDP regard this as a high priority and have initiated activities in both waste management (DEC, Joku personal communication 2006) and in broadening the parameters to be considered (UNDP, Bade personal communication 2006). However, many lessons are still to be learned. We continue to exploit our natural resource base unsustainably, especially in mining, petroleum and forestry, and use the income generated on questionable development activities which often ignore the poverty of many of our people and the decline in services, both rural and urban.

Few government documents or statements refer to the *National Sustainable Development Strategy*, though occasionally sustainable development is referred to in lieu of social and economic development. DEC documents do refer to 'environmentally sustainable development' (Department of Environment and Conservation 1996a, 1996b), and the Department of National Planning does refer to 'integral human development and sustainable livelihoods' (Office of National Planning 1999). However, even a consultancy report on sustainable development funded by UNDP at that time failed to mention the agreed strategy (McMaster personal communication 1999). Notably, the Department of Mining does have a sustainability policy (Banks 2001; Filer 2002). Yet the 2005 Medium Term Development Strategy 2005–2010 (MTDS) scantly or only indirectly refers to sustainability or sustainable development (Department of National Planning and Rural Development 2004).

Quite often it has been hoped that the *National Sustainable Development Strategy* would be resurrected. In preparation for the ten-year review of Agenda 21, the United Nations (UNDP) in Papua New Guinea advertised the position of a project coordinator (*Papua New Guinea Post-Courier* 25 January 2002) to manage a secretariat for Papua New Guinea's preparation for the World Summit on Sustainable Development ('Rio + 10'), to act as the secretary for the Papua New Guinea national steering committee and to prepare the national assessment report. Such a national review was required to document Papua New Guinea's progress in implementing Agenda 21. The report was prepared by a team from UPNG (University of Papua New Guinea 2002), but it was never accepted , nor presented by the government at Johannesburg, due to its critical nature. However Papua New Guinea did submit its own report in 2004 to the Barbados Programme of Action for the Sustainable Development of Small Island Developing Countries. (Government of Papua New Guinea 2004). In early 2005 the government of Papua New Guinea advertised for a position of coordinator for Goal 7 of the Millennium Development Goals.

DEC Environment Review

Despite the package of enlightened legislation passed between 1978 and the early 1980s, its implementation has been very weak, enforcement poor and in most areas ineffective. The *Environmental Planning Act*, 1978 required all development projects which might have a significant environmental impact to comply with environmental impact assessment (EIA) procedures, including the submission of an environmental impact statement (EIS) or plan. This has not been strictly followed. Approvals to proceed with development required approval of the EIS and of a subsequent environmental management and monitoring plan (EMMP); these working documents were intended to safeguard the project through its life and to ensure environmental best practice. The system needed effective enforcement, which was seldom catered for within DEC, which lacked an adequate budget and manpower support. This requirement for an EIA was followed in the mining sector, only in the last fifteen years in forestry, and in recent years to a lesser extent in agricultural, fisheries and infrastructural projects and a few other projects. In infrastructure projects, especially roads and bridges, EIAs were undertaken as a donor requirement and DEC and line departments such as the Department of Works and Implementation were targeted for staff training. But the process has been cumbersome and often ineffective due to limited funding and human resources. Some proponents, particularly in the agriculture and forestry sectors, either ignored the whole process or paid scant attention to it.

In 1978 parliament introduced the *Environmental Contaminants Act,* which aimed to reduce pollution and to control the use of hazardous chemicals such as pesticides and industrial chemicals. By the mid 1990s regulations existed for pesticides but not for other hazardous chemicals, and pollutants were not controlled except through legislation concerning discharges into waterways. Guidelines were introduced in the early 1990s for registration and labelling. The latter are ignored fifteen years later. All importers, distributors and users are required to be familiar with the FAO *Pesticide Code* (Food and Agricultural Organization 2003) but most are unaware of this code of best practice.

After twenty years there was general agreement that environmental management was not very effective.

Consequently, in 1995 DEC (which was responsible for implementation of the legislation), with the assistance of AusAID, embarked on a review of its mandate and mission and proposed a totally new environmental regulation framework and new strategic directions. The department made public its proposals and requested comment.

In a publication entitled Strategic Directions for 1996–1998 (Department of Environment and Conservation 1996a), DEC stated as one of its key objectives:

> To develop and maintain a regulatory framework to safeguard the air, water, land, wildlife and marine environment by ensuring effective management of industrial and domestic wastes, hazardous chemicals and unsustainable use of resources.

Another DEC publication, released in March 1996 (Department of Environment and Conservation 1996b, 5–6), outlined a proposed new regulatory framework for environmental protection. This is outlined in more detail below. The new regulatory framework was said to be based on an number of important principles, namely: certainty and integrity, transparency, consultation and communication, flexibility and practicality, cost-effectiveness and efficiency, 'polluter pays', the 'precautionary principle', and integration of economic and environmental decision making.

In 2000, a new *Environment Act* was passed, consolidating three existing acts (Environmental Planning, Environmental Contaminants, and Water Resources), with the intention of providing a more efficient assessment, approval and monitoring system. The legislation became effective in January 2004.

The new regulatory framework distinguishes three different levels or streams of regulation, depending on the magnitude and significance of the activity (Department of Environment and Conservation 1996b; Department of Environment and Conservation 2004a):

Level 1 activities are those that require a minimum level of environmental protection. Regulation of such activities is based on standards, codes and regulations which set benchmarks for environmentally acceptable activities. For example, maximum discharge levels, ambient quality standards for receiving environment, codes of practice, guidelines for best/acceptable practice. In cases of non-compliance, environmental protection orders, clean-up orders and emergency directions may be issued.

Level 2 activities are those that require a framework of environmental approvals allowing for water discharge permits, or licensing for importation, sale and use of environmental contaminants and for site-specific environmental conditions to be set for these activities which have more significant potential impacts. Level 2 activities are regulated by means of conditions in environmental permits, environmental improvement plans and environmental management programs.

Level 3 activities cover those with the potential of major environmental impact and are projects of national significance or of a large scale. Such activities are subject to a process of public and detailed considerations of environmental implication through the EIA process.

It is expected that most forms of environmental management will focus on Level 1 and Level 2 activities, with hazardous environmental contaminants and important pollutants subject to Level 2 regulatory mechanisms, and only Level 3 activities requiring an EIA (See Figures 10.1 and 10.2.).

Associated with implementation of the new act, DEC introduced a series of important new regulations (see, for example, Department of Environment and Conservation 2004b, 2004c, 2004d) and an operational manual for its staff (Department of Environment and Conservation 2004a). Some of these regulations/guidelines now need review and updating. Also, a number of codes of practice are now in place (covering solid waste/landfills, fuel storage, motor mechanics workshops, oil palm operations and environmental guidelines for roads and bridges, as well as a Logging *Code of Practice* for forestry (Department of Environment and Conservation and National Forest Authority 1995)). The effectiveness of some of these codes of practice is open to question and a number are proponent-driven, with an understaffed DEC. A review of the overall effectiveness of the new act and its implementation is urgently needed.

During a long process of self-review and AusAID 'DEC strengthening' (AusAID 1999), DEC received substantial funding cuts; many staff were made redundant and the department was downgraded to an office. At the end of 2001 it was upgraded again to department status. However, four years after this long and much needed review, DEC seems to still lack direction and financial capacity; it suffers from a scarcity of personnel skills and experience, and the decision-making process lacks accountability and is not seen as sufficiently transparent either by officers within the department or by the community. Policy is not implemented or enforced effectively.

A useful review of priority environmental concerns in Papua New Guinea was done by Nicholls for the International Waters Programme (Nicholls 2002). He identified ten areas: increasing land degradation; increasing environmental risk from hazardous materials; declining water quality in rivers and coastal areas; disturbed or unpredictable hydrological regimes; loss of critical habitats and biodiversity; declining coastal and marine resources; inadequate or unsatisfactory water supplies; declining air quality in urban area; noise pollution; and climate change. Given poor environmental governance in Papua New Guinea and people's lack of awareness about and/or poor attitudes towards the environment the few efforts to address these issues have had little success and certainly have not been sustained.

DEC from 2004 to 2006 initiated a much-needed review of chemical management in Papua New Guinea. This followed Mowbray's review of chemical management (*National Profile on Chemical Management*) (Mowbray 2000). With financial assistance from UNEP and funding from the Global Environment Facility (GEF) through the Stockholm Convention, the Papua New Guinea POPs (Persistent Organic Pollutants) Project reviewed the use of DDT and PCBs, the production of furans and dioxins, and the use of chemicals in agriculture, forestry and industry; it also carried out reviews of legislation and of education and training, conducted awareness activities on chemicals, and updated the 2000 National Profile (Mowbray 2005). An action plan was prepared to be submitted to the Stockholm Convention Conference of Parties in 2006 (Department of Environment and Conservation 2006). This was done jointly with several government departments and non-government persons.

There are many problems facing DEC in effectively carrying out its mission. These include mobility of staff at all levels, lack of job security, continually changing organizational structures, office machines and telephones that do not work, and absenteeism. Many of these and other problems were noted in a *National Profile on Chemical Management*, in which forty-three recommendations were made to improve chemical management in Papua New Guinea (Mowbray 2000). These points were reiterated in the 2004 update of the National Profile (Mowbray 2005). DEC and provincial governments must be given the capacity to implement the new environmental regulatory framework, and DEC needs the firm support and political will of Papua New Guinea's leaders.

Despite the new act, Sivusia-Joyce (2005) notes in a brief review that DEC has been under-resourced and deprived of its powers resulting in neglect of environmental regulation, monitoring, evaluation and compliance issues. Few if any prosecutions have been made for causing environmental harm. There are many continuing breaches of the pesticides regulations — both unregistered pesticides being imported and sold and Papua New Guinea labelling guidelines being ignored. Chemicals continue to be used unsafely due to lack of adequate chemical regulations, the absence of a licensing system for high-risk users (such as pest-control and timber treatment operations) and inadequate occupational health and safety standards and practices. Where DEC has requested information from companies on discharges and emissions, responses have not being forthcoming.

One added constraint in Papua New Guinea is that there are few 'environment-orientated' NGOs in Papua New Guinea; most are active in conservation and forestry-related activities. Hence there is no 'watchdog' organization monitoring or auditing what DEC does and does not do on environmental issues. Likewise, some companies can ignore the law, or requests from DEC, and not be answerable to anyone.

Figure 10.1 PNG's Different Regulatory Streams

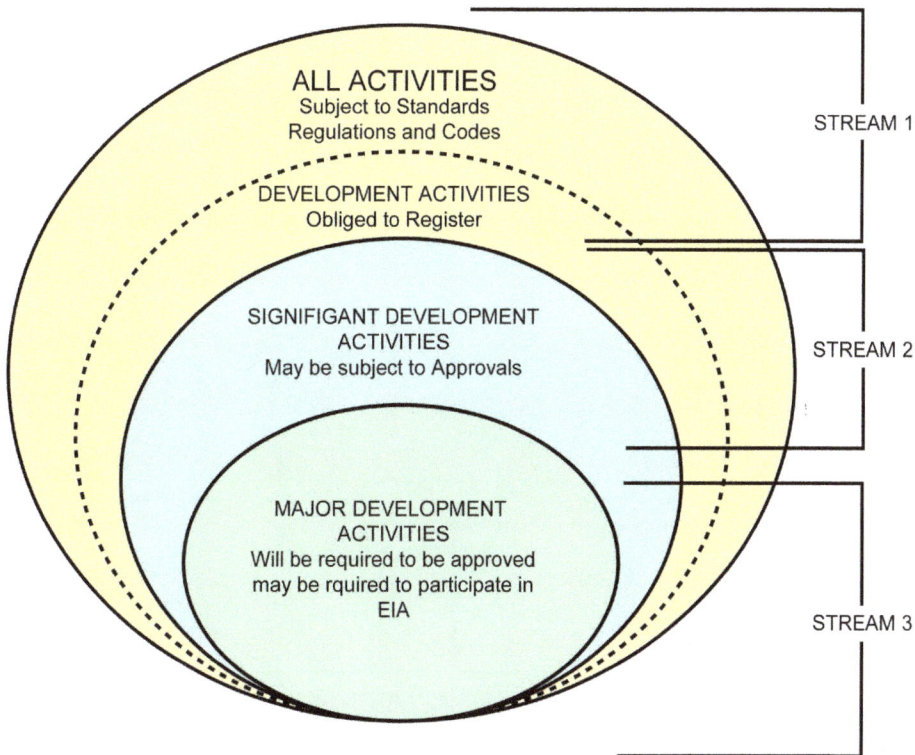

Source: Department of Environment and Conservation (1996b)

Figure 10.2 PNG's Environment Regulatory Framework under the Environment Act

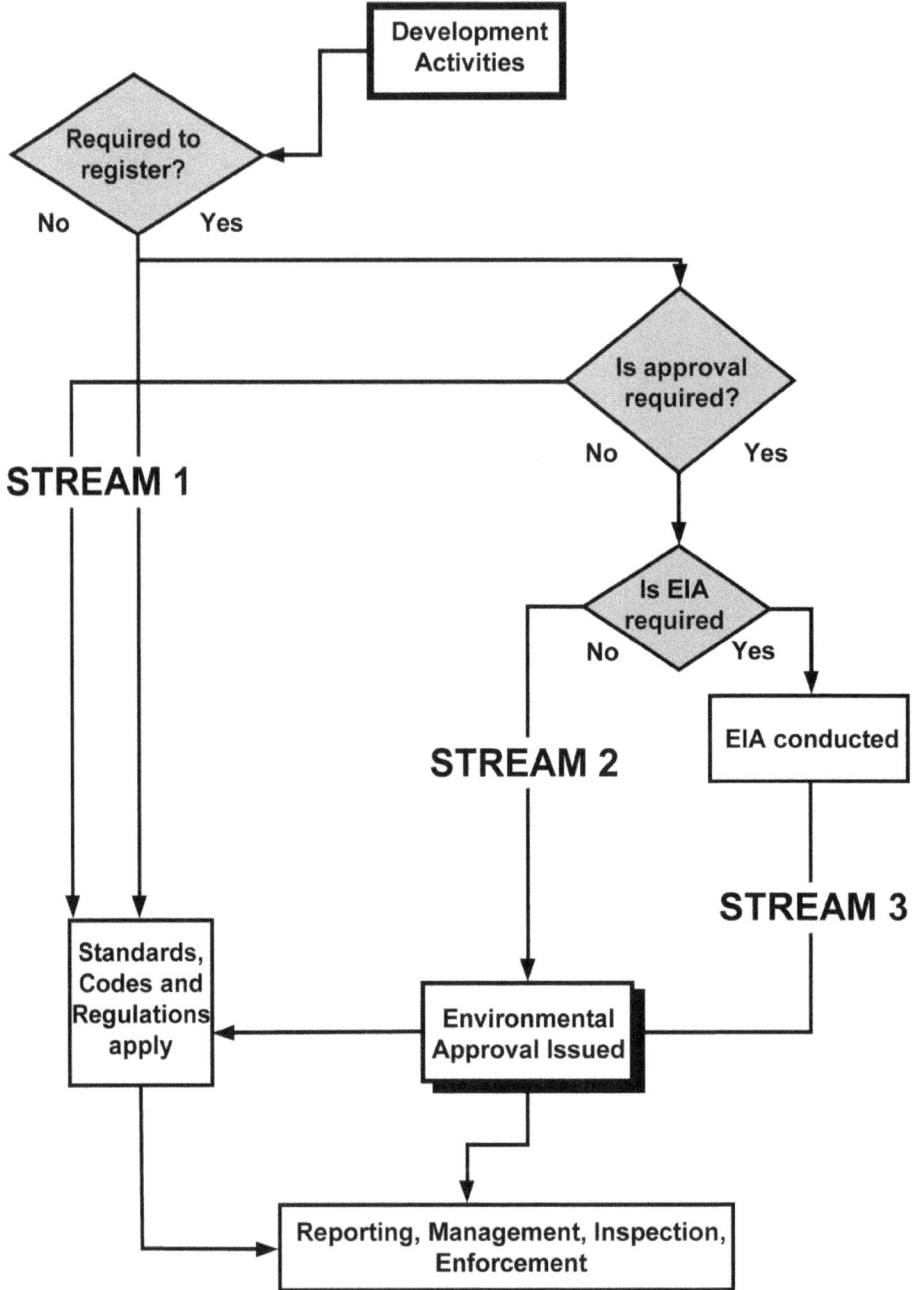

Source: Department of Environment and Conservation (1996b)

DEC Conservation Review

It is generally accepted that conservation policy in Papua New Guinea has not worked for over two decades. Three outdated conservation acts — the *Conservation Area, National Parks, and Fauna (Protection and Control)* acts — also need to be replaced (Unisearch PNG 1992).

Unfortunately, most responsibility for conservation on the ground seems to have been passed to provincial and local-level governments, who have neither the capacity nor funds to do very much. Much of the work in conservation is now done by NGOs working with local communities. But a new legislative framework needs to be developed, taking into account wildlife management areas (currently the main type of protected area), integrated conservation and development (lCAD) (Saulei and Ellis 1997) and conservation/protected areas, and biodiversity conservation. This will be difficult in a country with clan-based land tenure. There are many competing forms of land use, and trade-offs will be necessary. Conservation of marine areas is also new to Papua New Guinea and lacks appropriate legislation.

Various reviews of conservation and conservation policy were conducted in the 1990s by DEC, the World Wide Fund for Nature (WWF) and UNDP, covering protected area management rehabilitation (WWF and DEC 1992); conservation strengthening (WWF and DEC 1993); and the Conservation Resource Centre/ICADs (Sekhran and Millar 1994; Ellis 1997; McCallum and Sekhran 1997; Saulei and Ellis 1997; Van Heldon 1998). National parks as such are probably irrelevant in the Papua New Guinea land tenure context, but wildlife management areas (WMAs), ICAD projects, and new types of multipurpose protected marine areas need to be established. Furthermore, if conservation management is to work, it needs to involve people at the provincial level as well as the national government and local communities and landowners, and the plethora of local and overseas NGOs.

Over recent years the World Bank and AusAID have, intermittently, conducted feasibility studies of sustainable forest management and conservation (including a component on conservation planning and management (AusdAID 2000; World Bank 2000), and a study for a *Biodiversity Strategy and Action Plan* (World Bank 1998)). In 2002 proposals were invited for provision of consulting services to assist in the preparation of a National Biodiversity Strategy, Action Plan and National Report, with funding from the Global Environment Fund (GEF). Nothing happened until 2005, when DEC began holding consultations to develop a *National Biodiversity Strategy and Action Plan* and an important up-to-date review and proposal was prepared by Kwa (Kwa 2005) and discussed in a stakeholder workshop in Port Moresby in September 2005.

Through 1997–2000 the Papua New Guinea BioRap Project conducted a national biodiversity assessment and developed computer models useful for biodiversity planning in Papua New Guinea (Nix *et al.* 2000). Such models incorporated opportunity costs associated with agriculture and forestry, conservation commitments, and areas to be excluded because of high land-use and population density, and developed a set of conservation priority areas. Progress in using these models and incorporating environmentally sensitive and vulnerable areas has been ongoing but slow. Meanwhile a small number of new conservation areas has been gazetted under existing legislation.

Important reviews of conservation law have been conducted by Kwa (2004) and Whimp (1995, 1997). An ongoing review of conservation areas (known as the RAPPAM review) is presently being coordinated by WWF (Yamuna personal communication 2005). WWF has also initiated a local marine management area (LMMA) (Samuel personal communication 2005) and a marine 'ecoregions' project covering the Bismarck and Solomon Seas.

Similarly, with MacArthur Foundation funding, WWF, the Nature Conservancy and UPNG have been jointly developing a conservation area planning and capacity building training program entitled *Strengthening Conservation Capacity within PNG*. This project entails the production of training modules and postgraduate short courses, and certificate and diploma courses in conservation. A 'conservation leadership initiative' and training program, involving training in the teaching of conservation and environment curricula, has also been introduced by the University of Goroka, jointly with an NGO, Research and Conservation Foundation (Tiu personal communication 2005).

The development of a Conservation Trust Fund is another positive development supplementing government action. The *Mama Graun* Trust Fund has been established to support biodiversity conservation and related sustainable development initiatives. Its overall goal is stated as 'providing resource owners and managers with a long term source of funding', by attracting donor support for conservation in Papua New Guinea. More specific objectives include: to integrate conservation of biodiversity into sustainable development programs and activities; to conserve — and when necessary restore — priority natural biodiversity resource areas; to strengthen the capacity of resource owners to conserve and sustainably manage their own biological resources; and to enhance the knowledge and information base needed to monitor and achieve sustainable resource management and biodiversity conservation (Papua New Guinea Conservation Trust Fund Limited 2000; The Nature Conservancy and Papua New Guinea Conservation Trust Fund 1999). Unfortunately with the abandoning of the World Bank based National Forestry and Conservation Project, the implementation of the Trust Fund has been put on hold, although the Nature Conservancy hopes to resurrect it in the near future.

DEC conservation staff numbers have also been severely reduced, with many experienced staff leaving and joining NGOs. This severely limits DEC's capacity in relation to conservation, and greater responsibility therefore rests with provincial and local-level governments, and especially with NGOs and communities.

There are many conservation NGOs in Papua New Guinea, actively involved in education and awareness, in ICAD projects and assisting in community support and legal assistance. Some provide legal services to communities where environmental damage occurs or human rights are infringed. They are especially vocal on forestry activities and conservation matters. Though they tend not to be very critical of government, they provide crucial support both for communities on the one hand and for government on the other, especially DEC and the National Forest Authority.

An added complication for environment and conservation policy is the post-1995 provincial and local-level government reforms. These reforms have transferred many of the responsibilities of the national government to the provinces without concomitant financial and manpower support. This includes responsibilities for environmental management and conservation, and environmental governance. The present lack of capacity in the provinces for environmental and conservation management is a major problem.

Looking beyond 2006

A number of important processes occurring internationally and nationally are impinging on how conservation and biodiversity strategies, environmental protection, and sustainable development can be implemented in Papua New Guinea. These include globalization, democratization, deregulation, privatization, downsizing of government, cost-recovery, corruption and poor environmental governance, and insufficient training and capacity building. These processes will impact on the way things are done. They will require us to think of new ways of doing things in environmental management. A potentially important contribution to such a discussion is a review of environmental governance in Papua New Guinea (with a focus on multilateral environmental agreements) published by the United Nations University as part of their Inter-linkages Programme (Piest and Velasquez 2003).

But while new approaches to environmental protection and conservation management must be considered, we need first to take into account some key constraints affecting environment and conservation strategies in Papua New Guinea. We must acknowledge the weak influence of DEC; the lack of coordination between departments; the limited capacity but increasing strength and potential of environmental NGOs; the declining capacity of universities and training institutions; the dominance and territoriality of sectoral departments; the prevalent ideologies of development; community attitudes and pragmatism; and the move to decentralize powers and activities without concomitant support.

We must also recognize that all the key players in environmental protection and conservation, be they national or provincial governments, aid donors, development facilitators, international NGOs, local NGOs or communities, have different agendas (for example, see Martin 1999) and different expectations and ways of measuring successful outcomes of environment and conservation initiatives.

The capacity of agencies at the provincial and local levels to handle important environmental issues, for example in relation to forestry projects, must be given high priority by the national government and donors; capacity building at the provincial and local levels in environmental management and conservation is essential. DEC must be made relevant, and universities must play a larger role, especially in training but also in research, consultancy and outreach activities. Yet both DEC and universities have had their funding seriously cut and staff morale in both has been undermined by government policies and lack of sufficient donor funding. Insufficient emphasis has been placed on training in environmental management and conservation to meet the changing needs across the country.

A number of questions must be asked:

• How can the influence of DEC both in government and in the community be strengthened? Is the most effective institutional arrangement to have environment policy implementation the responsibility of an independent environmental ministry? From experience elsewhere (see Ebisemiju 1993), we would suggest it is, but what are the options and are there new ways DEC might do things?

• How do we change the dominance and territoriality of sectoral departments? Unless the relationships between DEC and key departments in areas such as finance, planning, mining, forestry and agriculture change, environment and conservation policies will remain ineffective.

• How can coordination between departments be improved to achieve complementary objectives, policies and programs, and resolve disagreements in policy?

• How can environmental NGOs more effectively sell their vision of conservation and development?

• Can we ensure the benefits of aid to Papua New Guinea do not stop when the donor leaves? Donor agencies need to put greater emphasis on ensuring sufficient capacity building and on linking up with local training institutions from the beginning of a project.

• Can we ensure the donor is 'on tap, not on top ' (Carew-Reid et al. 1994)? The recipients, not the donor, must set the agenda and timeframe.

• How do we deal with decentralization of powers and activities without concomitant support?

- How do we cope with ideologies of (economic) development which are constantly changing to meet the latest fashion (ESD, poverty alleviation, capacity building, good governance, and so on)?
- Which is more important — natural, human, man-made or social capital? Do we accept weak or strong sustainability? Priority is still given to mining and forestry, which can provide visible financial returns, but are weak on sustainability.
- Environment and conservation, and indeed ecologically sustainable development, are not seriously considered by most decision makers. Why?
- How do we respond to prevalent community attitudes? Most local communities are pragmatic and understandably will accept the best 'development package' offered, since government services do not meet their needs. How can we convince local communities to accept development projects that can deliver longer-term benefits and sustainability rather than promises of quick returns? How do we engender 'conservation conviction'?
- How do we improve communication between the various players and stakeholders in environmental protection and conservation, particularly local communities, given our different, often conflicting, backgrounds, visions and world views?
- How do we ensure that the recent commitment to environmental sustainability (Goal 7 of Millennium Development Goals) together with the National Sustainable Development Strategy is integrated into the next Medium Term Development Strategy, and effected?

Various authors have repeatedly stressed that DEC lacks influence and bargaining power (for example, see Filer and Sekhran 1998). Indeed, government generally will lack legitimacy until attitudes towards the right of the state to control people's activities change (Whimp 1997). It has even been suggested that a moratorium on forest activities might achieve more than piecemeal and ineffective conservation policies. The 1998 downgrading of the DEC to an office (OEC) reflected the lack of government commitment to environment and conservation and had a dramatic effect on the image of environment and conservation among the Papua New Guinea community and internationally, as well as on staff morale. Although the OEC was upgraded to department status again in 2001, some people have suggested that it has lost its vision and that the underlying principles stated in the 1996 discussion paper (Department of Environment and Conservation 1996b) need to be revived.

There needs to be more meaningful stakeholder participation and consultation and public awareness in environment and conservation policy formation. Perhaps new forms of consultation and conflict resolution in environmental and natural resource management are required, drawing on traditional cultural and social mechanisms. Universities and other training institutions, whose credibility and integrity have been questioned in recent years, must assist in training and creating awareness in the community of environment, conservation and development issues. Distance education and postgraduate courses in environmental sciences, biology, environmental management, conservation and community development need to be expanded, despite decreasing staff and financial resources.

The challenge is to spread environmental awareness and conviction, and to get environmental governance right, by determining the right mix of responsibilities for government, the community, NGOs, and the private sector, within the context of a policy of ecologically sustainable development.

References

Australian Agency for International Development (AusAID). 1999. *Department of Environment and Conservation Institutional Strengthening Project, Papua New Guinea Project Completion Report*. Port Moresby: Australian Agency for International Development.

Australian Agency for International Development (AusAID). 2000. *PNG Sustainable Forest Management/Forestry and Conservation Project — Feasibility and Design Study*. http://www.ausaid.gov.au/business/tender/summary.cfm?tenderid=99/096

Banks, G. 2001. *Papua New Guinea Baseline Study Final Report Mining, Minerals and Sustainable Development Project*. Canberra: Unisearch, Australian Defence Force Academy University of New South Wales.

Carew-Reid, J., R. Prescott-Allen, S. Bass and B. Dalal-Clayton. 1994. *Strategies for National Sustainable Development. A Handbook for their Planning and Implementation*, IUCN and IIED. London: Earthscan.

Department of Environment and Conservation. 1996a. *Managing Papua New Guinea's Unique Environment — Strategic Directions 1996–1998*. Port Moresby: Department of Environment and Conservation.

Department of Environment and Conservation. 1996b. *Proposed Environmental Regulation Framework*. A Discussion Paper. Port Moresby: Department of Environment and Conservation.

Department of Environment and Conservation. 2004a. *Environment Act 2000 Operational Manual*. Port Moresby: Department of Environment and Conservation.

Department of Environment and Conservation. 2004b. *Guideline for Conduct of Environment Impact Assessment and Preparation of Environment Impact Statement*. Information Guideline DEC Publication GL-Env/02/2004. Port Moresby: Department of Environment and Conservation.

Department of Environment and Conservation. 2004c. *Guideline for Preparation of Environment Inception Report*. Information Guideline DEC Publication GL-Env/01/2004. Port Moresby: Department of Environment and Conservation.

Department of Environment and Conservation. 2004d. *Notification of Preparatory Work on Level-2 and Level-3 Activities*. Information Bulletin DEC Publication IB-ENV/01/2004. Port Moresby: Department of Environment and Conservation.

Department of Environment and Conservation. 2006. National Implementation Plan for Management of Persistent Organic Pollutants in PNG. A plan of action for Government of Papua New Guinea in fulfilling its obligations under the Stockholm Convention in POPs. Draft Report. Port Moresby: Department of Environment and Conservation.

Department of Environment and Conservation and Department of Foreign Affairs. 1992. *The PNG Response to Rio. Report of the Post-United Nations Conference on Environment and Development (UNCED) Seminar for Sustainable Development in Papua New Guinea*. Port Moresby.

Department of Environment and Conservation and National Forest Authority. 1995. Key Standards for Selection Logging in Papua New Guinea. In *Towards Sustainable Forest Management*, ed. National Forest Authority. Port Moresby: National Forest Authority.

Department of Environmental Science, University of Papua New Guinea and Policy Co-ordination and Monitoring Committee, Department of the Prime Minister and NEC. 1993. *Stretim Nau Bilong Tumora* (in English, Tok Pisin and Hiri Motu editions). Port Moresby: Salvation Army Press.

Department of National Planning and Rural Development. 2004. *Medium Term Development Strategy 2005–2010. Our Plan for Economic and Social Advancement*. Port Moresby: Department of National Planning and Rural Development.

Department of Planning and Monitoring. 1999. *Papua New Guinea National Population Policy 2000–2010*. Port Moresby: Population and Human Resource Branch, Department of Planning and Monitoring.

Diesendorf, M. 1997. Principles of ecological sustainability. In *Human Ecology, Human Economy*, ed. M. Diesendorf and C. Hamilton. Sydney: Allen and Unwin.

Ebisemiju, F. S. 1993. Environmental impact assessment: making it work in developing countries. *Journal of Environmental Management* 38: 247–73.

Ellis, J. -A. 1997. *Race for the Rainforest II. Applying Lessons Learned from Lak to the Bismarck-Ramu Integrated Conservation and Development Initiative in Papua New Guinea.* Port Moresby: Department of Environment and Conservation (PNG) and UNDP-GEF UNOPS-PNG/93/G31.

Filer, C. 2002. Sustainable Development in Policy and Sustainability Planning Framework for the Mining Sector in PNG — Policy Development Framework — draft. Port Moresby: Department of Mining.

Filer, C. and N. Sekhran. 1998. *Loggers, Donors and Resource Owners, Papua New Guinea Country Study.* London: IIED (UK) and National Research Institute, Papua New Guinea.

Food and Agricultural Organization (FAO). 2003. *International Code of Conduct on the Distribution and Use of Pesticides.* Rome: FAO.

Gladman, D., D. Mowbray and J. Duguman. 1996. *From Rio to Rai: Environment and Development in Papua New Guinea.* Six volumes. Port Moresby: University of Papua New Guinea Press.

Government of Papua New Guinea. 2004. *Papua New Guinea's National Assessment Report on the Implementation of the Barbados Programme of Action for the Sustainable Development of Small Island Developing States.* Port Moresby.

Government of Papua New Guinea and United Nations in Papua New Guinea. 2005. *Millennium Development Goals — Progress Report for Papua New Guinea 2004.* Port Moresby.

Kwa, E. 2004. *Biodiversity Law and Policy in Papua New Guinea.* Port Moresby: Papua New Guinea Institute of Biodiversity.

Kwa, E. 2005. Papua New Guinea Biodiversity Strategy and Action Plan Working Draft. Port Moresby: Department of Environment and Conservation.

Martin, R. 1999. Integrating Conservation and Development in a Papua New Guinean Community. *Monash Publications in Geography and Environmental Science* Number 52. Melbourne: Monash University.

McCallum R. and N. Sekhran. 1997. *Race for the Rainforest: Evaluating Lessons for an Integrated Conservation and Development 'Experiment' in New Ireland, Papua New Guinea.* Port Moresby: Department of Environment and Conservation (Papua New Guinea) and UNDP-GEF UNOPS-PNG/93/G31.

Melnick, D., J. McNeely, Y. K. Navarro, G. Schmidt-Traub and R. R. Sears. 2005. *Environment and Human Well-being: A Practical Strategy. Summary Version.* New York: UN Millennium Project Task Force on Environmental Sustainability.

Mowbray, D. 2000. *Papua New Guinea National Profile of Chemical Management 1997–2000.* Canberra and Port Moresby: National Centre for Development

Studies, Australian National University and Department of Environmental Science, University of Papua New Guinea.

Mowbray, D. 2005. Papua New Guinea National Profile of Chemical Management 2000–2004 (draft). Prepared for PNG POPs Project. Port Moresby.

Nicholls, S. 2002. The Priority Environmental Concerns of Papua New Guinea. Draft Report. *Strategic Action Programme for the International Waters of the Pacific Small Island Developing States*. Port Moresby: Global Environment Facility, United Nations Development Programme and South Pacific Regional Environment Programme.

Nix, H. A., D. P. Faith, M. F. Hutchinson, C. R. Margules, J. West, A. Allison, J. L. Kesteven, G. Natera, W. Salter, J. L. Stein and P. Walker. 2000. *The BioRap Toolbox. A National Study of Biodiversity Assessment and Planning for Papua New Guinea*. Consultancy Report to the World Bank. Canberra: Centre for Resource and Environmental Studies, Australian National University.

Office of Environment and Conservation. 1976. *Environment and Conservation Policy — A Statement of Principles*. Port Moresby: Office of Environment and Conservation.

Office of National Planning. 1999. *Papua New Guinea Human Development Report 1998*. Port Moresby: Government of Papua New Guinea and United Nations Development Programme.

Papua New Guinea Conservation Trust Fund Limited. 2000. *Papua New Guinea Mama Graun Conservation Trust Fund*. Operations Manual. Port Moresby.

Piest, U. and J. Velasquez. 2003. *Environmental Governance in Papua New Guinea: A Review — Interlinkages: Synergies and Coordination among Multilateral Environmental Agreements*. Tokyo: United Nations University.

Quarrie, J. ed.) 1992. *Earth Summit '92 The United Nations Conference on Environment and Development Rio De Janiero 1992*. London: The Regency Press.

Saulei, S. and J. -A. Ellis. 1997. *The Motupore Conference: ICAD Practitioner Views from the Field*. Port Moresby: Department of Environment and Conservation and UNDP.

Sekhran, N. and S. Millar. 1994. *Papua New Guinea Country Study on Biological Diversity*. Port Moresby: Conservation Resource Centre, Department of Environment and Conservation and Africa Centre for Resources and Environment (ACRES).

Sivusia-Joyce, B. 2005. Environment policies hopes dashed. PNG has poor record of regulations, monitoring and compliance. *Papua New Guinea Post-Courier* 13 July 2005, 11.

The Nature Conservancy and Papua New Guinea Conservation Trust Fund. 1999. *Papua New Guinea Conservation Trust Fund. Trust Deed.* Port Moresby.

Unisearch PNG. 1992. *Papua New Guinea National Report to United Nations Conference on Environment and Development — Prepared for the Government of the Independent State of Papua New Guinea.* Port Moresby: University of Papua New Guinea.

United Nations Development Programme (UNDP). 1994. *Yumi Wankain: Report of the United Nations Joint Inter-Agency Mission to Papua New Guinea on Sustainable Development.* Port Moresby: United Nations Development Programme.

United Nations Development Programme (UNDP). 2003. *Human Development Report 2003.* Millennium Development Goals: A Compact Amongst Nations to End Human Poverty. New York: Oxford University Press.

University of Papua New Guinea, 2002. Papua New Guinea National Assessment Report: Response to Rio and Agenda 21. In *From Rai to Johannesburg,* ed. D. Mowbray. Port Moresby: University of PNG Printery.

Van Heldon, F. 1998. Be*tween Cash and Conviction: the Social Context of the Bismarck-Ramu Integrated Conservation and Development Project.* The National Research Institute (Papua New Guinea) and UNDP Global Environmental Facility. UNOPS-PNG/93/G31. Port Moresby.

Whimp, K. 1995. *Legislative Review Report 2 Conservation.* Department of Environment and Conservation Strengthening Project. Port Moresby: AusAID.

Whimp, K. 1997. Governance, law and sovereignty. In *The Political Economy of Forest Management in Papua New Guinea,* ed. Colin Filer. Port Moresby: National Research Institute, IIED (UK), Papua New Guinea Biodiversity Conservation and Resource Programme and Australian National University, Resource Management in Asia-Pacific Project.

World Bank. 1998. *Papua New Guinea. Enabling Activity Proposal in Biodiversity — Papua New Guinea Biodiversity Strategy and Action Plan.* Activity Funding Proposal from the World Bank to the Global Environment Facility. Washington: World Bank.

World Bank. 2000. *Papua New Guinea Forestry and Conservation Project.* Washington: World Bank.

World Wide Fund for Nature (WWF) and Department of Environment and Conservation (DEC). 1992. *Review of the Management and Status of Protected Areas and Action Plan. Papua New Guinea Protected Areas Programme.* Port Moresby: World Wide Fund for Nature and Department of Environment and Conservation.

World Wide Fund for Nature (WWF) and Department of Environment and
Conservation (DEC). 1993. *Papua New Guinea Conservation Areas
Strengthening Project 1994–2000, Project Document*. Port Moresby: World
Wide Fund for Nature, South Pacific Program and Department of
Environment and Conservation.

Yaru, B. T. and N. Bulina. 2005. *Evaluation and Assessment of the Legislative
Framework for Chemical Management in PNG. Prepared for PNG POPs
Project*. Port Moresby: Neconsult.

Endnotes

[1] Now known as the Department of National Planning and Monitoring, originally the National Planning Office.

[2] Including the Rio Declaration on Environment and Development, Agenda 21, the Framework Convention on Climate Change, the Convention on Biological Diversity, and the Statement on Forest Principles (Quarrie 1992).

Chapter 11

Forest Sector Policy Making and Implementation

Hartmut Holzknecht and Martin Golman

The total forested area of Papua New Guinea is estimated at around 36 million ha. (Louman and Nicholls 1995, 155). Of this, an estimated 13.5 million ha. is regarded as potentially commercial 'production forest' (Filer 1997b, 225). Exported forest products, particularly unprocessed logs, provided some 18.6 per cent of export earnings in 1994 but there has since been a steady decline in both the FOB value and the volume of forestry exports. While the reported 1993 timber harvest of 3.5 million cu.m. was said to be at the estimated sustainable yield nationally (Duncan 1994), logging in certain areas was well in excess of the sustainable yield, especially in West New Britain and New Ireland.

Traditionally, the forests of Papua New Guinea have been an important part of the production systems on which most people depend for their sustenance and livelihood. The high rate of logging, both controlled and uncontrolled, seriously threatens not only environmental stability in some areas but also species endemism. While there are millions of hectares of forest accessible for timber extraction, the diversity of tree species and the low density of commercially known species in accessible areas makes commercial exploitation problematic.

Three main factors underlie the difficulties of managing Papua New Guinea's forest resource. First, not enough is known about the ecological requirements of commercial timber species. Hence it is difficult to estimate a sustainable rate of logging, whether overall for a mixed forest or for individual species. Secondly, the volume of exploitable species per hectare is small and many species are virtually unknown in world markets. Thirdly, virtually all land (more than 97 per cent) is owned and inherited according to customary practice; thus the power of the state to control and manage land use is limited.

Policies at independence

The colonial administration recognized customary land tenure systems and customary ownership of trees and forests but was not particularly interested in finding ways in which customary owners could participate in forestry development, except as employed labour. Charles Lane-Poole, as forestry adviser to the Commonwealth government from 1922 to 1924, was an early visionary who saw the value Papua New Guinea's forests could have for commercial timber and for conservation. A report prepared by Lane-Poole in 1925 recommended a policy to regulate access to forests; this was not implemented at the time, but a gold rush in the 1930s and resulting exploitation of the forest eventually produced a forest ordinance.

John McAdam, the first director of Forests, obtained approval in 1948 for a forest resources survey, a program of forest reservation, research and management, a working plan for forests, and approvals for staff training (Carson 1974, 6). Three years later, Percy Spender, the then Australian minister for Territories, issued the first comprehensive forest policy statement, which placed emphasis on the production of sawn timber for post-war reconstruction and on the clearance of land for agriculture.

His successor, Paul Hasluck, made a further policy statement in 1957, which became the basis for a five-year program, 1968–1973. Included in this were the acquisition and reservation of a permanent forest estate, of 4 million acres within ten years and 10 million acres within twenty years; establishment of a forestry training centre, a forest research institute, and botanical collections and identification; research on timber utilization and preservation; and a reforestation program (including the reforesting of the extensive highlands grasslands). Subsequently the administration saw a need for forestry development, to generate revenue with a view to the eventual independence of the colony (Downs 1980).

The colonial policy for the extraction of timber from customarily-owned ('native') forests was developed over time through the mechanism of a 'timber rights purchase' (TRP) agreement, which was a way of purchasing so-called 'timber rights' from customary owners of forests, but not alienating the land. Virtually all logging companies in the colonial period were Australian-owned or Australian-based. Some of these did a degree of processing locally, but most timber was exported as round logs.

The legal framework for forest exploitation had three main elements:

Timber Rights Purchase (TRP). Under this arrangement the state acquired timber rights where customary owners were willing to sell. The state then issued a permit or licence to remove the timber on agreed terms and conditions, including the payment of royalties, a portion of which was passed on to customary owners. The TRP arrangement was intended for large-scale exploitation and was managed by the Department of Forestry.

Timber Authority (TA). Timber authorities could be issued, on payment of a fee, to enable any person to purchase a very limited quantity of timber directly from a customary owner. Without a TA no one other than a Papua New Guinean could purchase forest produce from a customary owner. However, there was no management control over TAs other than limitation on the quantity of timber purchased.

Forestry (Private Dealings) Ordinance, 1971 (which became an act in 1974). This enabled customary owners to dispose of their timber to whomever they wished, provided that (a) the interests of the owners were protected, (b) there was no conflict with national interest, (c) prospects for economic development were considered, and (d) the administrator gave his approval (Carson 1974, 11–12; also see below). At the time, many forestry officers were concerned about these private dealings, since their impact was diametrically opposed to proper management of the forest resource.

Forestry policy at independence was based on a 1973 National Forest Policy document, which clearly recognized of the customary ownership of forests and the need to link forestry development to national needs. Its main features are summarized below:

- To have the forest resources of Papua New Guinea managed as a national asset in the interests of the present and future generations of the people (who are the forest owners);
- to preserve, develop and maintain through reforestation such forest areas as will enable domestic needs to be met as far as possible and is warranted, and will also enable full advantage to be taken of export opportunities;
- to accept the need for protection and management of watersheds, control of soil erosion, conservation of animal and plant communities, and the use of forests for recreational and other indirect benefits;
- to encourage the development of permanent forest industries and to provide opportunities for the forest owners to become involved in these industries;
- to promote research into forest technology in order to improve the efficiency of forestry and forest industries, to reduce imports and increase export earnings, and to improve the social and economic benefits to the nation and the forest owners;
- to promote education in all branches of the forest industry and to encourage a better understanding by the people of the value of their forests in both their own and the national interest;
- to provide the laws, the organisation and funds to manage effectively the country's forests having regard to overall development policies and forestry's ability to compete successfully with other demands on the nation's resources (Carson 1974, 7–8).

Policy making since independence[1]

After independence there was little immediate change in forestry policy. The forestry sector thus operated under two very different laws: the highly interventionist *Forestry Act* and the relatively *laissez-faire Forestry (Private*

Dealings) Act. Under the *Forestry Act*, only the state could acquire timber rights from customary owners, under a standard TRP agreement. Customary owners received a set royalty but had no say over the way the resource was logged. In contrast, the *Forestry (Private Dealings) Act* permitted customary owners to sell their timber privately; the usual procedure was for a 'landowner company' to acquire timber harvesting rights from customary owners and then sell these rights on to a foreign logging company. Provided there was ministerial approval, loggers could operate without a timber permit and with minimum state supervision (Taylor 1997, 249).

However, changes were taking place in the forestry sector. From the early 1980s, virtually all of the existing Australian interests in logging in Papua New Guinea were taken over by Southeast Asian interests who brought to Papua New Guinea and to the sector their own ways of doing business. Though small groups of Papua New Guinean entrepreneurs among customary resource owners were kept happy by their close association with these foreign logging interests, there gradually arose a chorus of complaints and accusations of gross mismanagement of the extractive timber industry. These were augmented by vocal environmental groups and other NGOs, which began to emerge in Papua New Guinea at this time, and by their international partner NGOs, who began campaigning internationally against degradation of Papua New Guinea's unique environmental and biodiversity legacy.

This resulted in setting up in 1986 of a Commission of Inquiry into Aspects of the Forestry Industry. The Commissioner, Justice T. Barnett, began work in 1987 and by July 1989 had produced some twenty volumes and a *Final Report*. The Barnett Inquiry documented a timber industry out of control, characterized by pervasive corruption, rampant transfer pricing, and reckless logging practices. A detailed list of recommendations included:

- the formulation of a national forest policy;
- the enactment of revised forestry legislation;
- the establishment of a single forestry service under national control;
- full involvement of provincial government in provincial and national forestry planning;
- the inclusion of detailed requirements for sustained-yield forestry and environmental protection in every permit over land intended for future forestry use;
- provincial governments to have powers to veto projects in their own province;
- outside recruitment of experts to lead planning initiatives, resource surveys, monitoring of operations, marketing control and effective on-the-job training for local officers;
- formal consultation arrangements between national, regional and provincial bodies to prepare and update national and provincial plans;

- the full involvement of landowners and provincial governments prior to allocation of permits in discussions of desired future land use and the conditions to be imposed on the developer by the timber permit...;
- the National Forest Development Programme (i.e. harvesting projections) to be revised drastically downwards;
- outside assistance to be sought to enable an accurate professional survey of all forest resources;
- no future allocation of any area unless resource survey information and social and environmental impact reports are available and a detailed project-specific management plan for sustainable yield forestry (if appropriate) is in place;
- a review of all existing permits to introduce appropriate management conditions, revise harvesting rates, and reform logging practices;
- a new approach to improve the effectiveness of the monitoring of operations;
- a system of three-yearly review and assessment, on a company-by-company basis, to involve all aspects of operations, environmental damage, performance of permit conditions and marketing practices;
- radical changes to reduce transfer pricing, based on the Commission's very detailed investigations into this problem;
- far greater insistence on up to date and efficient local processing and the introduction of reprocessing techniques;
- a major increase in benefits for landowners and more effort to ensure that permits and licences protect their interests;
- the enforcement of conditions of permits which are designed to promote the interests of the local community (Barnett 1992, 104–107, reproduced in Filer *et al*. 2000, 13).

In addition, the Barnett Inquiry put forward a list of names for prosecution for various criminal and leadership offences, and recommended a series of measures to clamp down on political corruption.

The incoming government began to implement the recommendations in 1988. A new National Forest Policy was approved in 1990; a new *Forestry Act* was passed in 1991 and gazetted in 1992; and the *Forestry (Private Dealings) Act* was removed from the statute books.

The new *Forestry Act* incorporated the Papua New Guinea Forest Authority (PNGFA) as the responsible body for timber industry regulation under a National Forest Board; this had previously been an Office, then a Department, of Forests. As in the old act, the state reserved to itself the monopoly on the right to enter into a Forest Management Agreement (FMA) with customary forest owners. Once a FMA was agreed upon, the National Forest Board selected a registered logger to implement it. The act also required the development of a National Forest Plan, to which all forest activities had to conform. This was done through the National Forestry Development Guidelines (see below), a development program and a statement of annual allowable cut. Provincial forest development plans were also required, and provincial forest management committees were set up to make recommendations to the National Forest Board.

The FMA process, summarized in Figure 11.1, involved several steps (see Kwa 2000 for a detailed discussion). Of these, the three most contentious were the requirements for a 'development options study', the 'formation of land groups', and 'corporate formation'.

Development Options Study

In the early days of the formulation of the National Forestry Development Guidelines, the development options study was the first step. It involved taking a look at what resources a community or group of communities controlled, and recommending whether forestry or some other kind of resource development would be best suited to the area. If forestry were the best option, the next steps could be taken. However, the PNGFA felt this requirement would be too time-consuming and costly, and it was moved down in the process, to a point where the decision to proceed with a forestry project had already been taken. As a result, the development options studies undertaken to date have been very limited and virtually useless.

Formation of Land Groups

The new *Forestry Act* required participation by customary resource owners either through the formation of land groups, according to the procedures set out in the *Land Groups Incorporation Act*, 1974, or by the agreement of 75 per cent of the customary owners. Without knowing who all of the customary owners are, it has been impractical to follow the latter practice. Nor has the formation of incorporated land groups (ILGs) gone smoothly. Logging companies paid minimal funds for forestry officers to undertake the work required to identify and incorporate ILGs in as short a time as possible. Sometimes they hired people to pay customary owners to put their names down as ILGs, just to complete this requirement. In some (perhaps many) logging projects there has been a high degree of complicity between logging companies and principals of 'landowner companies', resulting in superficial adherence to the legal requirements.

Corporate Formation

The formation of corporate structures has been another area of concern. Before the FMA process came into being, partly as a result of the previous 'private dealings', 'landowner companies' had been created which were often headed by a local entrepreneur (frequently a provincial or national MP) who was not representative of the interests of the majority of customary resource owners (see, for example, Wood 1997). Almost invariably, the leadership of these organizations supported 'their' logging company in any disputes between loggers and individuals or communities from the areas in which they logged. Typically, they maintained a high lifestyle, usually in the provincial capital or in Port Moresby, supported by landowner company funds.

Figure 11.1 Resource Development and Allocation Process

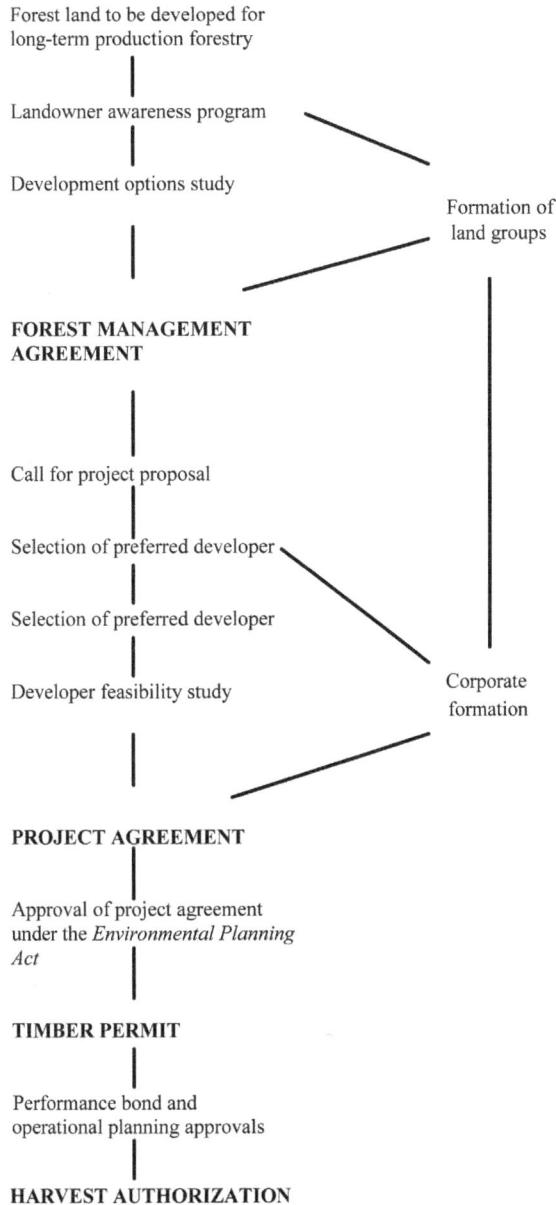

Forest land to be developed for
long-term production forestry

Landowner awareness program

Development options study

Formation of
land groups

**FOREST MANAGEMENT
AGREEMENT**

Call for project proposal

Selection of preferred developer

Selection of preferred developer

Developer feasibility study

Corporate
formation

PROJECT AGREEMENT

Approval of project agreement
under the *Environmental Planning
Act*

TIMBER PERMIT

Performance bond and
operational planning approvals

HARVEST AUTHORIZATION

[Source: PNG 1991:5]

The new *Forestry Act* required landowner companies to register with the PNGFA and, in so doing, conform to the act's requirements with regard to the representativeness of their membership lists, sound and transparent management of company funds, and so on. But when the PNGFA began trying to implement this requirement of the act, landowner companies and their logging company allies raised such a political storm in the media that the minister at the time, Andrew Posai, suspended that part of the act. To our knowledge it has not been reactivated.

Policy implementation

Between 1989 and 1991 when government set up a Forestry Transitional Management Council, there is evidence of a growing involvement of the World Bank (see Filer 1997a). Major policy reviews and statements concerning the forestry sector reflect pressures by the World Bank to achieve certain political, policy and practical outcomes. These pressures contributed to increasing tension in the relationship between the government of Papua New Guinea and the World Bank in this period.

Such tensions were already evident in: the setting up of the Tropical Forest Action Plan (TFAP) for Papua New Guinea; its restructuring into a National Forest Action Plan (NFAP); the circulation of draft National Forest Policy documents; the framing of the new *Forestry Bill*; statements from the minister of Forests about criteria for exempting projects from the moratorium he himself had announced and implemented; the setting up of a Technical Support Project to support the NFAP; World Bank supervisory missions; and the setting up of a World Bank-funded Forest Management and Planning Project. A third draft of the *Forestry Bill* (including last-minute amendments that had the effect of watering down some important provisions) was finally enacted by National Parliament in 1991. The World Bank reiterated its concern about the continued non-gazettal of the new *Forestry Act*; this was finally done in June 1992.

The formation of the Forestry Transitional Management Council in February 1992 brought in a number of outside experts to work on the establishment of the new Papua New Guinea Forest Authority. After another change of government, and another change in the minister of Forests, the PNGFA came into being, and the National Forest Board held its first meeting in December 1992. The NFAP was transformed into the National Conservation Action Programme (NFCAP).

Early in 1993 the National Forestry Development Guidelines (NFDG) were circulated. Soon after, the first of many amendments to the new *Forestry Act* was approved, reducing the size of the National Forestry Board and separating the position of managing director from that of general manager of the National Forest Service. Later in the year national members of parliament, prompted by landowner companies associated with logging companies, tried to amend the act again, but were opposed by the minister and eventually defeated. Cabinet finally approved the NFDG in December 1993. In May 1994 the government signed a log-export monitoring contract with an international firm, Société-Général Surveillance (SGS), and the following month a major fire destroyed a building containing offices and the basic filing system and project files of the PNGFA.

By September 1994 there was another new government in Papua New Guinea, and a new minister who promised to revise the NFDG to reflect the concerns of resource owners. From this point, the Papua New Guinea government came into increasing conflict with the World Bank over its Economic Recovery Plan (ERP) and associated requirements of a structural adjustment program (SAP). Issues to do with 'land reform', remaining from another World Bank project (the Land Mobilization Project), were integrated into the SAP but hurriedly dropped after public outcry and demonstrations. Further amendments to the *Forestry Act* were proposed, the managing director was sacked, pressures were increased to produce a National Forest Plan, there were visits by World Bank supervisory missions, a new forest revenue system was implemented, and there were threats of non-release of World Bank funding unless certain actions were carried out by the government and the PNGFA.

Following a further change of government in 1997, a World Bank team visited Papua New Guinea to discuss loan conditions (171 in all) for a second SAP, while another Bank mission came to design a Forestry and Conservation Project. By mid 1998, however, a further upheaval in the relationship between the Papua New Guinea government and the World Bank, associated with the appointment of the former World Bank country manager as chief economic adviser to the Papua New Guinea government, marked the beginning of a period of concerted attempts by the government to bypass the World Bank and find loan funding elsewhere. However, by early 1999 negotiations between a World Bank/IMF delegation and Papua New Guinea government officials re-opened.

When the Morauta government came to power in July 1999 it quickly put into place several key planks of a structural reform program designed to address a general 'crisis of governance' and restore the lost confidence of the donor community, particularly the World Bank. Forest policy reform was initially not part of this program, but the World Bank persuaded the government that even tougher measures than those imposed in 1997 and 1998 would be required as loan conditions, and a major condition was a moratorium on the issue of new timber permits and extension of existing permits. At the same time, World Bank staff continued to modify the design of the proposed Forest and Conservation Project so that it would complement the forestry and conservation projects notionally to be funded by other international donors.

By the end of 1999 the World Bank had reached broad agreement with other members of the donor community (including international NGOs) about the direction of forest policy in Papua New Guinea for at least the next five to six years. Questions remained about the new government's capacity to develop real ownership of a reform process which now seemed even more driven by external forces.

The new reform agenda

The main focus of the new Structural Reform Programme (SRP) was 'good governance'. The World Bank had laid down a SRP policy matrix which had 9 objectives, 39 first tranche conditions and 33 second tranche conditions. Civil society organizations gradually became more and more vocal in their objections to many of these conditions.

One of the fiscal measures adopted in the mini-budget of 1999 was the restoration of the log export tax. This came under fire from the Forest Industry Association (FIA), which predicted substantial falls in log production with consequent reductions in monthly foreign exchange earnings. A further review of the forest revenue system was called for by the FIA; this had already been signalled by World Bank. The 2000 budget addressed a number of conditions attached to the seventh of the SRP's objectives, namely 'to improve the management of the forestry sector to ensure sustainability and optimal returns to the country'.

Three other conditions called for NEC Decision 59/97 (on agricultural conversion and road-building projects in forested areas) to be rescinded. The first required a 5 per cent increase in the PNGFA's budget and called on the government to disburse the allocation to forestry 'in a timely fashion'. A further condition in the policy matrix was a moratorium on all new forestry licences and extensions until existing licenses and extensions had been reviewed for compliance with the *Forestry Act* and associated regulations. The independence and integrity of the National Forest Board had been called into question by the way the Kamula-Dosa extension in Western Province had been allocated.[2] The World Bank made it clear that a number of PNGFA decisions threatened the proposed new Bank-funded project. These included:

- a major extension to the largest timber concession in Papua New Guinea through a process that bypassed normal procedures;
- directions to provincial forest management committees to 'fast-track' a number of new logging operations;
- amendments to the *Forestry Act* to legitimate the fast-tracking of approvals for logging operations;
- the elimination of the SGS log export monitoring program for purposes of export tax avoidance;

- reduction of the PNGFA's budget allocation and staffing, undermining the Authority's capacity to support major forest projects;
- changes to the log export tax structure, resulting in logging firms paying virtually no tax; and
- the withdrawal of a forest concession to The Nature Conservancy (in Josephstaal, Madang Province) and its allocation to a commercial operator (Choi 1999).

In the 2000 budget papers, the Papua New Guinea government accepted the World Bank's dim view of the PNGFA's recent performance:

> Governance has been particularly poor in the area of forestry, with the side effect of promoting corrupt practices and undermining environmental sustainability in logging activities. The Government is committed to introducing a moratorium on all new forestry licenses, to ensure that proper procedures are followed, that logging practices are not carried out in an unsustainable way, and that landowners get their fair share of benefits from resource use (Papua New Guinea 1999, 18).

A World Bank forestry adviser (Choi 1999) saw a proposed Forest and Conservation Programme (FACP) as an integral part of the SRP. While there was a forestry component in this project (which also set up a $US17 million Conservation Trust Fund, financed in part by the Global Environment Facility), the focus appeared to be on a Landowner Development Options Unit (LDOU). A number of reviews of forestry and operating timber projects was carried out through the FACP, however the program was terminated by agreement between the government of Papua New Guinea and the World Bank, freeing the government to push for further large-scale commercial logging projects (some ten new projects were said to be in the pipeline).

PNGFA headquarters has produced a number of new draft policy documents — on reforestation, downstream processing and ecoforestry — but these have yet to be approved and implemented; since the suspension and dismissal of the PNGFA managing director in 2004, the PNGFA has effectively been in caretaker mode with many staff unsure of their futures and unsure of the organization's direction. The National Forest Policy and the National Forest Plan have not been reviewed or revised since their creation fourteen years ago.

There have been further attempts to tinker with the *Forestry Act*, the most recent amendment approved by National Parliament having the effects of short-circuiting the consultation processes with both the provincial forest management committees and customary resource owners, and of reducing civil society's voice on the PNGFA board.

Overview and conclusion

It was recognized after the Barnett Inquiry that lack of regulation and monitoring allowed all kinds of dubious activities to flourish. Simply blaming the loggers for the problems in the industry does not explain what was going on at that time nor help find ways of solving the problems. There were systemic failures within government, and manipulation of the vast majority of ordinary Papua New Guineans by a small number of their fellow citizens, many of them in positions of elected authority; there were systemic failures, also, in customary practices, which proved unable to control self-seeking individuals seduced by promises of short-term gains.

It was hoped in the early 1990s that reform of forest policy and the establishment of new instruments and processes would move the industry in the direction the mining industry had taken (R. Taylor, personal communication). The mining industry seemed to have responded sufficiently well to legislative and organizational reform that it no longer attracted carpetbaggers and fly-by-night (or *traiim tasol*) entrepreneurs.

In the event, these hopes have only partially been met. The forest sector, though now certainly better regulated, remains a happy hunting ground for operators, both Papua New Guinean and foreign, from high officials to grassroots people, who still seek quick personal gain with no regard for the long-term economic, social and environmental costs for their communities, their province or their country.

There are several issues that need to be addressed in policy making:

• Rights over forest resources tend to be group rights; the forestry sector needs to be reminded that the state's monopoly over access to those rights remains tenuous, despite the fact that colonial and post-independence governments have given themselves the legal right to control such access (Holzknecht 1997). The state, in conjunction with customary resource owners, must develop better ways to involve customary owners in managing and benefiting from these resources.
• In 2002 the PNGFA was circulating a number of draft policy documents. These included: a policy on plantations (or 'reforestation' or 'resource replacement' — the terminology changes from time to time); a policy on downstream processing; review of the National Forest Development Guidelines (originally approved by NEC in 1993, but without substantive effect in the intervening period); and a policy on small-scale saw-milling, to be developed in conjunction with a European Union-funded eco-forestry project.

Other policy documents were in preparation, including papers on extension services, and non-timber forest products. Some of these draft policies seem draconian and implicitly assume that the state has complete control over forestry.

An area of critical importance in the medium and long-term is the long-ignored issue of post-harvest forests. Natural regeneration almost always produces a non-commercial ('rubbish') forest that cannot be logged when/if a harvesting cycle eventually returns to the area. The PNGFA should be advising customary forest owner groups on the best ways they can support productive regeneration of the more valuable but slower-growing timber species.

Registration of landowner companies, along the lines envisaged by the new *Forestry Act*, is long overdue; large amounts of money have been misused.

There is an urgent need to develop a cadre of land group facilitators, and to train and supervise them in working with customary resource owner communities. They should not be beholden to either line departments or logging companies, and should be able to do their work without fear or favour. The World Bank's Forest and Conservation Project may assist in this development.

The PNGFA needs to think carefully about how it can do its job better, especially in the field where communities are becoming better informed and motivated to undertake their own activities (for example, see Arentz and Holzknecht 1991 on the use of mobile sawmills). To date the PNGFA has had little interest in local-level activity, though there seems to be some notice being paid at the provincial level. It has been the non-government organizations which have made the running in developing mobile sawmill operations. This is in contrast to the situation in Vanuatu, where the national Department of Forests is actively involved with mobile sawmills and village-level forestry.

The forest sector needs to better cooperate and coordinate its programs and activities with other line departments and agencies. A whole-of-government approach to planning and implementation, linked to local communities' own efforts, seems to be needed. The decentralization process in the forestry sector specifically needs to be reviewed.

Despite the difficulties identified above, it is important to acknowledge that by and large PNGFA staff have carried on in the face of increasing workloads and decreasing numbers, while battles have raged around them, battles involving the Papua New Guinea government, politicians and some senior public servants, sector organizations such as the FIA, international and national NGOs, and international bodies such as the World Bank. It should also be acknowledged that the ongoing involvement of the World Bank, in particular, and AusAID has been critical in moving reform agendas forward in the forestry and conservation sectors.

Looking to the future, Papua New Guinea's timber resources simply cannot sustain the present approach to forestry. Strategies in relation to forests and forestry need to be critically reassessed, as a matter of urgency, to develop appropriate ways in which the PNGFA can facilitate medium- and smaller- scale projects in which the customary resource owners play much more prominent roles. More emphasis needs to be placed on achievable regeneration of forests, whether as plantation or as forest, and less emphasis on extracting resources without considering sustainability in the sector. Such a critical reassessment of strategies and approach, however, appears not to be a high priority at present.

References

Arentz, F. and H. Holzknecht. 1991. *Evaluation of the Wokabaut Somil Training Programme: Report for the United Kingdom Foundation for the Peoples of the South Pacific*. London: Forestry and Land Use Programme, International Institute for Environment and Development.

Barnett, T. 1992. Legal and administrative problems of forestry in Papua New Guinea. In *Resources, Development and Politics in the Pacific Islands*, ed. S. Henningham and R.J. May, 90–118. Bathurst: Crawford House Press.

Carson, G. 1974. *A Report on Forestry and Forest Policy in Papua New Guinea*. Port Moresby: Office of Forests.

Choi, N. 1999. Landowners to gain from World Bank funded forest project. *The Independent*, 11 November.

Downs, I. 1980. *The Australian Trusteeship in Papua New Guinea 1945–1975*. Canberra: Australian Government Publishing Service.

Duncan, R. 1994. Melanesian forest sector study. *International Development Issues* 36. Canberra: Australian International Development Assistance Bureau (AIDAB).

Filer, C. 1997a. Key events relating to World Bank involvement in PNG forest policy reform process, 1988–98. In *The Political Economy of Forest Management in Papua New Guinea*, ed. C. Filer, 249–268. NRI Monograph 32. Boroko: The National Research Institute and London: International Institute for Environment and Development.

Filer, C. 1997b. A statistical profile of Papua New Guinea's log export industry. In *The Political Economy of Forest Management in Papua New Guinea*, ed. C. Filer, 207–248. NRI Monograph 32. Boroko: The National Research Institute and London: International Institute for Environment and Development.

Filer, C. with N. Dubash and K. Kalit. 2000. *The Thin Green Line. World Bank Leverage and Forest Policy Reform in Papua New Guinea*. NRI Monograph 37. Boroko: The National Research Institute and Canberra: Resource Management in Asia-Pacific Project, Research School of Pacific and Asian Studies, Australian National University.

Holzknecht, H. 1997. Two sides of the coin: the case of forestry. In *Compensation for Resource Development in Papua New Guinea, Law Reform Commission of Papua New Guinea*, ed. S. Toft, 94–104, Monograph No. 6 and NCDS Pacific Policy Paper 24. Canberra: Resource Management in Asia-Pacific, and National Centre for Development Studies, Australian National University.

Holzknecht, H. 1999. Papua New Guinea's rainforests: policy, practice, stakeholders and resource management. In *Environment Papua New Guinea*, ed. J. Rivers, F. L. Bein and P. Siaguru, 107–120. Collected Papers Series, Volume 1. Lae: Environmental Research and Management Centre, Papua New Guinea University of Technology and New Delhi: UBS Publishers' Distributors.

Kwa, E. 2000. Freezing customary land rights for forestry resources development projects. In *Culture and Progress. The Melanesian Philosophy of Land and Development in Papua New Guinea*, ed. N. Sullivan, 101–123. (Papers from the Divine Word June 2001 PNG Land Symposium). Madang: Divine Word University Press.

Louman, B. and S. Nicholls. 1995. Forestry in Papua New Guinea. In *PNG Country Study on Biological Diversity*, ed. N. Sekhran and S. Miller. Waigani: Department of Environment and Conservation, and Nairobi: Africa Centre for Resources and Environment.

Papua New Guinea. 1991. *National Forest Policy*. Hohola: Papua New Guinea Ministry of Forests.

Papua New Guinea. 1999. *2000 Budget Papers — Volume 2, Part 3: 2000 Estimates of Development Expenditure for National Departments, Statutory Authorities and Provincial Governments*. Port Moresby: Ministry of Finance and Treasury.

Taylor, R. 1997. The state versus custom: regulating Papua New Guinea's timber industry. In *The Political Economy of Forest Management in Papua New Guinea*, ed. C. Filer, 249–268. NRI Monograph 32. Boroko: The National Research Institute and London: International Institute for Environment and Development.

Wood, M. 1997. The Makapa Timber Rights Purchase: a study in project failure in the post-Barnett era. In *The Political Economy of Forest Management in Papua New Guinea*, ed. C. Filer, 84–108. NRI Monograph 32. Boroko: The National Research Institute and London: International Institute for Environment and Development.

Endnotes

[1] This section draws on the work of Filer and others, especially Filer (1997b) and Filer, Dubash and Kalit 2000).

[2] The Ombudsman Commission subsequently investigated the board's decision to extend the Kamula-Dosa timber permit into the area already allocated to Wawoi-Guavi, against the recommendation of the Forest Service management.

Chapter 12

Policy Making on Decentralization[1]

R. J. May

The division of the powers and responsibilities of government between national, provincial and local levels is a critical element of Papua New Guinea's political and administrative structure, and one which has important implications for governance generally and for service delivery in all sectors of government, as other chapters in this volume demonstrate. It is also an area that has been subject to virtually continuous contestation, recurrent review, and one major restructuring. As such, a study of decentralization might be expected to highlight some of the major issues which arise in policy making and implementation in Papua New Guinea, and elsewhere.[2]

The origins of provincial government in Papua New Guinea

During the Australian colonial period, Papua New Guinea had been administered through a number of administrative districts, each headed by a district commissioner; there were eighteen districts at the end of the colonial period. In 1975 one district was divided in two, and these nineteen districts, renamed provinces, together with the National Capital District, became the basis on which a system of provincial government was established. Local government councils had also been established, commencing in 1949, and in 1970 area authorities, comprising mostly local government council nominees, were created at what was then district level, primarily to serve as advisory bodies to the district commissioner.

In the lead-up to independence in 1975 there were calls for the political decentralization of a system which many saw as highly centralized. In its *1st Interim Report* of September 1973, the pre-independence Constitutional Planning Committee (CPC) discerned the emergence of a 'clear majority view' that a system of district government should be introduced with greater powers for districts than those vested in area authorities (CPC 1973a, ll). Two months previously the CPC had been presented with a demand for immediate district government in Bougainville and a detailed draft (prepared by the Bougainville Special Political Committee (BSPC)) of the form which it should take. In its *2nd Interim Report* in November l973 the CPC noted that the Bougainville proposal had been accepted by cabinet 'subject only to the condition that any agreement which might be reached must be within a general legislative framework to be applied to the country as a whole' (CPC 1973b, 1/7).

Between November 1973 and its final *Report* of 1974, the CPC received a *Report on Central Provincial Government Relations* by consultants W. Tordoff and R. L. Watts, which outlined options and offered recommendations, 'bearing in mind the (CPC's) firm commitment to the development of a strong form of provincial government (which is a decentralized form of government within a unitary system, subject to political control at the (then) district level)' (Tordoff and Watts 1974, i). The final recommendations of the CPC on arrangements for provincial government were set out in chapter 10 of its 1974 Report, which also contained a schedule of proposed national, provincial and concurrent powers.

Following the tabling of the CPC Report, however, a government 'White Paper' (*Proposals on Constitutional Principles and Explanatory Notes* 1974), challenged the CPC recommendations on several points. Though it 'strongly supported' the principle of provincial government, the White Paper expressed four major reservations:

• 'that the C.P.C. proposals could result in an undue concentration of power at the provincial centre';
• 'that the law should also safeguard the interests of local government bodies';
• that 'The type of near-federal system proposed by the C.P.C. would create many legal and administrative problems if introduced suddenly'; and
• that 'the schedule...dealing with the functions and powers of provincial governments should be used only as a guide....The devolution of powers and the speed and methods of arranging this should be left to negotiations between the governments concerned' (the government also argued that it was not essential for all provinces to reach the same stage of decentralization) (Papua New Guinea 1974, 35–37).

Following conclusion of the House of Assembly debate on the provincial government proposals, an inter-party Follow-up Committee was created to draw up an organic law. A first draft was completed in July 1975, but the same month the House of Assembly, meeting as the Constituent Assembly, voted to exclude the provincial government provisions from the constitution.

Notwithstanding this reversal, preparations for the introduction of provincial government continued, including the establishment of the Bougainville Interim Provincial Government in July 1974 and the creation of constituent assemblies in several other provinces. Then, on the eve of independence in September 1975, frustration over unsatisfied demands in Bougainville resulted in a unilateral declaration of independence by Bougainvillean leaders. Negotiations between Bougainville and the national government culminated in the Bougainville Agreement of August 1976 and contributed to the decision to reinstate the provincial government provisions through amendment to the constitution and the passage of an organic law. *The Organic Law on Provincial Government* (OLPG) was enacted in March 1977.

The OLPG differed from the earlier Tordoff-Watts/CPC recommendations in several important respects but retained the broad features of the fully-decentralized-unitary-system model put forward in 1974. The subordinate status of the provincial governments was reflected in several provisions of the constitution and the OLPG, notably in the National Parliament's powers to disallow a provincial law 'if in its opinion the disallowance is in the public interest' (S.37 of OLPG) and to suspend provincial governments (S.187E of the Constitution and Ss.86–98 of the OLPG). On the other hand, the division of legislative powers set out in Part VI of the OLPG (plus the delegation to provincial governments of executive responsibility in areas in which they did not have legislative power) gave the provinces a potentially wide field of operation. This resulted in the development of an essentially *political* system of decentralized government. The virtues of such 'essentially flexible' arrangements were argued by Yash Ghai and Mani Isana (both lawyers who were involved in the implementation process):

> The Organic Law intended to lay down a broad framework for Provincial Government and the establishment and further evolution of the system was, in large measure, left for consultation between the Provincial and the National Governments (Ghai and Isana 1978b, 3–4).

Elsewhere, however, the same authors described the OLPG as 'complex, legalistic and difficult to operate' and argued that the various provisions of the constitution, the OLPG and the provincial constitutions 'do not add up to a very coherent picture of the status of provincial Governments and their place in the overall national system' (Ghai and Isana 1978a, 1, 4).

As late as January 1977, the assumption seemed to be, as described in an information paper from the Public Services Commission:

> At proclamation, each Provincial Government is to ... select the particular packages of functions, ministry by ministry, which it wishes to assume executive authority over....The packages can be expected to differ Province to Province. Phasing of their introduction can also be expected to vary. The pattern of Provincial legislative action is also likely to vary widely. So the situation, across all Provinces, is expected to be complex, and changing from time to time as devolution proceeds according to each Province's desires and capacity (PSC 1977, 1).

Faced with continuing uncertainty about how to implement provincial government, and resistance amongst some public servants, in April 1977 the government employed consultants McKinsey and Co. to draw up a plan for implementation. A program based on the recommendations of McKinsey was accepted by the NEC in September; it involved the transfer of functions, uniformly for all provinces, in three stages during 1978. As I have argued elsewhere (May 1981, 16–17, 25), one of the unfortunate effects of this strategy was to tie the implementation of decentralization in all provinces to what was being demanded in that province which was the strongest supporter of decentralization and had the greatest capacity for financial autonomy.

Decentralization, 1978–1995

The structure of provincial government

Although some non-elected interim provincial governments put off elections for as long as they could, by mid 1980 all nineteen provincial governments had elected assemblies. All broadly followed the essentially Westminster model of the national government, though in four provinces[3] the head of government (the premier) was directly elected by the people. Most provincial constitutions provided for up to three appointed members of the assembly and some used this provision to appoint women and church representatives. In 1981 the OLPG was amended to make members of the National Parliament non-voting *ex officio* members of their provincial assemblies (though in most cases MPs seldom took the opportunity to attend provincial assembly meetings). Following the Westminster model, provincial executive councils (PECs) were appointed by the premier from the floor of the assembly (Manus was the only province to take up a CPC suggestion that provincial assemblies might consider a parliamentary committee system), and in the general absence of political party systems, large PECs (in Eastern Highlands and East New Britain at times more than half the assembly) were used as a means of discouraging votes of no confidence in the government.

Having decided against separate national and provincial administrative services, arrangements were made in the OPLG to assign to provincial governments control and direction of public servants and teachers carrying out transferred functions. Recognizing that Bougainville and East New Britain had already appointed some provincial staff, however, allowance was made for a locally-appointed 'provincial secretariat' of up to six people, headed by a 'provincial secretary'. Initially, 'in part to shield public servants from political pressure' (May and Regan 1997, 35), personnel matters concerning assigned national public servants were delegated to an 'administrative secretary' appointed by joint approval of the provincial and national governments. Both secretaries were answerable to the PEC. Although provision was made in the OLPGF to deal with the apparent ambiguity of this administrative structure, it was a source of some confusion and potential tension, and in the early 1980s, in all but two provinces, the 'provincial secretaries' were absorbed into newly-created departments of the provinces and the 'administrative secretaries', confusingly renamed provincial secretaries, were placed at the top of a single line of authority.[4]

With the creation of departments of the provinces, a line of authority was established back to the national Public Services Commission. Confusion over the respective roles of the provincial and national governments with respect to personnel management continued, however, and in 1984 the Morobe provincial government challenged the arrangements (following dispute over an appointment by the national government) and the Supreme Court ruled that the departments of the provinces were contrary to the OLPG. Some provinces took the opportunity to establish new administrative structures, though most simply replicated the old departmental structures. By the early 1990s most provinces had also established provincial management teams (PMTs), chaired by the provincial administrator and comprising the heads of the major sectoral divisions, and in many cases district management teams (Peasah 1994, 275–278).

By the latter part of the 1980s there were increasing complaints of politicization of appointments by provincial governments — including appointments of some provincial secretaries. On the other hand, the performance of national public servants responsible for service delivery at provincial level frequently left a lot to be desired.

The arrangements of the OLPG for division of legislative powers between the provincial and national governments were complex. A few areas were preserved to the national government, and a few to provincial governments, but most areas of potential legislation were left open to both levels of government, in the belief that such 'flexibility' would allow the system to accommodate the evolution of decentralization. Within this shared field, some subjects were listed as 'primarily provincial', in which provincial laws would take precedent over national laws, and some were placed in an 'unoccupied field' (which included defence and national security), in which national laws took precedence, but most were listed as 'concurrent', though here also national laws prevailed in the case of inconsistent legislation. As noted above, however, the essentially unitary nature of the system was reflected in the National Parliament's ultimate power to disallow a provincial law if it considered this to be 'in the public interest'. The national government used this authority only once: to prevent the Enga provincial government from extending the term of its provincial assembly in 1990.

In fact, after an initial burst of activity to pass basic implementing legislation (mostly drafted by national government officers), most provincial governments were fairly inactive legislatively, several doing no more than pass their annual appropriation acts. One of the reasons for this was that most of the activities of provincial governments were transferred to them by the national government and exercised under national legislation — an arrangement which, as Regan observes, 'largely ignored the spirit — and arguably the letter — of the OLPG and tended to give the national government greater control over provincial governments than was intended by the OLPG' (May and Regan 1997, 33).

There were, however, a few notable instances of provincial legislative initiatives, including those of the East Sepik provincial government in relation to customary land registration, Manus in relation to marine and forest resources management, and New Ireland in relation to compensation payments.

Local-level government[5]

Consistent with the recommendations of the CPC, the OLPG gave responsibility for local government to the provincial governments — despite the reservations expressed in the 1974 White Paper (see above). In thirteen provinces, provincial governments simply passed new legislation to perpetuate the existing structure of local governments; in two provinces councils continued to operate under national legislation, while four replaced local government councils by community governments, following a model already introduced in Bougainville. During the 1980s several provinces moved to replace councils in urban centres by appointed statutory authorities.

Already by 1977 local government councils were in decline in many parts of the country, with most facing resistance to the payment of council head taxes and participation in council activities. Local-level government funding was said to be under review in 1981, but nothing seems to have come of this. By the early 1990s, deprived of funding and human resources, local governments in most provinces were barely functioning. Regan observed that 'in the...struggle for power, resources and prestige, local government has been perhaps the biggest loser under the provincial government system' (May and Regan 1997, 28). In 1991 a committee of the Premiers' Council (responding to the report of the Hesingut Committee — see below) recommended that local governments be represented in provincial assemblies (up to 25 per cent of elected members) and be guaranteed 10–20 per cent of national government transfers to provincial governments, but no action was taken at the time.

Intergovernmental financial relations

Intergovernmental financial relations pose problems for most federal-type systems, and Papua New Guinea has been no exception. The financial arrangements of the OLPG contained several elements.

A minimum unconditional grant (MUG) was intended to ensure that each province had the basic funding necessary to carry out the functions transferred to the provinces in 1977; it was based on the level of expenditure by the national government on the transferred functions in the year prior to the introduction of provincial government, adjusted annually for movements in the consumer price index or in government revenue, whichever was smaller, less the salary cost of public servants assigned to the province by the national government (which were paid directly by the national government). From the outset, there were problems with the MUG. For one, in 1978 it was decided that provinces which had not attained 'full financial responsibility' (FFR) would not receive the full MUG.[6] The eleven provinces which did not achieve FFR received most of their funding directly through the national budget. This arrangement probably contravened the provisions of the OLPG, but the provinces without FFR did not object because the funding they received was greater than they would have received under the MUG formula. Secondly, the formula took no account of population increase or rising costs of carrying out the transferred functions — particularly rising salary levels (which were determined by a national tribunal, and were therefore beyond provincial control); as a result, the salary deductions taken from the MUGs of the provinces with FFR took a progressively larger part of the MUG (rising, on average, from 47 per cent in 1978 to 72 per cent in 1988).

A second category of grant, *additional unconditional grants* (AUGs), was initially intended to be the principal vehicle for equalization amongst provinces. It was envisaged that the AUGs would be of a significant amount, allocated at the discretion of the national government on the advice of the National Fiscal Commission (see below). In fact, the amount paid in AUGs was small, and after 1984 none were paid, funds being diverted instead to the national government's five-year rolling plans for non-recurrent expenditure (the National Public Expenditure Plan (NPEP) to 1985 and the Public Investment Program (PIP) from 1987). The NPEP did include a Less Developed Areas Program, through which several provinces with integrated rural development programs (East Sepik, Southern Highlands, Enga and Milne Bay) received funding, but only limited amounts of NPEP/PIP funding were directed to the provinces — less than 20 per cent in most years — the rest being allocated to projects of national government agencies. Analysis of NPEP expenditure suggested no evidence of provincial equalization (see May 1999, 131); indeed the process of competitive bidding for funds was very likely to disadvantage the less developed provinces, in which administrative capacity was generally also less developed. The need for an equalization element in financial transfers was argued before the review committee in 1981 (May 1981, 26–29).

A third source of provincial funding was a *derivation grant*, calculated on the export value of production originating in the province, less any royalties payable to the provincial government. This was designed essentially to placate the wealthier, or resource-rich, provinces, notably Bougainville — though it was rationalized as also giving provinces an incentive to encourage economic development. In addition, from 1990, a special support grant was introduced for those provinces hosting a major mining or petroleum project, based on the export value of minerals and petroleum production in the province. A fourth category of grant, conditional grants, for purposes agreed between the national and provincial governments, was used only sparingly, to finance town sanitary services in rural centres.

The proceeds of certain national government taxes were also transferred to provinces, the most important initially being royalties, of which the main recipients were North Solomons and Western provinces, and to a lesser extent Milne Bay, Enga, Southern Highlands, and New Ireland. Subsequently, the national government took over responsibility for the collection of retail sales/value-added tax, returning proceeds to provinces on the basis of derivation. The OLPG reserved certain revenue sources for the exclusive use of provinces, but internal revenue was a relatively minor source of funding, ranging in 1988 from 23 per cent in Bougainville to 2 per cent in the Southern Highlands. From 1978 (when the national government provided a grant and a K100,000 interest-free loan for the establishment of provincial 'development corporations') all provinces had business arms, but with poor management and frequent political interference in their operations, by the early 1980s most were running at a loss and few survived.

As early as 1979 there were demands for a review of intergovernmental fiscal arrangements (prompted primarily by the problems associated with the MUG arrangements), and in 1980 the Department of Finance and the Premiers' Council separately initiated review processes. Consultants' reports were commissioned and submitted in 1981 to a Committee to Review the Financial Provisions of the Organic Law on Provincial government (Chelliah 1981; May 1981); a Premiers' Council report was submitted the following year. This led further to the establishment of a specialist committee which reported to the Premiers' Council conference in 1984,[7] but nothing was done to implement the recommendations of the committee until 1988. Amendments to the OLPG were drafted and introduced into parliament in 1990, but they lapsed when parliament rose in 1992 without having debated them.

Intergovernmental relations

Given the emphasis on the flexibility of the decentralization introduced in 1977, the OLPG sought to encourage intergovernmental consultation, and several issues were made non-justiciable. Reporting in 1980, however, the General Constitutional Commission (GCC) expressed the view that, 'Although there has been some consultation between National Government and Provincial Governments the extent to which this has been carried out has been extremely poor' (GCC 1980, 31).

The main institutional elements to achieve this were a Premiers' Council and a National Fiscal Commission. The Premiers' Council, comprising provincial premiers and the prime minister and national ministers for Finance and Provincial Affairs, was required to meet at least once per year, and seldom met more often. It provided a useful forum for discussion of provincial concerns and occasionally played a role in helping resolve issues of contention between the two levels of government, but there was little follow-through on Premiers' Council resolutions[8] and it scarcely succeeded in achieving its stated objective of avoiding legal proceedings between governments (OPG S.84), which occurred with increasing frequency from the mid 1980s. By the early 1980s informal meetings of regional premiers (Islands, Highlands, Momase or North Coast and Papua or South Coast) were also taking place.[9]

The National Fiscal Commission (NFC) was intended to be an independent expert commission, along the lines of fiscal commissions in several federations, with the principal tasks of advising the national government on the distribution of additional unconditional grants (see above), and helping to resolve disputes over provincial taxes and other fiscal matters. In fact, however, the NFC as constituted was more eminent than expert, and it was generally perceived by provinces as being 'in the pocket' of the Finance Department (May 1981, 41–43). After 1985 it effectively lapsed.

Suspensions

The constitution and the OLPG of 1977 included complex provisions to safeguard the autonomy of the provincial governments. Already in 1979, however, the then minister for Decentralisation, John Momis, was pressing for amendments to make it easier to suspend provincial governments. This was eventually done in 1983 and the first suspension took place the following year. By 1995 all but five provinces had been suspended at least once, mostly on the ground of financial mismanagement[10] — though in several instances political animosities between provincial politicians and national MPs also seem to have come into play (May and Regan 1997; Barter 2004), and apart from a few prosecutions little attempt was ever made to address the problems that led to suspension.

The politics of provincial government and the call for change

The decentralization of 1977 had a difficult birth, and the provincial government system continued to generate controversy. Some of the early critics of provincial government remained convinced that the transfer of functions to the provinces was a mistake; local government councillors, who became increasingly marginalized in most provinces, often supported calls for change in the system; and, in particular, backbenchers in the National Parliament, who frequently saw provincial politicians as a threat to their political support bases, began looking at ways of reasserting their authority (the 1981 amendment to the OLPG which made national MPs ex officio members of provincial assemblies, was in large part a reflection of this,[11] as was the 1983 amendment which made it easier to suspend provincial governments). In addition, Regan argues, 'there was not (in the early period of provincial government) the mass mobilization around the new provincial governments that had been anticipated by the CPC', except perhaps in Bougainville and East New Britain (May and Regan 1997, 61). Unfulfilled expectations at provincial and local level, complaints about the high cost of the provincial government system,[12] evidence of mismanagement and corruption, and the general excesses of some provincial politicians, all combined to generate demands for change.

Administratively, the creation of departments of the provinces, which brought personnel assigned to provinces back under the control of the national Public Services Commission, the 'full financial responsibility' arrangements which saw the national Department of Finance retain control of funds intended to go to provinces, and the introduction of the NPEP/PIP for the allocation of non-recurrent spending, combined with the demise of the 'additional unconditional grants' (see above), were all designed to limit, if not to actually reverse, the process of decentralization. Elsewhere, in the departments of Health, Education, Primary Industry, and Forests, national agencies continued to exercise control over provincial activities through a variety of administrative procedures (see, for example, May and Regan 1997, 63–64 *et passim*), often with the passive acceptance of provincial governments.

In the early 1980s, opposition to provincial government became more overt. After being returned as prime minister in 1982, Somare initiated a move to replace the OLPG by an ordinary act of parliament, telling a Premiers' Council conference the following year that if there were a parliamentary vote on the abolition of provincial government, the vast majority of MPs would support it. The proposed legislative change was strongly opposed by the premiers of the Islands Region and some other prominent political leaders, and was not pursued. However, in 1984 Somare raised the issue again, this time proposing a referendum on the future of provincial government. Again, he was opposed by leaders in the Islands Region, who this time threatened to secede, and the proposal was dropped (see May 1999). However a parliamentary select committee, chaired by Anthony Siaguru, was set up to look at the working of the provincial government system. In 1985 Somare lost a parliamentary vote of no confidence and was succeeded by Paias Wingti, who — though himself no supporter of provincial government — terminated the work of the Siaguru committee. Wingti himself lost office in 1987, but told the press that if returned he would move to abolish the provincial government system (*Papua New Guinea Post-Courier* 4 November 1988).

The following year, 1988, saw the beginnings of the conflict on Bougainville, and in 1990 its declaration of independence. Regan has argued that the demise of the Bougainville provincial government — 'long held out as the model of what was possible under the system' and a potent force opposing the critics of provincial government — encouraged moves to abolish the system (May and Regan 1997, 70). Following a further change of government in 1988, in 1990 another parliamentary select committee on provincial government was set up under the chairmanship of Morobe MP Henu Hesingut. The Hesingut Committee left no doubt about its antipathy to provincial governments: its final recommendation was for the abolition of elected provincial governments and their replacement by provincial bodies composed of heads of local-level governments, which were to be brought under national government control (National Parliament 1990).

In reaction to this, the Premiers' Council established a Premiers Sub-committee on Provincial Government Review, essentially to counter what the premiers saw as the Hesingut Committee's 'consistently expressed...negative view of the provincial government system' (National Premiers Council 1990, 2). The sub-committee complained of the lack of response to resolutions of the Premiers' Council (see above), and argued that increased national control of public servants in the provinces had left them unable to efficiently manage staffing matters and had restricted their ability to take quick and decisive disciplinary action. It accused the Hesingut Committee of unwillingness to hear views in support of provincial government, and failure to consider previous reports on the system, concluding, 'It is the belief of the Premiers' Council that the real mission of the Select Committee is to lay foundations for the abolition of the provincial government system rather than conduct a constructive review' (*ibid*. 15).

Also between the preliminary and final reports of the Hesingut Committee, a private member's bill was introduced into parliament seeking the creation of district development authorities to take over most of the functions of provincial governments. The bill proposed district coordinating committees, chaired by the open MP (districts being the administrative level below provinces, and broadly corresponding with open national electorates) to oversee development projects at district level. Although the bill lapsed, an outcome of the parliamentary debate was the passage of the *Electoral Development Authorities Act*, 1992 which gave MPs a role in the distribution of funds in their electorates — what became known as 'slush funds' (see below).

In 1992 Paias Wingti again became prime minister, and announced his intention of overhauling the provincial government system. Within weeks of taking office, his government introduced a Village Services Programme, which Village Services and Provincial Affairs Minister John Nilkare described as 'the most fundamental policy shift in our national history' (*Papua New Guinea Post-Courier* 14 August 1992, 24–25. Also see *The Times of Papua New Guinea* 12 November 1992, 32–33 and Department of Information and Communication 1993, 41–42). It was designed to empower some 240 community governments through a structure of district centres and community councils linking the national government with village groups, largely bypassing provincial governments.

In a subsequent statement, Prime Minister Wingti said he would reduce the number of provincial politicians and give greater power to national MPs; he described the provincial government system as costly and divisive, and marred by gross mismanagement and corruption. In October 1992, the National Executive Council agreed to the abolition of the system of elected provincial governments established in 1977, and legislation was drafted for amendment of the constitution to enable the repeal of the OLPG. The then opposition leader, Sir Michael Somare, endorsed the decision.

Many welcomed the Wingti government's initiatives, but there was strong opposition from within provincial governments, and in the New Guinea Islands region there were renewed threats of secession and talk of creating a Federated Melanesian Republic if demands for greater autonomy were not forthcoming. In the face of this opposition, (as well as threatening to suspend the Islands provinces and prosecute their leaders) Wingti set up a Bi-partisan Parliamentary Select Committee on Provincial Government, chaired by New Ireland MP Ben Micah. After public consultations, the Bi-partisan Committee presented a final report in August 1993 which recommended a comprehensive restructuring of the provincial government system. The NEC endorsed the committee's report and created a Constitutional Review Commission (CRC) to implement its recommendations.

Draft legislation was tabled in the National Parliament early in 1994. The legislation proposed to do away with the elected provincial assemblies, replacing them with provincial governments comprising the national MPs from the province and heads of local-level governments, with provision also for a small number of traditional chiefs and appointed members (including a woman representative). It sought to incorporate districts in the new structure and to empower local-level governments. In explaining the general thrust of the proposed new organic law, the CRC described it as one 'of greater decentralisation...in that more powers are decentralised further to local level governments' (quoted from a CRC brief published in *The Times of Papua New Guinea* 7 April 1994, 31–42). Others, however, saw it as a re-centralization, in that it did away with elected provincial members and enhanced the role of national MPs. Continuing opposition from the provinces and some national MPs resulted in amendments to the draft legislation, including its financial provisions, in favour of the provincial governments.

The amended legislation still did not have an easy passage, with continuing threats of secession by the Island premiers, and the acknowledged father of provincial government in Papua New Guinea, John Momis, predicting that the new legislation would create 'an administrative nightmare'; not only was the local government system 'almost dead in most provinces', he said, but the new arrangements would 'make many provincial governments tools in national level conflict on a level and to a degree of intensity never before imagined' (*Papua New Guinea Post-Courier* 4 April 1995). Nevertheless, in June 1995 the new *Organic Law on Provincial Governments and Local-Level Governments* (OLPGLLG) was finally passed. In recognition of the special circumstances on Bougainville, the recently established Bougainville Transitional Government was initially exempted from the provisions of the OLPGLLG. Special arrangements were also made for the National Capital District. Sir Julius Chan, who had replaced Wingti as prime minister in 1994, welcomed the new arrangements, claiming that Papua New Guinea had been freed from the burden of a provincial government system that had handicapped the country for the best part of twenty years.

Several cabinet members, including Sir Michael Somare, opposed the passage of the OLPGLLG and as a result were dropped from the cabinet; a by-product of this was a split in the Pangu Pati which led to the emergence, under Somare's leadership, of the National Alliance.

Decentralization since 1995

The new structure of decentralization

Under the arrangements introduced in 1995, the governor, who is head of the provincial government and chairs the provincial assembly, is normally the member of the national parliament representing the provincial electorate. If the provincial member accepts an executive position in government, or becomes leader or deputy leader of the opposition or speaker or deputy speaker of the National Parliament he/she must be replaced by another MP.[13] The deputy governor is elected from among the representatives of the local-level governments. The governor is constitutionally responsible to the minister for provincial and local-level governments.

The former ministerial system at provincial level was replaced by a committee system. The provincial executive council comprises the governor and deputy governor and the chairpersons of the committees, not exceeding a third of the membership of the assembly. Since the governor appoints the committee chairs, this provision gives the governor considerable authority.

Administratively, provincial departments were abolished under the OLPGLLG, their operations coming under the relevant national departments through a provincial administrator, who is the chief executive officer of the provincial government and 'the administrative head of the staff in the province' (Ss.73–74). In fact, however, the shift from provincial departments to provincial administrations made little difference to the way things were done at the provincial level (except there was no longer an allocation to provincial departments in the national budget) and the role of the provincial administrator *vis-à-vis* the heads of national departments in Port Moresby has been ambiguous. The OLPGLLG provides that the provincial administrator be chosen by the National Executive Council from a list of persons nominated by the provincial executive council. In practice, however, the appointment of provincial administrator has been a subject of controversy in several provinces since 1995. In Southern Highlands Province at one stage there were three provincial administrators, appointed under different governors, contesting the position (and all drawing salaries), and this situation was more or less replicated at district level. At least one other province, Enga, has also for a time had more than one provincial administrator.

The framers of the OLPGLLG foresaw a decentralization of administration from Waigani to the provinces and from provincial capitals to the districts. In fact, however, the provisions of the OLPGLLG have been a source of some confusion: although the provincial administrator 'shall maintain overall supervision and direction' over all public servants in the province (excluding law enforcement agencies), and 'shall co-ordinate and monitor the roles and functions' of the national departments and agencies (S.74[1][d],[e]), it was not initially clear how this authority related to the chain of command within national departments and agencies, nor what control the provincial administrator exercised over district administrators. For example, under the *Public Finance (Management) Act* the provincial administrator is responsible for the accountability of the provincial administration, but has no formal power to direct staff responsible for keeping accounts. This has been a particular source of contention in the Health sector. Responsibility for rural health services (a sub-national function) rests with the provincial administrator, who is advised by a provincial health board (of which he is the chair); a provincial health adviser, appointed by a panel chaired by the provincial administrator and sometimes including a representative of the national Department of Health, sits on the board. The provincial health adviser has local responsibility for hospitals (a national function) but ultimate responsibility rests with the Department of Health. He/she reports to the provincial administrator; attempts by the national Department of Health to institute a system of dual reporting have not succeeded. At the local level, community health workers report to the district administrator, rather than the provincial health adviser. It has been argued that these structural arrangements do not make for effective delivery of Health services (see Thomason and Kase in this volume).

Under the OLPGLLG provinces retained their primary powers, including financial powers, but concurrent powers reverted to the national government. Local-level governments were also given significant law-making powers, covering such subjects as labour and employment, self-help schools (excluding curriculum), dispute settlement, local environment, and local aidposts (see

Ss.42–45). However, the OLPGLLG also provided that in the event of any inconsistency between provincial and local-level laws and national laws, the latter will prevail. There has, however, been confusion about which level of government is responsible for what (see below).

A significant amendment to the OLPGLLG (S.33A) in 1996 provided for the establishment of a joint provincial planning and budget priorities committee (JPPBPC) and joint district planning and budget priorities committees (JDPBPCs) in each province. Each JDPBPC consists of the MP representing the open electorate (as chair), the provincial MP, the heads of the local-level governments in the district, and up to three other members appointed by the open MP in consultation with heads of the district's local-level governments. The role of the JDPBPCs is to oversee and coordinate district planning (including a rolling five-year development plan) and budget priorities 'for consideration by' the provincial and national governments; to determine and control budget priorities for local-level governments, and to approve local-level government budgets. The JPPBPC has similar functions at the provincial level. In some districts (especially those around the provincial capital) the JDPBPCs have played an effective role; in others they have met infrequently, and often outside the district (in several cases in Port Moresby). A critical factor in this is the role played by the open MP (see below). Apart from the question of whether the JPPBPC/JDPBPCs work effectively, there is an inherent problem in these arrangements in that such 'bottom-up' planning means that provincial priorities are not necessarily consistent with national priorities laid down in the MTDS and embodied in the policies of national departments.

Local-level government

In presenting the new legislation in 1995, the CRC claimed that 'the reform is not "centralizing" powers as claimed by critics. This reform is in fact decentralizing powers further to the Local Level Governments'. As noted above, however, some commentators were more sceptical. As one assessment in 1997 suggested:

> It must be seriously questioned whether local-level government will have the capacity to carry this load....In the absence of a strong local-level government structure, the new system is likely to increase substantially the political role of national MPs. Arguably, this was the real objective of the reforms (May 1999, 144–145).

Local-level governments (LLGs) are defined as urban authorities or councils, community governments, local government councils, 'traditional form(s) of governmental structure', or some combination of these (S.26), though outside of the provincial capital most provinces have retained the long-established local government council structure. The OLPGLLG removed from provincial governments the power to make laws about local-level government. A 'normal maximum' of three rural local-level governments was set for each district.[14] Within each LLG is a structure of wards, around which have developed ward committees (not provided for in the OLPGLLG).

The administrative functions allocated to local-level governments are spelled out in the *Local-level Governments Administration Act* of 1997. They include the preparation of a rolling five-year development plan and an annual plan and budget, construction and maintenance of infrastructure for which LLGs are responsible, initiating and implementing programs for youth and women, and organizing forums to discuss renewable natural resources.

Until 2007, in most districts, little has been left of the small amount of revenue received by LLGs after allowances (fixed by the national Salaries and Remuneration Commission) have been paid to councillors. In 2007 this was addressed by replacing staffing grants with goods and services grants. In an attempt to re-mobilize local-level governments and give them a source of locally-generated revenue there has been a move to reintroduce head taxes. [15] The national government passed enabling legislation in 2004 and several local-level governments have passed the necessary legislation, but only a few have actually begun revenue collection and it is likely that many will never do so.

Special Purpose Authorities

The OLPG of 1977 contained provision for the establishment of special purpose authorities at local level. Four such authorities were then already in existence.[16] In 1989 the Porgera Development Authority was created, as part of the arrangements negotiated for the Porgera gold mine in Enga Province, and five years later the Nimamar Community Government was transformed into the Nimamar Development Authority during negotiations over the gold mine on Lihir, New Ireland.

The Local-level Governments Administration Act of 1997 provides for the creation, on a recommendation of the minister for Inter-Governmental Affairs and advice of the NEC, of special purpose authorities to assist in the implementation of functions of one or more local-level governments. Special purpose authorities have been seen as a means of devolving powers to locally-based corporate bodies whose operations are 'at arms length' from local-level governments (Filer 2004, 3). Their functions may vary; those of the Porgera Development Authority, for example, include the control, management and administration of the Porgera District, assistance to local government councils in carrying out their functions in the district, receiving and distributing royalties from the provincial government, maintaining the local airstrip, advising on liquor licensing, and assisting the provincial town planning board. Since 1995 several new authorities have been created or proposed, notably for Koiari (which covers the source of Port Moresby's water and hydro-electricity supply), Kikori, Kutubu and Hides (the last three associated with gas and petroleum resource projects). In addition an Ok Tedi Development Foundation was established in 2001 by Ok Tedi Mining Ltd (OTML) to deliver a range of services around the Ok Tedi mine in Western (Fly River) Province and PNG Sustainable Development Ltd was set up to receive income from the Ok Tedi mining operation and channel the funds to sustainable development projects in and beyond the province. While there have been attempts to use special authorities 'as "fronts" for the misappropriation of government funds' (*ibid*. 5), there has been some support for the special purpose authority model, specifically in areas where major resource projects generate substantial revenue, and create special problems of governance. (For a more detailed discussion of this topic see Filer 2004.)

Financial arrangements

To supplement their internal revenue sources, and the payment of proceeds from specific tax revenues collected by the national government (principally now the GST), provision was made for the provinces to receive six forms of grant from the national government: a provincial and local-level administration grant, a provincial infrastructure development grant, and a local-level government and village services grant (all based variously on population and land and sea area); a town and urban services grant (based on urban population); a provincial and local-level staffing grant (related to provincial administration and teaching service salaries, but administered through the national payroll system in Port Moresby), and a derivation grant (based on the export value of commodities produced in the province) and special support grants provided for in natural resource agreements. There was also provision for conditional complementary support grants to provincial and local-level governments 'to support any specific or contingency need', but this provision has not been used. In 1996, associated with the creation of Joint Provincial and District Planning and Budgetary Priorities Committees, a provincial and district support grant was added to the funding package. In 1998 the OLPGLLG was again amended; the minimum level of the provincial/district support grant was set at K0.5 million per electorate, half of which was to be paid to the JP/DPBPC to fund rural action and urban rehabilitation programs,[17] and half to the MP in the electorate, to be allocated at his/her discretion within district support grant guidelines (in some cases, MPs leave the allocation of the entire district support grant to the JDPBPC but in most cases MPs have retained control over the discretionary element, and this has been a continuing source of controversy).[18] (For an assessment of the electoral development / district support grant system see Ketan 2007).

The OLPGLLG also provided for the creation of an independent National Economic and Fiscal Commission (NEFC) with broad fiscal and economic functions, including oversight of provincial finances — a successor to the long moribund National Fiscal Commission established under the OLPG of 1977. In fact, it was not until 1998 that the NEFC was established, and then to ratify the Skate government's decision to pay the provincial and local-level governments amounts less than were prescribed under the grant formulae. Subsequently, the NEFC became the leading force in pushing for a review of the intergovernmental financial arrangements. The NEFC identified a number of problems. These include: the inability of the national government, in its present fiscal circumstances, to meet the requirements of the OLPGLLG; some uncertainties about fiscal responsibilities ('We do not even know clearly exactly what each level of government is responsible for')[19] ; wide disparities between provinces and districts in the costs of providing services; the fact that national priorities are not always given priority in provincial budget allocations; and the fact that 'only a small proportion of provincial funding is going into goods and services'. [20]

Intergovernmental relations

Under the new decentralization arrangements the Premiers' Council lapsed, though a provincial governors conference has met annually (without a statutory mandate) and there is an annual meeting of provincial administrators. As noted, the moribund NFC was replaced by the NEFC. However, a new institution, the National Monitoring Authority (NMA), formally titled the Provincial and Local-level Service Monitoring Authority (PLLSMA),[21] was established under the OLPGLLG with a range of functions, including:

a. coordination and monitoring of the implementation of national policies at the provincial and local level;
b. establishment and monitoring of minimum development standards for rural and urban communities;
c. assessment of the effectiveness and efficiency of sub-national governments, and
d. ensuring that all appointments to offices at sub-national level are based on merit.

The NMA/PLLSMA comprises heads of the major sectoral departments and the NEFC, and is chaired by the secretary, Department of Provincial Government and Local-level Government Affairs (DPLGA). Several meetings of the NMA were held in the latter part of the 1990s, with little concrete output; thereafter it lapsed until it was re-activated in 2004 (see Barter 2004, 134–135).

Suspension

The OLPGLLG effectively removed the national government's authority to suspend provincial and local-level governments, 'except where there is a war or national emergency or where a Provincial or Local-level Government undermines or tries to undermine the authority of the National Government'. However, the national government's powers to withdraw functions and finances from provincial and local-level governments (Ss.51–57), though subject to referral to an independent national investigation committee set up under the OLPGLLG, appeared to remain substantial. During the latter part of the 1990s four highlands provinces had powers withdrawn. In 2000 the governor of the Southern Highlands Province appealed against the withdrawal of his government's powers by the national government, on constitutional grounds, and his appeal was upheld. Commenting on this in 2004, Barter said:

> As a result, even where flagrant abuses have been demonstrated — such as stacking of a Provincial Assembly by nominees of the Governor rather than by representative Heads of LLGs — the national government has been unable to act (Barter 2004, 137).

The constitution has since been amended (as part of a package to retrospectively authorize the collection of GST by the national government) to broaden the national government's powers, but the new provisions have not been tested, and further draft legislative amendments submitted to a parliamentary committee had not been taken up at the end of 2006. Meanwhile, the national government appears to be powerless to remove a provincial governor.

The 1995 reforms in practice.

In early 1997 then Provincial and Local Government Affairs Minister Peter Barter told the National Parliament that 'it will definitely take time, maybe five years or more before the results of the system are realised' (Draft Hansard 11 February 1997). Three months later he told a seminar in Port Moresby that 'in the 22 months since the reforms commenced, little improvement has been achieved in the operations of provincial administrations and almost nothing in most of their sub-units, the districts' (quoted in *The Independent* 30 May 1997).

Since 1995 there has been growing criticism of the new decentralization, and renewed calls for reforms — ranging from the revival of elected provincial governments, on the one hand, to a more comprehensive decentralization to local-level governments on the other (see below). There has been no systematic study of provincial and local level government performance under the 1995 arrangements, however a number of problems have been identified:[22]

• To give effect to the new decentralization arrangements, a range of new legislation and amendments to existing legislation was required; much of this has not been done.
• The division of government responsibilities between three levels of government has made for a very complex form of decentralization, in which

functional responsibilities are not always clearly understood, contributing to poor service delivery.

• In the context of deteriorating economic and fiscal circumstances, the financial provisions of the 1995 Organic Law have proved unworkable, resulting in the underfunding of provincial governments (that is, provincial governments have received less — by the early 2000s about 60 per cent less — than mandated by the funding formulae of the OLPGLLG), and consequent legal challenges. An additional problem is that provisions for some 'equalization', or redistribution of funds from the richer provinces to the poorer, provided for in both the 1977 and the 1995 arrangements, have never been put into effect.

• Financial accountability is weak, with little scrutiny of provincial budgets by the national Treasury and weak oversight by DPLGA. As Barter (2004, 141) said, with specific reference to finance and audit of lower-level governments: 'There are widespread double payments, misappropriation, unauthorized advance payments of salaries, illegal borrowing, and payment of sitting allowances when there are no meetings' (Barter 2004, 141).

• Underfunding, poor capacity and deteriorating infrastructure, mismanagement and corruption, lawlessness, and the politicization of provincial, district and local-level administration, have contributed to poor service delivery in many parts of the country, especially the more remote areas. At the district level, cash offices and post office and banking facilities had been withdrawn in most district headquarters by the 1990s, most were without power as generators became unserviceable or lacked fuel, and government housing was sold off or vandalized.

• During the 1990s and early 2000s there also appears to have been a decline in the capacity of the DPLGA to support provincial and local-level governments and carry forward the changes introduced by the OLPGLLG. For example: in 2005 the DPLGA's Local-level Government branch had a staff of only ten to oversee some 300 local-level governments, most of which were struggling to deliver services, and the funds available for travel to provinces to enforce proper oversight of spending was totally inadequate.

In 2004–5 a group from the Australian National University, the National Research Institute and the Divine Word University undertook a pilot study in five provinces[23] to gather information about district and local-level governance. Some of the findings of the study are summarized below.[24]

District management

In some parts of the country there have been complaints that district administrators (DA) are frequently absent from their posts, that JDPBPCs (which are legally required to meet at least four times per year) seldom meet, and often meet outside the district, and that MPs dominate the JDPBPC process. Predictably, responses to the survey suggest that situations vary widely between provinces, and within the one province between different districts and local-level governments. In East New Britain, for example, in the two districts surveyed there was a high level of collaboration between the open member, the JDPBPC and the district administration; both open members were said to make regular electoral visits, to be on good terms with all local-level governments, and to meet regularly with the district administrator. The DAs also visited local-level governments and projects funded by the JDPBPCs on a regular basis. Civil society (churches, private businesses, NGOs and village communities) were said to play an instrumental role in the development of the district and the province. Relations between the district administrations and the provincial administration were generally good. In contrast, in Madang Province (where there was an ongoing dispute over the governorship) the Madang District JDPBPC had met only once in 2004 — in Port Moresby — and the DA was in Manus at the time. The open member was accused of 'stacking' the JDPBPC. In the conflict-ridden Southern Highlands, there were at one stage three provincial administrators, appointed by successive governors and all drawing salaries, and in most districts more than one DA. Not only public servants in the province, but also LLG presidents and councilors had been politically appointed. Mendi District was without an open MP (the local member having been removed from office after being found guilty of misappropriating funds); the DA was said to be often absent from the district, and the JDPBPC had seldom met, and then in Port Moresby or Goroka. In the absence of an open MP, the JDPBPC was said to be controlled by associates of the provincial governor. Many public servants had fled to escape the ongoing conflict and had not returned; those who remained were generally reluctant to travel around the district.

District planning

All districts are required to have rolling five-year plans as a basis for defining needs and setting priorities. Most do, though frequently, it seems, there is no clear matching of plans and budgetary resources. The Minister for Inter-government Relations has remarked that 'Until recently, approval for provincial and local-level budgets was without consideration of the planning dimension....Overall inadequacy of funding has meant that district Development Plans remain a dream, with little relation to budgets or implementation....The history of District 5-year and 10-year strategic development plans — where they exist — is miserable' (Barter 2004, 135, 142, 147). Until 2004 district plans were lodged with the Department of National Planning and Rural Development (DNPRD) without a copy going to DPLGA.

Service delivery

There are complaints about poor service delivery across the country, but this is particularly a problem in remote areas with poor transport networks and other infrastructure, and areas plagued by security problems. Confusion about the distribution of functions between levels of government, and politicization of service delivery were also identified as problems.

In the Southern Highlands Province, where most of the country's petroleum resources are concentrated and some landowning groups have benefited from the Porgera mine in the adjoining Enga Province, there has been an almost complete breakdown of provincial government, district administration and local-level government, and demands for a new Hela Province in the west. Inter-group fighting, utilizing high-powered weapons, has not only resulted in the loss of many lives, it has destroyed infrastructure, impeded the movement of people and goods and services, and caused a number of businesses to withdraw from the province. Many teachers and public servants have also left their posts in the province, while leaders of landowner groups and politicians from the Southern Highlands spend much of their time in Port Moresby (see Haley and May 2007). An audit of the provincial government by private auditors contracted by the national government in 2003 recorded comprehensive fraud and financial mismanagement, but at the end of 2005 no prosecutions had resulted. In the 2002 national elections, polling in six of the province's nine electorates was declared void and elections had to be conducted again. Attempts to address the problems of the Southern Highlands through the withdrawal of functions were frustrated by Governor Agiru's successful challenge to the national government's powers (see above). In 2006 a state of emergency was declared in the Southern Highlands (which was challenged by Governor Hami Yawari) and PNGDF troops deployed to assist police and help enforce a surrender of weapons. Under the state of emergency, some order was restored in the province and at the end of January 2007 twenty-four people had been charged with fraud (*The National* 31 January 2007).

The Southern Highlands is an extreme case, but nonetheless reflects some of the problems of governance in the provincial and local-level government system.

The shifting of provincial and local-level audit functions from DPLGA to Finance had done little to change what seemed to have become an entrenched culture in many provinces.

Reforms since 1999

In the context of the public sector reform program initiated by the Morauta government in 1999 and continued under the Somare government of 2002–2007 (see chapter 3 above), [25] there has been an explicit recognition that governance and service delivery cannot be improved without a concerted effort to improve performance at the sub-national level. Indeed, the government's Medium Term Development Strategy 2005–10 stated:

> ...in the years since the passage of the Organic Law (the OLPGLLG), service delivery has deteriorated. On the whole service delivery systems

are dysfunctional and there remains widespread confusion over functional (who does what) and financial (who pays for what) responsibilities across the three levels of government (MTDS, 9–10).

In 2000–2001 the Morauta government negotiated a National Development Charter as a mechanism for delivering priority services at subnational level, primarily through matched national and donor funding and district funds allocated through the Rural Action Program/district support grants. The National Development Charter appears to have lapsed around 2002 (Barter says that in 2004 DPLGA could not find a copy of it), but was restored in 2004, with proposals for a Planning Systems Support Program (to support the implementation of a uniform planning system across all levels of government), a Provincial Services Cadetship program (to support tertiary students interested in a career in provincial and district administration), and provincial medium term development strategies. In 2005 a District Roads Improvement Program (DRIP) was added, under which provincial governments and JDPBPCs are to receive matching national government and donor funding for specified road projects, and it was planned to introduce similar programs in health and education.

The MTDS 2005–2010 included a number of activities 'designed to identify practical solutions to the functioning of the decentralized system of government' (MTDS, IV, chapter 4). Among a number of initiatives introduced since 2002 in the area of decentralization have been: a program to strengthen the Department of Provincial and Local Government Affairs (DPLGA); the revival of the NMA/PLLSMA and the development of systems to monitor provincial government performance in relation to minimum service delivery standards; the launching of a Provincial Performance Improvement Initiative (PPII), initially in three provinces (East New Britain, Eastern Highlands and Central)[26], intended to improve provincial accountability and the integrity of budget systems; a District Services Improvement Program (DSIP) to support local-level governments; a District Treasury Roll-out program which aims to bring not only Treasury facilities but also banking and postal services to all district headquarters;[27] and encouragement for the (re)establishment of provincial and district management teams (PMT/DMT) designed to achieve improved coordination of provincial and local-level government activities (though the relationship between PMTs and JPPBPCs remains unclear, and some provincial administrators have complained that the PMTs usurp the position of the provincial administrators). Also, between 2002 and 2006 the NEFC undertook detailed studies, first, to specify functional responsibilities for the three levels of government — 'who decides, who actions and who pays' (see Simonelli 2003); secondly, to measure the relative costs of providing services at district level; and, thirdly, to assess the relative revenue-raising capacities of the provinces (see NEFC 2005). On the basis of these studies it recommended new intergovernmental financial arrangements designed to achieve some degree of fiscal equalization amongst the provinces; draft legislation to this effect had passed the first reading stage in the National Parliament in late 2006. A less developed districts grant program (for districts identified by the NEFC and DNPRD) was introduced as part of a package of interim proposals for new intergovernmental financial arrangements in 2003.[28] AusAID has strongly supported (if it has not in fact initiated) these initiatives, in part through its Sub-national Initiative (which in 2006 was upgraded to a Sub-national Strategy).

All these initiatives presume the continuation of the broad arrangements established by the 1995 OLPGLLG. However there have been continuing demands for fundamental structural change to the provincial government system, notably from opposition leader Peter O'Neill, who in 2006 succeeded in having the National Parliament amend the OLPGLLG and pass a *District Authorities Act* intended to do away with provincial governments and shift responsibilities to district authorities (composed of the open MP, LLG presidents and some appointed members) and local-level governments.[29] Former Inter-Government Relations minister, Sir Peter Barter, has given (qualified) support for O'Neill's proposals (Barter 2004 fn.10), and reports of the Public Sector Reform Advisory Group (PSRAG 2002, 2005)) have argued similarly for a further decentralization to district and local level. In fact, this has been a recurring theme of decentralization reform proposals since the early 1990s, starting with the *Electoral Development Authorities Act* and the Village Services Program, following on through the recommendations of the Bi-partisan Parliamentary Committee on Provincial Government and the Constitutional Review Committee, to the 1996 amendments to the OLPGLLG which created the JPPBPCs/JDPBPCs. There is, therefore, no guarantee that a new government will not review the system yet again. [30]

Meanwhile, following the conclusion of the Bougainville Peace Agreement in 2001, the Autonomous Bougainville Government has been set up, with elections in May 2005, and the newly elected government is addressing the challenges of autonomy. [31] Encouraged by the Bougainville example, East New Britain is now pressing for an autonomous government and there have been tentative moves in at least one other province (Morobe).

Conclusion

From its very beginnings, decentralization in Papua New Guinea has had a chequered history. There is little doubt that for the period between 1978 and 1995 one cause of problems was the initial decision to institute a uniform decentralization across all provinces, irrespective of capacity. But it is also clear from the record that successive national governments made little attempt to address emerging problems, even when (as, notably, in the case of financial arrangements) they had clear and sensible recommendations before them.

A major reason for this was that the interests of national politicians and public servants at the national level do not necessarily coincide with those of political actors and public servants at the provincial, district and local levels. The 'reforms' of 1995, which abolished elected provincial assemblies nominally in the interests of greater decentralization but in reality with the effect of placing greater power in the hands of national politicians, owed much to a growing antipathy between national MPs and provincial MPs from the same province, the latter being frequently seen as undermining the power bases of the former. As predicted by some commentators in 1994–1995, one effect of the arrangements introduced under the new organic law seems to have been the increasing politicization of administration and service delivery at sub-national level.

The 1995 reforms envisaged a substantial transfer of functions to the sub-national governments, but failed to clarify the respective roles of the provincial administrators/district administrators and the national departments, and failed to align functions and funding; indeed there has been some further shifting of functions from the national government to sub-national governments since 1999 while funding to provinces has steadily deteriorated. This has contributed to the ongoing decline in service delivery at provincial, district and local level.

But if the arrangements introduced in 1995 have not measured up to popular expectations, this is not to say that a solution lies in yet another fundamental restructuring of intergovernmental relations, as some people are proposing. As in other areas of policy making and implementation, improved service delivery and greater equity between provinces and districts requires policies to effectively address clearly identified problems, rather than wholesale changes in institutions, policies and personnel. Since 1999 there has been a proliferation of initiatives aimed at improving governance at provincial, district and local level, much of which has been driven by external donors. In many cases initiatives have not been followed through; where they have, lack of capacity in most provinces, weak institutional memories and sometimes poor understanding of policies, and frequently inadequate support from the national government have often limited the effectiveness of the measures.

In a culturally diverse, geographically challenging, and fractious country like Papua New Guinea, achieving good governance across the nation is extraordinarily difficult, but, as other chapters in this volume suggest, given that much of the responsibility for service delivery rests with sub-national governments, without effective policies on decentralization, good policy outcomes in health, education, agriculture, economic development, law and justice, and other sectors will be difficult to achieve.

References

Axline, W. A. 1986. *Decentralisation and Development Policy: Provincial Government and the Planning Process in Papua New Guinea.* Monograph 26. Port Moresby: PNG Institute of Applied Social and Economic Research.

Axline, W. A. 1988. *Reform of Intergovernmental Fiscal Relations in Papua New Guinea Trends in Provincial Government Finance, 1978–1988.* Port Moresby: PNG Institute of Applied Social and Economic Research.

Axline, W. A. 1993. *Governance in Papua New Guinea: Approaches to Institutional Reform.* Port Moresby: Institute of National Affairs.

Badu, Nao, n.d (2004?). *Costs and Benefits of Decentralisation.* Unpublished paper.

Barter, Sir Peter. 2004. *Blunt Assessment, Hope and Direction. Lower Level Government in Papua New Guinea.* Paper for the Public Sector Reform Advisory Group, April 2004. Reprinted in *Governance Challenges for PNG and the Pacific Islands*, ed. Nancy Sullivan, 132–154. Madang: DWU Press.

Bi-Partisan Parliamentary Select Committee on Provincial Government. 1993. *Final Report of the Bi-Partisan Parliamentary Select Committee on Provincial Government* (Micah Report). Waigani: The National Parliament.

Chelliah, R. J. 1981. *Provincial Revenue and Mechanism for Fiscal Adjustments in Papua New Guinea.* New Delhi: National Institute for Public Finance and Policy.

Constitutional Planning Commission (CPC). 1973a. *First Interim Report.* September. Port Moresby.

Constitutional Planning Commission (CPC). 1973b. *Second Interim Report.* November. Port Moresby.

Department of Information and Communication. 1993. *Government Policy Initiatives.* September 1993.

Filer, Colin. 2004. *Horses for Courses: Special Purpose Authorities and Local-level Governance in Papua New Guinea.* State, Society and Governance in Melanesia Discussion Paper 2004/6. Canberra: Research School of Pacific and Asian Studies, Australian National University.

General Constitutional Commission (GCC). 1980. *Interim Report.* Port Moresby.

Ghai, Y. P and M. Isana. 1978a. Report on Provincial Government, March. Unpublished.

Ghai, Y. P and M. Isana. 1978b. Review of the Constitutional Laws on Provincial Government. Paper presented to a workshop on Constitutional and Legal

Issues in Provincial Government, September. Port Moresby: Administrative College.

Ghai, Y. P. and A. J. Regan. 1992. *The Law, Politics and Administration of Decentralisation in Papua New Guinea*. Monograph 30. Port Moresby: National Research Institute.

Haley, Nicole and R. J. May eds. 2007. *Conflict and Resource Development in the Southern Highlands of Papua New Guinea*. Canberra: ANU E-Press.

Ketan, Joseph. 2007. The Use and Abuse of Electoral Development Funds and Their Impact on Electoral Politics and Governance in Papua New Guinea. *CDI Papers on Political Governance* 2007/02. Canberra: Centre for Democratic Institutions, The Australian National University.

May, R. J. 1981. *National-Provincial Government Relations in Papua New Guinea; Consultant's Report to the Committee to Review the Financial Provisions of the Organic Law on Provincial Government*. Working Paper No.4. Canberra: Department of Political and Social Change, Research School of Pacific Studies, Australian National University.

May, R. J. 1999. Decentralization in Papua New Guinea: two steps forward, one step back. In *Central-Local Relations in Asia-Pacific. Convergence or Divergence?* ed. Mark Turner, 123–148. Houndmills: Macmillan Press. Reprinted in R. J. May, *State and Society in Papua New Guinea. The First Twenty-Five Years*. Adelaide: Crawford House Publishing, 2001/Canberra: ANU E-Press, 2004.

May, R. J. 2006. *The public sector reform process in Papua New Guinea*. Public Policy in Papua New Guinea — Discussion Paper 2006/4. Canberra: The National Research Institute, Papua New Guinea and the State, Society and Governance in Melanesia Program, Research School of Pacific and Asian Studies, Australian National University.

May, R. J. and A. J. Regan with A. Ley eds. 1997. *Political Decentralisation in a New State. The Experience of Provincial Government in Papua New Guinea*. Bathurst: Crawford House Publishing.

National Economic and Fiscal Commission (NEFC). 2004. Review of Intergovernmental Financing Arrangements (RIGFA) Information Paper: Least Developed Districts Grant (Draft). Port Moresby: NEFC.

National Economic and Fiscal Commission (NEFC). 2005. *Review of Intergovernmental Financing*. Consultation Paper. Port Moresby: NEFC.

National Parliament. 1990. *Progress Report of the Select Committee on Provincial Government Review* (Hesingut Committee). Port Moresby.

National Premiers Council, Premiers Sub-committee on Provincial Government Review. 1990. *Report on Provincial Government Review*.

O'Neill, Peter. 2003. Establishing District Authorities in Provinces. Unpublished paper.

O'Neill, Peter. 2006. The proposal to establish district authorities in the provinces of Papua New Guinea. In *Two Papers on the Proposed Decentralisation in Papua New Guinea*. Public Policy in Papua New Guinea — Discussion Paper 2006/2. Canberra: The National Research Institute, Papua New Guinea and the State, Society and Governance in Melanesia Program, Research School of Pacific and Asian Studies, Australian National University.

Papua New Guinea. 1974. *Proposals on Constitutional Principles and Explanatory Notes* (Government White Paper). Port Moresby: Government Printer.

Peasah, Joseph A. 1994. *Local-Level Government in Papua New Guinea. A Study in Change and Continuity in the Development of Liberal-Democratic Self-Determination at theLocal Level*. Monograph 31. Port Moresby: National Research Institute.

Public Sector Reform Advisory Group (PSRAG). 2002. *Report No.1*. Waigani: PSRAG.

Public Sector Reform Advisory Group (PSRAG). 2005. *Second Report. Improved Decentralisation. Getting people Involved in Democracy, Strong Civil Society, Peace and Good Order, and Self-Reliance*. Port Moresby: PSRAG.

Public Services Commission (PSC). 1977. *Organisation and Management of the National Public Service of Papua New Guinea in the Provinces*. Discussion Paper. Port Moresby.

Regan, Anthony. 2008. *Bougainville/Papua New Guinea: KREDDHA Autonomy Mapping Project*. Kreddha Europe. http://www.kreddha.org/mapping/downloads/080212_Bougainville.pdf

Review of Intergovernmental Fiscal Relations in Papua New Guinea. Report of a Committee established by the National Executive Council, on the Recommendation of the Premiers' Council, on 1st December 1983. 1984. Port Moresby.

Simonelli, Tony. 2003. *Study into the Distribution of Responsibilities Accross Different Levels of Government and Administration in Papua New Guinea*. Working Paper prepared for the National Economic and Fiscal Commission. Port Moresby.

Tordoff, W. and R. L. Watts. 1974. *Report on Central-Provincial Government Relations*. Port Moresby.

Tuck, Graham. 2006. Improved decentralization: the work of the Public Sector Reform Advisory Group. In *Two Papers on the Proposed Decentralisation in Papua New Guinea*. Public Policy in Papua New Guinea — Discussion

Paper 2006/2, 15–23. Canberra: The National Research Institute, Papua New Guinea and the State, Society and Governance in Melanesia Program, Research School of Pacific and Asian Studies, Australian National University.

Wolfers, Edward P. 2006. *Bougainville Autonomy — Implications for Governance and Decentralisation.* Public Policy in Papua New Guinea — Discussion Paper 2006/5. Canberra: The National Research Institute, Papua New Guinea and the State, Society and Governance in Melanesia Program, Research School of Pacific and Asian Studies, Australian National University.

Endnotes

[1] I am indebted to Kathy Whimp for her comments on a draft of this paper.

[2] This chapter will focus on decentralization under the *Organic Law on Provincial Government*, 1977 and the *Organic Law on Provincial Governments and Local-level Governments*, 1995. It will not, except incidentally, look at local-level government, nor will it examine the autonomy arrangements under the Bougainville Agreement of 2001 or the operations of special purpose authorities (which are mentioned briefly below). For more detailed analyses of decentralization in Papua New Guinea see Ghai and Regan (1992), May and Regan (1997) and Axline (1986, 1993).

[3] North Solomons (Bougainville), Enga, Manus (from 1988) and East New Britain (from 1993).

[4] In the late 1980s, several provinces, either dissatisfied with public service performance or seeking additional sources of patronage, reestablished provincial secretariats.

[5] For a detailed study of local-level government before 1995 see Peasah (1994).

[6] For a detailed discussion of these issues see May (1981) and the sources cited in footnote.1 above.

[7] Review of Intergovernmental Fiscal Relations in Papua New Guinea. Report of a Committee established by the National Executive Council, on the Recommendation of the Premiers' Council, on 1st December 1983 (Port Moresby 1984).

[8] In 1990 a premiers' sub-committee of the Premiers' Council complained that between 1978 and 1990 the Premiers' Council had passed a number of resolutions – calling for the updating of national laws; proposing an intergovernment commission to conduct periodic reviews of the provincial government system; setting up the review of intergovernmental fiscal relations which led to the establishment of a committee by the NEC and recommended amendments to the OLPG; calling for assistance in the area of financial management, and so on – but that there had been no effort on the part of the national government to implement these resolutions or to address the problems identified by the Premiers' Council (see National Premiers Council 1990, 8-9. Also see May 1981, 43-45).

[9] From around this time also the Premiers' Council was generally referred to as the National Premiers' Council.

[10] May (1981, 33-39) identified a number of problems of accountability and audit (including the fact that after three years of decentralization in nineteen provinces the auditor general had produced only two – of a mandated fifty-seven – provincial audit reports) and recommended a number of remedial actions, but there was little follow-up.

[11] The amendment originated in a private member's bill which sought to give national MPs full voting rights in the provincial assemblies.

[12] In fact, calculations by Axline (1988) suggest that the actual costs of maintaining provincial governments were not large, and were fairly stable between 1982 and 1988.

[13] This has not always happened. In East Sepik Province, where in 2002 the provincial member, Sir Michael Somare, became prime minister and his replacement, Arthur Somare, later became a minster, then lost his portfolio, then again became a minister, a local-level government representative was, controversially, governor in 2004-2005. A local-level government representative was also for a while governor in Central Province.

[14] Because the boundaries of local government councils and community governments did not necessarily coincide with those of open electorates, it was necessary to carry out an extensive redrawing of local-level government boundaries. A number of provinces with more than three local-level governments in an open electorate also had to amalgamate councils or community governments.

[15] A *Review of Intergovernmental Fiscal Relations* in 1984 reported that there was head tax legislation in four provinces but only one (Bougainville) had raised 'a significant amount of revenue' (K170,000 in 1982) from the tax, and even there 'relatively few persons are paying the tax'. It went on to say: '…the tax is now difficult to collect…some provincial governments have explicitly abandoned any attempt to impose and collect the tax, either at provincial or local level. It is unlikely that head tax will ever raise significant revenue again, even if local level government again becomes effective. It was causing collection difficulties from the early 1970s'.

[16] The Higaturu-Oro Bay Services Authority, the South Bougainville Roads Authority, the Finschhafen-Kabwum Planning and Development Authority, and the Southern Highlands Development Authority.

[17] The Rural Action Programme replaced the controversial former Electoral Development Fund (commonly known as the 'slush fund').

[18] The legislation initially provided for a minimum of K0.3 million. Having been raised to K0.5 million in 1998, the amount was further increased to K1.5 million in 2001. Under a structural adjustment program with the World Bank, it was agreed that only K0.5 would be paid to MPs and JDPBPCs; the remaining K1.0 million was to be subject to a set of guidelines and procedures under the control of the Office of Rural Development. The amount was reduced back to K0.5 in 2002.

[19] Nao Badu, Chairman, National Economic and Fiscal Commission, 'Costs and Benefits of Decentralisation', n.d. (2004?).

[20] Amendments to the OLPGLLG in the constitution recommended by the NEPC were eventually passed by the National Parliament in 2008.

[21] Since the latter part of 2006 the NMA has reverted to its formal title (PLLSMA).

[22] This list is based largely on Sir Peter Barter's critique of decentralization under the OLPGLLG, written soon after he became minister for Inter-Government Relations (see Barter 2004), discussions with colleagues in DPLGA and NEFC, and my own fieldwork in the East Sepik Province. See also PSRAG (2005) and Tuck (2006).

[23] East New Britain, Eastern Highlands, Southern Highlands Madang, and Central. In each province two districts were selected for study.

[24] The unpublished report of the study is available online at http://rspas.anu.edu.au/melanesia/conference_papers/0506_PNGDistrictGovernance_pilotstudy.pdf.

[25] For a more detailed account of the reform process since 1999 see May (forthcoming).

[26] The PPII is part of an AusAID Sub-national Initiative, which in 2006 was expanded to become the Sub-national Strategy.

[27] The District Treasury Roll-out program was always an ambitious initiative. It involves the provision of office and staff accommodation and computer facilities in district headquarters which usually lack such infrastructure for existing staff and where power comes from generators which are chronically short on fuel, and where security is frequently a problem. In July 2006 the former Finance minister, Bart Philemon, said that he had personally opened 42 (of a planned 83) district treasuries in seven provinces (though some of these appear to have become moribund). He lamented the fact that progress appeared to have stopped after his loss of portfolio, and that the K50 million DSIP which was to have commenced in 2006, complementing the Treasury Roll-out, had not proceeded (see *The National* 13 July 2006).

[28] See NEFC (2004). Funds (amounting to K3.3 million in 2005) allocated for less developed district grants were in fact diverted elsewhere (mostly for expenditures in the Southern Highlands).

[29] See O'Neill (2003, 2006) (the latter reproduces the *District Authority Act*). However, there has been no move to implement the act, which at various points seems to clash with the OLPGLLG. (See also Tuck 2006.)

[30] Following the election of Sir Michael Somare as Prime Minister in 2007, a Taskforce on Government and Administration, chaired by Sir Barry Holloway, was appointed to review the structure of government and administration in Papua New Guinea, including intergovernmental relations.

[31] (For a review of the Bougainville experience see Wolfers 2006; Ryan 2008.)

Chapter 13

Thirty Years of Law and Order Policy and Practice: Trying To Do 'Too Much, Too Badly, With Too Little'?

Sinclair Dinnen

Set against a background of significant levels of crime, violence, and conflict, concerns about 'law and order' have become prominent in public debate and private reflection throughout Papua New Guinea. 'Law and order' is a capacious term that relates to threats to personal and societal security, as well as to institutions, mechanisms and processes aimed at preventing or controlling these threats. In a country noted for its acute socio-linguistic diversity and limited sense of shared identity, discussion about 'law and order' has become a genuinely 'national' discourse. Whether in the rural village, urban settlement, suburban home, or government office — everyone has an opinion about 'law and order'.

Beyond this broad agreement, however, there lies a bewildering array of views about the nature of these problems, their perceived causes and impacts, and how they can be effectively addressed. These perceptions vary between different individuals and groups, as well as along lines of gender, class, and location. For women in many parts of the country, the main issue is that of personal security and freedom of movement, including the threat of family and sexual violence from intimates and strangers alike. Members of the business community voice their concerns in terms of the risk of theft, robbery, fraud, bribery, corruption, and the interruption of commercial operations, as well as the attendant costs of private security and insurance premiums. For many living in the towns and cities, it is the spectre of raskolism or violent street crime that poses the most persistent source of insecurity. In parts of the Highlands Region, it may be the threat of inter-group conflict or tribal fighting that poses the most pressing concern. For criminal justice professionals, it is the apparent impotence of the state's principal instruments of crime control — the police, courts and prisons. For political leaders and international donors, Papua New Guinea's law and order problems tend to be conceived primarily in development terms, as major obstacles in the way of much-needed foreign investment and the prospect of economic growth. More recently, concerns about transnational crime and 'terrorism' have been added to the discursive mix; these derive, in large part, from new global and regional security discourses that have emerged in the aftermath of the dramatic attacks against the United States in September 2001 and the ascendancy of the Washington led 'war on terror'.

Viewed from a criminological perspective, there are complex historical and structural factors that have contributed to Papua New Guinea's fragile internal security. These include high population growth unmatched by economic development, growing levels of poverty and social exclusion, corruption and poor governance, deteriorating infrastructure and government services, pressures on land, internal migration and urbanization, uneven patterns of development, and the high levels of social dislocation accompanying Papua New Guinea's difficult integration into the global economy. Combined with the fragility and limited reach of state controls, and the erosion of traditional structures in many areas, these factors make for a fertile setting for dispute, conflict and criminality.

Although regularly acknowledging the deeper sources of conflict and lawlessness, the law and order policy responses of successive post-independence governments in Papua New Guinea have typically comprised crime control measures. Like their counterparts elsewhere, Papua New Guinea's political leaders have often resorted to short-term fixes reliant on relatively high profile (and expensive) control strategies, such as curfews and special policing operations, and, of course, increased penalties for offenders.

Despite the tough 'law and order' rhetoric, the actual implementation of announced policies and special measures has been regularly thwarted by lack of adequate resources and capacity on the part of government and its relevant agencies. This capacity deficit has become increasingly evident over the past thirty years, with state controls progressively overwhelmed by their internal weaknesses and the sheer scale of demands placed upon them. In light of the shortcomings of key agencies like the police, substantial levels of donor assistance, primarily from Australia, have been provided to Papua New Guinea. This, in turn, has made donor assistance an important factor in the shaping and implementation of policy in this area.

While few would deny the many institutional deficiencies in the workings of police, courts and prisons in Papua New Guinea, and the need to address them, it is important to understand these issues in the broader context of the relatively short history of modern criminal justice in Papua New Guinea and the enormously challenging and diverse social environment in which it operates. Expectations of the criminal justice system, particularly the police, have been unrealistically high. These agencies have been expected to deal with the complex fallout from broader processes of social and economic change over which they have little control but are nevertheless regularly blamed when levels of lawlessness and disorder increase.

The relatively weak presence of the state in parts of the country means that access to modern justice is severely restricted for many citizens. This situation has worsened in line with the overall deterioration in government services in recent years. State institutions, including police and courts, remain predominantly urban-based, while approximately 85 per cent of the population lives in poorly serviced rural areas. From the vantage point of the ordinary villager, accessing the nearest police post, magistrate, or, indeed, telephone, might involve a lengthy and difficult journey by foot, truck, or canoe. In such cases, reliance for everyday security needs is more likely to be placed on available community-based structures and local kinship associations than on the formal law enforcement system. Likewise, the only option for addressing outstanding grievances may be resort to informal mechanisms of dispute resolution involving village leaders and elders rather than formal courts. The effectiveness of such mechanisms varies significantly. In some places, they may work reasonably well. In others, they are susceptible to capture by bigmen and other local elites and have been used to reinforce the subordinate position of more vulnerable groups, such as women or youth. Just as the capacity of the state has declined, so too has that of many 'traditional' and community-based approaches to the prevention and management of conflict.

The issue of whether, and how, to engage with the plurality of social control traditions and practices found in Papua New Guinea is another recurrent theme in discussions about law and order, as in other parts of the island Pacific. In its comprehensive review in 1984, the Clifford Report identified two basic ways in which the phrase 'law and order' has been used in Papua New Guinea. The first of these is a notion of peace and order as a state of affairs generated and maintained within a given community without any state participation (Clifford *et al.* 1984, 6). It is an aspiration of ordinary people who view it as essential to their fundamental wellbeing. This meaning, according to Clifford *et al.*, is the 'traditional' view of law and order in societies, as was the case in Papua New Guinea, which existed in the absence of any state. It is contrasted with a second meaning that vests the state with the dominant role in the maintenance of law and order. This is the state-centred view that provides the rationale for the elaborate systems of justice and law enforcement that exist in modern nation-states. More than thirty years after Papua New Guinea's independence, the inherent tension between these two competing philosophies of 'law and order' remains extant.

This chapter provides an overview of law and order policy in Papua New Guinea in the thirty years following independence (1975–2005). The aim is to identify broad patterns in policy thinking about law and order rather than provide an exhaustive account. This includes an attempt to differentiate, where possible, between policy intent and actual practice — what was implemented and what was not. After a short historical introduction to the law and order (now called law and justice) sector and its larger operating environment, the pattern of policy making and, in particular, the crisis-management approach that was adopted during the first twenty years after independence is examined. There follows an account of some important, and more hopeful, developments that have taken place over the last decade, notably the relative stability achieved through the adoption of the 2000 national law and justice sector policy, the gradual move towards a sector-wide approach, and the accompanying adjustments in donor involvement with the sector. The longer history of Australian development assistance to the law and justice sector is then examined in more detail prior to some concluding remarks.

The law and order (law and justice) sector: history and context

Popular accounts of Papua New Guinea's deteriorating law and order situation often give the impression that this is a recent phenomenon and is, moreover, largely the result of the mismanagement and personal shortcomings of incompetent and corrupt agency officials and political leaders. While the decline in recent times has been noticeable, and while incompetence and corruption have contributed, the real story is, as one might expect, somewhat more complicated. As Morauta (1986, 8) has pointed out, 'the seeds of today's social and institutional problems were sown well before 1975'.

The modern criminal justice system, like the modern state of which it is an integral part, has had a relatively short history in Papua New Guinea. Throughout most of the colonial period, there was no discrete system of criminal justice for local people. Instead, the policing, judicial, and penal powers of government formed part of an undifferentiated system of 'native administration' embodied in a set of paternalistic 'native regulations' that was aimed primarily at maintaining stability and a semblance of order among colonial subjects rather than delivering justice. This system was personified in the office of the patrol officer or *kiap*, who acted simultaneously as government agent, police officer, prosecutor, magistrate, and gaoler. The primary role of the 'native constabulary' (the forerunner of the Royal Papua New Guinea Constabulary (RPNGC)) was the extension of government control and only secondarily the control of crime. Given the limited aims and capacities of colonial administration, most Papua New Guineans continued to rely on customary or traditional means for the resolution of all but the most serious local disputes and for the provision of personal and community security.

This was to change gradually with the process of institutional modernization — or 'state-building' in today's parlance — that commenced in the 1950s and picked up pace in the 1960s. While *kiap* justice was a pragmatic strategy for the gradual expansion of administrative influence, it was considered inappropriate for the long-term governance of the Territory. Paul Hasluck, the long-serving and reform-minded Australian minister for Territories (1951–63), was intent on building a system of justice consistent with what he saw as the future political needs of the Territory. Replacing the old colonial model with a centralized justice system administering a uniform body of law was viewed as a necessary condition for the self-government that would one day follow. The adoption of an Anglo-Australian system of law and justice was proposed in a major review of judicial administration, the so-called Derham Report (Derham 1960). This report became the blueprint for the system of law enforcement and judicial administration that Papua New Guinea inherited at independence in 1975.

An early priority was to establish a separation of powers between judicial, administrative, and executive arms of government. This meant supplanting the administrative model of colonial order with an independent, institutionally differentiated and professionally staffed justice system. A separate Prisons Branch was established in 1957 under the *Corrective Institutions Ordinance*. The police force was separated from the Department of Native Affairs in 1961 and in 1966 it was removed from the control of the Public Services Commission in order to ensure its neutrality. Mobile squads were established after the police reorganization in 1966 and were used in response to a revival of tribal conflict in the highlands, as well as growing anti-government protests in a number of areas. The transition from the old colonial style of policing to a professional and independent constabulary was a difficult one and, in some respects, remains a work in progress.

The system of courts also underwent significant changes from the mid 1960s, with the introduction of more formal court procedures applicable to both indigenes and foreigners. Local and district courts were established in 1963 and connected through appeal to the superior courts. Most of the old 'native regulations' were repealed in 1968, and the new inferior courts were mandated to administer summary offences codified in modern criminal statutes modelled on Australian legislation. Provision was made for training Papua New Guinean magistrates at the Administrative College established in Port Moresby in 1964. Indictable offences continued to be provided for under an outdated version of the Criminal Code of Queensland.

By 1975, Papua New Guinea had acquired the institutional framework of a modern Anglo-Australian justice system. However, these institutions and their operations remained unfamiliar to many Papua New Guineans. The emphasis on due process, individual responsibility, and punishment rather than restitution, caused confusion in many rural areas where they often clashed with local perceptions about how disputes should be resolved (Strathern 1972). Rapid localization resulted in the replacement of many seasoned officials with less experienced personnel, which compounded the difficult birth of the modern law and justice system. The police force was arguably 'the most crippled of any government agency' (Dorney 2000, 304). Its coverage in 1975 extended to only 10 per cent of Papua New Guinea's total land area and 40 per cent of the population (quoted in Dorney 1990, 296). Many of its problems were attributed to inexperienced and untrained staff, including an acute shortage of commissioned officers and senior NCOs (Dorney 2000, 304).

A range of social and political problems emerged during the decolonization period that were to challenge the authority and capacity of the independent state. While most of these were already evident in the final period of the colonial administration (Nelson 2003), once independence was granted the 'fundamental opposition between indigenous people and colonial powers was displaced by a far messier array of local divisions' (Otto and Thomas 1997, 4). Some of these related to the aggravation of longstanding antagonisms between local groups, while others arose from divisions and tensions of more recent origin. The most serious manifestations included micronationalist movements in some of the more developed regions, notably Bougainville and the Gazelle Peninsula; the revival of tribal fighting in parts of the highlands; and the rise of street crime in the main urban centres.

The incidence and intensity of tribal fighting have increased in the post-independence period. Growing numbers of fatalities and serious injuries have resulted from the introduction of modern firearms (Burton 1990, 25). Crime control responses, consisting primarily of the deployment of mobile squads, have had little positive impact and, in the opinion of some observers, have often served to prolong fighting (Mapusia 1986, 108). Recent evidence suggests that tribal conflict — long viewed as a rural phenomenon confined to certain highlands provinces — has become a major source of tension and violence in some of the larger towns, including Port Moresby (Haley and Muggah 2006).

The most notorious manifestation of Papua New Guinea's law and order problems has been the steady rise in violent urban crime, widely attributed to raskol gangs comprising adolescent boys and young men. By the second half of the 1980s, criminal gangs had entrenched themselves as a menacing feature of the urban landscape, with sophisticated networks extending across the country (Harris 1988). The widespread availability of small arms and light weapons, often sourced illegally from the defence force and the police, has added greatly to problems of criminal violence (Alpers 2005). Raskolism has also spread to many rural areas. Violence against women, including rape, is a problem throughout the country. In a series of studies in the 1980s, the Law Reform Commission documented endemic violence within marital relationships (Toft 1985, 1986). Sexual assaults are also commonplace outside of marriage. High levels of rape and sexual abuse have, in turn, contributed to the prevalence of STDs and rapid spread of the HIV/AIDS epidemic currently gripping Papua New Guinea.

With an establishment of just over 5,000 sworn officers, the size of the RPNGC has not grown significantly since independence despite the population having more than doubled from 2 million to over 5 million people during the 1975–2005 period. [1] The police to population ratio in Papua New Guinea was estimated at 1:1121 in 2002, substantially below the 1:380 ratio in 1975 and well under the U.N. recommended ratio of 1:450 (Public Sector Reform Management Unit 2002, 63). Policing problems are a significant part of the difficulties facing the administration of criminal justice in Papua New Guinea. While the RPNGC appear incapable of successfully undertaking routine criminal investigations and apprehending suspects, prosecutions often fail for lack of adequate evidence and preparation. Lengthy delays in the processing of court cases have resulted in large numbers of detainees on remand awaiting their hearings, while mass escapes from the country's prison system are a regular occurrence.

Charges of ill-discipline and serious human rights abuses are levelled regularly against the RPNGC (Human Rights Watch 2005). Although susceptible to exploitation by vexatious litigants, a significant proportion of civil claims against the state originate in allegations of police violence. A 2004 review of the RPNGC commissioned by the Papua New Guinea government concluded that 'policing was close to total collapse' in many parts of the country (Administrative Review Committee 2004, 40). Responsibility for this alarming state of affairs was attributed to a lack of government support and direction; ineffective police leadership; inadequate and unreliable provision of resources to do the job; unpaid allowances and entitlements; barely adequate salaries; system-wide lack of discipline, accountability and self-respect; almost total absence of community trust and respect; and political interference in police operations.

Policy responses — rhetoric and practice

1975–1997: managing crisis

Early law and order policy was *ad hoc* and reactive. Weaknesses included a lack of strategic planning, monitoring and evaluation, chronic policy inconsistency, and an absence of coordination between the principal agencies. Budget appropriations were more often the result of competitive negotiations between senior officials than the outcome of a rational assessment of the needs of individual agencies. The sheer number of agencies and departments make this one of the most challenging sectors of government. At present, the law and justice sector is made up of the Department of Justice and Attorney General, National Judicial Staff Services, Ombudsman Commission, RPNGC, Correctional Services, Magisterial Services, Office of the Public Prosecutor and Public Solicitor. Since the late 1990s, the Department of National Planning and Rural Development has taken a lead role in attempting to improve coordination and planning across the sector. Each department and agency has their own structures, operating procedures and corporate plans. Constitutional doctrines such as judicial independence impose further limits on inter-agency coordination.

Over the years, there have been numerous reports and policy reviews, and various attempts to establish mechanisms for coordination, as well as efforts — usually with significant donor input — to strengthen the institutional capacities of particular agencies. Policy reviews and crime summits have generated long lists of recommendations aimed at improving the functioning of agencies, enhancing inter-agency cooperation, strengthening crime control, reforming the law, and, more broadly, measures to address the underlying causes of lawlessness. While there may be some value in such exercises, they often produce extensive 'wish lists' that lack overall coherence and that make few concessions to the reality of resource constraints and limited institutional capacity. Moreover, these lists often fail to prioritize recommendations, provide costing or implementation plans, or integrate proposed changes with ongoing programs and plans in the agencies concerned. Implementation of recommendations arising from reviews is invariably partial and selective.

Lack of government support and effective leadership in the agencies has been a persistent problem. As in many other areas of policy, there has been little consistency between different governments and departmental administrations. New ministers and senior officials have sought to make their individual mark, often by deliberately distancing themselves from their predecessor's initiatives. There has been a preference for setting up new mechanisms and initiatives rather than improving existing structures. Many of the same recommendations appear time and again, indicating the gap between policy rhetoric and implementation, as well as a serious lack of corporate memory among decision makers. Political leaders have been more concerned with responding to public pressure for quick-fix solutions than with engaging in the less glamorous task of sustained capacity building and reform aimed at improving the effectiveness of the criminal justice system. As in many other countries, the concerns and attention spans of politicians have often been short-term with a focus on symptoms rather than upon systemic problems.

There are numerous examples of this haphazard approach. In the first decade of independence, a crisis management approach evolved that was to prevail for the next two decades. Periodic crime crises contributed to mounting public anxiety and highlighted the acute limitations of routine law enforcement procedures as a deterrent to criminal violence. Various attempts were made to enhance coordination among the law and order agencies but pressure for immediate results usually inclined political leaders towards high profile crime control measures aimed at achieving short-term impacts. Reviewing the first ten year's of Papua New Guinea's law and order policies, Louise Morauta remarked that:

> Government response to law and order problems has frequently been a
> response to crises in public opinion or particular events, and is marked

by fluctuations of interest. It also reflects the dispersed nature of government efforts: with a considerable number of different agencies making rather independent contributions. There has also been uncertainty about appropriate coordinating mechanisms (Morauta 1986, 8).

The growing focus on law and order as a major policy challenge is evident from the early 1970s. Concerns with the revival of tribal fighting led to the establishment of an official investigation that, among other things, 'heard many complaints of a lack of judicial and police presence at village level and considers this lack as one of the prime causes of increased lawlessness in the Highlands' (Papua New Guinea 1973, 7). *The Inter-Group Fighting Act* was passed in 1977. It provided for the declaration of 'fighting zones' in affected areas and a reversal of the onus of proof in certain criminal proceedings. However, the Supreme Court later declared a number of its provisions unconstitutional (Constitutional Reference No. 3 of 1978, Re *Inter-group Fighting Act* 1977, *Papua New Guinea Law Reports* 1978). In 1979, the government resorted to the declaration of a state of emergency in all five highlands provinces in response to tribal conflict.

The need for juvenile justice, police and prison reform, and improved coordination between agencies, were identified by a Peace and Good Order Committee set up to investigate rising urban crime (Papua New Guinea 1974). An international seminar on crime prevention in Port Moresby in 1975 led to the setting up of a Crime Prevention Council comprising senior agency officials. The seminar report advised that Papua New Guinea's crime problems were closely linked to the weakness of its policing system (Biles 1976).

In 1977, the government commissioned a wide-ranging review of the role and needs of the RPNGC. The task force conducting the review made various recommendations, including the need for a clear and concise policy on policing, improved training, and the streamlining and review of the pay system (RPNGC 1977). While the government accepted the report, there was no systematic implementation of its findings. In 1981, the Port Moresby Committee for the Promotion of Law and Order was established at the instigation of the prime minister to provide a community voice on law and order matters. Following this, an Inter-Departmental Committee of Review on Law and Order was created in 1982 in an attempt to coordinate expenditure and funding of the main law and order agencies. However, this committee became 'largely a trading exercise by the law enforcement departments for a share of the available financial cake' (Clifford *et al.* 1984, 117).

Two major reports were published in 1984. The first of these was from the Committee to Review Policy and Administration on Crime, Law and Order established by the National Executive Council (NEC (cabinet)) under the chairmanship of a senior public servant, Leo Morgan (Department of Provincial

Affairs 1983 [the Morgan Report]). [2] This report originated in a recommendation made by a sub-committee on law and order established at a meeting of the Premiers Council at Arawa, North Solomons Province, in October 1982. The terms of reference laid down by the NEC called for a comprehensive review of government policy and administration relating to law and order. As well as examining the law and order agencies, the report dealt with many social and economic issues in discussing the wider genesis of lawlessness. Key recommendations included:

• creation of a Crime Commission to integrate the planning and coordination of individual agencies;
• creation of a Commission of Employment and Production to generate employment, particularly for youth;
• creation of a youth management team to plan and implement youth policy;
• control over production and consumption of alcohol;
• establishment of ward committees and more urban village courts;
• extension and strengthening of the Leadership Code;
• strengthening of party discipline in parliament.

The second report was a joint initiative between the Institute of National Affairs, a private-sector think tank, and the Institute of Applied Social and Economic Research, a government-funded research body (Clifford *et al.* 1984). An anthropologist with longstanding Papua New Guinea experience, a former National Court judge, and the director of the Australian Institute of Criminology wrote the report. It documented the shortcomings of individual agencies and was critical of the weakness of planning and budgeting across the sector. Instead of inter-agency coordination, it stated that planning was conducted in isolation, while budgeting was a process of competitive negotiation between agencies pursuing their own institutional interests. A separate Law and Order Policy Development Unit staffed by non-agency personnel was proposed. This unit would advise the NEC and line agencies on law and order policy, evaluate programs, and monitor the implementation of NEC decisions.

A distinguishing feature of the Clifford report was its emphasis on the need to reduce the perceived gap between the realm of formal state justice and the myriad informal institutions of social control operating at community levels. In this regard, the report recommended a gradual shift in policy towards one that sought to incorporate informal (non-state) mechanisms in the maintenance of order and dispute resolution, while gradually reducing what it viewed as over-reliance on formal (state) structures (*ibid.* 252–253).

The radical character of the Clifford report was its move beyond a conventional focus on formal state agencies and its emphasis on the need to try and accommodate community-based mechanisms prevailing in rural and urban village settings. At its core was a critique of the appropriateness and sustainability of institutionalized criminal justice in Papua New Guinea and recognition of the existence of non-state resources that could be mobilized to enhance security and safety at local levels. Commenting on the evident deficiencies of the formal agencies, the report stated that:

(T)he possibility that existing services may be defective or inefficient — not because they are starved of resources but because they are either irrelevant to the situation in Papua New Guinea or refusing to work with communities — does not seem to have detained people long (*ibid*. 125).

Clifford *et al*. made the case for improving the articulation between state and non-state approaches to the maintenance of order and resolution of disputes. Engaging with 'traditional' and other community-based mechanisms was — and remains — a major challenge to those working in the formal justice sector. For many, such a move is viewed as threatening to their institutional and professional domains, as well as being potentially corrosive of the rule of law. The Clifford analysis also raised — without providing many answers — difficult practical issues about how to render operational the community engagement being proposed.

Detailed consideration of these two reports was diverted by an escalation of violent crime in Port Moresby in late 1984. Following a series of widely publicized criminal attacks, including the pack rape of a New Zealand woman and her daughter, which provoked the largest public demonstration in the capital's ten-year history, the NEC agreed to a package of forty-nine crime control measures. These measures, many of which were distilled from the Morgan and Clifford reports, provided 'something for everyone in cabinet' and lacked any 'clear overall theme' (Morauta 1986, 9). One of the authors of the Clifford report complained of the 'great difference of emphasis' between the report and the government's announced measures (Bill Clifford quoted in INA 1991, 2). The latter included proposed changes to laws, strengthening law and order agencies, support for village courts and urban local governments, improved police-community relations, ID cards, street lighting, and a review of urban settlement policy. More draconian proposals included mandatory corporal punishment for rape and violent crimes, boom gates for the major towns, and a review of the *Vagrancy Act*.

A small part-time implementation task force — replaced by a full-time body in 1985 — was formed to report to a Ministerial Committee on Law and Order. It prepared an NEC submission to review implementation of the forty-nine measures and identify funding priorities. However, a further spate of criminal violence in Port Moresby persuaded the government to take even more drastic action and the submission was never considered. In June 1985, Prime Minister Somare declared a state of emergency in the National Capital District (NCD), stating that the police were incapable of controlling the deteriorating situation using their normal powers (*Draft Hansard*, Tenth Day, 12 June 1985, 20). As mentioned earlier, a state of emergency had been declared in the highlands in 1979 but this was the first and only time it was used against urban crime. The 1985 emergency allowed the government to deploy the defence force in a civil capacity, increase police powers, prohibit public demonstrations, and impose a nightly curfew. For most Port Moresby residents, this measure brought welcome, albeit temporary, respite. Despite an estimated cost of K2.9 million (*Papua New Guinea Post-Courier* 2 October 1985), it also provided the government with an unequivocal expression of its commitment to confronting crime. Restrictions on movement and the presence of large numbers of police and soldiers ensured a significant reduction in reported crime. Raids by security personnel resulted in numerous arrests, seizure of stolen property, and the recapture of approximately 160 prison escapees.

The 1985 emergency set in motion what was to become a familiar pattern of reactive responses to localized outbreaks of criminal violence. These have typically included the announcement of an elaborate package of crime control measures with 'something for everyone', special policing operations, and, in the most serious cases, the imposition of temporary restrictions on movement. Prior to 1987, a curfew could only be imposed under the auspices of a state of emergency declared under the constitution. However, the *Curfew Act* of 1987 provided for the declaration of a curfew independently of a state of emergency. This served to normalize curfews as a routine instrument of crime control. Defence Force and Correctional Service personnel — the other two components of Papua New Guinea's 'disciplined services' — have also been used to supplement over-stretched police on such occasions. While relatively few of the announced measures are implemented, the immediate impact of curfews and special security operations was the temporary restoration of public order and confidence until the next build-up when the whole process would be repeated again (Dinnen 2001, 63–71).

This normalization of emergency powers was, among other things, an acknowledgement of the weakness of institutionalized criminal justice practice in the face of serious escalations in violence and disorder. Supplementary measures were aimed at restoring order in designated areas through a combination of restrictions on movement, punitive raids, and orchestrated displays of militaristic strength. These displays belied the actual capacity of Papua New Guinea's security forces to control crime and disorder on any significant scale. While providing short-term relief in the areas concerned, curfews and other special operations had little lasting impact on crime. Once the restrictions were lifted, crime rates begin to rise again. Such strategies were also extremely costly and further reduced resources available for general policing and other law and justice services. In addition, the arbitrary targeting of 'suspect communities' and the violence that routinely accompanies police raids, served to further aggravate high levels of distrust between police and many local communities. The concentration of crime control measures in particular areas also contributed inadvertently to the expansion of criminal networks as suspects moved to other towns and areas to avoid apprehension.

On assuming office in mid 1988, the Namaliu-led government promptly identified law and order as one of its policy priorities. A Ministerial Committee on Law and Order was established with wide terms of reference. These included the formulation of law and order policy; liaising with relevant government agencies; coordinating and monitoring law and order policy; and advising on crime rates, types of crime, treatment of offenders, and the effectiveness of the criminal justice system. Papua New Guinea's first National Law and Order Policy, prepared by the Ministerial Committee chaired by Justice Minister and former judge Bernard Narokobi, was announced in August 1988.

The policy comprised an extensive set of recommendations aimed at improving the workings of justice and law enforcement agencies, as well measures to address underlying causes, such as enhanced law awareness, education, labour and employment, and urban development. There was also an ambitious plan to create a 'super ministry' — the Ministry for Law, Order and Social Justice headed by either the prime minister or deputy prime minister assisted by assistant ministers or ministers of state (Papua New Guinea 1988, 43). This single ministry would be responsible for the entire array of law and order related agencies, including the courts and tribunals, the state solicitor, public solicitor, public prosecutor, police, correctional service, public curator, registrar-general, juvenile justice, secretary and principal legal advisor, ombudsman commission, law reform, and censorship board. Needless to say, the considerable practical and constitutional difficulties entailed in bringing so many institutions and agencies together ensured that no such 'super ministry' eventuated. It was also recommended that a permanent Law and Order Secretariat be established outside the Justice Department to coordinate programs among different agencies and departments, and non-government organizations. Provincial law and order committees would provide coordination in the provinces.[3] There was also a proposal to establish a Law, Order and Justice Foundation to engage with the wider community and secure funds for local programs.

The Foundation for Law, Order and Justice (FLOJ) was formed out of the Papua New Guinea Community Law Awareness Program in 1989. FLOJ was incorporated as a private company and initially received support from government and the private sector. Its objectives were to undertake research, policy development and advice, program design and implementation, and coordination between government law and order agencies. NEC later approved a merger between FLOJ and the existing Secretariat for Law and Order and the merged body was given the task of advising the Ministerial Committee for Law,

Order and Justice. However, the Ministerial Committee was abolished in 1990 as part of a government cost-cutting exercise (INA 1991, 21). FLOJ survived for several years as an independent proponent of crime prevention and community-oriented justice initiatives. It was also the basis for another NGO, Peace Foundation Melanesia, which emerged in the second half of the 1990s.

Following another law and order crisis in Port Moresby, a National Crime Summit was held in February 1991. The Namaliu government announced a package of crime control measures that included the reintroduction of capital punishment for murder, rape, and drug offences; the tattooing of convicted offenders; additional maximum security prisons; identity cards; vagrancy laws; and the forcible repatriation of 'unemployed people and troublemakers' (*Papua New Guinea Post-Courier* 15 March 1991). Foreshadowing developments more than a decade later, the Summit also called for the deployment of Australian police in line positions in the RPNGC. Capital punishment was subsequently re-introduced as an available sentence in the case of convictions for wilfull murder. In response to the summit, the prime minister's department — echoing earlier calls — requested the setting up of a National Crime Council to coordinate all crime control and prevention measures, advise government, and monitor the overall crime situation (INA 1991, 30).

The Namaliu government also threw its support behind a controversial proposal to establish a National Guard. In March 1991, NEC approved the establishment of a National Guard Task Force to provide one year of national service training to all young men aged between thirteen and nineteen years with an emphasis on military training, discipline and community work (*Papua New Guinea Post-Courier* 15 March 1991). Karl Stack, the minister for Forests and originator of the scheme, announced that a force of up to 5,000 Nepalese Gurkhas would conduct the training. However, the prospect of Gurkha-trained youth roaming the towns and countryside on the completion of their national service led to growing opposition to the proposal. Despite attempts to replace the militaristic model with one that stressed personal development and vocational training, the scheme was never implemented (*Times of Papua New Guinea* 6 June 1991).

In mid 1991, the government published a strategic paper, *Security for Development*, with the stated aim of integrating its response to the earlier crime summit into a comprehensive and planned approach to law and order. The paper noted that:

> Previous attempts to deal with crime in Papua New Guinea have sometimes suffered from rushed decision-making, based on insufficient information, analysis, and allocation of resources, and followed by inadequate implementation and feedback (Papua New Guinea 1991, 2).

It also acknowledged that the security forces (police and Defence Force) were unable to cope with rising levels of lawlessness and disorder and that the most serious security threats facing Papua New Guinea were internal rather than external. This view was shared in Canberra, and in the same year the Papua New Guinea and Australian governments released a joint statement announcing that Papua New Guinea would give the highest priority to internal security needs, while Australia would assist Papua New Guinea's disciplined forces maintain internal security.

Security for Development called for an expert body to monitor and give advice on crime, and the establishment of an Office of Security Coordination to provide policy advice on security needs. An Office of Security Coordination and Assessment (OSCA) was subsequently established in the Department of the Prime Minister, in mid 1991, to coordinate, in consultation with law and order and security agencies, the implementation of government policy.

Paias Wingti became prime minister in 1992 and set up a National Law, Order and Justice Council (NLOJC). FLOJ served as a secretariat to the new Council which was charged with making recommendations to the Policy Coordination and Management Committee (PCMC) in the prime minister's department and through it to the National Planning Council. Its principal task was to develop a new law and order policy and detailed program of implementation. Approved by the NEC in late 1993, the aims of this — the second — national law and order policy were:

• to control, reduce and prevent crime, and provide a safe and secure environment for human development;
• to increase community participation in the preservation of social order, and to take local direction on law and order maintenance and problem identification;
• to improve the efficiency with which resources in the law and order sector and supporting agencies are used; and
• to develop disciplined and professional law and order personnel and agencies which have good working relationships with the people they serve and to foster efficiency and honesty among political and bureaucratic officials and institutions responsible for law and order policy and programs (Papua New Guinea 1993).

Various working groups comprising agency officials and representatives from the non-government sector convened to finalize programs and implementation strategies in six broad areas:

1. local level relations and relations with wider social and economic concerns;
2. research and information systems;
3. manpower, facilities and equipment;
4. coordination and efficiency;
5. corruption and management;

6. budgeting and planning capacity for the sector.

The working groups did a great deal of work in 1994 and a number of projects were ready for implementation. There was also an attempt to integrate the recommendations of yet another law and order report that had been prepared independently by an adviser to the prime minister in 1994 (Spencer Report 1994). The latter included proposals for greater integration of the functions of the disciplined forces, improved national planning and training, emphasis on mediation and conflict resolution, and enhanced national awareness of law and order developments. While devoting considerable time to policy development, the Wingti administration was not immune to more reactive responses in the face of periodic crime crises. For example, in 1993 it announced a familiar package of repressive measures. Measures implemented included the passing of the controversial *Internal Security Act*, which was consistent with the broader trend of normalization of emergency powers and allowed for severe restrictions on freedom of movement and association in areas affected by high levels of crime or social disorder (Dinnen 1993). In reality, the capacity of the Papua New Guinea state to implement such measures beyond narrowly prescribed localities was — and remains — extremely limited. In addition, the Supreme Court in 1994 upheld a constitutional challenge against certain sections of the act on the grounds that they were inconsistent with due process provisions of the constitution.

Sir Julius Chan succeeded Paias Wingti as prime minister in August 1994 and replaced the former Council (NLOJC) with a new Law Order and Administration Committee chaired by a senior bureaucrat. The committee was tasked with preparing the Chan government's policy on law and order, but, as far as is known, no policy was ever produced. Most of the energy of the new administration was expended on addressing Papua New Guinea's rapidly deteriorating fiscal situation. Measures adopted included the devaluation of the national currency (the *kina*) in mid September, followed by its flotation in early October 1994. Calls to declare a state of emergency or impose a curfew in Port Moresby were dismissed by senior police officers as 'too expensive' (*Papua New Guinea Post-Courier* 24 November 1994). Continuing public concern with urban crime led Prime Minister Chan to declare 1996 'the year of law enforcement' and announce a series of measures to increase 'police firepower' and target 'hard-core criminals' (*The National* 6 November 1996). Late the following year, a nationwide curfew was introduced, initially for two months but subsequently extended for an unprecedented period of nine months in the NCD (*The National* 11 August 1997). The Chan government lost office in 1997 in the wake of the tumultuous Sandline Affair (Dinnen *et al.* 1997). It was succeeded by the volatile Skate administration, which was, in turn, replaced by the reformist government led by Sir Mekere Morauta in 1999. During the Skate administration, a Law and Order Summit in Port Moresby resulted in the announcement of a package of (over 50) familiar strategies designed to counter lawlessness. A Plan of Action for Law and Order 1999–2002 was prepared as an NEC submission but never formally approved.

By the mid 1990s, the most critical problems facing Papua New Guinea's struggling criminal justice system were well known. These included:

• the paucity of reliable criminal justice data on which to base planning, forecasting, and the evaluation of particular initiatives;
• a growing backlog of cases in the court system;
• a low success rate for arrest, investigation and prosecution of crimes;
• limited access to legal aid;
• over-reliance on the formal justice system and custodial sentences and lack of articulation with community-based dispute resolution processes and use of alternatives to imprisonment;
• a very high prison remandee population;
• mass prison breakouts;
• widespread abuse of police powers;
• large numbers of outstanding civil actions against the state arising from police actions and the loss of large sums as a result of successful claims;
• systemic problems of financial and personnel management;
• inadequate levels of government support; most agency budgets were directed to salaries, allowances and utilities, with little, if any, funding remaining for goods, maintenance and other services.

These problems had been exacerbated by the chronic lack of policy consistency and absence of coordination between agencies in the sector. As stated in a joint review of the law and order sector in 1993 under the Papua New Guinea-Australia Development Cooperation Programme:

> (T)he development of functions for justice agencies is plagued by *'too much, too badly, with too little'*. With regular shifts in government thinking on law and order, it becomes both problematic and unrewarding for agencies to engage in even medium term planning exercises. Lack of consultation across the sector exacerbates the difficulties in planning. These difficulties are further compounded by the focus, in the consultation that does occur, on budgets and expenditure control to the exclusion of any consideration of the merit of program-based arguments (Papua New Guinea-Australia Development Cooperation Program 1993, emphasis added).

1997 and beyond: Towards a measure of stability?

A serious attempt to move beyond this sorry state of affairs commenced in 1997. This began as a low profile effort initiated by concerned senior law and order bureaucrats. The Office of National Planning — a key central government agency

— convened two workshops on the Law, Order and Justice Sector, in May and July 1997. An initial aim was to familiarize policy officers in the different agencies with the earlier work of the National Law, Order and Justice Council. The main objective was to develop an overall sector plan with strategies for implementation at national, provincial and local levels. A Law and Justice Sector Working Group comprising senior officials from the main law and justice agencies was set up and began to meet regularly under the auspices of the Office of National Planning. Rather than coming up with yet another policy, the Working Group set out to integrate previous policies and recommendations into a single policy framework for the whole sector. It was, in essence, a task of consolidation rather than innovation, and was entrusted to experienced sector professionals rather than politicians.

After reviewing past initiatives and undertaking consultations with stakeholders, the Working Group finalized a draft National Law and Justice Policy and Plan of Action in December 1999 and this was subsequently endorsed by the NEC in August 2000 (Papua New Guinea 2000). The 2000 policy provides a broad vision statement for the sector as a whole. Replacing the term 'law and order' with 'law and justice' reflected, among other things, a desire to move away from the singularly reactive approach associated with the former term. The fact that the policy has survived to date, notwithstanding a change of government, distinguishes it from its predecessors and has provided a welcome element of stability and continuity.

The contents of the policy are organized around three broad pillars. The first recognizes the need to continue to improve the efficiency of the formal criminal justice system through capacity building with individual agencies and initiatives aimed at strengthening multi-agency approaches and greater community participation in areas such as juvenile justice, law reform, rehabilitation strategies, and anti-corruption. The second pillar addresses the critical issue of sector-wide coordination and the need for appropriate coordinating structures, systems and processes. It is premised on, among other things, the high level of interdependence between the law enforcement and justice agencies in practice and the need to move towards a sector-wide approach in the area of criminal justice. The third pillar addresses the need to develop effective crime prevention and restorative justice strategies in partnership with community-based organizations, particularly at local levels. As such, it echoes the Clifford Report's concern with improving the articulation between formal and informal realms of justice.

In early 2003, the government established a National Coordinating Mechanism (NCM) as the principal vehicle for promoting sector-wide coordination at the national level, as envisaged in the policy. The NCM comprises the heads of the sector agencies and is chaired by the secretary of the Department of National

Planning and Rural Development. [4] Meeting on a monthly basis, the NCM's role is to set policy, decide strategies and priorities, and promote coordination across the sector. While the NCM remains light on civil society representation, the fact that regular meetings are now being held between senior executives of the principal agencies is a significant step forward. Strengthening coordinating mechanisms at provincial levels is the next step. The Law and Justice Sector Working Group acts as a secretariat to the NCM. This group, formed in the late 1990s, has been a critical driver of policy reform and sectoral coordination at the operational level.

Consistent with the Papua New Guinea policy and larger changes in Canberra's approach to development assistance, Australian aid has shifted progressively from support of individual agencies to a sector-wide approach. As stated in a joint review in 2000 of the law and justice sector under the Papua New Guinea-Australia Development Cooperation Program:

> Australia is now well placed to assist in a more integrated way and could not have contemplated sectoral approaches when key elements within the sector were not addressed. This fundamental sector objective for future Australian assistance not only acknowledges the high levels of interdependence between each sector component but also provides practical support and encouragement to sector agencies seeking to implement the National Law and Justice Policy that Australia has agreed to support (Papua New Guinea-Australia 2001, ix).

Australian support is now channelled through a single facility, the Law and Justice Sector Program (LJSP). The LJSP is designed to work through Papua New Guinea's own management systems and includes the provision of imprest account funding, technical assistance, infrastructure, training, procurement of materials and equipment, disbursement of grants, and support for community-based initiatives.

A Community Justice Liaison Unit (CJLU) was established as an innovative mechanism to promote the engagement of civil society organizations in the law and justice sector with a focus on crime prevention, restorative justice and partnerships for change. The kind of work undertaken by the CJLU includes:

- training, awareness raising and advocacy;
- restorative justice initiatives and research;
- targeted interventions with women, youth and other vulnerable groups;
- partnerships for change, personal and community development;
- intervention appraisal, design, monitoring and evaluation.

The program approach in the law and justice sector is being implemented initially over a 5-year period and Australia has committed $A170 million for this purpose for the period 2003-8. An Australian-funded Justice Advisory Group (JAG) has also been set up to provide independent technical advice to the Papua New Guinea government and AusAID on the performance of the law and justice sector. The JAG, which will be phased out in 2008, aims to:

- provide independent advice to support the Papua New Guinea government in its role of sector monitoring and evaluation of performance of the law and justice sector, including impact and outcomes of government and donor funding;
- advise on policy, structural, financial or other issues for the law and justice sector;
- provide specialist technical advice in relation to policy, management and/or organizational matters;
- assist in the promotion of sector coordination and monitoring, the development of agreed sector outcomes and indicators, and the collection of sector performance information.

While Australian assistance previously struggled for traction in Papua New Guinea's uncertain and fluid policy environment, it is obviously easier to integrate donor activities now that Papua New Guinea has a relatively well established policy framework. Integration in this sense is also facilitated by the adoption of a sector-wide approach by both the Papua New Guinea government and AusAID.

The changing character of Australian assistance to the Papua New Guinea law and justice sector

Conventional institutional strengthening

Australia's development assistance program has undergone a series of changes since independence, moving progressively from budget support (the primary form of assistance from 1975 to 1989) to program aid in the 1990s. In the thirty years following independence, more than $A240 million was provided to strengthen Papua New Guinea's law and justice system. Reflecting concerns with the deteriorating capacity of the police and a conventional view of the centrality of police systems in the management of crime and disorder, 69 per cent of this assistance was directed at the RPNGC (AusAID 2003, 36). Prior to 1989, numerous police training courses, missions, police postings and consultancies were undertaken through AIDAB (now AusAID), the Australian Federal Police (AFP), and various Australian state police forces. A series of design and appraisal missions developed a proposal for a RPNGC development project. Phase I of the project began in 1989 with a core focus on organizational development, human resource management, and development of training and management systems. Commencing in January 1993, Phase II provided operations support and training. The focus was on advisers facilitating improvement rather than directly implementing change. Phase III began in March 2000 and was extended until 2005 before being folded into the new sector-wide law and justice program. It represented a departure from the first two phases and attempted to improve the capacity of the RPNGC to effectively enforce law and to work with the community to preserve peace and good order. This phase also had a significant capital works component.

Despite the criticisms leveled at the RPNGC development project, there is little doubt that it contributed in a number of technical areas, though how sustainable the benefits were remains an open question. Against a domestic context of chronic under-resourcing and other problems, it has also been argued that, 'the project helped maintain the constabulary's operations at an acceptable level' (Wan 2000, 112). In other words, without the material support provided by the project, the condition of the RPNGC would probably have deteriorated even faster than it has. However, few would disagree with the general conclusion that the results of over fifteen years of institutional strengthening have been disappointing. In terms of overall improvement in police performance, positive outcomes are hard to discern.

Such an assessment is by no means confined to the RPNGC development project. All of the criminal justice agencies have experienced varying degrees of difficulty in absorbing, implementing and sustaining the new ideas and practices promoted through large-scale institutional strengthening projects operating within strict budgetary and contractual timeframes. In addition, the perennial problem of inadequate and poor management of resources facing the principal agencies has served to marginalize 'development objectives until operational priorities, such as payment of wages, utilities, food bills, vehicle and equipment maintenance, are met' (Pitts 2002, 0113).

As outlined in Table 13.1, Australia has supported institutional strengthening activities with most of the principal agencies, including the Attorney General's Department, courts, prisons, the ombudsman and the public legal services.

New security agendas

In mid 2003, there was a significant shift in Australia's strategic thinking and engagement with the Pacific islands region, including Papua New Guinea. This entailed the adoption of a more robust stance with an emphasis on timely and tangible outcomes and a growing insistence on securing 'value for money'. The broader context of these changes was the dramatically changed international security environment following the attacks against the United States on 11 September 2001. Subsequent 'terrorist' attacks closer to home, notably in Indonesia, accentuated the potential security risks posed by struggling states in Australia's immediate neighbourhood.

Table 13.1 Australian Development Assistance to the Law and Justice Sector (up to 2005)

Agency/Scope	Project Title	Duration	Cost ($A million)
Attorney General's Department	Attorney General's Department Institutional Strengthening Project	1999–2003	7.673
Correctional Institutions Services	Correctional Services Development Project	Phase I: 1992–1995 Phase II: 1996–2002	2.100 10.000
Royal Papua New Guinea Constabulary	RPNGC Development Project	Phase I: 1989–1992 Phase II: 1993–1998 Interim: 1999 Phase III: 2000–2005	29.700 79.000 4.000 41.200
Ombudsman Commission	Ombudsman Institutional Strengthening Project	1997–2002	5.950
Sector-wide	Justice Advisory Group (JAG)	2002–2005	4.500
Sector-wide	Law and Justice Sector Program	2003–2008	170.000

Source: AusAID Website, www.ausaid.gov.au

One practical outcome was the progressive securitization of Australian development assistance with a strong emphasis on enhancing the security capabilities of neighbouring states viewed as vulnerable. An effective law and justice system and, in particular, efficient police structures, was seen as a critical bulwark against insecurity and instability. The focus on security has also been accompanied by a shift in modes of delivery, with increasing resort to the direct insertion of Australian personnel, including police officers, into 'inline' positions in institutions being strengthened, rather than the former reliance on advisers working alongside local counterparts. There is also growing emphasis upon a whole-of-government approach to capacity building, with a range of Australian government agencies involved in development assistance work.

This changing approach was manifested in the short-lived Enhanced Cooperation Program (ECP) in Papua New Guinea. The ECP was a bilateral assistance package initially agreed at the Australia-Papua New Guinea Ministerial Forum in Adelaide in December 2003. It involved substantially increased Australian assistance to policing, other law and justice agencies and border management, as well as economic and public sector management. Australian personnel, drawn from the Australian Federal Police (AFP), other state forces, and a number of government agencies, were to be placed into inline positions in the RPNGC and other key Papua New Guinea institutions. The policing component, involving up to 230 Australian police officers, was costed at $A800 million over a five year period and was to be additional to the existing aid program to Papua New Guinea.

The first batch of civilian officials under the ECP was sent to Port Moresby in mid February 2004. However, disagreement between the two governments over conditions of deployment caused lengthy delays in the implementation of the program. Canberra insisted that Australian police and certain other personnel be provided with immunity from prosecution under Papua New Guinea law, while Port Moresby refused to grant blanket immunity. Eventually a compromise was agreed between the two governments. Australian police began arriving in September 2004. Around twenty officers were sent to Bougainville, while others were deployed in stages to Port Moresby. Despite overwhelming public support in PNG for the deployment of Australian police, reservations were expressed by a number of Papua New Guinea leaders. There was also considerable resistance from elements in the RPNGC. In May 2005, Papua New Guinea's Supreme Court delivered its judgement on a constitutional challenge to the immunity provisions under the ECP initiated by Morobe governor and former judge, Luther Wenge. The court ruled unanimously that certain provisions of the enabling legislation, including those dealing with immunity, were unconstitutional (*Papua New Guinea Post-Courier* 19 May 2005). This resulted in the immediate withdrawal of the Australian police personnel although non-police officials deployed under the ECP continued their work. Subsequently, a 'watered down' version of the police component of the ECP commenced implementation in 2006, though, this time, with Australian police advisers rather than inline police officers.

Conclusion

Papua New Guinea has significant law and order problems. Many of these arise from structural factors and processes whose origins lie well beyond the law and justice sector. Responding to them requires policy interventions across a range of government sectors. Law and order is, in other words, a cross-cutting issue demanding the attention of the entire spectrum of social and economic policy areas. Part of the problem in Papua New Guinea has been the often quite unrealistic expectations of the key law and order agencies. International evidence establishes the important limitations of law and order responses, including policing, in the control of crime and disorder. As Bayley (1994, 10) remarks:

> It is generally understood that social conditions outside the control of the police, as well as outside the control of the criminal justice system, determine crime levels in communities.

Ultimately, getting this sector of government to work depends in large part on getting other sectors — notably essential service delivery — working effectively. In addition, the uncritical promotion of conventional deterrence-oriented law enforcement measures detracts from the need to develop appropriate crime and conflict prevention strategies.

Having said that, there is no doubt that the criminal justice system, including the RPNGC, can and should operate much more effectively than it currently does. This requires attention to the particular needs of individual agencies, as well as those of the sector as a whole. It is a major and long-term challenge that, if successful, is likely to consist of incremental improvements rather than any rapid and dramatic transformation. There are no quick-fix solutions. As in many other jurisdictions, policy formulation in this area has regularly been subordinated to the exigencies of immediate responses to crises. There has been a continuous tension between the longer-term perspective needed for capacity-building, policy development and reform, on the one hand, and more pressing short-term law enforcement requirements, on the other. This is where the 'politics of law and order' often serve to accentuate existing problems of lack of capacity. Where progress has occurred, as in recent years, the initiatives have tended to come from law and justice professionals in the relevant agencies, rather than from elected leaders pursuing short-term political agendas. Political leadership is, of course, important and where effective can be a critical factor in progressing reform. It nevertheless remains a two-edged sword.

As we have seen, the law and justice sector is one of the most complicated of government sectors, comprising many different agencies and institutions, each with its own corporate identity, goals and institutional culture. This makes for a particularly challenging policy environment. Given the level of operational interdependency between the various institutional components of the sector, some degree of coordination and cooperation between them is required. The establishment of the NCM in 2003 and gradual adoption of a sector-wide approach are positive developments that should facilitate coordination, though it would be unwise to underestimate the difficulties this presents in practice.

Policing remains a critical challenge in Papua New Guinea and, as documented in the 2004 review, the RPNGC is in urgent need of repair. The fact that the police have been recipients of significant levels of development assistance over many years indicates the enormous difficulties of capacity building in this area. It is neither simple nor something that can be achieved over a short period of time. While it is important to develop new approaches to capacity building, it is equally clear that there is no single or fully adequate strategy. A significant part of the problem with the police, as with other agencies, has been prolonged government neglect and the failure to provide the RPNGC with the resources required to fulfil its duties. Development assistance has traditionally focused on the provision of training and generally shies away from addressing these more fundamental resource issues on the grounds of sustainability (or lack thereof). Such assistance also appears to work most effectively when there is a stable domestic policy environment and where donor and domestic policy objectives coincide. Problems arise when there are significant differences — real or imagined — between the objectives of donors and domestic authorities. This appears to have contributed to the difficulties of the ECP, which was in large part conceived as part of the Australia's own domestic security agenda.

The tensions between local approaches to dispute resolution that prevail in large parts of Papua New Guinea and the state-centred basis of the modern justice system present additional challenges. They also present opportunities and it is important to move beyond seeing these community-based strategies primarily as an obstacle to the consolidation of the rule of law. The arguments put forward by the Clifford Report remain as valid today as they were when originally proposed over twenty years ago. As we have seen, the current law and justice policy reiterates the need to develop more effective linkages between formal and informal sectors and the establishment of the Community Justice Liaison constitutes a modest step towards this end. The relative success of community-based approaches in a variety of different contexts from Bougainville through to urban settlements provides, at the very least, a case for exploring the potential for more innovative and socially attuned approaches to community security and safety in Papua New Guinea. This is not to understate the real difficulties, including human rights abuses, which can attach to community-based strategies. Nor is it proposed as an alternative to building state capacity. As stated at the outset of this chapter, Papua New Guinea's law and order problems reflect weaknesses in the regulatory capacities of both state and local (non-state) institutions. The long-term challenge is to build both and enhance complementarity between them. State justice needs to be rendered more accessible, accountable, and responsive to local needs, while community justice practices need to brought into a human rights regulatory framework. Among other things, the successful mobilization of local cultural resources — at little or no cost to the state — will relieve some of the pressure on the over-burdened and extremely costly formal justice system.

References

Administrative Review Committee. 2004. Royal Papua New Guinea Constabulary. Draft Report. Port Moresby: Administrative Review Committee.

AidWatch. 2005. *Boomerang Aid: Not good enough Minister!* Response to Australian Foreign Minister Downer's comments on Boomerang Aid. AidWatch, June 2005. http://www.aidwatch.org.au/

Alpers, Philip. 2005. *Gun-Running in Papua New Guinea: From Arrows to Assault Weapons in the Southern Highlands*. Special Report. Geneva: Small Arms Survey.

AusAID. 2003. *The Contribution of Australian Aid to Papua New Guinea's Development 1975–2000*. Provisional Conclusions from a Rapid Assessment. Evaluation and Review Series No. 34. Canberra: AusAID.

Bayley, David H. 1994. *Police for the Future*. New York: Oxford University Press.

Biles, David. 1976. *Crime in Papua New Guinea*. Canberra: Australian Institute of Criminology.

Burton, John. 1990. Tribal fighting: the scandal of inaction. *Research in Melanesia* 14: 31–40.

Clifford, William, Louise Morauta and Barry Stuart. 1984. *Law and Order in Papua New Guinea* (Clifford Report). Port Moresby: Institute of National Affairs and Institute of Applied Social and Economic Research.

Department of Provincial Affairs. 1983. *Report of the Committee to Review Policy and Administration on Crime, Law and Order* (Morgan Report). Port Moresby: Department of Provincial Affairs.

Derham, David P. 1960. *Report on the System for the Administration of Justice in the Territory of Papua and New Guinea*. Canberra: Department of Territories.

Dinnen, Sinclair. 1993. Internal Security in Papua New Guinea. *Criminology Australia* 5(2): 2–7.

Dinnen, Sinclair, Ron May and Anthony J. Regan eds. 1997. *Challenging the State: The Sandline Affair in Papua New Guinea*. Canberra: Australian National University, National Centre for Development Studies, Pacific Policy Paper 30; and *Regime Change and Regime Maintenance in Asia and the Pacific*. Discussion Paper 21, Department of Political and Social Change, Australian National University.

Dinnen, Sinclair. 2001. *Law and Order in a Weak State. Crime and Politics in Papua New Guinea*. Honolulu: University of Hawai'i Press.

Dorney, Sean. 1990. *Papua New Guinea: People, Politics and History since 1975*. Sydney: Random House.

Dorney, Sean. 2000. *Papua New Guinea: People, Politics and History since 1975*. Fully revised edition. Sydney: ABC Books.

Haley, Nicole and Robert Muggah. 2006. Jumping the Gun: Armed Violence in Papua New Guinea. In *Small Arms Survey 2006*: *unfinished business*, 164-187. Oxford: Oxford Univesity Press.

Harris, Bruce M. 1988. *The Rise of Rascalism: Action and Reaction in the Evolution of Rascal Gangs*. Discussion Paper 54. Port Moresby: Institute of Applied Social and Economic Research.

Hughes, Helen. 2003. Aid has failed the Pacific. *Issues Analysis* 33. Sydney: Centre for Independent Studies.

Human Rights Watch. 2005. *'Making Their Own Rules'. Police Beatings, Rape, and Torture of Children in Papua New Guinea*. New York: Human Rights Watch. http://www.hrw.org/

Institute of National Affairs (INA). 1991. *Developments in Law and Order*. Working Paper 15. Port Moresby: INA.

Mapusia, Mike. 1986. Police policy towards tribal fighting in the Highlands. In *Law and Order in a Changing Society*, ed. Louise Morauta, Political and Social Change Monograph 6, 57–69. Canberra: Department of Political and Social Change, Australian National University.

Morauta, Louise. 1986. Law and order in Papua New Guinea: a tenth anniversary report. In *Law and Order in a Changing Society*, ed. Louise Morauta, Political and Social Change Monograph 6, 7–19. Canberra: Department of Political and Social Change, Australian National University.

Morauta, Mekere. 2005. The Papua New Guinea-Australia relationship. *Pacific Economic Bulletin* 20(1): 159–161.

Nelson, Hank. 2003. Our great task. *Meanjin* 62(3): 123–143.

Oram, Nigel. 1973. Law and order: maximum participation at all levels. *New Guinea* 8(1): 4–22.

Otto, Ton and Nicholas Thomas, Nicholas eds. 1997. *Narratives of Nation in the South Pacific*. Amsterdam: Harwood Academic Publishers.

Papua New Guinea-Australia Development Cooperation Program. 1993. *Final Report of the Law and Justice Sector Working Group*. Canberra: AusAID.

Papua New Guinea. 1973. *Report of Committee Investigating Tribal Fighting in the Highlands*. Port Moresby: Government Printer.

Papua New Guinea. 1974. *Report of the Peace and Good Order Committee*. Port Moresby: Government Printer.

Papua New Guinea. 1988. *Policy on Law and Order*. Port Moresby: Ministry of Justice.

Papua New Guinea. 1991. *Security for Development: Integrating the Government's Response to the National Summit on Crime into a Comprehensive and Planned Approach to Law and Order*. Port Moresby: Acting Government Printer.

Papua New Guinea. 1993. *National Law and Order Policy*. Port Moresby: National Law, Order and Justice Council.

Papua New Guinea. 2000. *The National Law and Justice Policy and Plan of Action — Toward Restorative Justice 2000–2005*. Port Moresby: Department of National Planning and Monitoring.

Pitts, Maxine. 2002. *Crime, Corruption and Capacity in Papua New Guinea*. Canberra: Asia Pacific Press.

Public Sector Reform Management Unit (PSRMU). 2002. *A Review of the Law and Justice Sector Agencies in Papua New Guinea: Opportunities to Improve Efficiency, Effectiveness, Coordination and Accountability*. Port Moresby: Public Sector Reform Management Unit, Department of Prime Minister and the National Executive Council.

Royal Papua New Guinea Constabulary (RPNGC) Task Force. 1977. *RPNGC Role and Functions. Report One*. Konedobu: Royal Papua New Guinea Constabulary Task Force.

Spencer Report. 1994. National Law and Order Policy and National Law and Order Programme, Stage II 'Implementation'.

Strathern, Marilyn. 1972. Official and Unofficial Courts: Legal Assumptions and Expectations in a Highlands Community. *New Guinea Research Bulletin* 47. Port Moresby: New Guinea Research Unit.

Toft, Susan ed. 1985. *Domestic Violence in Papua New Guinea*. Monograph 3. Port Moresby: Law Reform Commission.

Toft, Susan ed. 1986. *Domestic Violence in Urban Papua New Guinea*. Occasional Paper No.19. Port Moresby: Law Reform Commission.

Wan, Jim. 2000. Overview of AusAID assistance to the Royal Papua New Guinea Constabulary, 1988–1998. In *Australia and Papua New Guinea. Crime and the Bilateral Relationship*, ed. Beno Boeha and John MacFarlane, 106–114. Canberra: Australian Defence Studies, Australian Defence Force Academy.

Endnotes

[1] The estimated population in 2009 stands at over six million people.

[2] Though dated 1983, the report became publicly available in 1984.

[3] The *Inter-Group Fighting Act* of 1977 provided for the establishment of peace and good order committees in each province as the mechanisms for declaring 'fighting zones' under the provisions of the act. In practice, the effectiveness of these committees has varied considerably between different provinces. In some, they meet regularly and play an active role in advising on provincial law and order matters, while in others they have remained largely inactive.

[4] Membership of the NCM comprises the chief justice, police commissioner, commissioner of Correctional Service, chief ombudsman, chief magistrate, attorney general, public solicitor, public prosecutor, and secretary of the National Judicial Staff Service. Further details can be viewed on the Papua New Guinea Law and Justice Sector homepage: http://www.lawandjustice.gov.pg/www/html/7-homepage.asp

Chapter 14

Policy Making in Defence

R. J. May and James Laki

At independence the Papua New Guinea Defence Force (PNGDF), under the command of a Papua New Guinean officer, was widely regarded as one of the best trained and most cohesive institutions of the new state — though defence policy was still largely determined by Australia. The PNGDF's successful intervention in support of the newly independent government of Vanuatu, in the 'Santo rebellion' of 1980, further boosted its image and morale (see Gubb 1994). Over the years — against a background of growing problems of internal security culminating in the Bougainville conflict of 1988–2001, increasing pressures on government resources, occasional tensions between the PNGDF and civil authority, and recurring problems of discipline within the PNGDF — the objectives of defence policy, and the role of the PNGDF, have been reviewed on several occasions. Measuring the effectiveness of defence policy, in the absence of a visible external threat, is always difficult, and Papua New Guinea has enjoyed a relatively benign external security environment. However, the PNGDF has also played a significant role in supporting the Royal Papua New Guinea Constabulary (RPNGC) in internal security operations, where its performance has been more visible. As in other areas of policy, the record of policy making and implementation in defence has been a mixed one, with changing (and sometimes conflicting) objectives, poor follow-through in policy decisions, and a perception, both within the PNGDF and amongst many outsiders, that the resources allocated to defence have been less than adequate and often poorly managed.

This chapter provides a brief overview of the record.[1]

The colonial inheritance

In the decade or so before independence there was some debate as to whether Papua New Guinea needed a defence force, and especially about whether an army, if there were to be one, should have any role other than that of defending the country against external aggression. There were some who supported the idea of a paramilitary force with police and military functions, and some who suggested not only that there should be a defence force but that it be represented in cabinet.[2] Others, seeing Papua New Guinea's emerging military as a 'super tribe', saw it as a potential threat to a post-independence democratic state. In the event, the Constitutional Planning Committee (CPC) proposed that Papua New Guinea have a defence force, but it expressed the view that the defence force should be 'firmly oriented towards external defence' and added:

> ...we have very serious reservations about the possibility of a future Papua New Guinea Government using the army against its own people in any but the most extreme cases of civil disorder, and then subject also to specific conditions (CPC 1974, chapter 13 p.3).

The CPC report provided the basis for the constitutional provisions defining the functions of the PNGDF (see Constitution Ss 201–205). Following the CPC's recommendation that there be 'a dual but integrated structure' in which the minister for defence would be advised 'by senior civilian and military officers of equal status' (CPC 1974, chapter 13 p.4), the constitution recognized the commander, PNGDF as principal military adviser on matters relating to the Force, and an officer of the public service (in practice the secretary of the Defence Department) as the civilian adviser, with powers prescribed by legislation. A *Defence Act* was passed in 1974 and a Department of Defence created the same year. Coordination of defence policy was achieved through the creation of a Defence Council, comprising the minister, Defence secretary, and PNGDF commander. Broader questions of national security policy are referred to a ministerial National Security Council, and a National Security Coordinating Committee.

The Pacific Islands Regiment (PIR), the forerunner of the PNGDF, was created during the Second World War, disbanded in 1946 and re-formed in 1951. It was, however, until 1964, part of the Australian Army's Northern command, with headquarters in Brisbane. In that year PIR headquarters were established in Port Moresby, but Australian officers continued to predominate and orders came from Canberra. A marked expansion of the force took place in the 1960s, in the context of perceived expansionist threats from Indonesia, and a program of localization was commenced. The PIR's first Papua New Guinean officers, Ted Diro and Patterson Lowa, graduated from Officer Cadet School at Portsea in Australia in 1963. In 1973, what had become Joint Force Papua New Guinea was redesignated Papua New Guinea Defence Force (PNGDF), and two years later Brigadier-General Diro became its commander.

Defence policy post-independence

At independence, the underlying assumption of defence policy in Papua New Guinea was that if Papua New Guinea were attacked, the PNGDF's role would be to mount a holding operation until its allies — principally Australia — arrived to assist. There was, however, no formal treaty between the two countries; until 1987 defence relations were covered, in fairly broad terms, in an exchange of letters. In that year defence was included in a Joint Declaration of Principles between the two countries (amended in 1992), but an undertaking to consult in the event of external armed attack still fell short of a firm security commitment by Australia. In the event, the relationship has not been put to the ultimate test.

In 1975 the PNGDF consisted of a Land Element (comprising 1PIR based at Taurama and 2PIR based at Moem), and a Maritime Element (comprising a Patrol Boat Squadron based in Manus and a Landing Craft Squadron based in Port Moresby). An Air Element, based in Lae, was added, and an Engineering Company, established in 1973, was upgraded to battalion status in 1976. With an actual force size of 3614 the PNGDF included 490 Australian officers and men (14 per cent of the Force). By 1979 this number had been reduced to 141 and by 1988 to 30 (most of whom were with the Air Transport Squadron).

It was clear, however, that if defence spending after independence were to be maintained at anything like its pre-independence levels Australian assistance would be required, and this has been provided through the Australian Defence Cooperation Programme (DCP). The DCP has met the salaries of Papua New Guinean personnel training in Australia, and certain mutually agreed projects. An Australian Defence Cooperation Management team, based in Port Moresby, oversees the DCP with Papua New Guinea. In 1991 Australian Defence sources estimated that about 90 per cent of the PNGDF officer corps had trained or studied in Australia. In addition, the two countries carry out joint exercises, and until 1999 the Australian Army maintained a civil engineer works unit in Papua New Guinea (based in the Southern Highlands).

In 1985 incoming PNGDF commander Tony Huai called for a diversification of Papua New Guinea's defence relations. As well as agreements with New Zealand and the US, Papua New Guinea has established military ties with Indonesia, Malaysia, Singapore, China and Fiji, and has purchased military aircraft from Israel and Spain.

Writing in the same year, former PNGDF chief of staff Colonel Colin East criticized what he saw as Australia's failure in 1975 to do other than undertake 'cosmetic surgery to the existing Australian service components' of the PNGDF. 'The result', he argued:

> ...is the present PNGDF, its individual elements meaningful in the framework of the Australian Defence Force of a decade ago, tailored in the Australian military tradition and reflecting that approach. As a separate force, it is militarily unbalanced, expensive and non-viable (East 1985, 11).

Notwithstanding this, the basic structure of the PNGDF underwent little change until the 1990s. The Defence Department initiated a review of the PNGDF in 1978, and subsequently received assistance under the DCP to carry out specialist studies of the Maritime and Air Transport elements and of Special Forces. A report, completed in 1982, provided the basis for the government's first post-independence defence policy statement. This endorsed the PNGDF's 'prime role in defending the nation' (*Defence Report* 1982, 1) and placed emphasis on its greater participation in national development, and on the increased importance both of maritime surveillance and of patrolling the border with Indonesia.

Following this, a review of defence policy was carried out by a ministerial committee. Its 1983 report resulted in a decision to undertake several policy changes, namely: to shift the patrol boat base from Manus to Port Moresby (a decision reversed the following year) and the Air Transport Squadron from Lae to Nadzab (see below); to establish a forward infantry company base near the Indonesian border at Kiunga and upgrade the Vanimo outstation; to relocate the Engineer Battalion from Port Moresby to Lae; to form a special forces unit to be located at Nadzab; to undertake a long-term re-equipment program, including the purchase of helicopters; and, for budgetary reasons, to reduce the force strength ceiling to 3050.

The National Executive Council (NEC) also endorsed a list of six PNGDF 'priority functions', based on the 1982 policy statement. This placed security against external threat, securing the nation's borders, and maritime surveillance as the top priorities, and assistance to the police when required in maintaining internal security at the bottom. In fact, few of the decisions were implemented at the time, though steps were taken — in the face of opposition within the defence establishment — to reduce force size.

From as early as 1977–78 there were complaints about inadequate force size and structural deficiencies in the PNGDF, specifically the under-manning of infantry battalions, lack of adequate reserves of materiel, and inadequate mobility, especially with regard to air transport (see *Defence Report* 1977–78). Such complaints were repeated in subsequent years. In 1981 the assistant secretary, Finance and Programming Branch commented that, with limited manpower and deteriorating equipment capability, there was no way the Defence Force could effectively meet any serious contingency (*Defence Report* 1980–81, 4). Four years later, Colin East observed that the 'acute shortage of funds over recent years' had resulted in a major reduction in patrolling and training of soldiers, restrictions on flying time and naval operations, and obsolescence of vehicles, weapons and equipment, all of which had impacted on morale and leadership (East 1985, 4). In 1984 a defence manpower review had revealed a wastage rate among officers of 7.7 per cent and among other ranks of 15.8 per cent (*Defence Report* 1984–85, 44). The following year it was reported that discipline in the force was 'below the required standard' (*ibid.* 39).

Less than a year after independence, in 1984, the PNGDF was called out to support the civil authority, during a state of emergency declared in response to rising criminal activity in Port Moresby. This was followed by several other deployments to assist police in law and order operations in the national capital and in the highlands and other provinces (see May 1993).

In 1985 Prime Minister Somare promised an increase in defence spending, but his government lost office soon after. Two years later the new Defence minister, former PNGDF officer James Pokasui, sought to increase force strength to 5000, improve salaries, initiate a review of military equipment, and deploy PNGDF troops overseas; but before these proposals had passed through cabinet there was a further change of government. In 1988 the *Defence Report* noted that most operational units were 70 per cent below strength and that the PNGDF was having difficulty retaining specialists.

That year, however, the government produced a *Defence Policy Paper* which contained proposals for a ten-year program to replace major equipment, reorganize force structure to emphasize operational mobility, enhance capabilities in several areas, and generally make Papua New Guinea more self-reliant in defence matters. Cabinet approval for the PNGDF's Ten-Year Development Plan did not come until late 1991, after the government had undertaken a review of internal security. However, several policy changes were initiated in 1988–89, against the background of the emerging Bougainville conflict. These included decisions to increase force strength to 5200 by 1995, and to proceed with plans (approved in 1985) for the development of a reserve force. It was further announced in 1991 that a military base was to be established, for a proposed engineer and infantry unit, in the highlands at Banz, and that from 1992 women would be recruited into the PNGDF.

In 1989 PNGDF troops were deployed to Bougainville to assist police in what was initially seen as a law and order problem. The 'Bougainville crisis' quickly escalated into an armed rebellion which continued up till a ceasefire in 1998 and a Bougainville Peace Agreement in 2001. The PNGDF did not come out well from the Bougainville conflict: while some blamed the government for indecision in its dealings with the Bougainville rebels and the PNGDF, it became clear that the PNGDF lacked the resources, strategy and training to conduct a successful guerilla campaign in unfamiliar territory (see, for example Liria 1993; Rogers 2003). Frustrated by their inability to contain the rebellion, and resentful of what they saw as lack of commitment on the part of the government, elements of the PNGDF became involved in human rights abuses and acts of defiance against the civilian authority. The PNGDF also made several incursions into Solomon Islands' territory in pursuit of the Bougainville Revolutionary Army and its supporters, creating tensions between the two countries.[3]

In 1991 the Defence minister told a PNGDF passing-out parade that 'the real future of our Defence Force is to assist the civil authority deal effectively with (internal) threats'. Following a review of the Australian DCP it was announced that Australia would give highest priority to internal security needs.

Between 1988 and 1992, the appropriation for Defence rose from K33.4 million to K56.5 million, and its percentage of total government spending from 3.7 to 4.5. However, from 1987 actual spending on Defence substantially exceeded budget estimates: by 1991 Defence spending had risen to K92.0 million, 81 per cent above the appropriation for Defence. The Defence Department justified this by arguing that its budgetary allocation was inadequate, especially in view of the cost of the Bougainville operation, and that in the restoration of government services in Bougainville, Defence had had to meet costs which should properly have been met by other departments (such as Health, Public Works, and Provincial Affairs). By 1993 this had become a source of tension in civil-military relations.

Notwithstanding the increase in Defence spending, from at least 1990 there were complaints from local suppliers that PNGDF bills were not being paid. In August-September 1993 the PNGDF was said to be owing more than K3 million to businesses in Rabaul (*The Times of PNG* 12 August 1993) and naval and air craft could not be used because of lack of funds (*Sydney Morning Herald* 14, 15 September 1993). In Port Moresby, soldiers returning from Bougainville attacked the pay office when they did not receive due pay and allowances; at this stage unpaid special allowances and compensation payments were said to total K4.8 million.

In presenting the 1993 budget the minister for Finance announced new strategies in the law and order sector, which included a 'scaling down' of the PNGDF. In future the PNGDF was to be 'more involved in civic action, more involved with the village and community, more coordinated with other agencies in both the law and order and other sectors, and better disciplined' (1993 Budget Documents, vol.I, 122). This was to be achieved through an expansion of the civic action program (CAP) and a shift in training to engineering, construction, infrastructural development and community relations. The shift to civic action was to be accompanied by a reduction in force strength, through attrition, from the current level (4200) to 2500–3000; most of these would perform CAP activities at the village level, but a core group of 1000–1500 would 'receive specialized combat training to prepare them to effectively counter any major internal threat' (*ibid.*).

Thus, in 1993 there were two contradictory policy positions on defence: one, embodied in the Ten-year Development Plan, foresaw an expanded and re-equipped defence force, oriented primarily towards external defence; the other envisioned a reduced force, geared primarily towards civic action. Both policies had been endorsed by cabinet, and no one seemed to be concerned about their incompatibility. In practice, the contradiction was alleviated by the fact that little attempt was made to implement either policy.

Two years later, in March 1995, Australian defence experts Paul Dibb and Rhondda Nicholas[4] were commissioned by then Defence minister, Mathais Ijape to prepare a report on the future role and structure of the PNGDF. The report was to serve as an input to a policy review. The Dibb Report (as their report became known) was submitted towards the end of 1955. [5] It recommended changes to the structure and organization of the Defence Force 'to reflect more accurately Papua New Guinea's strategic outlook'.

Dibb and Nicholas foresaw no external threat but argued that Papua New Guinea needed to demonstrate that it could manage to protect its territorial integrity against any low-level incursions which might occur in the future. They also argued for close attention to the PNGDF's contribution to internal security and national development tasks, which they saw as 'the most serious and credible challenges to Papua New Guinea's future stability'. To meet the tasks of protecting territorial integrity and resources, assisting with internal security, and performing civic action tasks, the Dibb Report argued, the PNGDF required a geographical presence 'in those key areas of the country where security problems are likely to arise', improved training, communications and surveillance equipment and intelligence, and greater involvement with the community (Dibb and Nicholas 1996, 1–2). Restructuring was recommended to provide a smaller, more balanced, and operationally more effective force. Specifically, Dibb and Nicholas recommended an immediate reduction in force size, from 4375 to around 3100 (to be achieved by retrenching some 1260 personnel on the reserve short list/unallotted list), at a saving of some K12 million per year; recruitment of additional infantry and pioneers/engineers, over five years, however, would bring force size back to around 3700. The effect of restructuring would be to reduce the proportion of the Defence budget spent on personnel from 68 per cent in 1994 to around 50 per cent over five years, and to substantially increase spending on operational costs and equipment and facilities. Recommended contracting out to the private sector of maintenance of aircraft, patrol boats and vehicles, and support services such as catering, security, stores and clerical support, as well as sharing some support facilities with the Royal Papua New Guinea Constabulary (RPNGC), was seen as a further source of saving. For the longer term, once restructuring was completed and the recommended savings achieved, the government should consider a third infantry battalion, to augment the Force's capabilities for border patrolling, resource protection, internal security operations, and civic action, with a corresponding increase in Defence spending (to K70 million per year).

The Dibb Report was not received with great enthusiasm either within the PNGDF or by the government, but it provided a basis for a new Defence White Paper, Defence in National Development, which was accepted by the National Parliament in 1996. Brigadier General Singirok, who became PNGDF commander in 1995, had a substantial hand in the drafting of the White Paper. In a preface,

Defence Minister Ijape said: 'While the fundamental functions of the defence of PNG remain unchanged, emphasis is now being placed on the role that Defence must play in nation building and development' (Defence White Paper 1996, 1).

Echoing the Dibb Report, the White Paper asserted that strategic assessments indicated no identifiable external threat. Notwithstanding the benign external security environment, however, the White Paper acknowledged Papua New Guinea's vulnerability to 'low level incursions', including air and maritime space intrusion, illicit activities such as arms smuggling and drug trafficking, terrorist acts and piracy, and exploitation of the country's EEZ by illegal foreign fishing vessels (*ibid.* 7–10). The last of these had become a significant problem, particularly in the 'Dogleg' area in the Papuan Gulf. A more serious concern for Papua New Guinea's security planners, however, was seen as arising from within:

> Internal security is a major concern with increased law and order problems in the urban areas and the escalation of the land compensation disputes....Our country's politics is unpredictable and Parliamentary groupings have been loose. Personalities and political and regional groupings have given rise to a high rate of votes of no confidence. Ethnic aspirations based on regionalism and the push for greater autonomy have the potential to become the source for wider and serious internal security concerns....Future uncontrolled ethnic and secessionist movements will be very costly as protagonists would be better prepared and armed than is the case now (*ibid.* 9–10).

Spelling out the defence management implications of this analysis, the White Paper concluded that what the PNGDF needed was 'a small balanced response force' that was rapidly deployable, operationally mobile, and versatile, with improved surveillance and intelligence capability (*ibid.* 10–12).

The principal elements of the proposed new defence strategy, which was given the title 'Banis Strategy' (perimeter defence strategy), were fourfold.

First, it argued for a rationalization of the existing force structure, to achieve a small, balanced, responsive force with appropriate guerilla and conventional warfare skills, adaptable to the country's internal security needs.

Secondly, it supported diversification of Papua New Guinea's defence relations and military sources of assistance. It acknowledged Australia's 'generous assistance' through the DCP, but endorsed the recommendation of a 1994 Defence Co-operation Evaluation for DCP in Papua New Guinea for a shift in policy 'from one which is predetermined by Australia's DCP priorities in PNG, to one determined by those priorities that are consistent with Papua New Guinea's Defence Policy'. It supported the idea of PNGDF participation in UN peacekeeping operations, recommended formal defence and security arrangements with neighbouring South Pacific countries, and supported the formation of a regional peacekeeping force. It also supported joint intelligence arrangements, joint exercises, and bilateral security operations, while noting (with specific mention of the Joint Declaration of Principles with Australia) that such arrangements did not offer a 'total security guarantee'.

Thirdly, the White Paper recommended decentralization of Defence Force establishments — engineer, infantry, air and maritime — to the country's four administrative regions. As part of this it proposed improved capability of the engineer battalion and the construction of four engineer bases, at Banz, Madang, Port Moresby and Kimbe. It also proposed that under a Defence Civic Action Program the PNGDF should assist provincial works programs and participate in public tendering (*ibid*. 22). Other measures included improved capability of the medical platoon and the creation of a mobile field hospital (which could assist communities in remote areas), improved capacity to assist in emergency and disaster relief operations, and improved national surveillance capability.

Fourthly, having identified internal security and law and order as the country's 'credible threats' to peace, stability, and socio-economic prosperity, the White paper stated that, 'defence's priorities should be directed at internal security responsibilities through closer co-operation between the Papua New Guinea Defence Force and the Royal Papua New Guinea Constabulary' at all levels, including joint internal security operations, joint intelligence, and joint training (within a joint internal security operational doctrine). Noting that the government had 'directed the establishment of a para-military force (the Rapid Deployment Unit (RDU)) whose basic function is to maintain law and order and internal security', it called for the formation of a third battalion, within the existing manpower ceiling, and for the RDU to be made part of the proposed third battalion, which would be based at the Goldie River training establishment.

As part of its guidelines for defence policy development, the White Paper further endorsed the principle that 'Defence must become a major participant in nation-building and development', though it should move away from 'the traditional civic action concept to a more constructive approach with new commitments' (*ibid*. 15). (In fact there had been virtually no civic action program since 1988.)

The following year the Papua New Guinea and Australian governments signed a New Defence Partnership, which placed emphasis on improved management and strategic planning, capacity building and rehabilitation of infrastructure.

The 1996 White Paper generated expectations of some restructuring and improvements in defence capability, equipment and training. Once again, however, policy recommendations were overtaken by events. In March 1997, in the celebrated 'Sandline Affair',[6] the PNGDF commander, Brigadier General Singirok denounced a secret government contract with 'military consultants' Sandline International, aimed at ending the Bougainville conflict, detained and subsequently deported Sandline personnel, and called on the prime minister, deputy prime minister and defence minister to resign. Prime Minister Chan accused Singirok of 'gross insubordination bordering on treason', and dismissed him. In the ensuing national elections Chan lost his seat and there was a change of government.

While Singirok's actions in the Sandline Affair received widespread popular support, they exacerbated existing factional tensions within the PNGDF. Specifically, there was resentment of the role played in the affair by the Special Forces Unit which had been set up by Singirok following the recommendations of the 1996 White Paper, but which was disbanded by Singirok's successor General Nuia and replaced by a Special Operations Group chosen by Nuia. There were also divisions along regional lines, particularly between soldiers from the Momase Region, who had supported Singirok, and those from the Islands Region.

Singirok was later reinstated by the new prime minister, Bill Skate, and in late 1998 it was announced that the PNGDF would undergo 'a change of culture', with greater emphasis on civic action, and that in accordance with the recommendations of the White Paper a new PNGDF engineers base was to be established in the Western Highlands.

Apart from that, little progress had been made toward the implementation of the 1996 White Paper before the Skate government announced that it was to review the PNGDF's priorities. This review resulted in the publication in 1999 of a new PNGDF white paper, titled *Service to Others*, which replaced that of 1996. Although it did not represent a radical departure from the previous policy, the 1999 white paper argued that the defense force should de-emphasize its internal security role and focus its efforts on the three other roles laid down in the constitution: defending sovereignty and national interests, contributing to regional and collective security, and nation building and development.

In 1997 98 the PNGDF had played an important role, with Australian army support, in delivering emergency supplies to rural communities affected by a major drought and frost which impacted heavily on food gardens in the highlands (see chapter 16).

The shift in emphasis in the 1999 White Paper reflected events in Indonesia, where, following the demise of President Suharto, East Timor voted for independence and separatist tendencies in West Papua gathered strength, fuelling concerns about further instability along the border with Indonesia. In a departure from its earlier policy position, in 1999 the PNGDF offered to take part in coordinated operations with the Indonesian army, following a hostage-taking incident attributed to the OPM (though this policy change does not appear to have been pursued).

As part of its commitment to nation building and development, the defense force finally began work on a Regional Construction Engineers base in the Western Highlands, with plans to establish two more such bases in Madang and West New Britain. Other priority areas included improved maritime capacity (with proposals to acquire two additional patrol boats and an operations support ship); strengthening of the air element (including fixed and rotary wing aircraft to provide air transport, medical evacuation, search and rescue, surveillance, and minimal capability for close air support for ground troops and maritime interdiction); and the creation of a third army battalion 'to strengthen the PNGDF's overall capacity to maintain a credible operational land force'. The new white paper endorsed the 1996 recommendations for a smaller, more mobile and capable force, and for improved intelligence. It also proposed the reactivation of the PNG Volunteer Rifles as a reserve force capable of assisting in law and order and internal security operations, and the reintroduction of a school cadet scheme. Following another recommendation, the PNGDF recruited its first women soldiers in 1999. The 1999 white paper envisaged a reduction in PNGDF force size by about 18 per cent to 4309, with an additional reserve force of 112. At the end of 1999, however, force size stood at 4500, a reduction of only 100 from the previous year.

Also in 1999, a publication, Foundations of Maritime Doctrine, set out the basis for the PNGDF's maritime operations, focusing on illegal fishing, drug and arms trafficking, and people smuggling. It was also announced that Papua New Guinea's surveillance capacity was to be enhanced by the construction of a satellite earth station network supported by the Defence Force National Surveillance Organization and the National Fisheries Authority (NFA). (In 2002 a memorandum of agreement between the PNGDF and the NFA formalized arrangements for regular patrols by the PNGDF Maritime Element throughout Papua New Guinea's EEZ, with the NFA contributing to the cost of operations.)

In July 1999 the Skate government lost office. The incoming government of Sir Mekere Morauta suspended General Singirok (and appointed as acting commander one of several senior officers who had been retired by Singirok in 1998); however it supported initiatives to strengthen the capability of the PNGDF and address problems of discipline and morale. Nevertheless, problems remained. In September 1999 troops on Bougainville threatened to withdraw in protest against poor food (due largely to non-payment of local suppliers) and non-payment of salaries and allowances. In early 2000 soldiers staged a protest outside the Department of Defence, demanding a 100 per cent pay rise (they eventually received 5 per cent). Then in September, as celebrations of Papua New Guinea's twenty-five years of independence were under way, soldiers at the Second Pacific Islands Regiment's Moem Barracks went on a rampage, burning down the regimental headquarters and officers' mess and causing visiting Papua New Guinean and Indonesian dignitaries to flee. The following week PNGDF personnel were involved in another incident, in which about 100 soldiers marched on the Port Moresby General Hospital to retrieve the body of a colleague shot dead by police following an armed holdup. Rocks were thrown and a police vehicle set alight in suburban Port Moresby, and rumours that soldiers were about to march on the National Parliament forced the parliament to postpone its session.

In the aftermath of this, a parliamentary Ministerial Task Force on Defence, headed by Defence Minister Muki Taranupi, reported on the status of the PNGDF. Introducing the report to parliament in October, Prime Minister Morauta spoke of a 'culture of instability' in the PNGDF and commented: 'the PNGDF and the Defence Department cannot provide the protection that the people of Papua New Guinea need'; if hostilities or a national emergency occurred, 'a credible force could not be mobilised in less than 30 days'. The institutional breakdown of the Force, he said, was a result of years of neglect and mismanagement. The report itself argued that the basic needs of Defence members were not being met, that basic management structures and systems were not appropriate or not working, and that critical issues relating to the mission and purpose, capacity, resourcing and structure of the Force needed to be examined by government. The prime minister foreshadowed a 'radical overhaul' of the PNGDF and said he would ask the Commonwealth Secretary-General for assistance in this. The government would consider the possibility of creating a coast-guard-type air and maritime service and a highly mobile specialist unit, 'the latter possibly as part of the police'. There was also talk of reducing force size from 4200 to around 3000 at the end of 2000 and 1500 by mid 2001. Following talks with the Australian government, it was announced that Australia would increase its support for the PNGDF under the DCP, from $A8 million to $A25 million, and would provide up to thirty defence advisers. The bulk of the financial assistance was to be a once-off payment to enable the PNGDF to pay entitlements owed to soldiers and meet other outstanding debts, and to cover the costs of downsizing.

In November 2000 a Commonwealth Eminent Persons Group (EPG), headed by a former New Zealand secretary of defence, arrived in Port Moresby to undertake yet another review of the PNGDF. Its report was presented to the government in January 2001. The EPG report made a number of observations about structural imbalance, maintenance and supply deficiencies, financial and personnel management, and discipline. One of its key recommendations, however, was a dramatic reduction in force size, from the current 4150 to 1900 within six months, through a Voluntary Release Scheme. While the recommendation of a cut in force size was not new, PNGDF personnel were not adequately consulted about the EPG recommendations and after the report had been accepted by cabinet in March, rumors of imminent downsizing generated anger amongst the troops. Within PNGDF HQ at Murray Barracks, where there was already a large number of soldiers who had been made redundant but were still awaiting redundancy payments, a group of soldiers called on the government to resign, and there were reports of soldiers breaking into the armory. The soldiers also called for the removal of Australian military advisers, a reaction to the Australian government's offer to underwrite the cost of the PNGDF downsizing. In the event, the dispute was resolved fairly quickly, but only by the government's agreement to rescind the cabinet decision to reduce force size (though in fact force numbers continued to decline).

Following the incidents at Murray Barracks, yet another review of the PNGDF was completed in mid 2001. This review, conducted within the Department of Defence and entitled Defence Organisational Restructure 2001, largely endorsed earlier proposals for restructuring of the PNGDF to achieve a small, balanced, mobile and effective force, and a decentralized operational command structure. Under the proposed arrangements, an elite rapid response Joint Task Force headquarters was to be set up, headed by a second brigadier general, to command forces in operations and conduct low-level operations, but without its own force. The review also recommended that defense policy and resource control roles be separated from PNGDF HQ, and supported earlier calls for a reduction in force size, from 3340 (at June 2001) to 2000 over three years, but building back up to 2500 over ten years. This downsizing would fall most heavily on the land element. It was subsequently announced that certain financial powers had been decentralized down to unit commanders.

Soldiers' grievances again came to the fore in the latter part of 2001. Soldiers claimed that while retrenched soldiers were still awaiting funding for their repatriation, and serving soldiers had not received outstanding allowances and leave fares, money had been lost through financial mismanagement and fraudulent deals involving Defence Department officials. In representations to newly-appointed Defence Secretary John Vulupindi, the soldiers demanded a commission of inquiry into the affairs of the PNGDF and the Department of Defence. Vulupindi, who had been highly critical of management within the PNGDF and the Defence Department, was himself replaced as Defence secretary. This was the sixth change in Defence secretary since 1997; in the same period there had been six changes of commander (substantive or acting) and seven different ministers of Defence.

Subsequent to this, Prime Minister Morauta announced that his government had allocated an additional K35 million in 2001 to help meet the costs of Phase One of the PNGDF rebuilding program. Most of this amount was to be spent on redundancy payments and other outstanding entitlements due to PNGDF personnel. The new initiatives identified in the 1999 White Paper appeared to have been shelved.

Problems persisted. In early 2002, mutinous soldiers and retrenched personnel took control of Moem Barracks in Wewak, burning down buildings, raiding the armoury, and chasing some officers and their families out of the compound. In a 13-point petition presented to then opposition leader Sir Michael Somare (a resident of Wewak) the soldiers listed, as well as industrial demands, calls for the resignation of the prime minister and of the commander PNGDF, and several other political demands, including a halt to the privatization of government assets and proposed land mobilization. After negotiations between the soldiers and a PNGDF crisis team failed to resolve the dispute, the Barracks was retaken in a military operation and around thirty soldiers arrested. In a sequel to this, the Wewak courthouse was burned down just before the soldiers' scheduled trial.

In the lead-up to the 2002 national elections, a new Defence minister was appointed and changes in senior PNGDF positions were announced, but deferred after a legal challenge. A Defence Intelligence report to the PNGDF commander, Commodore Peter Ilau (a naval officer who had been appointed in October 2001), suggested that this reshuffling was 'election-related' and evidence of a plot to halt the retrenchment exercise and change the current command structure. Amid allegations that the PNGDF was being subjected to 'outside (political]) influences', it was decided that the PNGDF would not be used in routine operations to assist police in providing security during the 2002 elections. (In 1997 troops had been so used, but some soldiers had been accused of acting in a partisan way, and several had been arrested.) Subsequently it was reported that some soldiers, as well as the civilian Defence secretary, had taken part in the election campaign, and several were later charged with electoral offences. Notwithstanding this, troops were deployed in the Southern Highlands in 2003 during new elections in six electorates where polling had been declared void in 2002, and later assisted police during a state of emergency in that province aimed at restoring law and order and enforcing a surrender of weapons in civilian hands.

The September 11, 2001 attacks on New York and Washington had little impact on Papua New Guinea's perceptions of external security threats but following the Bali bombings of 2002 the foreign minister, Sir Rabbie Namaliu, called for an urgent review of Papua New Guinea's preparedness to deal with a terrorist attack and of its internal security and intelligence gathering resources. From around 2002 some stability seems to have returned to the PNGDF, and restructuring has been under way, with force size down to about 2000 by the end of 2003 and some new recruitment commencing, and an increased budgetary allocation for defence.

In recent years there has been support for the idea of PNGDF troops participating in UN peacekeeping operations. In 2002 the then Defence minister dismissed the idea, saying that Papua New Guinea lacked the resources, but the idea persists. Meanwhile some ninety PNGDF infantry and engineers took part in the Regional Assistance Mission to the Solomon Islands (RAMSI) in 2003 —

PNGDF's first overseas engagement since its successful operation in Vanuatu in 1980 — and a smaller PNGDF presence (a platoon once every twelve months on a four-month rotation with Fiji and Vanuatu) has been maintained.

In 2005 the PNGDF produced a publication, Foundations of Papua New Guinea Military Doctrine, setting out its 'philosophical approach to the conduct of military operations', ostensibly based on the security objectives identified in the 1999 White Paper but implying some further shifts in priorities. The first security objective was identified as the defence of Papua New Guinea territory and interests from direct threat; the others were stated as contributing to regional security, supporting global interests, and peacetime national tasks. The overall approach was elaborated in the opening chapter:

> The PNGDF has traditionally trained for limited conventional operations, and must continue to do so. The PNGDF must be flexible enough to meet the challenges of international efforts to counter asymmetric threats, assist in containing the fallout from intra-state warfare and support efforts to counter transnational criminal activities. This can only be achieved in an environment where the PNGDF develop conventional niche capabilities in support of mid to higher end coalition operations or peace support operations ...

The PNGDF achieves this by developing an affordable and fit for purpose force that has multiple-roles, and capabilities. The PNGDF applies this force by taking the 'Banis Strategy' of home defence and developing it into manageable niche capabilities (PNGDF 2005, 1-2–1-3).[7]

The appropriate 'military response operations' (MROs) were listed, in order, as: surveillance; border security; force security operations; coalition operations, and civil military cooperation.

The emphasis on surveillance and border security reflected longstanding but increasing concerns about illegal fishing, people smuggling, and securing the border with Indonesia. During the Bougainville conflict patrolling of the border with Indonesia virtually ceased, though incidents continued to occur along the border. In September 2004 the PNGDF was deployed to the border following reports that members of the Organisasi Papua Merdeka (OPM) had attacked a Papua New Guinea citizen, and that people from across the border were poaching in Papua New Guinea. The PNGDF border post at Kiunga in Western Province (closed in 1998) was re-established during 2004 in a move to strengthen surveillance of the border.

Taking up the idea of participating in overseas peacekeeping operations, the Foundations of Papua New Guinea Military Doctrine went on to say:

> It is unlikely that future major operational deployments by the PNGDF will be unilateral in nature, but rather a part of a coalition or major UN

peace support operation. These factors form the basis that (sic) the PNGDF doctrine and policy that will guide the development of higher level doctrine within the force (*ibid.* 1–4).

Although civil-military cooperation was listed last amongst the MROs, continuous reference was made to the PNGDF's role in nation building. Apart from its deployment to assist the RPNGC in the Southern Highlands by-elections in 2003, a significant new initiative was the decision, in 2005, that, as part of 'Operation Green Revolution', PNGDF aircraft would be used to assist remote communities transport coffee and other agricultural produce to markets (though in 2006 there were complaints that little had been done to implement this policy).

By 2006, the downsizing of the PNGDF had been largely accomplished, measures had been introduced to strengthen command and control and management systems, and the Australian government had promised further support for the PNGDF, with some thirty projects, including assistance in the building of offices and housing, providing improved weapons control, strengthening of the air transport wing, and support for the PNGDF deployment to Solomon Islands. However, reports of the disappearance of a small number of weapons from a warehouse at Murray Barracks and the disclosure that outside contractors had received substantial unauthorized payments, suggested that some problems of capacity and management remained.

Conclusion

At independence, the retiring Australian colonial government left Papua New Guinea with a defence establishment it was unlikely to be able to maintain, even with assistance through the DCP. The fact that Papua New Guinea did not face a significant external threat made it even more likely that these high standards would not be kept up. Even before the Bougainville crisis, the PNGDF had become substantially involved in internal security (that is, law and order) operations in support of the civil authority — though many in the defence establishment did not welcome this involvement, and there was early evidence of emerging problems of morale and discipline. The PNGDF's inability to contain the conflict on Bougainville after 1989 highlighted weaknesses in defence planning and capacity, problems of troop discipline and morale, and tensions in relations between elements of the military and civil authorities.

These problems have been recognized and partially addressed in a series of defence reviews, which, since the late 1980s, have recommended changes in force structure to achieve a smaller, more mobile and highly trained force and more involvement in civic action. What stands out from this account, however, is that the frequency of reviews and recommendations has not been matched by action (indeed, setting up another review seems, in several instances, to have been an alternative to taking unpopular or unaffordable action). Few of the recommendations of successive reviews and enquiries have been fully implemented. For example, the downsizing of force strength, first mooted in 1993, had not been fully achieved in 2006, despite Australian assistance in covering the cost of the exercise; the proposed engineers base in the highlands, announced in 1991 and said to be under construction in 1999, has yet to be realized; and plans for a third battalion, around since at least 1996, remain unfulfilled. The high turnover of PNGDF commanders, Defence secretaries and Defence ministers throughout the 1980s and 1990s undoubtedly contributed to weak policy commitment. Meanwhile ageing assets and facilities have not been adequately maintained, and there was substantial damage to the Wewak barracks during the riots of 2001 and 2002. There has been no published report for the Department of Defence since 1994, and there are recurring allegations of financial mismanagement.

As against this, the military coup predicted by many observers at the time of independence has never occurred, and there seems to have been greater stability and consolidation in the Force since the early 2000s. PNGDF personnel have performed creditably in joint exercises with the Australian and other defence forces and as part of the RAMSI contingent in Solomon Islands. It remains to be seen whether this will provide a basis for a new direction in defence operations (though one suggested as early as 1985 following the success of the PNGDF intervention in Vanuatu), namely deployment of the PNGDF in international peacekeeping operations.

References

Claxton, Karl. 1998. Bougainville. 1988–98. *Five Searches for Security in the North Solomons Province of Papua New Guinea*. Canberra Papers on Strategy and Defence No.130. Canberra: Strategic and Defence Studies Centre, Research School of Pacific Studies, Australian National University.

Constitutional Planning Committee (CPC). 1974. *Final Report*. Port Moresby.

Defence Board of Enquiry, Papua New Guinea. 2007. Report Prepared by Chairman and Commissioner Honourable Justice Gibbs Salika, CSM, OBE, Supreme Court Judge of Papua New Guinea, General (retired) Anthony Huai, CBE, Deputy Chairman and Commissioner, and Mr Daniel Liosi, Commissioner. 13 December 2006–16 March 2007.

Dibb, Paul and Rhondda Nicholas. 1996. *Restructuring the Papua New Guinea Defence Force. Strategic Analysis and Force Structure Principles for a Small State*. Canberra: Strategic and Defence Studies Centre, Research School of Pacific Studies, Australian National University.

Dinnen, Sinclair, Ron May and Anthony J. Regan eds. 1997. *Challenging the State: the Sandline Affair in Papua New Guinea*. Canberra: National Centre for Development Studies and Department of Political and Social Change,

Research School of Pacific and Asian Studies, Australian National University.

Dorney, Sean. 1998. *The Sandline Affair: Politics and Mercenaries and the Bougainville Crisis*. Sydney: ABC Books.

East, Colin. 1985. PNGDF: colonial legacy, or independent force? *Pacific Defence Reporter* 12(5): 11–13, 60.

Gubb, Matthew. 1994. *Vanuatu's 1980 Santo Rebellion. International Responses to a Microstate Security Crisis*. Canberra Papers on Strategy and Defence No.107. Canberra Strategic and Defence Studies Centre, Research School of Pacific and Asian Studies, The Australian National University.

Laki, James. 2000a. Challenges for a 'new look' Defence Force, Internal challenges for the Defence Force, and Civil military relations: what are the lessons to be learned? In *Issues and Trends in National Development*, ed. Beno Boeha and James Robins. Searchlight on Papua New Guinea. January-June 2000, Vol.1, 57–66. Port Moresby: The National Research Institute.

Laki, James. 2000b. Streamlining the Defence Force, Defence relations: Australia and Papua New Guinea and New look defence: an independent perspective. In *Issues and Trends in National Development*, ed. Beno Boeha and James Robins. Searchlight on Papua New Guinea. July-December 2000, Vol.2, 67–68. Port Moresby: The National Research Institute.

Liria, Y. A. 1993. *Bougainville Campaign Diary*. Melbourne: Indra Publishing.

May, R. J. 1993. *The Changing Role of the Military in Papua New Guinea*. Canberra Papers on Strategy and Defence No.101. Canberra: Strategic and Defence Studies Centre, Research School of Pacific Studies, Australian National University.

May, R. J. 2001/2004. *State and Society in Papua New Guinea. The First Twenty-Five Years*. Adelaide: Crawford House Publishing, reprinted by ANU E Press, Canberra.

May, R. J. and Matthew Spriggs eds. 1990. *The Bougainville Crisis*. Bathurst: Crawford House Press.

O'Callaghan, M-L. 1999. *Enemies Within: Papua New Guinea, Australia, and the Sandline Crisis: the Inside Story*. Sydney: Doubleday.

Papua New Guinea Defence Force (PNGDF). 2005. *Foundations of Papua New Guinea Military Doctrine*. DDP 0.0. Port Moresby: Corporate Express.

Rogers, Trevor. 2003. The Papua New Guinea Defence Force. Vanuatu (1980) to Bougainville (1990). Unpublished PhD thesis, Australian National University.

Spriggs, Matthew and Denoon Donald eds. 1992. *The Bougainville Crisis. 1991 Update.* Bathurst: Department of Political and Social Change, Research School of Pacific and Asian Studies, Australian National University in association with Crawford House Press.

Endnotes

[1] For more detail see May (1993; 2001/2004, chapters 10,11), Dorney (1998), the annual reviews in *Asia Pacific Security Outlook* (Tokyo and New York: Japan Centre for International Exchange), Laki (2000a,b), and Rogers (2003).

[2] The early debate over defence and the defence force is reviewed in May (1993, 3-13).

[3] For more detail on this see May and Spriggs (1990), Spriggs and Denoon 1992), Dorney (1998), and Claxton (1998).

[4] Dibb, then head of the Australian National University's Strategic and Defence Studies Centre, was a former deputy secretary in the Australian Defence Department and director of the Joint Intelligence Organisation; Nicholas, a Canberra-based lawyer, had previously worked in the Australian Defence Department.

[5] The report was subsequently published as a discussion paper by the Strategic and Defence Studies Centre of the Australian National University (Dibb and Nicholas 1996).

[6] For details of the Sandline affair, see Dinnen, May and Regan (1997), Dorney (1998), and O'Callaghan (1999).

[7] The concept of 'niche warfighting' was referred to again at 4.2 and 4.30 of the document.

Chapter 15

Women, Policy Making and Development

Anne Dickson-Waiko

Women and gender issues have received increasing attention, partly as a result of the United Nations International Year of Women (1975) and first Decade for Women (1976–85). New bureaucratic structures have been set up with an explicit mandate to bring women's interests into the policy-making process (Miller and Razavi 1998; Staudt 1998; Tsikata 2000; Jahan 1995). Feminist activists and scholars have scrutinized and contested the role played by various state institutions and development agencies in sustaining gender inequalities through their structures, procedures and policy outcomes. There has been debate among feminists about whether to engage with or disengage from the state, an institution viewed by many feminists as 'a vehicle for social justice versus a protector of male interests' (Miller and Razavi 1998, 4). But feminists who have attempted to gender the discipline of politics identify other considerations of which Papua New Guinea women in policy making should take note — especially since women tend to look to the state for any development activity to do with women, including the development of a women's movement:

> To date the government is fed up with the current fragmentation and rivalry amongst women, and is determined to establish a coordinated, united and solid organization and movement for women in PNG (Women's Division c.1993).

This view is reiterated in a vision statement on women's policy.

Organized women in Papua New Guinea should take note of the post-structuralist argument that the state is not a unified body and that power is dispersed throughout various institutions of the state which do not necessarily act in concert (see Rai 1996, 18). From what is cited above, obviously the majority of organized women in Papua New Guinea, that is those whose voices we can hear, wish to be engaged with the state and its various bureaucratic structures. But what kind of a relationship must women construct with the state? This discussion of women's policy will therefore include problems women of Papua New Guinea face in their attempts at feminist engagement as well as the engagement strategies used in promoting change within existing bureaucratic structures. The struggle should not be limited to a unified struggle (see Rai 1996, 19) as suggested by officers in the Women's Division of the Department of Home Affairs and Youth, [1] which is itself an entity of the state. Thus there are spaces within the state where various struggles can be launched through negotiation, cooperation, opposition, and 'subversion not only of rules but also of articulated intentions of state forms' (*ibid.*). Papua New Guinea women can begin to construct a multifaceted approach to the state through a strong but varied women's movement.

Historical background

Prior to 1973, women were considered part of welfare and social development (before 1945 'welfare' referred specifically to education and health). During the colonial period women, as part of welfare, would have come under Native Affairs if they were considered at all. The provisional postwar administration in 1946 created an expanded public service but social welfare was not among the newly created departments. Women came under District Services and Native Affairs, reorganized in 1956, 1964 and 1969 into the Department of the Administrator (Jinks 1971, 131). It is conceivable that women were also considered under Native Labour and under Health and Education. A Maternity and Child Welfare Section was inaugurated in 1952 as part of the Department of Health (Mair 1970, 240). A reorganization of the colonial public service became necessary in the late 1960s when it was recognized that field staff of the Department of Administrator 'no longer spent most of their time enforcing law and order, but must now play a vital part in development and welfare' (Jinks 1971, 131, emphasis added). Thus a Department of Social Development and Home Affairs was created.

Until the first five years of statehood, women, if considered at all in government policies and processes, carried a welfare orientation reflecting a 'traditional' Western perception that women are primarily concerned with reproduction and household maintenance. The purpose of the welfare approach introduced in the 1950s and 1960s was to bring women into development as better mothers (Moser 1993, 59). It was based on three assumptions: that women are passive recipients of development, rather than participants in the development process; that motherhood is the most important role for women in society; and that childrearing is the most effective role for women in all aspects of economic development (*ibid.* 59–60). This approach focused entirely on women's reproductive role, with programs initiated and implemented through the various women's clubs, emphasizing women's 'traditional' preoccupations with infant and mother's welfare, handicrafts, motherhood, cooking, and sewing. Women's broader economic roles were generally overlooked during this initial phase.

Many community activities were organized by the Department of Native Affairs, and welfare officers assisted by the old Department of Information and Extension Services. Though most of the participants were men, gradually specific courses for women were mounted through women's clubs and church women's groups, apparently becoming very popular in the mid 1960s and the early 1970s (Kekedo 1985, 32). The first welfare officers were recruited and trained in Ahioma, Milne Bay Province and in Fiji. They were to be responsible for both welfare and women's work. Despite feminist criticism of the welfare approach (Lee 1985; Schoeffel 1986), and modernization theory generally (Waylen 1996, 36–40; Moser 1993, 58–62), I believe that the approach was useful at a certain stage of women's development in Papua New Guinea, and in many areas of the country today a welfare approach is still considered appropriate, and is sought after by grassroots women themselves, particularly in the areas of health and nutrition.

The Women in Development framework

In 1973, 'Women's equal participation' became part of a national 'Eight Point Plan' (see King, Lee and Warakai 1985, 453) which was subsequently incorporated into the national constitution as the 'Eight Aims'. With respect to the Eight Point Plan, Fitzpatrick (1985, 23) explains: 'it was something of an afterthought'; the Faber Report (1973) did not mention women's equality. The authors of the Eight Point Plan were Tony Voutas, Steve Zorn and Michael Somare. Fitzpatrick (1985, 24) notes that 'there was only one difference between the first and final drafts of the Eight Aims, namely the inclusion of the seventh aim'. Curiously, he does not say on whose insistence the seventh point was included, only that 'promoting the participation of women, was included with some difficulty' (*ibid*.). Voutas (1981, 46) refers to the ambivalence of some ministers about the philosophy behind the Eight Aims, saying: 'it reflected an intellectual trend of the late sixties and seventies keenly felt by the expatriate Western liberals and by the Papua New Guinean graduates and undergraduates'. Somare's commitment to women's development can be surmised from his address as chief minister to the first-ever women's convention in May 1975:

> I believe this convention is the first of its kind to be organised and conducted in our country. And I am proud that this important initiative came largely from the women of Papua New Guinea. The support my Government has given this convention by providing the finance emphasizes the importance my Government places on the role of women in Papua New Guinea. As you know my Government is committed to a philosophy of equal participation by women and I believe this convention is a clear sign of my Government's desire to involve women in developing this country in partnership with the men (Boden 1975, 54–56).

The conceptual basis of women's equality was obviously Women in Development (WID), promoted by liberal feminists in the early 1970s as part of the intellectual debate waged by women in the reemerging feminist movement (Moser 1993; Waylen 1996).

In the late 1960s there was a growing perception of the failure of development, especially in the emerging criticism of the impact of modernization theory on Third World women coming from liberal feminists (see Jacquette 1982; Scott 1995). Not only was the 'trickle down' effect not happening, the impact of modernization or development was assessed to be different for men and women. Instead of improving women's rights and status, the development process appeared to be contributing to a deterioration of their position (Razavi and Miller 1995, 2–6).

The original WID approach recognizes 'that women are active participants in the development process, who through both their productive and reproductive roles provide a critical, if often unacknowledged, contribution to economic growth' (Moser 1993, 63). While it recognizes the negative impact of economic development, it is also concerned with fundamental issues of equality, which transcend development (*ibid.*). Thus we see sentiments expressed in the Eight Point Plan and the constitution; the second goal of the constitution comes directly from the seventh aim. The Eight Point Plan was important as the first public document to raise the issue of women's equal participation as citizens in the new, soon-to-be independent state.

The WID approach formed the second phase of Papua New Guinea's women policy development. WID was taken on board by the United Nations, its agencies and many bilateral donors (Razavi and Miller 1995), who provided the external push for Papua New Guinea government agencies to pursue women's programs and projects. Papua New Guinea joined the United Nations in 1975 and has struggled since then to keep up with the sustained pressure from UN agencies and to address gender and women's issues emanating from the various UN women's conferences. In fact, a high level of activity by both government and civil society groups tends to follow world conferences on women, lapsing into inactivity between conferences. Empowerment through women's organizations in Papua New Guinea has been a fractured process (Dickson-Waiko 2003).

Women and Development

The re-emergence of a global women's movement coincided with the birth of Papua New Guinea as a nation-state. This has proven to be fortuitous for female citizens. Two major government documents refer to women's equality: the Eight Point Plan (1973) and the constitution of 1975. The preamble to the constitution reaffirmed what had been the seventh point of the Eight Point Plan in stating its second goal to be: 'for all citizens to have an equal opportunity to participate in, and benefit from, the development of our country' (King, Lee and Warakai 1985, Appendix A, 453–4). The constitution formalized the relationship of women with the new state, surviving what had been a male-gendered colonial state (Dickson-Waiko 2001, 52–56).

The seventh point of the Eight Point Plan or Eight Aims, provided official recognition of women's disadvantaged position in society in calling for a 'rapid increase in the equal participation for women in all forms of economic and social activity' (King, Lee and Warakai 1985). This public statement generated a lot of interest among women in the urban areas between 1973 and the early 1980s, when educated women began to see themselves not just as members of families and clans, as in the Melanesian cultural context, but as individuals and, from 1975, citizens (King, Lee and Warakai 1985, 2–10, 32–177). Unfortunately, this early interest in women's rights and issues, also expressed in government documents describing women in typically WID terms as 'both beneficiaries and agents in the development process' (see Women's Policy 1990), did not lead on to the emergence of a women's movement. Women have become more vocal about issues which affect them, but we have yet to witness an effective women's movement.

Despite official *recognition* of women's subordinate status in society, in concrete terms development for the female citizens of Papua New Guinea can be best described as having a very low priority. For example, a review of the National Public Expenditure Programme (NPEP) found that between 1979 (when the first government funds were made available for women's projects) and 1982, the share of total NPEP funding for women's projects declined from a low 1.5 per cent to a mere 0.2 per cent (Department of Home Affairs n.d., 5). The Women's Division has since moved away from designating women's projects to be funded under the NPEP or Public Investment Programme (PIP), relying solely on donor funding and the annual departmental recurrent budget, which has been on a downward slide since 1990. The fact that the Women's Division (though renamed Gender and Development Division) is still located in the Department of Social Welfare and Development illustrates the fact that nothing much has changed since 1969. The adoption of WID by the United Nations and most countries around the world has seen the creation of separate Women's ministries/departments/machineries in many countries. Discussions were under way in 2005 for a Gender Unit to be located in the prime minister's department. Its main functions were expected to be policy development, research and monitoring (Kajoi, personal communication 2005). The link between the proposed new entity, the Gender Unit (formerly the Women's Division) in the Department of Community Development, and national and provincial councils of women remains unclear.

In the late 1980s the National Council of Women (NCW), under the presidency of Buntabu Brown, was working towards replacing the NCW with a National Commission for Women. This progressive move was frustrated by some better-educated women members of the group, Women in Politics (WIP), headed by Maria Kopkop, and women officers from the Women's Division, Department of Religion, Home Affairs and Youth. At the NCW convention in Lae in 1990, they managed to disrupt proceedings and oust the Brown executive (personal communication Au Aruai and Ume Wainetti; see also *Times of PNG* 4 January 1990, p19).[2] The 'women's movement' has never quite recovered from this experience.

Implementing the Second National Goal

Between 1982 and 1987 the first coordinated government strategy on women was put in place. It was known as the National Women's Development Programme (NWDP). The idea was to have an integrated program emphasizing training, income-generating activities, family health, network building, and educational programs for women. It reflected a shift in approach from welfare to 'equal and productive partners', arising from the changing discourse on Women in Development. Network building and mobilization dominated the first phase of the NWDP, which involved setting up provincial councils of women and convincing provincial governments to establish positions for women's affairs officers. Up till 1983, many provincial governments had welfare officers but not women's officers. Network building required a close working relationship between the provincial governments, the official women's machinery (the Women's Division), and the NGO women's machinery, the NCW (personal communication Jane Kesno, Marilyn Kajoi 2001). The NCW, which came to include twenty provincial councils, was recognized as an alternative vehicle through which women's programs, information and educational training could be delivered.

This was the most productive period of policy making, policy implementation and resource allocation for women's programs by government. Staff from the Women's Division spent most of their time in the provinces mobilizing women and establishing provincial councils of women. They ran numerous workshops and training programs on issues ranging from food preparation, family health, and how to run meetings, to family planning, leadership training, appropriate technology and literacy (personal communication, Kajoi 2002). There was at least one women's officer in each province, and in the districts community women's organizers (CWOs) were appointed to mobilize women and set up the provincial councils. CWOs were volunteers; they were given a daily allowance to cover transportation and food costs and undertook the groundwork in the rural areas. Between 1982 and 1985 the National Youth Programme (NYP) and the NWDP worked closely together. In fact, many of the concepts used in the NWDP, such as the idea of using volunteers as community women's organizers, were developed by the NYP.

A National Women's Coordinating Committee (NWCC) was set up in 1983. Its role was to advise the ministry on policy, programs and training for women. Its membership included six church women's groups, provinces whose women's organizations were not members of the NCW, the NCW, and other women's groups such as the Young Women's Christian Association (YWCA), the Country Women's Association (CWA) and the Women's Division as the convenor. The NWCC was dominated by church women's groups, as the NCW was still relatively weak in the early 1980s.[3] The NWCC was reconstituted in 1989 as a result of the restructuring of the NCW after a period of dormancy between 1986 and 1988. Had this committee idea worked, it would have provided an important pressure group within the NWDP. The NWCC suggested that the NWDP be expanded in the areas of training, communication and networking. This recommendation was endorsed by an internal review conducted by the Women's Division in Kundiawa in 1988, where it was decided that new components would be added on to the NWDP.[4]

The NWDP was successful in establishing a women's agenda, within both the bureaucracy and civil society, and in raising awareness about women's participation in development. The program also paved the way for the development of the National Women's Policy. There had been calls for a National Women's Policy since 1982, when initial work on such a policy had begun. Intensive consultations on policy began in 1987. But while women-oriented policymakers worked outside the state apparatus, the training of those who worked within the bureaucracy was overlooked.

The most active period of policy making and implementation in the early 1980s coincided with the presence of a coterie of female social planners who guided various policy initiatives from the Women's Division through the National Planning Office. One of these, Margaret Nakikus, became the director of the National Planning Office. In hindsight, what contributed to the loss of the momentum of the early 1980s was a failure to adequately cultivate the insider-outsider dynamics of women's development within the bureaucracy, and to find negotiating spaces within the state.

Other components of the NWDP included the 1990 National Training Package co-funded by the United Nations Population Fund (UNFPA) and the International Labour Organization (ILO), and training for CWOs and provincial women's officers supported by grants from the national department. CWOs worked under the supervision of the provincial women's development officer. They supervised projects and activities of women's groups within the districts. A communication and network-building component saw the publication of Nius Blong Meri, a quarterly newsletter focusing on women's issues, concerns and achievements. A UNIFEM (United Nations Development Fund for Women)-funded project, Mobilization of Women Through Communication, which operated from 1989–92, focused on training women leaders about media relations, lobbying, public speaking and fundraising skills. Practical exercises were conducted in writing press releases and newsletter articles, and preparing radio information pieces (Nakikus *et al*. 1991). A Women's Resource Directory was also produced.

Other components of the NWDP came on stream after the launch of the Women's Policy in 1991 and were incorporated under the policy. These included the first credit scheme launched in 1991 under the Credit Assistance Component. It had been piloted in the East Sepik and Simbu provinces in 1989. Seven other provinces came into the scheme in 1991. Other credit schemes have since been introduced, including Meri Dinau (Women's Credit Scheme). A few provincial governments have supported women's credit schemes by offering capital for lending, one of the more successful being that of the Western Highlands Province under Governor Robert Lak. The Women's Division was also engaged in several inter-departmental training activities, including the Health Department's sensitizing of women leaders on HIV/AIDS and other sexually-transmitted diseases. This project was funded by UNICEF (the United Nations Children's Fund). A National Women's Literacy Committee was established to liaise with the Literacy Council on adult literacy for women and to work with NGOs involved in literacy projects targetting women. A donor-supported Women in Fisheries Project was developed in 1989 in cooperation with the Fisheries Department. It was piloted in Milne Bay, with plans to expand it to Momase and the New Guinea Islands regions. The idea was to increase women's participation in fish handling, processing and marketing. Direct funding by the Commonwealth Fund for Technical Assistance (CFTA) and the Canadian International Development Agency (CIDA) ceased in 1997. Other international donors funded feasibility studies and technical assistance, including the Asian Development Bank, the South Pacific Commission, USAID Fisheries Program and the International Centre for Oceanic Development. Over six hundred women and youth were trained in various post-harvest fisheries activities in rural areas (Sungu 1999). The Women in Fisheries Project was transferred without funds to the Department of Home Affairs in1997. The Women's Division failed to raise funds for its continuation.

By the mid 1990s, when a new provincial government system was put in place, the Women's Division was implementing a credit scheme, and a family health and family planning project funded by the Asian Development Bank (ADB).

National Women's Policy

The development of the Women's Policy took almost ten years and probably involved the widest community consultation of any government policy, through women leaders at the national and local levels, the National Council of Women, church women's groups, and government agencies and departments (personal communication Kajoi, Kesno 2001; Nakikus *et al*. 1991). Many workshops were held to consider various policy drafts, and consultations were held in every province at district level (*ibid*.). The policy was finally completed in 1990 and launched by Prime Minister Wingti in 1992. It spelled out the government's role in women's development issues by placing responsibility on a number of key government departments, such as Health, Education, Agriculture and Planning, to better plan policies and programs with consideration of their impact on women. The policy delineated the roles of the Women's Division and the National Council of Women and urged the government to strengthen the National Council of Women and other non-government organizations of women.

The policy also introduced a new approach, that of gender mainstreaming. Under this approach, line departments were to include women's projects within their particular policy mandates, while the Women's Division was to facilitate and monitor implementation. Unfortunately, most departments have not taken the Women's Policy seriously. Despite the wide consultation with various stakeholders in formulating the policy, line departments need specific guidance from the Women's Division or gender specialists as to how gender mainstreaming is to be incorporated within the policy units of the line departments. The rationale behind sending a large government delegation to the Fourth World Conference on Women, in Beijing, was to give female officers an insight into how to mainstream gender within their respective departments. The delegation included women from line departments, including the prime minister's department, and representatives from two provincial governments and the social sector. Two years after 'Beijing + Five', only four government agencies have lived up to that expectation, namely the Departments of Agriculture and Livestock, Education, Mining, and the University of Papua New Guinea.

Implementing the Women's Policy

Many of the activities under the NWDP were continued as part of the implementation strategy of the Women's Policy. But beyond that, the Women's Policy appears to have been shelved. A Five Year Management Plan (FYMP) for the Women's Division was developed by a consultant in 1994, setting out an implementation guide. The plan outlines a year-by-year implementation schedule which the department is supposed to follow, strengthening existing administrative structures and culminating in the establishment of a proposed Office of the Status of Women (OSW). The passage of the Organic Law on Provincial Governments and Local-level Governments in 1995 made the FYMP redundant, because the organic law transferred the major functions of the department to the provinces under a new system of decentralization. The Women's Policy has yet to be reviewed to incorporate this change, and to include the various international commitments that the government has agreed to, such as the ratification of the United Nations Convention on the Elimination of

Discrimination Against Women (CEDAW) and the Beijing Platform for Action (1995). Parliament ratified CEDAW without reservation in 1994, some fifteen years after its adoption by the United Nations General Assembly, but there is no new women's policy in the offing. While resources allocated to the Women's Division have declined, the Division's workload has increased as various international organizations step up the pressure on member countries to address gender issues, through, for example, CEDAW, the Beijing Platform for Action, and other international agreements such as the Commonwealth Plan of Action on Women and Development. This was highlighted by an internal review of women's policy by officers of the Women's Division in 1999.

Constant reorganization and restructuring has also contributed to the demoralization of staff and consequent inaction. A number of inappropriate appointments to senior management has not improved the situation. No government, with the exception of the first Somare-led government, has paid attention to gender issues in a systematic way. Recognizing women's disadvantaged position and encouraging them to participate in all forms of public life is one thing; recognizing gender as a development issue is quite another. Some implementation of women's policies has taken place, but it has been *ad hoc*. Several provinces, including New Ireland, Oro, Gulf and Sandaun, however, have gone ahead to plan their own provincial women's policies/plans.

A review of the NWDP in 1988 revealed that the Women's Division had anticipated that in the second phase of the NWDP, with sufficient training programs for women's officers and CWOs, provinces would be able to develop their own women's programs and, after 1992, their own Provincial Women's Policy modelled on the national one (personal communication, Molly Manuyakasi). Indeed, had the second phase of the NWDP proceeded as envisaged, provincial gender units would have been well placed to accommodate the 1995 provincial and local-level reforms, which transferred functions to provinces and districts.

Institutional arrangements — women's machinery

A significant impediment to the development of a coherent women's policy has been the way in which bureaucratic structures responsible for women's interests were allowed to evolve in a disjointed manner. After the launch of the Eight Point Plan, the then chief minister, Michael Somare, appointed an adviser on women's affairs, Tamo Diro. A Women's Unit was established in 1974 in the Office of Home Affairs located within the Department of Decentralisation. The Women's Unit tried to appoint at least one women's activity officer in each province. In 1975 a coordinator was appointed to oversee Papua New Guinea women's involvement in the United Nations International Year activities; this included the holding of the first national convention for women. The National Council of Women (NCW) was formed at this historic convention. The establishment of the Council was formalized in 1979, with the passage of the *National Council of Women Incorporation Act* paving the way for the establishment of provincial councils of women (PCW) throughout the country. But the status of the NCW has been ambiguous: while formally a statutory body it has largely operated as a non-government organization, while at the same time functioning sometimes as an appendage or even a program of the Department of Social Welfare and Development. A grant of K94,000 was reportedly given by the Somare government in 1978 to run NCW programs (Brouwer *et al.* 1998, 51).[5] Dame Rosa Tokiel, the first president of the NCW, established a full-time secretariat to carry out its advocacy role.

The Women's Office in the prime minister's department was reorganized in 1978 and a Women's Activity Section was established in the Office of Social Development within the Department of Decentralisation. In 1980, Prime Minister Chan felt that social development lacked the attention it deserved and so the Department of Community and Family Services was created under the leadership of Rose Kekedo (personal communication 2001; see also Department of Community and Family Services 1981). Both welfare services and women came under the new department. This was the first serious attempt to implement the equality provisions of the constitution and the national goals. The short lifespan of the department, however, meant that it had little time to do anything but put together a first comprehensive policy document on women. The department was abolished after a year, and the women's functions transferred to the Office of Youth, Women, Religion and Recreation, located in the prime minister's department. In mid 1983 the Office of Youth and Recreation became a separate department, while Women, Welfare and Religion were separated into a new department of Home Affairs. The Women's Unit was upgraded to a division headed by an assistant director in 1983, with a staff strength of four. In 1988 Home Affairs, Youth and Recreation merged into the Department of Religion, Home Affairs and Youth (DRHAY). The staffing level rose to nine. This bureaucratic arrangement continued until the Department was downgraded to an office under the Skate government and transferred to the Department of Provincial Affairs in 1999, as the Office of Church and Family Affairs. That decision was reversed a year later when the Morauta government restored its departmental status. The department was renamed Social Welfare and Development in 2000. In 2002, for the first time a female member of parliament (the only female member of parliament), Dame Carol Kidu, was appointed minister for Social Development. Under her direction the department underwent a major restructuring, resulting in further reduction of staff in the Women's Division (which was renamed Gender and Development Division). The following year the Department was renamed yet again, as the Department of Community Development, reflecting the department's 'community development' focus.

Constant reorganization has contributed to the Women's Division's inability to plan for systematic implementation of the 1990 Women's Policy. Decentralization has further contributed to confusion and frustration. Meanwhile, in the provinces and districts, the WID and GAD units have not been properly addressed with usually one officer in charge of women, welfare, sports, youth, and other functions.

A UNIFEM Gender Mainstreaming Project mounted in 1988 led in 1992 to the establishment of a Gender Unit in the Department of Planning and Implementation. The intent was to facilitate the mainstreaming of women's issues and concerns into project planning and implementation processes across all sectors. However, over the years, the one officer allocated to the unit has been given other responsibilities, such as justice, and law and order. Other gender units were established after the Beijing conference in 1995, in the Departments of Agriculture and Livestock, Commerce, Labour and Employment, Police, Education and (until 1997) Fisheries. Over the past five years, however, the effectiveness of coordination and monitoring by the Women's Division has been hampered by restructuring and retrenchment initiatives by the government, and the Women's Division has virtually collapsed.

The conceptual shift from WID to GAD was developed 'after recognition of the slow progress in equalizing power in gender relations' (Goetz 1997, 5). This involved a reassessment of concepts, analysis and approaches in gender equality. 'WID approaches had been based on a politics of access while GAD recognizes the importance of redistributing power in social relations' (*ibid.*). A permanent gender desk has since been established in the Department of Planning and Implementation, but given the number of projects, both donor-driven and government-initiated, budget preparations and the general workload on department staff, it is almost impossible for the person at the gender desk to keep track of the various projects from formulation, design and development through to implementation. The department has experienced its share of restructuring: at least four times since 1992. WID and GAD units in line departments are usually the first to be axed when budget cuts occur.

The 1995 *Organic Law on Provincial Governments and Local-level Governments* had a similar effect; indeed its impact has been more severe since it transferred control of women's programs to provinces (see National Monitoring Authority 1998). The Women's Division no longer runs programs from the national office. Decentralization has meant that, in most provinces, one officer is charged with women's affairs, often in conjunction with sports, welfare, youth, and other functions. In the 1980s, when the national government began implementation of the NWDP, liaison between the national department and provincial governments was much stronger, especially in provinces where a provincial coordinating committee (PCC) had been established. There was also coordination between various provincial agencies whose work covered women, such as non-formal education, health, agriculture, and business development. The provincial women's officer coordinated the meetings of the PCC. This made for better coordination of extension work with women, and facilitated parallel programs in the rural areas. By the 1990s this linkage had become difficult to maintain. The national department's ability to sustain projects under the NWDP declined, as Papua New Guinea experienced a series of economic and financial crises. The pivotal link between the national department, provincial governments, provincial women's councils and districts—the Community Women's Organisers (CWO) scheme — was gradually phased out. Some provincial governments re-engaged their CWOs, had them retrained, and appointed them as provincial women's officers. But the linkage between provincial and national departments has become tenuous at best, as provincial governments have shown a tendency to determine their own priorities and programs. Funding for women's programs is now dependent on the whim of provincial governors and their provincial administrations, specifically the joint planning and budget priority committees in the provinces. A few provincial governments, including Sandaun, Gulf, New Ireland and Oro have developed, or are in the process of developing, their own women's policy.

The national Department of Community Development now has the important role of monitoring the implementation of women's policy and programs at the provincial level. In general, the bureaucratic structures required to implement women's policy and women's development are not well developed. Those provincial governments which are doing fairly well with regard to women's development are, not surprisingly, also provinces which have well-organized provincial councils which are pushing for women's development. But most provinces suffer from bureaucratic and political indifference. Some are bewildered by constant changes caused by restructuring, retrenchment, reforms, and the high turnover of political leadership. One province which has gone ahead in mainstreaming gender is Manus: It has legislated the establishment of a single provincial women's policy mechanism bringing government and non-government machineries together in Pihi Manus. Pihi Manus has been incorporated into the Manus provincial government structure, ensuring government funding for its programs.

Women were mobilized into a 'movement', ostensibly to participate in development. But the training needs of those who worked within the Women's Division were often overlooked. Feminist academics became involved in the exciting new field of feminist scholarship, but the field of Women's Studies was virtually unknown in the various training institutions engaged in human resource development, such the University of Papua New Guinea and the Papua New Guinea Institute of Public Administration (the former Administrative College). Ironically, while certain women leaders began to demand a move away from welfare-oriented programs, most of the staff who were employed in the Women's Division graduated from the University of Papua New Guinea with Social Work degrees. While civil servants in other departments underwent specialist training, as career diplomats, agricultural officers, teachers, even *kiap*, women's officers received no such specialist training; women's officers were supposed to know how to institutionalize women and gender policies and processes because they happened to be women.

Feminist policy advocacy within the state in Papua New Guinea has never been an issue, while in Australia, Papua New Guinea's colonial forebear and mentor, it became highly developed (see Watson 1990; Sawer 1998). Further, women's policy development and implementation was never a government priority in Papua New Guinea. In the 1990s attempts were made through a number of donor-funded projects to institutionalize WID and GAD, but this proved difficult in an entrenched, male-gendered bureaucracy.

Conclusion

The implementation of the women's policy has thus suffered from a number of inconsistencies. First it is part of a sector that continues to be marginalized. Personnel changes at the political and bureaucratic levels have meant changes in policy, implementation, priorities, and emphasis. In particular, the constant reorganization of the bureaucratic structure has brought confusion, frustration and low staff morale, and diminishing state resources have worsened the situation. This has forced the Women's Division to rely on donor-funded projects, but donor assistance, especially that from multilateral institutions, comes with strings, which restrict the Division's ability to implement its own programs.

Women's policy underwent an internal review in 1999, but a planned external review has yet to take place. What is needed is a new policy that takes into consideration all the structural and functional changes that have occurred in the last ten years. A new policy needs to address gender mainstreaming in a more realistic manner within the state apparatus, extending down to provincial and local-level government. Coordination of government and non-government machinery, separate from social welfare, is well overdue. Policymakers and women's civil society groups need to strategize the relationship of Papua New Guinea women with the state, such that female citizens, regardless of class, ethnicity, religion and locality, begin to experience real changes in their lives.

Postscript

A number of developments have taken place since this chapter was first drafted. Preparation of a CEDAW report was at an advanced stage at the end of 2008. Papua New Guinea should be ready to present its first report to the UN some time in 2009. The new Office of the Development of Women has received funding from the government to appoint staff in 2009. The Office will eventually be located in the Prime Minister's Department. The Somare government has agreed to use Section 102 of the constitution and appoint three nominated women to the National Parliament. A process of nomination has been agreed to and three nominated women should be appointed to parliament in the first quarter of 2009.

The Somare government has also agreed to fund the National Council of Women to build a convention centre. Land has been secured for construction to begin. The National Council of Women Act has also initiated a consultative process to make amendments to its legislation.

References

Boden, D. 1975. Notes on conference, The First National Convention of Women in Papua New Guinea. *Administration for Development* 5(October): 50–61.

Brouwer, E., B. Harris, B and S. Tanaka. 1998. *Gender Analysis in Papua New Guinea*. Washington, D.C.: The World Bank.

Department of Community and Family Services. 1981. *Policy Document, Papua New Guinea*. Port Moresby.

Department of Home Affairs, n.d. *Women in Development*. Port Moresby.

Department of Home Affairs and Youth. 1987. *First Draft National Women's Policy, Papua New Guinea*. Port Moresby.

Department of Home Affairs and Youth. 1991. *Papua New Guinea Women's Policy*. Boroko.

Dickson-Waiko, A. 2001. Women, individual human rights, community rights: tensions within the Papua New Guinea state. In *Women's Rights and Human Rights, International Historical Perspectives*, ed. P. Grimshaw, K. Holmes and M. Lake, 49–70. London and New York: Palgrave.

Dickson-Waiko, A. 2003. The missing rib. Mobilizing church women for change in Papua New Guinea. In *Women's Groups and Everyday Modernity in Melanesia*, ed. B. Douglas. *Oceania* 74 (1&2): 98–119.

Fitzpatrick, P. 1985. The making and the unmaking of the Eight Aims. In *From Rhetoric to Reality: Papua New Guinea's Eight Point Plan and National Goals after a Decade*, ed. P. King, W. Lee and V. Warakai, 22–31. Waigani: University of Papua New Guinea Press.

Goetz, Anne M. ed. 1997. *Getting Institutions Right for Women in Development*. London: Zed Books.

Jacquette, J. S. 1982. Women and modernization theory: a decade of feminist criticism. *World Politics* 34(2): 267–288.

Jahan, R. 1995. *The Elusive Agenda: Mainstreaming Women in Development*. London: Zed Books.

Jinks, B. 1971. *New Guinea Government. An Introduction.* Sydney: Angus and Robertson.

Kekedo, R. 1985. The role of the Department of Community and Family Services in women's advancement. In *From Rhetoric to Reality: Papua New Guinea's Eight Point Plan and National Goals After a Decade*, ed. W. Lee, P. King and V. Warakai, 32–37. Waigani: University of Papua New Guinea Press.

King, P., W. Lee and V. Warakai eds. 1985. *From Rhetoric to Reality: Papua New Guinea's Eight Point Plan and National Goals After a Decade.* Waigani: University of Papua New Guinea Press.

Lee, W. 1985. Women's groups in Papua New Guinea: shedding the legacy of drop scones and embroidered pillowcases. *Community Development Journal* 20(3): 222–236.

Mair L. 1970. *Australia in New Guinea.* Melbourne: Melbourne University Press.

Miller, C. and S. Razavi. 1998. *Missionaries and Mandarins. Feminist Engagement with Development Institutions.* London: Intermediate Technology Publications in association with the United Nations Research Institute for Social Development.

Moser, C. 1993. *Gender Planning and Development. Theory, Practice and Training.* London: Routledge.

National Monitoring Authority. 1998. *Handbook on the Rules and Responsibilities of Different Levels of Government Under the Reforms.* Port Moresby.

Nakikus, M., M. Andrew, A. Mandie-Filer and B. Brown. 1991. *Papua New Guinea Women in Development Sector Review.* Port Moresby: United Nations Development Programme.

Overseas Development Group, University of East Anglia for the International Bank for Reconstruction and Development. 1973. *A Report on Development Strategies for Papua New Guinea* (The Faber Report). Port Moresby: Office of the Chief Minister.

Rai, S. M. 1996. Women and the state in the Third World: some issues for debate. In *Women and the State: International Perspectives*, ed. S. M. Rai and G. Lievesley, 5–22. London: Taylor and Francis.

Razavi, S. and C. Miller. 1995. *From WID to GAD: Conceptual Shifts in the Women and Development Discourse.* Geneva: United Nations Research Institute for Social Development.

Sawer, Marian. 1998. Femocrats and ecocrats: womens' policy makers in Australia, Canada and New Zealand. In *Missionaries and Mandarins, Feminist Engagement with Development Institutions*, ed. C. Miller and S. Razavi,

112–137. London: Intermediate Technology Publications in association with the United Nations Research Institute for Social Development.

Schoeffel, P. 1986. The rice pudding syndrome: women's advancement and home economics training in the South Pacific. In *Development in the Pacific: What Women Say*, 36–44. Canberra: Australian Council for Overseas Aid.

Scott, Catherine V. 1995. *Gender and Development. Rethinking Modernization and Dependency Theory*. Boulder: Lynne Rienner.

Staudt, K. 1998. *Policy, Politics and Gender, Women Gaining Ground*. Connecticut: Kumarian Press.

Sungu, Monica. 1999. Post Harvest Fisheries Technology. Information Supplement for Project Development, Women in Fisheries Development Programme in Papua New Guinea. Port Moresby: Women's Division, Office of Family and Church Affairs. Typescript.

Tsikata, D. 2000. *Lip-Service and Peanuts: The State and National Machinery for Women in Africa*. Ghana: Third World Network-Africa.

Voutas, A. C. 1981. Policy initiatives and the pursuit of control, 1972–74. In *Policy-Making in a New State: Papua New Guinea 1972–77*, ed. J. A. Ballard, 33–47. St Lucia: University of Queensland Press.

Watson, Sophie ed. 1990. *Playing the State. Australian Feminist Interventions*. Sydney: Allen and Unwin.

Waylen, G. 1996. *Gender in Third World Politics*. Boulder: Lynne Rienner Publishers.

Women's Division, Department of Religion, Home Affairs and Youth, 1990. *Status Report of National Women's Development Programme*. Department of Home Affairs and Youth, Port Moresby.

Women's Division, Department of Religion, Home Affairs and Youth, c 1993. Background Information. Port Moresby. Typescript.

Women's Division, Department of Religion, Home Affairs and Youth, 1988–1993. *Expansion of Women's Role in Development*. Department of Home Affairs and Youth, Port Moresby.

Women's Division, Department of Religion, Home Affairs and Youth, with assistance of The Asian Development Bank. 1994. *Women's Division, Department of Religion, Home Affairs and Youth, Five Year Management Plan 1994–1998*. Department of Home Affairs and Youth, Port Moresby.

Women's Division, Department of Religion, Home Affairs and Youth, n.d. *National Women's Development Programme*. Department of Home Affairs and Youth, Port Moresby.

Endnotes

[1] The Women's Division was initially part of the then Department of Home Affairs. In 1988, as a result of a departmental reorganization, it became part of the Department of Religion, Home Affairs and Youth. This and subsequent administrative reshuffling are detailed below.

[2] I discuss the source of these ongoing tensions between organized women in (Dickson-Waiko 2003, 102).

[3] Church womens' organizations such as the United Church Fellowship and the Lutheran Wokmeri had been around since the early 1950s (see Dickson-Waiko 2003).

[4] The concept of a coordinating committee was revived in the lead-up to the 1995 Fourth World Conference on Women. An Inter-Agency Committee was established, but was disbanded immediately after the Beijing conference.

[5] This piece of history has been incorrectly recorded. According to Louis Aitsi (general secretary of the NCW at the time) and Nelly Lawrence (an officer with the NCW), the money given by Somare was earmarked for the building of a Women's Resource Centre (personal communication, Louise Aitsi 1985 and Kajoi 2004).

Chapter 16

Foreign Policy Making

Edward P. Wolfers and William Dihm

Foreign policy is a notoriously elusive concept. A number of factors combine to blur the distinction between foreign and domestic policies (cf. Rosenau 1997; see also Rosenau 1992). Among the factors of particular contemporary relevance, both in the present case and generally, are: the domestic requirements and effects of globalization; the growing spread and depth of international cooperation and the increasing domestic acceptance and application of international law (which, together, affect almost all areas of public policy in Papua New Guinea, and impose increasingly tight limits on the internal discretion and activities of government across more and more); aid dependency (the more so when general budgetary support gives way to programs and projects requiring joint approval between donor and recipient), and the conditions attached to loans from international financial institutions, including the World Bank, the International Monetary Fund (IMF), and the Asian Development Bank (ADB). Specifically in Papua New Guinea since the late 1980s, they also include the Bougainville crisis and peace process, especially as these have required involvement in the work of the United Nations Human Rights Commission during the 1990s; the negotiation and management of relations with the South Pacific Regional Peace Keeping Force (SPRPKF) in 1994 (Papua New Guinea 1994), the neutral regional Truce and Peace Monitoring Groups (TMG and PMG) and the Bougainville Transition Team (respectively, 1997–98, 1998–2003, and 2003 (Wolfers and Dihm 1998)), and the United Nations observer mission in Bougainville (UNOMB, 1998–2005); and relations with foreign aid donors providing support for restoration and development, weapons disposal, and other aspects of peace-making and peace-building, including meetings in New Zealand and Australia between the national government and the Bougainville factions.

While other aspects of public policy may sometimes be defined in terms of the policies announced as applying to the functional responsibilities of particular government agencies or discerned in their behaviour, foreign offices (especially, their overseas missions and posts) not only have their own core and other assigned functions but characteristically serve as agents for other government bodies too, charged with pursuing policies which these bodies make, including representations on behalf of the private sector.

To complicate the picture still further, certain institutions and relationships at the critical centre of many countries' foreign relations, including significant elements of defence cooperation, are conducted with little or no provision for foreign offices' participation, while others, such as the World Bank and the IMF, make no provision for such participation at all.

Then there are the growing numbers of international meetings at which particular officeholders (members of parliament, ombudsmen, police commissioners, etc.) or representatives of government agencies in almost every area of government activity, including commodity boards, get together to exchange information or develop cooperative arrangements with counterparts from other countries and officials of the organizations to which they belong. The levels of inclusivity of these meetings and organizations extend from the bilateral through the sub-regional (Melanesian) and varying definitions of the regional (Pacific islands, South Pacific, and Asia Pacific) to the Commonwealth, the African, Caribbean and Pacific (ACP) Group, the functional or commodity-defined, such as the organizations through which cocoa, coffee, natural rubber and tropical timber-producing and exporting and other countries cooperate, to the United Nations (UN) and specialist organizations.

When it comes to trade and investment, the role of government tends to be limited to negotiating, participating in, and monitoring compliance with international agreements, regulation, and promotion. The substance of trade and investment in a market economy like Papua New Guinea's are primarily matters for the private sector, whether or not they come under the Department of Foreign Affairs or another agency (or agencies) as far as government policy is concerned.

In the case of Papua New Guinea foreign policy, the picture is further complicated by the changing — though, over the longer term, generally contracting — combination(s) of functions for which the Department of Foreign Affairs has been responsible: from foreign affairs, defence and trade, including customs and migration, for much of the 1970s, through foreign affairs and trade, without customs after the early 1980s, to foreign affairs (still including migration, recently described officially as immigration) from about 1985.

Despite the difficulty, already mentioned, of defining the term, foreign policy has tended to be, almost by definition, beyond the competence of all colonial regimes (external/foreign control over foreign relations is one of the defining characteristics of colonial or other dependency status). It has also been generally the last area of government activity, together with defence, handed over at independence — though in Papua New Guinea's case, day-to-day responsibility for the country's foreign relations was transferred on a de facto basis to Papua New Guinean control in March 1975, six months before the country became formally independent. It is, therefore, an area in which successor regimes have tended to have little experience at independence, though generally very powerful legacies to manage. These legacies include the treaties and membership of international organizations to which newly independent states succeed (see Papua New Guinea 1982, Appendices I and II), and, especially, the centrality of relations with the former colonial power (Boyce 1977 contains a detailed comparative history and discussion of the issues involved in the establishment of foreign offices in the context of decolonization, with particular reference to Papua New Guinea in Chapter 4).

The history of Papua New Guinea foreign policy to date can be usefully divided into four broadly defined, sometimes overlapping, periods: the period in which Universalism (in the broader sense, not just the first element discussed below) was the main theme, 1974–1979; a period of transition; followed by the *Foreign Policy White Paper* (Papua New Guinea 1982), which promoted active and selective engagement as the basic approach from 1981 on; and the period since about 1997, when the basic approach has not been as readily applicable in its original form — which may turn out to be another period of transition to what may prove to be a new foreign policy approach following further review.

A great deal of foreign policy, especially in multilateral *fora* such as the United Nations, can be essentially a matter of words. It can often involve little more than expressing a view and, if the matter is raised in an international organization, then voting — especially as far as small states without substantial diplomatic resources and global influence are concerned. The frequency with which potentially controversial issues are deliberately buried in complexly worded, even intentionally ambiguous, consensus resolutions means that votes are not always required, and are sometimes deliberately avoided. Thus, the distinction between policy and implementation, which can be difficult to make in almost any area of public policy, can be even more difficult — and sometimes close to impossible — to apply in relation to foreign policy.

Moreover, even more obviously than in other areas of public policy, implementation is often a matter of negotiation. Insofar as foreign policy objectives are pursued through international organizations or require cooperation based on mutual respect for the sovereign independence of states, there is really no alternative. In any event, quite apart from the niceties of formal diplomacy, a relatively small and not very powerful state like Papua New Guinea can rarely impose its will on other states even if it were disposed to try (which no responsible Papua New Guinean leader has ever even proposed).

Two major paradigms have been developed, in practice and theory, for making, and evaluating, foreign policy: the Realist and the Idealist. The first emphasizes the pursuit of national interests, and the second support for principles as the main considerations. In practical terms, the first often employs the second as its rationale or as an instrument of propaganda (for example, 'fighting for peace'), though it can also be used domestically to justify participation in international cooperation and support for important principles as being in the national interest. The second can sometimes disguise the first (take, for example, the claims to democracy advanced by states which present themselves as Marxist 'people's democracies' or as adhering to a particular — perhaps Asian or African — cultural form). In certain cases, the distinction is actively denied, obvious instances being the widely held view that the USA has a particular interest in promoting what many Americans see as universal values, such as democracy and respect for human rights, as part of its national mission around the world, and claims that foreign aid to support development in less developed countries serves such universal principles as equity and humanity, not simply the interests of donor or recipient states.

When it comes to performance, the difficulties already outlined in distinguishing clearly and usefully between policy and implementation, and of agreeing about the sincerity with which principles are espoused, make it almost impossible to achieve widely shared evaluations. In any event, some of the most important achievements of a successful foreign policy are often essentially negative — for example, avoidance of wars or crises, including setbacks to development strategies. The role of policy in avoiding alternative, negative outcomes can be very hard to demonstrate at all conclusively.

However, despite the reservations outlined above concerning the possibility of systematic comparison with public policy-making, policy and implementation in other areas of government activity in Papua New Guinea, the following discussion of Papua New Guinea foreign policy since independence is organized under the same subheadings and follows the same sequence as other contributions to this volume — to facilitate such comparisons as can be fruitfully made, and assist in highlighting both the differences and the similarities they reveal.

Policy at independence

Papua New Guinea is unusual (if not unique) among former dependencies in having had a foreign policy in place at independence — officially, not just in the political manifesto of a political party or the colonial government's successor regime. The main elements of Papua New Guinea's first official foreign policy were sketched out by the responsible minister, Sir Albert Maori Kiki, even before the Australian government transferred day-to-day responsibility for the actual conduct of foreign relations (and defence) some six months before independence (Papua New Guinea 1976). That policy owed a great deal to recent history and current concerns, as policies often do, in which the legacy of Australian rule was a major factor (see, for example, the preoccupation with Australia in Griffin (1974, passim), especially the contributions by the editor and Papua New Guinea's first two foreign ministers, Sir Albert Maori Kiki and Sir Ebia Olewale).

Like other United Nations trust territories, New Guinea, in particular — and, to a lesser extent, Papua, because of the impossibility of understanding the one without the other, especially after their 'administrative' amalgamation following World War II — were both involved in international relations well before independence (New Guinea had been a League of Nations' mandate between World Wars I and II, but the system then involved neither visiting missions nor any other form of direct interaction between the Permanent Mandates Commission and people from the territories under its purview, as it did when New Guinea became a United Nations Trust Territory after World War II). Certain governments went to some pains to maintain the distinction between the two territories (a French member of a United Nations Trusteeship Council visiting mission declined to accept an invitation to accompany his colleagues on a short visit to centres in Papua, other than the capital for the combined territory, Port Moresby, apparently, out of concern at the possible implications for United Nations' involvement in France's Pacific territories). But the reality was that policy and policy recommendations for the one had direct implications for the other, and, increasingly, applied without any distinction in both.

The triennial United Nations visiting missions provided occasional opportunities for Papua New Guineans to be actors, not merely objects of interest or concern, in at least one international forum (as confirmed in frequently cited memories of the first requests for self-government and early demands for Bougainville's secession at meetings with such missions during the early 1960s). So, to a lesser extent, did meetings of the Trusteeship Council at United Nations headquarters in New York, where selected Papua New Guineans attended and sometimes spoke, as members of the Australian delegation, in the annual debates on New Guinea (and rather more freely outside, for example at a cocktail party in New York in late 1971, when a prominent Papua New Guinean political leader, beer glass firmly held in his shirt pocket, demanded of a senior Indonesian diplomat when Irian Jaya would be allowed self-determination — notwithstanding the nationalist sensitivities of the official to whom he was speaking, or the United Nations-approved *Act of Free Choice* two years previously).

In a regional context, the South Pacific Conferences which were held under the auspices of the South Pacific Commission following World War II allowed — again, selected — aspirant Papua New Guinean leaders to interact with counterparts from other Pacific island territories. In addition to raising awareness of issues such as the transfer of West New Guinea from Dutch to Indonesian control (following a short United Nations interregnum), and providing opportunities for aspirant politicians to engage in informal exchanges of ideas outside the formal meetings about matters such as political party organization and platforms, these meetings were important in building the mutual understanding and institutional foundations for subsequent cooperation in the Pacific, both among island countries and region-wide.

Then, during the 1960s, increasing numbers of actual and potential Papua New Guinean leaders visited Australia on political education tours, where they met Australian political leaders and officials at different levels of government. Increasing numbers of senior Australian politicians and officials visited Papua New Guinea too.

Thus it was that, even as Papua New Guinea opened up to the wider world during the 1960s and 1970s, Australia remained, by far, the dominant external factor in Papua New Guinea's foreign relations at independence (and, arguably, not so very external when one considers the relative predominance of Australian aid not only in overall foreign development assistance but in government revenue; Australia's continuing contribution to foreign investment in and overseas trade with Papua New Guinea; the number of Australian public servants still on the job if, in certain respects, on the way out, as well as other Australian residents; and the ongoing, close educational, communications and cultural links, as well as the personal, even political, ties between Papua New Guinea and Australia).

The Australian legacy was, therefore, central to almost every aspect of Papua New Guinea's foreign relations at independence. That legacy was not just a matter of links and shared interests with Australia. It also affected the way in which the new state viewed, and dealt with, other parts of the world, notably the Pacific islands and Southeast Asia, especially Indonesia (as discussed below).

Thus, the process of opening-up further to other parts of the world, or diversifying Papua New Guinea's foreign relations, following independence implied some dilution of relations with Australia (not necessarily in absolute, but certainly in relative, terms, as Papua New Guinea began to deal with new players and relations with them grew). It has meant that, even today, important issues in, and relations with, other countries are often refracted through lenses in which Australian perceptions and sometimes suspicions of Australia have tended to have substantial influence on what Papua New Guineans (especially, those who were adults at independence) perceive, say or do.

The ready initial identification of Papua New Guinea with other Pacific island countries also owed a great deal to orientations and contacts successive Australian governments had encouraged before independence (through the South Pacific Commission and Conference, as well as the Central Medical School in Fiji). Christian missions which had close relations with counterparts, or were part of much bigger regional operations, played a significant part, too, in forging links and identifications across national boundaries, and with the wider region.

Relative inexperience in dealing with Asian governments and people — apart from residents of Chinese or Ambonese descent, and then mainly on the New Guinea side — was another aspect of the Australian legacy (the White Australia policy had applied to immigration to Papua New Guinea under Australian rule, and also to Papua New Guineans seeking entry to Australia (Wolfers 1975)). The combination of pre-independence experience and orientations in relation to the Pacific and Asia meant that members of the Papua New Guinea government and educational elite at independence had had relatively little direct involvement with or knowledge of the county's closest and largest neighbour, Indonesia. The sole exception of any significance was in relation to the (West) Papuans who had participated in South Pacific Conferences until 1962, those who had come to Papua New Guinea for education, including a number of doctors, and others who had entered and remained behind, sometimes without being officially noticed (like the 300 or so people from (West) Papua who lived on a hillside above the Port Moresby suburb of Badili during the mid-1960s, passing themselves off as people from Papua New Guinea's Western District), and other illegal border-crossers and refugees. Insofar as Papua New Guineans developed attitudes towards Indonesia, they were often likely to be influenced by experience and identification with those (West) Papuans they had met, as well as the residue of Australian fears of possible Indonesian expansionism during the Sukarno era.

Thus, the main reference to Asia in Papua New Guinea's first foreign policy was expressed in a metaphor whose practical implications and application were unclear: Papua New Guinea was — or aspired to be — a bridge or link between Asia and the Pacific, without any clear explanation of what, if anything, might be expected to follow in operational terms (the observations that the main role of a bridge is to be walked over and that a link in a chain is liable to be pulled from both sides, or even wound around someone's neck, were made publicly only some years later).

The Australian legacy was reinforced by the continuing presence of Australian personnel in key positions in government agencies engaged in border administration and related activities, the centrality of the common border in policy and interactions with Indonesia, and the apparent reluctance of some Australians to train, let alone trust, Papua New Guineans to deal responsibly with Indonesian issues and officials. A related time-lag that affected Papua New Guinea policy towards Indonesia was a tendency to deal with Indonesia and the border in a national-security framework which owed quite a deal to fears not only of Indonesia but of the likelihood and possible implications of Papua New Guineans identifying with the Melanesians to the west — hence the theme and title of the published proceedings of the first Papua New Guinea-Indonesia dialogue in 1984, *Beyond the Border* (Wolfers 1988), which attempted to take a broader view.

Policy-making since independence

Researching, analyzing and writing about the making, content and implementation of Papua New Guinea foreign policy since independence is complicated by a number of quite practical factors (apart from the requirements of public service confidentiality, respect for the records of previous governments, and the secrecy which applies to exchanges and a very small number of agreements with other governments).

While the Department of Foreign Affairs has not experienced as many changes of secretary as some other government agencies, it has certainly seen increasingly frequent changes of minister (there were twenty-four changes of foreign minister between 1975 and 2002), as well as repeated organizational restructuring and significant cutbacks in staffing. These changes, together with the recall and (re-)assignment of personnel which accompany the normal cycle of overseas postings, and political appointments at the level of head of diplomatic mission or consular post, have combined to weaken institutional memory. Funding cuts have meant that a very useful journal of record, the *Papua New Guinea Foreign Affairs Review*, has ceased publication. The physical reconstruction and rearrangement of offices in the mid 1990s, which followed a previous minister's desire for a larger ministerial suite, together with the subsequent removal of the department's headquarters from one building to another, have taken a heavy toll of the registry and the filing system (a departmental library which was finally becoming useful after years of painstaking collecting and cataloguing no longer exists).

Like its counterparts in other policy areas, the Permanent Parliamentary Committee on Foreign Affairs has not been a major player in the making, management or monitoring of Papua New Guinea foreign policy. It has, apparently, met only rarely, and barely (if at all) since committee allowances ceased to be linked to members' attendance.

Thus, many of the records required to write a well-researched history of the Papua New Guinea Department of Foreign Affairs in its various manifestations or of Papua New Guinea foreign policy, or to make systematic comparisons with other government agencies or policies, do not exist or cannot be readily retrieved, or, in the case of possible oral sources of information, are beyond ready access.

More generally, it is fair to say that foreign policy has not featured prominently among the issues in successive Papua New Guinea elections, in the reasons advanced for changes of government, or in parliamentary debate (the *Foreign Policy White Paper* containing the results of the first major review of Papua New Guinea foreign policy since independence was barely discussed when it was formally tabled in the National Parliament in 1981, and not reported in detail or depth in most media).

The only exceptions, where aspects of Papua New Guinea's foreign relations have been prominently on the public agenda, have been the political situation and future in Indonesian Papua (especially when large-scale border-crossings coincided with elections, which they tended to do during the 1970s and early 1980s); the Sandline affair in 1997, which was widely perceived by Papua New Guineans as a test of strength with Australia over the right of Australian media and officials to intervene, rather than, say, a moral issue; the Bougainville conflict, where Australia's role in providing logistical support for the Papua New Guinea Defence Force, and demands for external intervention to stop the conflict or safeguard human rights were significant political issues during the 1990s; and the Bougainville peace process, in which New Zealand and Australia have hosted important meetings, the United Nations has provided observers, and regional governments peace and truce monitors, and these, together with other organizations and states, have supported efforts to make and build peace. Even then, political interest in foreign policy issues other than the Bougainville peace process has tended to be occasion-specific, perhaps even somewhat opportunistic, with remarkably little carry-over into government of views expressed in media interviews or electoral context (one former minister for Foreign Affairs, when asked about the relationship of views expressed about Indonesian Papua during an election to his previous record and future policy implications, responded quite firmly that what he said then was for electoral purposes, not government).

However, insofar as electoral promises and demands depend on the availability, terms and uses of foreign aid, foreign investment and Papua New Guinean participation in development, including decision-making, ownership (in every sense) and employment, aspects of foreign policy have, of course, been implicit in many other issues.

Even so, foreign policy has generally been a significant concern only for educational and official elites, as well as communities on or close to the borders with Indonesia, Solomon Islands and, especially before the *Torres Strait Treaty* was concluded in November 1978, Australia.

One outcome has been relatively greater continuity in policy and, in this case, practice — or, at least, the basic approach — than in government personnel, especially until the late 1990s.

Foreign policy-making has, in practice, been largely a matter of government trying to take advantage of external opportunities or responding to external pressures (and sometimes seeing — and taking advantage of — opportunities in external pressures, and even crises, as shown in the initiatives which led to the *Treaty of Mutual Respect, Friendship and Co-operation* with Indonesia [MRFC — as in the acrostic in the treaty's preamble), and the *Joint Declaration of Principles Guiding Relations* (*JDP*) with Australia, when difficulties on the common border and in the aid relationship respectively provided openings to propose arrangements directed towards refocusing and restructuring relations).

As far as Papua New Guinea's first foreign policy is concerned (set out in some detail in Papua New Guinea 1976), it may be a *cliché* but it is nonetheless true that Universalism was clearly a product of history and circumstance. This policy had three main elements (not always expressed with absolute uniformity or even consistency, but nonetheless clear and persistent):

1. Willingness to open relations with any country that did not insist on placing conditions on Papua New Guinea's foreign policy (described, apparently spontaneously, by the then-minister, Sir Albert Maori Kiki, in the memorable phrase 'friend to all, and enemy of none');
2. identification with other Pacific island nations; and
3. a role as bridge or link between Asia, especially Southeast Asia, and the Pacific, notably the South Pacific, especially Pacific island countries.

The first was, in certain respects, an almost inevitable posture for the government of a newly-independent state concerned to display and maintain its independence. It focused on the most obvious and immediate priority of a newly-independent country, especially as far as formal diplomacy and diplomats (whose previous training and experience had focused on protocol) were concerned: the opening of formal diplomatic relations. In doing so, it addressed, and provided a very effective instrument for dealing with, a particular circumstance of the Cold War: the competition for diplomatic recognition and advantage of divided states, such as East and West Germany, North and South Korea, and China and Taiwan. It provided a rationale for resisting embroilment in rivalries where Papua New Guinea had little interest and even less capacity to affect outcomes by treating all-comers on a uniform basis, provided they respected Papua New Guinea's independence both formally as a state and diplomatically as an international actor.

The main shortcoming of (1) was that, over time and especially in the formulation that Papua New Guinea wanted to be 'friend to all, and enemy of none,' it did not provide a clear rationale for the future development of relations, especially as it might involve setting priorities or making choices. Once formal diplomatic relations had been opened with the major players in the Asia-Pacific, including countries in Europe and North America, it exhausted its original purpose and scope. Its relevance and application declined. The part came to be regarded as the whole as Universalism came to be widely described, even applied, in terms of the first theme on its own. The phrase became a slogan for continuous evenhandedness, even a rationale for timidity and inaction, giving rise to doubts and confusion in situations where the further development of relations was clearly to Papua New Guinea's advantage. Discussions about the wider implications of Universalism, including whether further development of relations in some cases might amount to a form of alignment, sometimes resembled those about the implications of neutralism for the neutrality of other newly-independent countries; the result was sometimes indifference to professed understandings of policy, and frequently similar to that described in a very different context as 'the tyranny of policy' (Galbraith 1999, 160–161), when adherence to established policy comes before all else, including the need for review and change.

Universalism provided the basis on which Papua New Guinea successfully opened formal diplomatic relations with the People's Republic of China in 1976, becoming the first state in the world that did not have to denounce Taiwanese aspirations — and each of the next few words is important — by declaring publicly it regards China as one country on both sides of the Taiwan Strait. But success here has, in certain respects, been the mother of subsequent problems, as succeeding governments have attempted to deal with Taiwan either ignorant of, or indifferent to, what has been achieved, or at least its significance.

The second element of Papua New Guinea's first foreign policy, often described as the natural product of ethnic similarities, was, in fact, equally a result of history: the contacts made and experiences gained through the South Pacific Conference and regional educational and church institutions, including the Central Medical School in Fiji, where Papua New Guineans went for medical training during the 1950s, and Christian missions which were organized on a regional basis (sometimes with their regional headquarters in Solomon Islands or another country in the Pacific). It was also, at least partly, the product of fears among Australian officials concerning the likely conduct of Papua New Guineans if they participated more actively in wider Asia-Pacific or specifically Asian settings (would they be corrupted or charmed? or might they identify strongly with their Melanesian neighbours in Indonesian Papua and cause difficulties for, or in Australian relations with, Indonesia?), and the consequent encouragement for Papua New Guineans to focus on and identify their country's future with other Pacific island countries. The last consideration might help explain — and was certainly reinforced by — the apparent reluctance of senior Australian officials employed by the Papua New Guinea government to involve Papua New Guineans in issues related to the common border with Indonesia (to the extent that some would not even discuss policy openly in the Department; they insisted on meeting for briefings outside). It certainly explains some of the difficulties that arose in managing the border — and dealing with Indonesia — in the mid-1980s, including the lack of relevant experience among Papua New Guinean officials, and the need for the almost-instant localization of key positions which followed.

The third element represented an early attempt to reach out to Papua New Guinea's Asian neighbours — cautiously, for the reasons just outlined. The main outcome was a number of statements promoting cooperation between the South Pacific Bureau for Economic Co-operation (SPEC, which later became the South Pacific Forum Secretariat, now the Pacific Islands Forum Secretariat) and the Association of South-East Asian Nations (ASEAN), and not-very-productive meetings between senior officials of the two regional organizations.

The feature shared by each of the three main elements of Universalism was that none of them, singly or together, provided clear guidance — indeed, to some extent they hindered the further development of Papua New Guinea's foreign relations (perhaps, incidentally, buying time for making much wiser decisions). Together, they helped to avoid the temptation of opening missions and posturing on issues where national interests and likely influence were not clear, which had bedevilled other countries in the first few years of independence, and sometimes led to subsequent closures and policy changes (Boyce 1977, 145).

The first element, in particular, provided a basis for resisting external pressures to embroil Papua New Guinea in rivalry between other states by being 'friend to all, and enemy to none'. The second, identification with other Pacific island countries, did not have an obvious basis in the interests of the new nation-state (as distinct from sentiment; culture or physical appearance — which are, obviously, not uniform throughout Papua New Guinea; clear sources of significant national interests, or adequate guides to the development of relations with other countries and international organizations). While identification and solidarity with other South Pacific (island) countries might be a source of support in contexts where states are equal and numbers count, such as the United Nations General Assembly, it did little to strengthen Papua New Guinea's role in the world. Insofar as it led others to see Papua New Guinea as part of a generally less important and less influential region in a remote part of the world, where Australian, New Zealand and other Western interests were dominant, it might even have weakened Papua New Guinea's international standing (the South Pacific has been, in certain respects, a source of weakness in some contexts, if a source of strength in others, as far as Papua New Guinea — the most populous country in the region, with the largest and most diverse economy, and a unique land border with an Asian country — is concerned).

If the metaphor of being a bridge or link between regions had been given operational significance, the third element might, at best, have defined a possible role — though its focus was not on Papua New Guinea's particular national interests (in which cooperation between regions could well be of greater or even exclusive benefit to other, smaller states, and might complicate relations with Indonesia over Indonesian Papua, for example). If it had any implications for questions of principle, such as contributing to regional or world peace, they were never clearly spelt out.

It was against the background outlined, including considerable awareness of the particular drawbacks identified above, that the then minister for Foreign Affairs and Trade, Hon. Ebia Olewale, who was also deputy prime minister, and the first secretary of the Department at independence, Anthony Siaguru, agreed there should be a foreign policy review, and obtained cabinet's endorsement in early 1979.

A combination of independent judgment and responsiveness to Papua New Guinean circumstances was achieved by having an external consultant (E.P. Wolfers), submit his findings and generally work to a committee of departmental heads (from Prime Minister and National Executive Council, Foreign Affairs and Trade, Defence, Finance, and Primary Industry) to review the *White Paper* in draft, before it was presented to the National Executive Council for final approval. Additional inputs into the process had been provided earlier in the process by participants in a conference of heads of Papua New Guinea's diplomatic missions and consular posts around the world, who travelled to Port Moresby for the purpose, as well as a variety of senior officials from other government agencies.

The key recommendation in the *Foreign Policy White Paper* (1982) was that Papua New Guinea should adopt a basic approach to foreign policy making of 'active and selective engagement'. The approach was described as involving:

• identifying issues, opportunities and problems which seem likely to be relevant to Papua New Guinea's national interests;
• selecting those issues and actors (including governments, international organizations, multinational corporations, etc.) which affect us and which we, sometimes only with the support of others, can affect;
• analyzing the relative advantages and disadvantages of alternative courses of action or inaction; and
• engaging actively with the issues and actors selected to secure our national interests.

The *White Paper* made clear that, far from providing guidelines for immediate implementation, it proposed an evolutionary approach by outlining a basis for ongoing policy-making (it was intended to help generate policy from time to time, not to provide a detailed blueprint for implementation). Thus:

> the objectives should be kept under continuous review, and adapted as Papua New Guinea's internal and external circumstances change. Such review will be facilitated by the basic approach (Papua New Guinea 1982, 19).

The new approach clearly looked to breaking out from the not-very-consistent-or-successful attempts at evenhandedness, the timidity and the inaction which had, by then, become features of Universalism in practice, by promoting a more outward-looking and purposeful posture towards Papua

New Guinea's foreign relations that allowed for clear distinctions to be drawn in the development of relations with different countries and international organizations (a point which was even clearer in the various strategies proposed). It envisaged the Department of Foreign Affairs and Trade being the key point of contact — and the chief engine for managing relations — with the external world. However, this role was only partly fulfilled. Relevant factors in the failure to promote the Department's role in coordinating all aspects of Papua New Guinea's foreign relations included: inter-agency rivalries; failure to set up adequate machinery to facilitate consultation and cooperation across the whole of government and with the private sector and civil society (as proposed in the *White Paper* (1982, 72, 90)); the way in which membership of international financial institutions is reserved to finance ministries and their representatives; the practice whereby high commissions have direct access to national government departments and other agencies; the role that meetings at the level of head of government play in international relations; and similar considerations. Other factors included the priority that successive governments have (quite properly) given to domestic development, the Department's and its senior officers' relative standing in the wider bureaucracy, and such internal issues as the relative (in)experience, seniority and turnover of staff.

In distinguishing between the basic approach towards foreign policy making and the particular policy priorities or catchphrase of the government or minister of the day (and successive governments and ministers for Foreign Affairs each wanted their own), the *White Paper* attempted to avoid some of the difficulties that had arisen with Universalism by focusing on ongoing policy-making, not immediate policy, and so on furthering perceived state interests, essentially on Realist lines, not simple rules-of-thumb. It did so by distinguishing the basic approach from the particular concerns and preferences of the government/minister of the day, and leaving space for the latter to be announced as the basic approach is applied and new priorities are identified as conditions change. It therefore proved to be possible for successive governments to endorse and apply the basic approach of active and selective engagement even as ministries, responsible ministers and their specific preferences and priorities changed, and new catchphrases to describe particular governments' and ministers' priorities were announced and turned from words into actions.

Thus, the basic approach was formally endorsed, and, as time passed, simply accepted and followed, by successive governments and ministers for Foreign Affairs.

However, having been prepared at a time when a key objective was still to open diversify, strengthen and deepen Papua New Guinea's foreign relations — and economic circumstances and prospects seemed to allow for ongoing budgetary growth, hence recruitment and training of staff, and the opening of new missions and posts — the basic approach pointed the way to expansion, not contraction. In doing so, it paid insufficient attention to the opportunity costs of implementation within Departmental and national budgets, especially in the more stringent economic and budgetary circumstances which developed from 1994 on. The same feature, therefore, became one of the reasons why the basic approach has become less and less relevant (at least, without modification) as cutbacks in funding, staff, and missions and posts, have become more usual orders of the day since the late 1990s.

The basic approach proposed in the *White Paper* led to, and was supported by, a three-pronged diplomatic strategy, which emphasized:

1. consolidation and extension of existing relations;
2. independent and constructive neighbourly relations; and
3. diversification and development of relations.

The particular policies/priorities/emphases/orientations and applications promoted by successive governments and ministers have included 'purposeful direction' (c. 1982), 'independent commitment to international cooperation' (c.1989), 'look North' (c. 1992), 'opportunity and participation' (c. 1994), 'look North and work the Pacific' (c. 1994) and 'reinforcing core relationships' (c. 1995).

In addition to ministerial statements presented to the National Parliament, occasional speeches and negotiated arrangements with various countries and international organizations, these policies were variously elaborated, notably in the United Nations Initiative on Opportunity and Participation undertaken by Hon. Sir John Kaputin in 1993–95, which resulted in the publication of quite a substantial book to promote the proposal (Kaputin 1993), and the subsequent convening of a panel of experts (with financial support from Papua New Guinea) at United Nations headquarters to prepare a report (UN 1995), and, separately, the *Pacific Plan* (Papua New Guinea 1995).

Consistent with one of its main general purposes, the United Nations Initiative on Opportunity and Participation proved to be a useful trial-run for officials (and others) who would later need to know what was involved in mobilizing support at the United Nations for the establishment of a United Nations presence to assist in the Bougainville peace process. This presence took the form of a United Nations observer mission in Bougainville, Papua New Guinea, which was invited to help implement the *Lincoln* and *Ceasefire Agreements* after 1998, and the *Bougainville Peace Agreement* from 30 August 2001. The mission was formally known in New York as the 'United Nations Political Office in Bougainville, Papua New Guinea' (UNPOB) because it was funded from the United Nations Department of Political Affairs, not the peace-keeping budget, until the mission was formally reconstituted for diplomatic, not substantive, reasons, as the 'United Nations

Observer Mission in Bougainville, Papua New Guinea' (UNOMB) for a final six months from the end of 2004, while still being funded from the same source (in both cases, the reference to Papua New Guinea was added by Papua New Guinean diplomats out of regard for — shared — nationalist sensitivities).

However, Papua New Guinea's economic orientation and relative lack of complementarity with other Pacific island countries' economies meant that the *Pacific Plan* served to reaffirm longstanding political commitments rather than produce tangible results (the minister responsible, Sir Julius Chan, since went on to become the architect of the *Pacific Plan* which the Pacific Islands Forum adopted in 2005).

General economic — hence fiscal and specifically budgetary — constraints since 1994 have coincided with an attempt to open formal diplomatic relations with Taiwan (in exchange for incredible claims of likely financial assistance) in mid 1999 and resulting tensions in the Department, compounded by allegations of irregularities and impropriety in the Migration Division, in particular, and growing instability of personnel. These developments have, in turn, given rise to questions about the continuing relevance of the basic approach, as well as capacity to implement or apply it effectively. The then minister for Foreign Affairs, Hon. Sir John Kaputin, therefore, announced a foreign policy review in 2000. A further review was announced by the minister for Foreign Affairs and Immigration, Rt Hon. Sir Rabbie Namaliu, in November 2005.

Implementation

Implementation, as already observed, can be hard to distinguish from policy making, either conceptually or in practical terms — generally, and in the particular case of foreign policy where words and votes in international organizations can be, in effect, actions. Both policy making and implementation in foreign relations are also often dependent on negotiation — more so in relation to foreign policy than other areas of public policy, because individual governments have so little authority or power over so many variables, especially in the case of states like Papua New Guinea which have only limited resources and influence for pursuing national interests and government policies internationally, and tend to have to rely on others for support.

However, even significant foreign policy initiatives can require little more than decisiveness and political will, though additional follow-up may be required if they are to produce optimal, ongoing results. Examples include the way in which a young Departmental officer travelled to, and obtained visitor status for Papua New Guinea at, a meeting of the Non-Aligned Movement, almost as soon as the proposal was formally floated in 1981 (Papua New Guinea has since become a full member, though, with the end of the Cold War, the wider significance of membership has, in certain respects, declined). They also include the decision to open formal diplomatic relations with Vietnam in 1989. Though it required substantial preparation and lobbying, the effort to re-inscribe New Caledonia on the United Nations list of non-self-governing territories in the late 1980s is another case in point — with far-reaching consequences for the people of New Caledonia, French policies and relations in the region, and, perhaps, for decolonisation more generally.

As previously observed, a substantial amount of foreign policy implementation takes the form of attending, participating and, as occasion arises, speaking, voting and making and following up on proposals for change at *ad hoc* or regular, scheduled meetings of international organizations and with significant bilateral partners. Instances in which Papua New Guinea governments have played a critical role have occurred at the United Nations — the re-inscription of New Caledonia as a non-self-governing territory and the Initiative on Opportunity and Participation are examples. Sometimes, they require the establishment of new international organizations, such as the Melanesian Spearhead Group in the late 1980s (an instance of an initiative in an area where, like bilateral relations with Indonesia, Australian officials and observers had previously feared what Papua New Guineans — in this case, with other Melanesians — might say or do). In other cases, they have led to new bilateral arrangements, as in the case of Indonesia and Solomon Islands, especially the *Treaty of Mutual Respect* and the *Framework Treaty Guiding Relations* respectively. Frequently, they have taken the form of gradually strengthening relations with or increasing participation in existing organizations — as in the way in which Papua New Guinea graduated from observer to special observer status at ASEAN in 1981, and was then able to persuade the other members to amend the *Treaty of Amity and Co-operation in South-East Asia* during the 1980s so that Papua New Guinea could accede. Papua New Guinea's experience at ASEAN has also influenced the establishment of the Post-Forum Dialogues in the Pacific.

Some initiatives begin as leaps of faith. Others are devised in the contexts of particular events (of which they are intended to take advantage). Examples include the exchange of letters in October 1984 guaranteeing the safety and providing safeguards for unauthorized border-crossers who return to Indonesia, the precise text of which is secret. Another is the *Treaty of Mutual Respect, Friendship and Co-operation* with Indonesia, signed in 1986, which was the first — and is still the only — treaty explicitly named and aimed to promote 'mutual respect' in the world. A further example is the *Joint Declaration of Principles Guiding Relations* (*JDP*) with Australia, which, though proposed in a somewhat different form and initially resisted by the Australian government, appears to have become the model for a similar arrangement between Australia and Nauru.

The immediate circumstances in which particular initiatives were first proposed, which have often seemed both vivid and urgent at the time, might fade from view, as in the case of the *Treaty of Mutual Respect* and the *JDP*, whose immediate origins — respectively, in a series of alleged border violations, and differences over future foreign aid arrangements — are rarely mentioned, if they are even remembered.

However, the outcomes may prove to be enduring — as evidenced in the public acknowledgement by other governments and independent experts of the contributions these agreements have made not only to bilateral relations but to the stability of the wider region testify (in regard to the *Treaty of Mutual Respect*, in particular, see the positive assessments by a former Australian Foreign Minister in Evans (1989, 178) and Evans and Grant (1991, 171), and the former chairman of a major investment banking and financial services firm, Merrill Lynch Asia Pacific in Dobbs-Higginson 1993, 244; see also the appraisals by an Australian diplomat and scholar that the *Treaty* has put the relationship between the two countries 'on a new and cordial footing' (Henningham 1992, 254), and by another Australian academic that it is 'a significant step ... to improve the foundations for amicable relations' between the two countries (Mediansky 1988, 213–4); though there are also sceptics and critics concerning the *Treaty*'s achievement and value, including the author of, and a number of others cited in, 'Mutual Respect, Friendship and Co-operation?' (May 1987)).

Some initiatives have, in fact, begun not so much as bold gestures or proposals but as a result of questioning the received knowledge on which previous arrangements were based. The mutual security provisions in the *JDP* with Australia are a case in point: they closely resemble provisions in the *Agreement on Mutual Security between Australia, New Zealand and the United States of America* (*ANZUS*), though they are, of course, of lesser status and force in international law. Reported to have been finally hammered out around the cabinet table in Australia, they defy the previous conventional wisdom that Australia would not agree to a stronger form of mutual security assurance for Papua New Guinea than that contained in the 1977 *Joint Statement on a Long Term Defence Arrangement* in which the prime ministers of the two countries committed their governments to consult 'on matters affecting their common security', and engage in joint training and technical cooperation. The *JDP* as a whole has since come to serve as a widely cited touchstone for the overall conduct and development of relations between the two countries.

Obviously, some initiatives are apparently implemented only to have their enduring importance questioned later (as in the case of efforts to place existing defence cooperation arrangements in the context of wider security co-operation). Some, such as Papua New Guinea's efforts to promote more comprehensive and deeper security cooperation among Pacific Islands Forum members during the 1990s, may produce only compromise, as with the 1997 *Aitutaki Declaration on Regional Security Cooperation*, only to be raised again subsequently — and still produce results, as with the *Bitekawa Declaration* of 1999, which commits the signatory governments to cooperate in meeting member states' security vulnerabilities. Another compromise arising from a Papua New Guinean initiative takes the form of the Joint Commercial Commission with the United States of America (USA) — which is a considerable step down from the high-level and wide-ranging consultations between Pacific island countries and the USA sought in response to a previous initiative by President George H. Bush in 1990.

However, Papua New Guinean initiatives are not the only — or even a necessarily helpful — measure of effective policy implementation. Sometimes working with others (for example, in establishing the Western and Central Pacific Tuna Commission) or simply seeking modifications to existing arrangements (as in the case of the *Lomé Convention*'s scheme to support stabilization of mineral export incomes, SYSMIN, during the late 1970s) can be, at least, as important.

Simply working through, and thereby reinforcing the effectiveness of, a body like the South Pacific Forum Fisheries Agency or the South Pacific Applied Geoscience Commission can achieve significant results too, both for an individual member state and for the organization as a whole.

The *Foreign Policy White Paper* was published at a time when a growing number (and proportion) of increasingly well-educated members were being elected to Papua New Guinea's National Parliament — and more of their number were beginning to enter the ministry — with ever greater experience, interest and self-confidence in dealing with foreign affairs.

At the same time, the Department of Foreign Affairs (and Trade) was localizing, gaining experience, and, above all, recruiting, training and promoting increasingly well-qualified Papua New Guinean staff.

Initiatives taken during the 1980s included the opening up of opportunities for secretarial staff to become diplomats, and the (quite separate) establishment of a multi-disciplinary, professionally-oriented, postgraduate program in international relations at the University of Wollongong, specifically tailored to the Papua New Guinea Department's and similar agencies' and governments' needs, subject in the case of Papua New Guinean students to the availability of scholarships from AusAID (the University of Wollongong's program drew positive comment from Papua New Guinea's first ambassador to the United Nations and the United States, and a previous secretary of the Department of Foreign Affairs and Trade, in Matane 2000, 61–2).

Throughout the 1980s, the proportion of foreign service career officers appointed as heads of Papua New Guinea's diplomatic missions and consular posts abroad continued to rise.

The prospects for successfully implementing the more outward- and forward-looking and purposeful approach proposed in the *White Paper* improved accordingly, until budget cuts beginning in the 1990s required the retrenchment of personnel, the repeated restructuring of the Department of Foreign Affairs, and, in 2001–02, the closure of a number of diplomatic missions and consular posts.

One measure of the Department's success in attracting, recruiting and building the capacity of its personnel is the way in which they have, in effect, 'colonized' other areas of the bureaucracy — where, at times, six or more of their number have been heads of other important government agencies. The head of the Department of Foreign Affairs has generally come from the Department's own ranks; the only exceptions have been personnel with previous high-level experience in another government agency — and then following service as a head of a diplomatic mission abroad.

However, following the budget cuts, retrenchments of personnel, closure of missions and posts which have come about (at least, partly) as a result of the 2001 functions review — itself part of the much wider, ongoing public sector reform program — and pending the outcome of ongoing public sector reform and the foreign policy review, it is appropriate to be sombre, though hopeful about the short- to medium-term future of Papua New Guinea's Department of Foreign Affairs.

Conclusion

Like every other area of public policy, Papua New Guinea foreign policy probably deserves a mixed review after twenty-five-plus years — though one in which the balance is all the more positive because of the comparative lateness with which foreign policy-making became a Papua New Guinean responsibility, the relative speed and completeness with which the staff of the Department of Foreign Affairs was localized, and the manner in which early achievements have generally been sustained (while some diplomatic missions and consular posts have been closed, Papua New Guinea has not deliberately breached any treaties or gone back on other international agreements, although the Supreme Court of Papua New Guinea found in 2005 that one, the treaty providing for the Enhanced Co-operation Program (ECP) with Australia, was inconsistent with the *Papua New Guinea Constitution* and had, therefore, to be considerably revised).

It is also important to note that, while the Department's functions have, in certain respects, been cut, the scope of its activities has grown, notably (though not only) in the way that the presence of neutral, regional monitors and the United Nations observer mission in support of the Bougainville peace process has given foreign actors, relations and so policy a fresh domestic dimension.

Implementation of the agreed arrangements for managing foreign relations in consultation and cooperation with the Autonomous Bougainville Government (ABG) under the terms of the *Bougainville Peace Agreement* and the constitutional provisions giving them legal effect will, in future, require the Department of Foreign Affairs to set up and remain mindful of the procedures required to allow the ABG to participate in specified aspects of Papua New Guinea's international relations in accordance with the *Agreement*.

As in other areas of public policy, major initiatives have often come from within — or, at least, from the minister and the Department, including diplomatic missions and consular posts abroad. The distinction promoted in the *Foreign Policy White Paper* between the basic approach (for the generation) of foreign policy and the particular emphases, preferences and catchphrases of successive governments and individual ministers has facilitated continuity and incremental development in key areas. The growing professionalization of the Department of Foreign Affairs, including the gradual increase in the appointment by cabinet of heads of mission and post from within, has supported the process in practice.

Though it is hard to document the case in detail — and there have been occasional departures — the pattern of steady growth (at least, until the cuts necessitated by the overall budgetary situation since 1997) has been supported by the way in which the making and management of what might be loosely described as the political aspects of foreign policy has generally occurred in a context where other materially important factors have also been taken into account, especially foreign aid, trade and investment. In a very particular sense, the latter have provided the ballast which has helped to restrain any tendency to the kinds of extravagances that have occurred (and then required even greater subsequent cutbacks) in other newly-independent, developing countries.

The experience of the Department of Foreign Affairs also underlines the importance of serious commitment to capacity building after recruitment — generally positively, but, in certain respects, negatively, when circumstances have imposed unusually serious limits on the availability of funds and personnel.

The sensitivity of the Department's responsibilities required an unusually early, firm and determined commitment by management to complete localization. The same sensitivity — which includes the role the Department plays in relation to foreign aid — makes it a difficult model to explain and promote more widely within the Papua New Guinea system of government. It is, therefore, perhaps of limited utility in seeking support for building capacity in other areas of public policy.

References

Boyce, P. J. 1977. *Foreign Affairs for New States: Some Questions of Credentials*. St Lucia: University of Queensland Press.

Dihm, William, and Edward P. Wolfers. eds. 1998. *Neutral Regional Truce Monitoring Group for Bougainville: A Collection of Key Agreements and Statements*. Waigani: Government of Papua New Guinea.

Dobbs-Higginson, Michael. 1993. *Asia Pacific: Its Role in the New World Disorder*. Melbourne: William Heinemann.

Evans, Gareth. 1989. Australia's regional security. Ministerial Statement. Reprinted in *Australia's Regional Security*, ed. Greg Fry. Sydney: Allen and Unwin, 1991.

Evans, Gareth and Bruce Grant. 1991. *Australia's Foreign Relations in the World of the 1990s*. Melbourne: Melbourne University Press.

Galbraith, John Kenneth, 1999. *Name-Dropping*. London: Aurum Press.

Griffin, James ed. 1974. *A Foreign Policy for an Independent Papua New Guinea*. Sydney: Angus and Robertson in association with the Australian Institute of International Affairs.

Henningham, Stephen. 1992. Australia and the South Pacific. In *Australia in a Changing World: New Foreign Policy Directions.*, ed. F. A. Mediansky. Sydney: Maxwell Macmillan Australia.

Kaputin, John R. 1993. *Opportunity and Participation*. Waigani: Papua New Guinea Department of Foreign Affairs.

Matane, Sir Paulias. 2000. *Coach Adventures Down Under*. New Delhi: UBS Publishers Distributors.

May, R. J. 1987. 'Mutual respect, friendship and co-operation'? The Indonesia-Papua New Guinea border and its effects on relations between Papua New Guinea and Indonesia. *Bulletin of Concerned Asian Scholars* 19(4): 44–52.

Mediansky, F. A. 1988. Australia and the Southwest Pacific. In *In Pursuit of National Interests: Australian Foreign Policy in the 1990s*, ed. F. A. Mediansky and A. C. Palfreeman. Sydney: Pergamon Press.

Papua New Guinea. 1976. *Universalism: Guidelines to the Foreign Policy of Papua New Guinea*. Port Moresby: Department of Foreign Affairs and Trade.

Papua New Guinea, 1982. Foreign Policy. *Papua New Guinea Foreign Affairs Review* 1(4).

Papua New Guinea. 1994. *Pasifik Pis. Report of the Papua New Guinea Government on the Staging of the Bougainville Peace Conference and the Introduction of the South Pacific Regional Peace Keeping Force*. Port Moresby: Ministry of Foreign Affairs and Trade.

Papua New Guinea. 1995. *Pacific Plan. Presented to the National Parliament*. Port Moresby.

Rosenau, James, N. 1992. Governance, order and change in world politics. In *Governance without Government: Order and Change in World Politics*, ed.

James N. Rosenau and Ernst-Otto Szempiel, 1–29. Cambridge: Cambridge University Press.

Rosenau, James, N. 1997. *Along the Domestic-Foreign Frontier: Exploring Governance in a Turbulent World*. Cambridge: Cambridge University Press.

United Nations. 1995. *Report of the United Nations Panel on Opportunity and Participation*. United Nations General Assembly, Document A/50/501, New York.

Wolfers, Edward P. 1975. *Race Relations and Colonial Rule in Papua New Guinea*. Sydney: Australia and New Zealand Book Co.

Wolfers, Edward P. ed. 1988. *Beyond the Border: Indonesia and Papua New Guinea — South-East Asia and the South Pacific*. Discussion and Documentation. Waigani: University of Papua New Guinea and Suva: the Institute of Pacific Studies.

Wolfers, Edward P. and William Dihm, William eds. 1998. *Neutral Regional Truce Monitoring Group for Bougainville: A Collection of Key Agreements and Statements*. Waigani: Government of Papua New Guinea.

Part 2. Policy case studies

Chapter 17

The 1997-98 Drought in Papua New Guinea: Failure of Policy or Triumph of the Citizenry?

Bryant J. Allen and R. Michael Bourke

The 1997 drought — natural disaster or national disaster

At first glance, the 1997–98 drought in Papua New Guinea was a natural disaster. Between December 1996 and March 1997 the Southern Oscillation Index (SOI), which is the standardized difference in surface air pressure between Darwin and Tahiti and is the oldest and simplest measure of the El Niño-Southern Oscillation (ENSO) phenomenon in the Pacific, fell from +12 to −25. This is the most spectacular fall in the SOI in the post-1950 history of ENSO events. In Papua New Guinea, usually one of the wettest and cloudiest places on the globe, rainfall declined across much of the country. Crops withered and died, local sources of drinking water dried up, and bushfires burned from the coast to the crests of the main mountain ranges, destroying economic trees, sago stands and dwellings. Above 2000 metres altitude, night time temperatures repeatedly fell below zero.

By October 1997 a partial assessment estimated that 150,000 people were eating 'famine' foods. By December, this estimate, based on a second nationwide assessment, had risen to 260,000. A further 980,000 people were assessed to be eating poor quality food in reduced quantities. Many people were forced to walk for hours to collect drinking water of questionable quality. Death rates in isolated places almost certainly increased, many schools closed, many health centres were not staffed and had no medical supplies anyway. In some centres town water supplies were threatened. The hydroelectric station at Sirinumu was forced to stop generating (in order to conserve drinking water in the dam) causing serious power failures in Port Moresby. The Ok Tedi mine closed for seven months because the Fly River became un-navigable and the Porgera mine closed for six weeks through lack of water for processing, resulting in a severe loss of hard currency to the Papua New Guinea economy.

From another point of view, however, 1997–98 was a national disaster for Papua New Guinea. The Papua New Guinea government was unable to come to terms with the severity and extent of the drought. For a number of weeks it did almost nothing and was forced into taking action by the international aid-giving community and in particular by the Australian government which paid for assessments and mounted a large assistance program, implemented by the Australian Defence Force (Lea *et al*. 1999; Barter 2001). Some provincial governments, missions, NGOs and large numbers of ordinary citizens did respond, and offered help to a hungry rural population. But mismanagement of the Papua New Guinea economy, exacerbated by the Asian economic crisis, saw the kina fall from around $US0.72 to $US0.48 between September 1997 and April 1998, and many citizens associated the fall of the kina with the drought. It is not drawing too long a bow to suggest that the precipitous fall in the value of the currency, and its continued decline to below $US0.30, set in train forces which contributed to the fall of the Skate government in 1999. Not the least among these forces were dramatic price rises for imported foods consumed largely in urban areas.

The 'dominant' or establishment view of natural disasters is that, although they are attributable to nature, good public policy, backed up by advanced geophysical and managerial capability, can prevent or ameliorate the impacts (Hewitt 1983). The net impact of a natural event is seen as the outcome of a 'battle' between the forces of nature and the institutional and technical counter forces of the state. This view of natural disasters sees good public policy, emergency measures, plans and relief and rehabilitation as critical. While scientific insights are important they are to be subordinated to action, usually carried out by military or quasi-military organizations.

The establishment view of natural disaster accords with the experiences of disaster events in developed countries. For example, much of the discourse around the recent bushfires in Australia is of a quasi-military character with 'headquarters' receiving 'intelligence' from satellites and aerial 'surveillance', 'bombing' from the air and fire 'fighters' 'attacking' the infernos, which are the work of a dangerous and malevolent Nature. Volunteer fire fighters are lauded as heroes. After the fires have abated, policy questions are debated. Many of them are about resources, regulations and control. Government departments and politicians manœuver for the greatest advantage or the least amount of blame.

But in developing countries, such as Papua New Guinea, the establishment view of natural disasters may not apply. In these countries, resources are chronically stretched, effective centralized control of education and health services, let alone quasi-military and military forces, is always questionable and technical capabilities are poor or non-existent. Hewitt argues that the establishment view may even warp and constrain other possible views of the event and hence better ways of managing future events. In arguing this point, Hewitt suggests that in developing countries, the outcome of a disaster is not as dependent upon the geophysical processes and existing policies as it is upon the values of the society and its institutions and the 'conditions of everyday life'. This alternative view implies that the expectations placed upon the Papua New Guinea state in 1997 by the international aid-giving community and the media were unrealistic and to a large extent unfair. It also explains why the responses to the disaster by Papua New Guinea civil society received little recognition during and after the event, even within Papua New Guinea.

This chapter first examines some of the reasons why the Papua New Guinea state was unable to quickly come to terms with the 1997–98 drought. Secondly, it describes how Papua New Guinea citizens responded to the event. Thirdly, it discusses what can be learned from the 1997 event for future policy-making, both in Papua New Guinea, in Australia and elsewhere. A fundamental dilemma is revealed for those who must make policy in Papua New Guinea and in neighboring relief-giving countries, such as Australia. If the establishment view does not apply, and it is argued that it does not in Papua New Guinea, how does the Papua New Guinea state and the international aid-giving community offer assistance to people who will be left to manage as best they can with their own resources? What alternative policy choices might be available?

ENSO and PNG

The Southern Oscillation is the term used to describe a phenomenon in which the temperature of the sea and the circulation of atmosphere over the Pacific and Indian Oceans move from one extreme to another in a regular pattern. At one extreme, known as El Niño, the eastern Pacific sea surface warms and air pressure falls, while in the western Pacific the sea surface cools and air pressure rises. Rainfall on the normally arid Peruvian coast increases while the higher pressure and cool seas in the western Pacific bring low rainfall conditions to Papua New Guinea. At the other extreme, known as La Niña, air pressure falls in the western Pacific and warm seas bring high rainfall to Papua New Guinea. The system does not oscillate with perfect regularity and is much of the time somewhere between the extremes. For a number of reasons, some not yet understood and some to do with Papua New Guinea's complex geography, extreme ENSO events do not all affect Papua New Guinea with similar severity. However El Niño conditions extreme enough to cause drought, such as that experienced in 1997, have probably occurred about once every 100 years for at least the last 6000 years (Haberle 2000), while less severe events have occurred on average around every thirteen years. Papua New Guinea is a high rainfall equatorial country and La Niña impacts are more difficult to identify, although it is possible that they cause longer and more chronic food shortages in areas dependent on sweet potato than the more spectacular but less common El Niño events (Bourke 1988).

The historical record in Papua New Guinea, which is a little over 110 years long in the lowlands and 50 years in the highlands, shows that severe droughts have occurred in 1914–15, 1941–42, 1972, 1982 and 1997. It is also likely, but more difficult to demonstrate, that severe droughts were experienced in 1887 and 1901–02. Documentary reports increase in frequency and geographical coverage over time, but even the early reports suggest widespread disruption to food supplies, fires and famine. In 1901 and 1902, 'famine' is reported from Rigo District and Goodenough Island, a 'complete crop failure' was reported from Milne Bay and the sago swamps at Cape Nelson burned. In 1914, E.W.P. Chinnery, the government anthropologist, reported that almost the whole population of New Ireland, including those normally dependent on sago, were 'wandering about in desperation'. He reported 'destructive bushfires along the whole line of the coast' and a 'great loss of life' (Chinnery 1929, 45). In 1941 'abnormal conditions and fires' were reported from Wau, Bulolo, Madang and Wewak, the New Britain coast was 'brown from drought or black from the effects of fires' with 'smoke everywhere like a thick fog' and sago swamps burned out on the Sepik River (*Pacific Island Monthly* November 1941, 6). Food supplies were 'critical' in Western Province and the 'inland mountain districts' of Papua (*Pacific Island Monthly* February 1942, 29). Oral accounts from the highlands include frost in Enga followed by mass migrations from the Upper Lai Valley in which 'many died on the road' (Dwyer 1952). From Tari in the Southern Highlands comes a description of a two year drought that occurred soon after the visit to Hoiebia by Taylor and Black in 1938 (Gammage 1998, 77) when a bushfire burned right across the central basin, the peaty swamp caught fire and a famine occurred 'much worse than what happened in 1972' (Allen *et al.* 1989, 289).

It is probable that severe ENSO events have been occurring for some thousands of years. The general success of Papua New Guinea food production systems in maintaining the population over that period suggests that these events do not have a long-term negative influence on food production, or that systems are adapted to cope. In pre-colonial times, because severe ENSO events occur only every three or four generations, knowledge of how to cope was recorded in oral accounts. The coming 'big one' was used by older people to cajole and threaten young men and women who did not want to work hard in their gardens: 'Work hard', they were told, 'because one day a big famine will happen and you will starve if you don't have large gardens'.

In a bureaucracy, however, an event which occurs only once every 100 years is not likely to be well remembered. In Papua New Guinea there was almost no administration to record the consequences of the 1901, 1914 or 1941 (in the highlands) events. The loss of experience at independence and concerns with other matters since then, means that in 1997, severe ENSO events were not at the forefront of most peoples' minds.

The 1972 event — ignorance, politics and food relief

In 1972, however, the Australian colonial administration was at its greatest geographical extent. It was about to hand over powers of internal government to a Papua New Guinea administration. The 1972 event was less severe than 1941 or 1997 by several orders of magnitude, but to public servants in the highlands it was their first experience of repeated frosts at elevations above 1800 metres. The spectacular destruction of sweet potato gardens by frost and the fear of widespread public disorder and tribal fighting as people began to migrate out of the worst affected areas led to a food relief program, managed by expatriate missionaries and administration officers and carried out with assistance from the Australian Army. At the peak of the program, 150,000 people were being fed. A parallel program distributed planting material of English potato and corn seed and collected sweet potato vines from lower altitudes and transported them into frosted areas, to enable the restoration of the food supply as soon as possible.

Following the completion of the food relief program in 1973, Eric Waddell argued in a report to the government (published as Waddell 1989) that the switch in policy from one that supported local coping in late 1971, to direct intervention by providing food in 1972, was brought about by the severity of the frost and widespread drought, the inability of the Australian administration to judge the severity of the situation because of a lack of knowledge of local agricultural systems, and the widespread belief that the local population had no capacity to cope with the situation. Waddell was primarily concerned that the relief effort had undermined longstanding adaptive strategies maintained by local people to deal with the frost hazard.

However, two serving Australian officers who commented on Waddell's report emphasized that changes in the broader political environment were an important part of the decision to provide food. Between August 1971, when the first frosts occurred, and April 1972, Papua New Guinea's first fully operative national government had taken office and the formal handover of self-government was due to take place in December 1973. Brian Scoullar, then the Department of Agriculture Rural Development Officer at Laiagam in Enga, argued that it was a Papua New Guinea government and not an Australian colonial administration that was responsible for decision-making in 1972 and that the decisions were based on two questions: how many people would die if nothing was done, and could the new government afford to be seen to be responsible for any deaths of highlanders under the political circumstances in force at the time (the new government was led and dominated by lowlanders and highlanders had accepted the move to self-government with some reluctance). John Wallis, Southern Highlands District Rural Development Officer in 1971, also notes that the 'crisis was fused politically' with an emphasis on national unity. Both Scoullar and Wallis believed that without feeding, many deaths would have occurred, mainly of the very young and the very old, and Scoullar saw this as part of the adaptive strategy. Both also commented on the almost complete lack of knowledge of indigenous food production systems, in particular the effect of frost on sweet potato production (published as part of Waddell 1989).

Waddell (1983, 35) later commented on the politicisation of the 1972 event, noting that 'the new government was concerned to strengthen the very fragile (and artificial) sense of national unity'. The Australian administration and the Christian missions were 'concerned to assume a strong interventionist role as was their custom, thereby countering possible criticism and suspicion....[T]he new government [saw] the relief program as a vehicle for affirming its leadership and demonstrating the solidarity of all New Guineans'.

Post-1972: crying 'Wolf!'

The 1972 event and the generally accepted conclusion that too many people were fed for too long had a number of repercussions for policies dealing with natural disasters. Partly in response to the revealed ignorance of food production systems, the first Papua New Guinea National Food Crop Conference was held in 1975 (Willson and Bourke 1976). Prior to 1972 it would have been impossible to find the resources to mount such a conference. Waddell's argument that food relief undermines local coping was widely accepted by concerned expatriates, but not by Papua New Guinea politicians. A pattern was established in which policy, thought to be sound and sensible, was made by expatriate experts and administrations, often supported by Papua New Guinea public servants, but was not supported by political leaders and their expatriate advisers, some of whom went out of their way to subvert what were supposed to be their own policies.

Decisions were increasingly influenced by those who stood to benefit most from having a 'disaster'. Thus in 1980 when food shortages were reported from many parts of the Southern Highlands, at the time heavily staffed by foreign agricultural, health and nutritional experts under a World Bank rural development project, the foreigners and senior Papua New Guinea public servants argued, against the urgings of local government councillors and provincial politicians, that food aid would cause a breakdown in 'local coping mechanisms' and that it was not warranted in the particular circumstances. The politicians won the day, however, and the National Executive Council approved the spending of K500,000 for 'relief operations to drought frost affected areas' (sic). This decision was recommended by the Papua New Guinea National Emergency Services (PNGNES) and the Papua New Guinea Defence Force (PNGDF). The PNGDF, which was tasked by PNGNES to distribute the food, was involved in flying national politicians in chartered helicopters on brief visits to affected areas before the decision was made. Very small amounts of food were distributed directly to some local areas and not to others. Provincial public servants were by-passed by the operation which was directed by local politicians. Clansmen who had not received food aid because they were of a different tribal allegiance to the local member of parliament took out their anger by joining a stone throwing mob in Mendi or by blocking roads and robbing trucks carrying relief supplies in Enga.

In February 1981 the public service was successful in blocking attempts to create a 'disaster'. The Pacific representative of the UN World Food Programme (UNWFP), an American based in Fiji, made his first ever visit to Papua New Guinea. At Mount Hagen provincial politicians took him to Tambul and showed him frost-affected sweet potato gardens and told him people were about to starve. As a result he placed a request directly with the UNWFP in Rome for food aid for 39,597 Papua New Guinea villagers 'totally deprived of subsistence food'. The request was sent back from Rome to Papua New Guinea for confirmation. In Port Moresby, the receipt of this request was the first that the national government knew of the situation. Phil Ainsworth, a retired Australian Army officer working in the National Planning Office (NPO) Coordination Section, pre-empted the director of PNGNES, a New Zealand-born Papua New Guinea citizen Leith Anderson, by establishing an inter-departmental committee known as the National Disaster and Relief Committee. The committee continued to be chaired by Anderson, but comprised senior public servants from Treasury, Finance, National Planning, Provincial and Local Government Affairs, the PNGDF and the police. In a report written by Ainsworth, the committee said that it found itself 'confronted by conflicting information' and noted that 'no objective survey' had been made. A 'technical appraisal team' was formed. It was led by Paul Wohlt, an American anthropologist who had spent 1972 in the field at Kandep, following migrating groups to the lower valleys and back again, and comprised a geographer, a nutritionist and a Papua New Guinean graduate working for the Simbu Land Use Project.

Before the appraisal team had reported, the PNGNES director leaked the details of the UNWFP offer to the press and implied that its acceptance was being held up by uncaring bureaucrats. Senior national politicians, including Paul Torato, then minister for Justice, lambasted the committee in the press, accusing it of ignoring 'my starving people' and stating that '150,000 are starving' and need food for six months. However the appraisal team found that the food aid was not required and the Papua New Guinea Department of Foreign Affairs formally declined the UNWFP offer, the first country ever to do so. The appraisal team's report contained evidence of senior national ministers having food delivered by helicopter and truck to communities in their electorates that had not requested assistance and did not need it. In the Rigo mountains, food received had been carefully stored in villages because people believed some mistake had been made and that it would have to be returned (Wohlt *et al.* 1982). A national election was to be held in 1982.

The only semblance of 'policy' at this time comprised public requests by vested interests, mainly politicians from affected areas, the military and the emergency services staff, that food should be distributed after almost every minor frost or alleged food shortage. Senior public servants and expatriate experts at the national and provincial level, who wanted objective assessments carried out first, opposed these requests. The ability of one side or the other to get their way was influenced to some extent by economic conditions in the country. In 1982, a relatively severe ENSO event that resulted in widespread frosts across the highlands, and a drought that stranded barges on the Fly River, coincided with a collapse in export commodity prices and a doubling of the price of oil. After the experiences of 1980 and 1981, a national ministerial 'assessment committee' was established and the national government refused to release funds until provinces had set up their own assessment teams and produced evidence of need. Provincial public servants, then smarting at levels of political interference that are now accepted as normal, made statements in newspapers that, at the urgings of provincial political leaders, villagers were exaggerating their needs and were hiding food from assessment teams in order to attract relief supplies.

By the end of 1982, a widespread climate of cynicism had developed in which villagers were portrayed as far from helpless in the face of natural disaster. They were viewed as clever and cunning and not only capable of coping, but of tricking supplies of rice and fish out of the government. In addition, the disinterested role of the military and emergency services was openly questioned. The PNGDF had produced a clearly inadequate report on the frosts which was again leaked to the press. This report recommended that the PNGDF be given K1.1 million with which to mount a relief program. This proposal was publicly mocked and rejected by senior Treasury officials. The sad irony was that many people probably suffered severe food shortages for some months in 1982.

1997 — a policy failure?

From 1982 to 1997, Papua New Guinea governments were distracted from making policy on natural disasters by a civil war and a series of economic crises. The PNGDF was engaged in Bougainville and lost interest in 'disasters' as a source of income. The PNGNES remained under the leadership of Anderson, who was seen by many senior public servants as compromised after 1981 and 1982. It was not properly funded and was allowed to run down to the point where it was almost completely ineffective. Rumours abounded in Port Moresby that senior PNGNES staff were receiving kickbacks from suppliers of emergency equipment such as tarpaulins and buckets. One way or another, the PNGNES was demoralized and incapacitated. But in the strange ways of Port Moresby, the director continued to have political support from within and was not replaced. While he remained it was difficult to reform the PNGNES. Various attempts to improve the organization, including aid projects, ran aground as senior officials played political games to ensure they maintained their positions of influence and control. The PNGNES continued to deal with calls for help from the odd village affected by a flood or a local landslide. But when the Rabaul volcanoes erupted in 1994, destroying the town and creating a large number of homeless, nobody seriously expected the PNGNES to be able to cope and a special task force was set up almost immediately which largely excluded the PNGNES.

Thus in 1997, as the drought increased in intensity, Papua New Guinea had no policy with which to deal with it and had an emergency service which was viewed as a joke by many observers. In June 1997, the Land Management Group at the Australian National University wrote to Anderson, pointing out that the SOI had taken the most precipitous fall for fifty years and that it was possible a severe drought and frosts would occur. He was sent photocopies of parts of a 334 page special edition of *Mountain Research and Development* which contained our knowledge of ENSO impacts in Papua New Guinea to 1985. No acknowledgment was received and phone calls were not returned. In Papua New Guinea, as the situation developed, provincial public servants did not know which agency or department to report to. In August 1997, in response to widespread frosts in the highlands, the Department of Agriculture and Livestock (DAL) organized a meeting in Mount Hagen. The Department of Provincial and Local Government Affairs (DPLGA) had teams in the field collecting information for a new Village Directory (a database of villages and local services), and was getting reports of problems in many locations.

The structure of government in Port Moresby meant that senior officials from DAL and DPLGA (such as Ted Sitapai and Brian Deutrom respectively) who knew that problems were developing in rural areas did not speak with each other. Rather they met Mike Bourke, an ex-DAL research agronomist now at ANU, by chance during a visit by him to Port Moresby in August and asked independently if it would be possible to carry out an assessment. Bourke directed them to the Australian High Commission to request assistance. But it was not until the *Sydney Morning Herald* published a front-page article by Lucy Palmer on 15 September 1997, entitled 'Cry for help as our neighbors start to die' complete with a colour photograph of a woman at Tambul prostrate on a parched and frost-damaged sweet potato mound, that things began to happen. In Papua New Guinea, Matthew Kanua of DAL used the 1989 *Mountain Research and Development* publication and Bourke's 1988 thesis on food shortages in the highlands to write a report to his department secretary. In Canberra, the Land Management Group at ANU was asked by AusAID if it was possible to carry out a national assessment of food supply and drinking water.

The outcomes of the two assessments and the drought and frost relief programs based on them have been described elsewhere (Allen 2000; Bourke 2000; Allen and Bourke 2001). Sixteen papers covering particular aspects of the 1997 event are included in the proceedings of the 2000 Papua New Guinea Food and Nutrition Conference (Bourke *et al*. 2001). This is not the place to re-visit suggestions for policies on climatic monitoring and ENSO prediction, crop systems research or ways of ameliorating impacts by ensuring schools and health centres remain open (Allen and Bourke 2001). Instead we want to examine how the Papua New Guinea state responded to the crisis that the event created. The question being posed is, should the performance of the Papua New Guinea government in 1997 be judged against the establishment view of natural disasters, or some other criteria.

Lucy Palmer's *Sydney Morning Herald* article, and others even more lurid that followed in quick succession in Australian newspapers, placed pressure on the Australian government to 'do something'. Almost certainly, questions from the Australian foreign minister to his Papua New Guinea counterpart were what stimulated a reaction from the Papua New Guinea government. Following from Mike Bourke's chance visit, a formal request was made for assistance to assess the impact of the drought and this was immediately approved in Canberra. The request was initiated by Brian Deutrom, an expatriate officer in the Department of Provincial and Local Government Affairs through the minister, Simon Kaumi. Shortly after this, Peter Barter, an Australian-born Papua New Guinea citizen and former minister of Health, was asked by Prime Minister Skate to chair a National Drought Relief Committee, the previous committees having quietly faded away between 1982 and 1997. Barter was well known as a relatively successful minister, although he had created unhappiness in some quarters of the public service by outspoken criticism of health staff who did not carry out their professional duties satisfactorily. He was also the owner of a tourist business including hotels, two ships and a personal helicopter. Membership of the new committee comprised senior politicians from all regions and from the government and the opposition, including Simon Kaumi, military and police officers, senior public servants, and NES staff. But before the committee had met, and while he was on a self-sponsored drought relief fund-raising trip to Australian RSL clubs, Barter was replaced by Peti Lafanama, the MP for Eastern Highlands Province and provincial governor. Barter was appointed 'liaison and implementation officer', with no terms of reference, to a committee that did not meet (Barter 2001, 262). Mr Lafanama was facing a court challenge to his election. He immediately left Port Moresby for Goroka and did not return for at least a month. This had a number of consequences.

First, the provinces and other Papua New Guinea institutions had no formal national body to report to, or to request information from. Every province was required to set up its own provincial drought relief committee and in most provinces these committees were sensibly organized, with membership from government, business, NGOs and missions, were active and made realistic and sound decisions. In general local political representatives were not active members of the provincial drought relief committees, and sought their own funds through political channels. The PNGNES set up a Coordination Centre in the Waigani government offices which was supposed to be manned twenty-four hours a day. The Centre quickly became unreliable, because of unexplained staff absences, incompetence and power cuts (it was set up in a room with no windows) and was soon largely ignored by those working on the assessments and relief planning, at least until Anderson was promised a knighthood and retired, when it was reorganized.

Secondly, with no active committee in place, political pressure built up on the Papua New Guinea government to do something. We are not familiar with the details of the funds made available through the Papua New Guinea government in 1997. However, before the assessment team's reports were received, the national government made an allocation of more than K1 million in total, direct to all MPs on the basis of the number of people resident in their electorates. This meant that MPs whose electorates were relatively unaffected by drought or frost received the same amount of funds, on a *pro rata* basis, as those whose electorates were severely affected. It seems likely that most MPs handed over the money to their personal staff and told them to buy food. In severely affected electorates, the funds were insufficient to feed the numbers of people seriously short of food for more than a few days. In many cases all the allocation was spent on food, with nothing left to pay for transport, and weeks went by while transport was sought. Commonly, business houses in Lae donated trucks to deliver the rice to highlands locations or PMV owners were contracted to pick up rice from Lae but were never paid. At Yonki in Eastern Highlands, for example, a shipping container was dumped outside the police station by the staff of the local MP, and people were told to take rice if they needed it, under police supervision. Old people and those distant from a main road received nothing and there was no accounting of who received the rice.

Thirdly, the international aid-giving community had no single central Papua New Guinea organization to talk to, or to get decisions from. In frustration, the Australian government side-stepped almost all Papua New Guinea government organizations, including the inactive Drought Relief Committee, and, with approval from Minister Kaumi, launched its own $A30 million relief program to areas accessible only by air and judged by assessment teams to be severely affected (Sudradjat 2001). In its early stages, this program liaised with Papua New Guinea officials only at the uppermost level of government.

Fourthly, a critical task given to the committee, to set up and manage a transparent trust fund into which all contributions to a Papua New Guinea relief fund could be paid, was not completed until December 1997. Foreign governments and international aid organizations refused to place funds into a general revenue account. But for a number of weeks the Papua New Guinea government insisted that all donations should go into a government-controlled account (Barter 2001, 261). Frustrated members of the diplomatic corps told senior Papua New Guinea public servants in language that was distinctly undiplomatic, that they would not deposit funds into anything other than a trust account because the money would be 'stolen'. As a result many charities directed their considerable funds to the Red Cross, Caritas, the Salvation Army and Oxfam. The Papua New Guinea NGO community formed their own committee under the Papua New Guinea Red Cross to coordinate their efforts.

This summary does not cover all Papua New Guinea government responses to the drought. The formal Papua New Guinea government response improved as time passed. A number of provincial governments (including Enga, Simbu, Milne Bay and Manus) responded with outstanding effectiveness and efficiency; others (including Western Highlands, Eastern Highlands, Morobe, East New Britain and New Ireland) set up effective provincial committees; while yet others did almost nothing. Government agencies became involved in rehabilitation projects using World Bank funds, and DAL organized a third assessment in 1998 with AusAID support. It is enough, however, to attempt to answer the question, was the chaotic response to the crisis in 1997 by the Papua New Guinea government a policy failure?

First, we have argued that in 1997, following of a loss of confidence in the 1980s in the institutions that are responsible for responding to natural disasters, there was very little policy in existence that can be said to have failed. Secondly, a policy is only as good as the ability of a government to implement it. In 1997, the Papua New Guinea government had almost no capacity to deal with a major natural disaster in the manner required of it by the establishment view of disaster management. The central coordinating office responsible for disaster management was demoralized, poorly trained and under-equipped. The disciplined forces were inadequately funded and equipped, frequently accused of being poorly disciplined and were suffering demoralizing defeats on Bougainville. The economy was in poor shape. The political organization of the country had just been reformed in a conscious attempt to remove conflict between provincial governments and the national government by doing away with the provincial governments. However, national government departments were poorly prepared to take over the tasks that the reforms demanded and provincial administrations did not know how to make the new system work. Funds became stuck at all levels of government. Even the best policy in the world could not have saved Papua New Guinea from itself in 1997. This was not a failure of policy, but a failure of governance.

Does it follow from this that Papua New Guinea should be encouraged and helped to make better policy about natural disasters and to fix up all of the things that did not work in 1997, and in general do not work very well most of the time? Or, since, at least in the medium term, it will be most unlikely that all parts of government in Papua New Guinea will function effectively all of the time, is there any point in having a policy that demands a highly managed and coordinated government response to implement it?

Before answering these questions, the response of Papua New Guinea civil society to the 1997 drought needs to be briefly considered.

A triumph of the citizenry?

The AusAID and Australian Defence Force (ADF) relief program provided food to more than 100,000 people in areas accessible only by air (Sudradjat 2001, 219). But the assessment teams estimated that 260,000 people had no food available and 980,000 had severely restricted amounts of food available from gardens. That implies that around 160,000 people who had no food and 980,000 who had insufficient food were left to be assisted by the Papua New Guinea government relief program. We know that Papua New Guinea government responses were inadequate to say the least. The Papua New Guinea national government purchased around 23,500 tonnes of rice for relief in 1997/98 (compared to around 9400 tonnes purchased by AusAID and 7000 tonnes purchased by individual provincial governments) but much of this food was delivered after the most critical period in December 1997 had passed (see, for example, Jonathon 2001, 212–213). How did these people survive?

First, they ate 'famine foods', either foods that are not eaten often, or that are only eaten in times of hunger. Secondly, in rural areas people raised small amounts of cash by killing and selling pigs, cooking and selling pork and vegetables, buying packets of cigarettes and selling them individually, and by selling artifacts. With the cash earned they purchased imported rice and flour. Thirdly, they moved to areas where food was available. A customary coping mechanism in frost-affected areas is to move to lower altitude valleys to stay with relatives. It was estimated that up to 75 per cent of people moved out of the Kandep and Marient basins during 1997 and walked over mountain passes into the Tsaka and Lai valleys. The problem with this response in 1997 was that the drought was so widespread and severe that food in these areas was also critically short. Many people moved further to stay with relatives in towns. For example, an estimated 20–25 per cent of the population from villages at Elimbari in Simbu migrated to Goroka, Lae and Port Moresby (Bourke 2000, 163). Anecdotal reports suggest that many public servants had standing room only in their houses at night and spent all of their salaries and savings on buying food. Fourthly, people employed in urban areas or at mines either sent money to their rural relatives or purchased rice and sent it home.

The overall outcome of these responses and the relief program was a 65,917 tonne or 38 per cent increase in the sales of rice in Papua New Guinea during 1997–98. The important point is that over 80 per cent (54,000 tonnes) of the additional rice was purchased through retail outlets (Bourke 2000, 160; Whitecross and Franklin 2001).This is the rice purchased by people who had sold their collection of empty bottles, or killed their pigs, or cooked vegetable stews, or sold cigarettes. It is the rice that people bought for their relatives visiting the towns and which people sent into the countryside to their home villages. It should be noted that Rice Industries, the importer of almost all rice into Papua New Guinea did not increase prices during 1997, despite the severe drop in the value of the kina (Whitecross and Franklin 2001).

So, although due credit must go to AusAID and the ADF for delivering food to inaccessible areas, credit must also go to the citizens of Papua New Guinea for feeding themselves or feeding their relatives, from their own resources, for around four to six months in 1997–98. They 'drew upon the "on-going and everyday". Their obligations to kin, their long-standing exchange relationships and a truly amazing ability to withstand suffering and hardship, saw them through' (Allen 2000, 120).

But an unknown number of children and older people died in 1997, directly or indirectly as a result of the food shortages. They died quietly, without fuss, out of sight of the glare of the international media, in out-of-the-way places. An AusAID-funded review of the relief program criticized the assessments of October and November/December 1997 on the grounds that they under-estimated the ability of people to cope using their own resources (Lea et al. 1999). On the evidence of the increased rice and flour sales in 1997–98, this is possibly true for the more accessible areas. The assessments certainly did not foresee the remarkable response of the Papua New Guinea citizenry in the feeding of their rural kith and kin. But other evidence that came to hand during 1997 strongly suggests that in isolated places death rates increased significantly (Dwyer and Minnegal 2000; Haley 2001; Lemonnier 2001; Robinson 2001).

The need for a bilateral policy

If 1997 was a 'failure of governance' and a 'triumph of the citizenry of Papua New Guinea', what does this teach us about the sort of policies that might be developed in Papua New Guinea and elsewhere to deal with the next ENSO event? What are the 'facts'?

Based on the evidence of past severe ENSO events and on evidence from remote areas in 1997, we conclude that considerably greater numbers of people, mainly small children and old people, would have died in Papua New Guinea in 1997 if there had been no interventions at all. The additional loss of life in 1997 due to the drought and frosts was greatest in the most isolated areas, where people do not have access to markets for cash crops, to government services, to information, and to effective political representation. Without AusAID's relief program, many more people in these places would have died.

On the other hand, AusAID's program probably damaged the long-term capability of the Papua New Guinea government to deal with future ENSO events. For many reasons that were justifiable in the circumstances, AusAID rode over the top of the inadequate responses of the Papua New Guinea government and put a well-oiled military operation into action. Many educated Papua New Guineans have jokingly suggested to me that Papua New Guinea was completely 'useless' in 1997 and had to be rescued by Australia from its own inadequacies.

If we argue that a policy of no intervention, or minimal intervention should be followed the next time, many people would starve and some would do it in public! Given the great attraction of disasters to the Australian and international media, it would be very tough governments, in Papua New Guinea and Australia, that could stand by and do nothing, with nightly TV pictures of people dying on the screen. Here is the dilemma: do nothing and watch some people die; do almost everything because the Papua New Guinea government cannot, and destroy local morale and the confidence that a crisis can be met with local resources.

However, this need only be a dilemma if Australian policy continues to be one of waiting until Papua New Guinea policy fails and then coming to the rescue with programs that resemble something out of *Apocalypse Now*. The solution would appear to be a joint bilateral agreement between Papua New Guinea and Australia to make policy together. The policy would recognize the strengths and weaknesses of both countries and would seek to use the strengths and avoid the weaknesses of both parties and approaches. Australia could continue to provide the advanced technical assistance, climate prediction, communications, satellite imagery, specialized aircraft, and even perhaps corporate memory. Papua New Guinea could provide local-level monitoring and liaison, knowledge of the country, knowledge of agricultural systems, language skills and so on. Papua New Guinea policy must recognize the importance of the private sector and its role in importing and distributing rice and flour, which are essential to the food security of the country. Both countries should make policies that ensure that rice and flour continues to be imported into Papua New Guinea and retailed at reasonable prices.

Elements of this approach were adopted by the Australian relief program in 1997 when circumstances demanded it. PNGDF soldiers were placed aboard ADF helicopters to act as interpreters, after a bunch of helpful bush-knife wielding villagers, who offered to unload a helicopter, terrified the ADF crew who mistook them for primitive savages with a blood lust. Australian monitors with experience in rural Papua New Guinea (a number were ex-patrol officers) were posted to provinces to work directly with provincial drought relief committees, where they were accepted and valued. The approach continues to be followed in a number of other ways. The responses to the next ENSO event will benefit from the detailed knowledge that was collected during 1997. Papers on the drought were presented to the PNG Food and Nutrition 2000 Conference, with the proceedings published by the Australian Centre for International Agricultural Research (Bourke *et al.* 2001).

A more sympathetic view needs to be taken of Papua New Guinea's inability to act like a developed country when it comes to natural disasters. Papua New Guinea is not a developed country and the establishment view of disasters will not work there. Australia and Papua New Guinea must make new policy together, policy that draws upon the best of the establishment view of disaster management and the best of the alternative view.

References

Allen, B. 2000. The 1997–98 Papua New Guinea drought: perceptions of disaster. In *El Niño — History and Crisis: Studies from the Asia-Pacific Region*, ed. R. H. Grove and J. Chappell, 209–122. Cambridge: The White Horse Press.

Allen, B. J. and R. M. Bourke. 2001. The 1997 drought and frost in PNG: overview and policy implications. In *Food Security for Papua New Guinea*, ed. R.M. Bourke, M.G. Allen and J.G. Salisbury, 155–163. Proceedings of the Papua New Guinea Food and Nutrition 2000 Conference, PNG University of Technology, Lae, 26–30 June 2000. ACIAR Proceedings No. 99. Canberra: Australian Centre for International Agricultural Research.

Allen, B., H. Brookfield and Y. Byron. 1989. Frost and drought through time and space, part II: the written, oral, and proxy records and their meaning. *Mountain Research and Development* 9(3): 279–305.

Barter, P. 2001. Responses to the 1997–98 drought in PNG. In *Food Security for Papua New Guinea*, ed. R. M. Bourke, M. G. Allen and J. G. Salisbury, 260–264. Proceedings of the Papua New Guinea Food and Nutrition 2000 Conference, PNG University of Technology, Lae, 26–30 June 2000. ACIAR Proceedings No. 99. Canberra: Australian Centre for International Agricultural Research.

Bourke, R. M. 1988. *Taim Hangre*: Variation in Subsistence Food Supply in the Papua New Guinea Highlands. Unpublished PhD thesis, The Australian National University, Canberra.

Bourke, R. M. 2000. Impact of the 1997 drought and frosts in Papua New Guinea. In, *El Niño — History and Crisis: Studies from the Asia-Pacific Region*, ed. R. H. Grove and J. Chappell, 149–170. Cambridge: The White Horse Press.

Bourke, R. M., M. G. Allen and J. G. Salisbury eds. 2001. *Food Security for Papua New Guinea*. Proceedings of the Papua New Guinea Food and Nutrition 2000 Conference, PNG University of Technology, Lae, 26–30 June 2000. ACIAR Proceedings No. 99. Canberra: Australian Centre for International Agricultural Research.

Chinnery, E. W. P. 1929. *Studies of the Native Population of the East Coast of New Ireland*. Territory of New Guinea Anthropological Report No 6. Canberra: Government Printer.

Dwyer, P. and M. Minnegal. 2000. El Niño, Y2K and the 'short, fat lady': drought and agency in a lowland Papua New Guinean community. *Journal of the Polynesian Society* 109(2): 251–273.

Dwyer, T. 1952. *Patrol Report Wabag No 2 of 52/53, Wabag. September 1952*. Papua New Guinea National Archives, Port Moresby.

Gammage, B. 1998. *The Sky Travellers: Journeys in New Guinea 1938–1939*. Melbourne: Miegunyah Press and Melbourne University Press.

Haberle, S. 2000. Vegetation response to climatic variability: a paleoecological perspective on the ENSO phenomenon. In *El Niño — History and Crisis: Studies from the Asia-Pacific Region*, ed. R. H. Grove and J. Chappell, 66–78. Cambridge: The White Horse Press.

Haley, N. C. 2001. Impact of the 1997 drought in the Hewa area of Southern Highlands Province. In *Food Security for Papua New Guinea*, ed. R. M. Bourke, M. G. Allen and J .G. Salisbury, 168–189. Proceedings of the Papua New Guinea Food and Nutrition 2000 Conference, PNG University of Technology, Lae, 26–30 June 2000. ACIAR Proceedings No. 99. Canberra: Australian Centre for International Agricultural Research.

Hewitt, K. 1983. The idea of calamity in a technocratic age. In *Interpretations of Calamity from the Viewpoint of Human Ecology*, ed. K. Hewitt, 3–31. London: Allen and Unwin.

Jonathon, A. 2001. The El Niño drought: an overview of the Milne Bay experience. In *Food Security for Papua New Guinea, ed*. R. M. Bourke, M. G. Allen and J. G. Salisbury, 209–213. Proceedings of the Papua New Guinea Food and Nutrition 2000 Conference, PNG University of Technology, Lae, 26–30 June 2000. ACIAR Proceedings No. 99. Canberra: Australian Centre for International Agricultural Research.

Lea, D., B. Broughton, B. Murtagh, B., M. Levett, C. McMurray and J. Amoako. 1999. *Australian Assistance to the 1997–98 PNG Drought*. Canberra: Australian Agency for International Development.

Lemmonier, P. 2001. Drought, famine and epidemic among the Ankave-Anga of Gulf Province in 1997–98. In *Food Security for Papua New Guinea*, ed. R. M. Bourke, M. G. Allen and J. G. Salisbury, 164–167. Proceedings of the Papua New Guinea Food and Nutrition 2000 Conference, PNG University of Technology, Lae, 26–30 June 2000. ACIAR Proceedings No. 99. Canberra: Australian Centre for International Agricultural Research.

Robinson, R. 2001. Subsistence at Lake Kopiago, Southern Highlands Province, during and following the 1997–98 drought. In *Food Security for Papua New Guinea*, ed. R. M. Bourke, M. G. Allen and J. G. Salisbury, 190–200. Proceedings of the Papua New Guinea Food and Nutrition 2000 Conference, PNG University of Technology, Lae, 26–30 June 2000. ACIAR Proceedings No. 99. Canberra: Australian Centre for International Agricultural Research.

Sudradjat, A. 2001. Australia's response to the 1997 PNG drought. In *Food Security for Papua New Guinea*, ed. R. M. Bourke, M. G Allen and J. G. Salisbury, 218–221. Proceedings of the Papua New Guinea Food and Nutrition 2000 Conference, PNG University of Technology, Lae, 26–30 June 2000. ACIAR Proceedings No. 99. Canberra: Australian Centre for International Agricultural Research.

Waddell, E. 1983. Coping with frosts, governments and disaster experts: some reflections based on a New Guinea experience and a perusal of the relevant literature. In *Interpretations of Calamity from the Viewpoint of Human Ecology*, ed. K. Hewitt, 33–43. London: Allen and Unwin.

Waddell, E. 1989. Observations on the 1972 frosts and subsequent relief program among the Enga of the Western Highlands. *Mountain Research and Development* 9(3): 210–223.

Whitecross, N. and P. Franklin. 2001. The role of rice in the 1997 PNG drought. In *Food Security for Papua New Guinea*, ed. R. M. Bourke, M. G. Allen and J. G. Salisbury, 255–259. Proceedings of the Papua New Guinea Food and Nutrition 2000 Conference, PNG University of Technology, Lae, 26–30 June 2000. ACIAR Proceedings No. 99. Canberra: Australian Centre for International Agricultural Research.

Willson, K. and R. M. Bourke. 1976. *1975 Papua New Guinea Food Crops Conference Proceedings*. Port Moresby: Department of Primary Industry.

Wohlt, P. B, B. J. Allen, A. Goie and P. W. Harvey. 1982. An investigation of food shortages in Papua New Guinea, 24 March to 3 April, 1981. *IASER*

Special Publication No. 6. Port Moresby: Institute of Applied Social and Economic Research.

Chapter 18

Privatization Policy in Papua New Guinea[1]

Timothy Curtin

Introduction

In its short history as an independent state, Papua New Guinea has gone full circle, from a mostly private enterprise economy through state capitalism and back to private enterprise, much more rapidly than many developed countries. In 1975 its public enterprise sector was quite small, and broadly limited to the classical public utilities of electricity, water and sewerage, transport (airways and harbours), posts and telecommunications, and central banking. Shortly before independence, the government acquired the local banking network of the Commonwealth Bank of Australia, renamed the Papua New Guinea Banking Corporation (PNGBC). In addition, the new government owned the Papua New Guinea Development Bank and the Investment Corporation. However by 1981 the central government had acquired direct interests in 34 public enterprises (with at least 49 per cent ownership in 28 of them), and indirect controlling interests in another 23 companies through the Development Bank and the Investment Corporation (Trebilcock 1982, 4). Similarly, while in 1975 the government had equity of 20 per cent in one mine (Bougainville Copper Ltd), in 1979–80 it took up 20 per cent in Ok Tedi Mining Ltd, and announced its intention to take up 10 per cent in the Porgera gold prospect. In 1986 it took up 20 per cent in the smaller gold mine at Misima, and from 1992 it held 22.5 per cent in the Kutubu, Gobe, and Moran oilfields; an initial 30 per cent in Lihir Gold was acquired in 1995.

As described below, various governments culminating in that of Sir Mekere Morauta (1999–2002) had succeeded in divesting themselves of most of this rather large portfolio of wholly or partly publicly-owned enterprises, so that by 2002 they had transferred the state's holdings in almost all mining and petroleum projects either to landowners and provincial governments in project areas or to Oil Search Ltd, and most of its shareholdings in oil palm plantations and other non-mining companies had also been sold. By July 2002 the Morauta government had also completed sale of PNGBC to the private sector bank, Bank of South Pacific, and had established a framework for privatizing Air Niugini,

PNG Power (formerly Elcom, the Electricity Commission), Telikom PNG, and the Harbours Board through a holding entity, the Independent Public Business Corporation (IPBC), but since then the Somare government (July 2002 to 2007) has stalled this process (see below).

The justifications usually advanced for the kind of expansion of the public enterprise sector that had occurred in Papua New Guinea in its first few years of independence included the argument that certain activities generate social benefits to the wider community greater than the benefits accruing to their private owners, with the implication that the private owners would not expand the activity to a scale commensurate with the potential social benefits. This argument had considerable force in the case of services like education and health, where inability of a proportion of the community to meet the costs of provision could lead to under-provision by the private sector, but was used more questionably to justify nationalizations, like those of the privately-owned copper mining industry in Zambia in 1970 (Faber and Potter 1971).[2]

Another commonly used argument for public ownership in Papua New Guinea was as a means of controlling 'natural monopolies', that is those industries where 'the total market can be served at lowest cost by a single firm', because of declining marginal costs (Trebilcock 1982, 8). Airlines are classic examples of falling-cost industries, as the Australian experience of recurrent collapses of Qantas's fare-cutting competitors demonstrates.[3] In Papua New Guinea telecommunications and electricity were also deemed to be 'natural' (i.e. falling cost) monopolies, without any evidence being advanced that this was indeed the case, given that the manifestly small domestic markets for these industries made it unlikely that they could achieve the economies of scale that lead to declining unit costs. After 1980 there was deregulation and privatization of state-owned telecommunications and power industries in many countries, led by Britain and New Zealand, but the regular demise of new entrants (like that of OneTel in Australia in 2001) suggests these industries may indeed be natural monopolies. Irrespective of the existence of falling costs, Papua New Guinea's telecommunications and electric power undertakings continue to enjoy *statutory* monopoly status, which still prevents new entrants to these industries.

Other arguments for expanding public ownership in Papua New Guinea included replacement of 'inappropriate' foreign ownership in cases where that was perceived to favour overly capital-intensive technologies, and a supposed need for government to be a direct participant in certain industries as a means of obtaining information needed to monitor the private sector participants, for example, logging (Trebilcock 1982, 9–11). In practice the government's joint ventures with various logging firms at Stettin Bay, Gogol, and Open Bay never yielded the expected inside information on transfer pricing and other unacceptable activities, perhaps because of the inevitable conflict of interest for the government in its roles as both shareholder and tax collector – a conflict present in all firms in which governments have shareholdings. Under Papua New Guinea's *Companies Act*, the government directors on the boards of companies in which it had shares had a primary fiduciary duty to all the shareholders of companies like Bougainville Copper and Stettin Bay Lumber, not just the government, and that duty would quite naturally include seeking to maximize company profits, irrespective of environmental costs, and to minimize taxes. The Papua New Guinea government's equity in Bougainville Copper Ltd, the Porgera Joint Venture, and Ok Tedi Mining Ltd created a striking conflict of interest in regard to the environmental impacts of those mines.

Papua New Guinea's public sector at independence

To any first-time observer of Papua New Guinea's economy in 1975, other than the staff of the World Bank and International Monetary Fund (IMF) that have constantly claimed that its public sector was too large, one of the most striking features would have been the very small size of the public sector, especially when measured by the number of employees, the proportion these were of the total population, and the availability of public services in general and public utilities and infrastructure in particular. At independence in 1975 the total number of public servants in the central government was 25,951. In addition there were 4,034 government-funded teachers (in 1971–72) and 6,137 health workers (1972–73). The total number of public servants was 44,981 in June 1973. (Administration of Papua New Guinea 1974, 226–229, 236). The increase to over 70,000 by 2005 is wholly accounted for by the increase in the number of teachers to over 30,000.

Thus public servants amounted to under 2 per cent of the total population of about 2.5 million in 1975. That meant large areas of the country other than the towns were innocent of any form of government presence, apart from some teachers and health workers in the larger rural settlements. The education system enrolled fewer than 250,000 pupils, about half of total school-age children, but with only 371 in Year 12 and 4,374 in Year 10 by 1975 (Curtin 1991, 158).

Such figures confirm Papua New Guinea's status as a Third World country when it became independent. With total internal revenue of $A93 million in 1973, and grant revenue from Australia of $A83 million, for total recurrent revenue of $A176 million or $A7 per capita, clearly the central government's resources were limited, while the local government councils were able to raise only $A5.5 million in local taxes, rates, and charges (Administration of Papua New Guinea 1974, 249, 261).

The country's public enterprise sector was even smaller than the administration, and provided services limited in the main to the towns, of which only three (Port Moresby, Lae, and Rabaul) had populations of more than 25,000 in 1971. For example, there were but 14,596 telephone subscribers in 1973, and electricity production amounted to only 474.3 million KWh in 1972, of which half was attributable to a single user, Bougainville Copper Ltd. (Administration of Papua New Guinea 1974, 226–229, 236, 295, 300). The postal and telecommunications services were provided by a government department until 1982, and there were few statutory authorities carrying on commercial activities, with the exceptions of the Harbours Board and Electricity Commission (Elcom), which had been set up broadly in their present form in 1962, and Air Niugini, set up in 1973 (Whitworth 1993, 4). In addition to such utilities, the new state's government was a minority shareholder in a few large private sector plantations, such as New Britain Palm Oil Ltd. The government was also directly involved in regulating various primary industries, such as coffee and copra, by the colonial legislation that had set up marketing boards, but was not itself engaged in production or ownership.

The most significant government involvement in private sector enterprises was in the financial sector. In addition to owning the largest commercial banking network (PNGBC), the government retained the Investment Corporation set up by the colonial administration as a unit trust for acquisition of shares in ownership of major foreign investments on behalf of Papua New Guinean subscribers to the Corporation's capital. The government also retained ownership of the Papua New Guinea Development Bank set up in 1965 (renamed Agriculture Bank and later, Rural Development Bank) that extended loans for agriculture and mainly small-scale industrial and commercial undertakings from resources provided initially by aid donors and later only by the government, without ever becoming a deposit-taking bank.

Thus, even if in 1975 privatization had been a concern of the government — it was not — there was little to privatize. To the contrary, the Allende government's nationalization program in Chile (including the US copper mining company Kennecott in 1971), and then the overthrowing of Allende by Pinochet, inspired some of the new nation's leaders, notably John Kaputin (the first national to be minister for Justice), to call in 1974 for expulsion of Kennecott from the Ok Tedi copper and gold prospect (Jackson n.d., 57). The World Bank's support of an influential report (Overseas Development Group 1973) recommending interventionist economic development policies after independence also stimulated the pre-independence Somare government's Improvement Programme of 1972 that called for 'government control and involvement in those sectors of the economy where control is necessary to achieve the desired kind of development'. This statement found its way into the Preamble and the Five National Goals of Papua New Guinea's constitution in 1975, which in effect retained this equivalent of Clause 4 of the British Labour Party's manifesto (May 2001, 309–310).[4]

In any event, shortly before independence the government successfully dislodged Kennecott from its Ok Tedi copper discovery (Jackson n.d., 70). Then, for a time the government in effect became a mining exploration company in its own right, through its wholly-owned Ok Tedi Development Company, which supervised various drilling programs at Tabubil until it finally succeeded in transferring the project to Australia's BHP in 1980, with retention of a minority equity stake of 20 per cent. [5]

After September 1975 the government also embarked on a policy of direct investment in and management of agricultural and industrial production. This was partly a response to the eagerness of many expatriate plantation owners to divest from Papua New Guinea, and the government saw 'buying back the farm' as an important tool in its program of redistribution of wealth and income (to which it was committed by the emphasis in the constitution's Five Goals on the redistribution of income rather than its growth). Apart from its minority equity in foreign oil palm estates and logging operations, the government acquired 100 per cent ownership of sundry normally private sector activities, such as piggeries, abattoirs, a hotel, a marine amusement park, and scattered rubber and cocoa estates. Clearly none of these amounted to the 'commanding heights' of the economy, and the only programmed interventions were the acquisitions of plantations, most of which would have ceased production without the government assuming ownership.

Development of state enterprise policy 1975–1983

The tendency at independence for the government to contemplate direct ownership and management of industrial and agricultural enterprises was soon moderated (except for mining), and by 1978 the minister for Finance (Julius Chan) had invited the IMF to review Papua New Guinea's non-financial public enterprises (Whitworth 1993, 5). In the following year Chan himself chaired a committee of inquiry whose report, *The Role of Government in Development*, criticized the tendency for the government to assume activities properly pertaining to the private sector (Ministry for Finance 1979).

The IMF's report was written by R. H. Floyd (1979), who noted that apart from the four main utilities, all other non-financial government enterprises had lost money, and that even the utilities were under-performing relative to the opportunity cost of capital (i.e. rates of return in the private sector). Floyd's key argument was that economic efficiency requires that prices paid by consumers for goods and services should cover the full opportunity cost of resources used as inputs, and that if services are proposed to be provided at prices fixed at below cost-recovery levels — as implicitly mandated by the constitution's Five National Goals — the government should provide explicit subsidies to the enterprise through the budget. He also recommended that to avoid hidden subsidies, state enterprises should be subject to the same taxes and duties incurred by the private sector, and that their investments should be determined within the overall framework of the government's capital expenditure budget (Floyd 1979, 24–39; Whitworth 1993, 7–8).

The Floyd Report met with a mixed reception. Only one of its recommendations was adopted immediately (ending of the exemption from company tax of the Harbours Board and Electricity Commission in 1980). Trebilcock (1982) criticized Floyd's proposal to make the government responsible for determining the enterprises' capital spending. It was not until 1983 that the crucial principle of commerciality (cost-based pricing and abolition of tax and import duty exemptions) was adopted for all four of the utilities, namely, Air Niugini, Harbours Board, Elcom, and Post and Telecommunications Corporation (PTC), which were thereafter known as the Commercial Statutory Authorities (CSAs).

The cabinet's decision (National Executive Council 163/1983, 1–5) defining the government's future relations with the CSAs also laid down that they should only undertake new investments if they earned at least the rate of return to be laid down from time to time by the minister for Finance in the annual budget, and that if a CSA wished to undertake a non-commercial investment for 'social/political reasons', it should seek a subsidy through the budget to cover any losses incurred by the investment. The minimum rate of return was announced only once in a budget, and that budget was rejected (in 1985), but the minister for Finance had in 1984 advised each CSA that an 'appropriate' rate of return would be in the range of 16–22 per cent already permitted to the private sector on price-controlled items (Whitworth 1993, 25).

These prescribed rates of return were rarely achieved by any of the CSAs. The average return on investment (ROI) of all four CSAs between 1985 and 1989 varied between a low of 11.1 per cent in 1985 and a high of 13.1 per cent in 1986 (World Bank 1992, 178). Those were the good years: from 1994 onwards Elcom's operating profits were usually less than its interest payments (partly because price controls prevented tariff increases to cover higher costs of imported fuel after the devaluation of the kina in 1994) and its ROI fell below 5 per cent, while the PTC's fell to 4 per cent in 1995, and Air Niugini incurred only losses after 1994 (World Bank 1999, 148–149).

The 1983 NEC decision directed the CSAs to pay dividends to the government from 1984 equal to 50 per cent of the previous year's after-tax profits. Initially this was complied with, at least for as long as the CSAs earned profits, but with adjustments in cases where the CSA obtained cabinet approval for netting off subsidies on unprofitable services it had been obliged to undertake without ever receiving the promised explicit budget subsidy. In this respect, also, the CSAs' performance began promisingly but without achieving the target, with total dividends paid by all four reaching K11.7 million in 1989 (the first year of a recorded subsidy) (World Bank 1992, 178). Thereafter dividend payments to government disappeared along with their profits.

The NEC decision had directed the CSAs to prepare annual rolling forward five-year capital investment programs for approval by cabinet, and this was complied with until they were corporatized in the late 1990s. The decision further stated that legislation would be drafted enabling the CSAs to vary their prices and charges to the level needed to achieve the required rates of return, but subject to the 'price justification' procedures laid down in the *Prices Regulation Act*.

The force of the cabinet's decisions on pricing and investments was considerably weakened by this failure to grasp the nettle of freeing the CSAs from the government's price controls. As the years went by, the CSAs found it more and more difficult to gain timely approval for price increases from the secretary of the Finance or Treasury Department, in his role as price controller, and this largely explains the CSAs' worsening profits performance noted above. But even in the good years their overall gross margin (i.e. total revenue less operating costs as a ratio of total revenue) was less than 20 per cent, whereas the private sector would aim for 40 per cent; and this shortfall reflected operating inefficiencies, inadequate sales relative to their large capital investments, and over-staffing.

Nevertheless there is some evidence of improvement in the productivity of the CSAs between 1984 and 1991. For example, they employed 6,636 persons on gross revenue of K208.7 million in 1984, or K31,449 per employee, and 7,259 persons for revenue of K369 million in 1991, or K48,656 per employee, an improvement of K17,207 (over 50 per cent) in revenue generated per employee. The average in 1991 conceals the dispersion between the capital intensive Air Niugini's K74,082 per employee and the Harbours Board's K34,339 per employee) (World Bank 1992, 178; Whitworth 1993, 1).

The government's rationale for subjecting the CSAs to prices justification was that each was supposedly a monopoly, but that was more by law (telecommunications, power, harbours) than from any evidence of falling marginal costs preventing new entrants to these industries. Even where some degree of competition existed, as on Air Niugini's domestic routes, price controls were enforced on both Air Niugini and its private sector competitors. However there are few if any absolute monopolies — for example, Elcom's declining efficiency led most large buildings and other big power users to install their own generators during the 1990s, an airline monopoly may well have to compete with other forms of transport such as shipping, and privatized harbours (e.g. in Lae and Madang, Rabaul and Kavieng, Alotau and Port Moresby) would have been able to compete with each other for traffic and for new 'foot-loose' industries to locate in their vicinity (see also Department of Finance and Planning 1992, 19).

It is evident that the response of the government in 1983 to the growing difficulties of the CSAs in the 1970s and early 1980s was not to contemplate privatization, which was rarely mentioned as a possibility, except by Trebilcock (1982, 115), but to accept Floyd's restructuring proposals by turning them into quasi-autonomous entities free to behave as if they were private sector firms, subject however to restrictions on price setting and staff emoluments. The implicit contradiction between Floyd's commercialization of the CSAs and their continued public ownership was either not noticed or justified on the grounds that given equal commercial efficiency public monopolies would somehow be more benevolent than private monopolies. Both the CSAs' autonomy and their ability to operate as if they were privately owned began to be eroded in the 1990s, for increasingly their boards and top management became the creatures of the current minister, and if he was removed or transferred to a new ministry, the new incumbent soon acted to replace both board and top management (Millett 1993, 27).

First moves to privatization 1983–1994

After the 1983 NEC decision on CSAs, the government began to turn its attention to its commercial investments. In some cases its hand was forced when many of its wholly-owned commercial enterprises either became defunct or sank into bankruptcy (e.g. Sea Park, the Food and Fish Marketing companies, Energy Development Company, Baiyer River Alcohol, and Kagamuga Natural Products) and were not bailed out. In 1987 the Wingti government initiated privatization of the wholly state-owned National Insurance Corporation (NIC) and a few of its minority shareholdings in joint ventures. The sale of NIC to Malaysian interests in 1988 was aborted at the last minute after a change of government, and no action was taken on the minority shareholdings. NIC remained a public entity until absorbed by PNGBC in 1998.

The first comprehensive privatization policy paper was overseen by a committee of officials chaired by the governor of the central bank but largely drafted by Jakob Weiss, an adviser to the central bank, and presented to the cabinet in 1991, after prompting by the World Bank in the context of its initial Structural Adjustment Programme in Papua New Guinea (World Bank 1992, 52–54; Millett 1993, 12). The Weiss paper stopped short of proposing privatization of either the CSAs or the state-owned commercial bank, PNGBC. It also failed to address the incomplete implementation of the 1983 decision. Instead, its main recommendations were establishment of a unit trust into which the government's shares in mining projects would be placed, and further sales of the state's minority equity holdings in plantations and the like to the national public — which overlooked the pre-emptive rights of the foreign shareholders that managed most of these concerns.

These proposals were superseded when the return to government of Paias Wingti after the elections in 1992 led to a much higher profile for privatization. The government's first act set up the Papua New Guinea Holdings Corporation as a statutory body under the prime minister with capital of K5 million, replacing the previous government's costless Privatization Committee of officials. The corporation became the statutory owner of all the government's non-mining enterprises, with full powers to proceed with privatization and retain all proceeds for its own purposes (Millett 1993, 40).

The Wingti government also moved to raise the state's involvement in the mining industry. The policy from 1980 until 1992 had been for the government to take up to 30 per cent of the shares in mining projects, and 22.5 per cent in oil projects, but in each case only when the projects — including their financing plans — had been approved. This meant that the government avoided the exploration and pre-development risks it had incurred between 1975 and 1980 at Ok Tedi. Payment for its equity in mining was paid up-front *pro rata* with its share of developers' previous exploration and pre-development costs. In the case of oil projects, the developers were obliged to 'carry' (i.e. finance) the state's equity, with recovery of their costs plus interest from the state's forgoing of its 22.5 per cent share of oil production until paid for.

In 1979 the joint venture of three mining companies (Placer Dome of Canada, and MIM and Goldfield Ltd of Australia) formed to develop the Porgera gold deposit had asked the government to determine the size of its equity in advance of the more intensive drilling program they proposed to undertake. The government chose to limit its holding to 10 per cent and signed the 1979 Shareholders Agreement on that basis, despite the precedent of its 20 per cent stake in Bougainville Copper Ltd and its intention to take 20 per cent in Ok Tedi. The large burden on the government's resources of financing its share of the Ok Tedi project explains its decision to limit itself to 10 per cent at Porgera, but the private joint venture partners were evidently keen to be sure of retaining at least 30 per cent each before embarking on a major exploration program.

The new drilling was successful in proving the existence of a larger and richer ore body than had been expected, and in 1985 the managing director of Placer's Australian subsidiary, Robert Needham, wrote to the prime minister seeking confirmation that the government would honour the Shareholders Agreement and limit itself to 10 per cent of the project. Sir Michael Somare replied in the affirmative. Placer Dome floated its Australian subsidiary, Placer Pacific, in 1986, and amidst controversy some of the government's ministers (including the new prime minister, Paias Wingti, and the minister for Finance, Julius Chan) acquired shares at what proved to be a heavily discounted float price, despite the restrictions of the Leadership Code.

By the time the second Wingti government took office in 1992, Porgera had begun production and proved for a few years to be the most profitable gold mine in the world. In September 1992 Wingti secured cabinet approval for removal of Mel Togolo, the chief executive of the Mineral Resources Development Company (MRDC), the government's holding company for its mining equity stakes, and his replacement by Robert Needham, the same Needham who, when managing director of Placer Pacific, had written to the prime minister about the government equity in Porgera the year before its float in 1986. Needham prepared demands presented by the prime minister to Placer and its partners claiming that the government had been 'misled' as to the potential richness of Porgera in 1979 and again in 1985 when it limited itself to only a 10 per cent stake and that therefore the companies should grant the government an extra 20 per cent stake in the mine, at a price based on the original cost rather than the current market value, taking it to 30 per cent. This demand looked to many to be akin to nationalization or even expropriation, but an agreement was eventually reached whereby the companies provided the government with an extra 15 per cent (for a total of 25 per cent), at a price based on market valuations rather than original cost, and payable from the future profits earned by the government's extra holding (World Bank 1993, 91).

The appearance of a new phase of direct state involvement in mining was strengthened when Wingti's and Needham's next move was to demand that Rio Tinto should grant the government an extra 20 per cent equity stake in the new Lihir gold project, taking it to 50 per cent, to be held on behalf of the government by the Malaysian Mining Corporation. Rio Tinto rejected what was seen as a move to replace its management by a team led by Needham — and the government's minister for Mining, John Kaputin, then refused to proceed with Rio Tinto's application for a special mining lease. In mid 1994 a faction of the government led by the then Finance minister, Masket Iangalio, succeeded in having Needham dismissed from MRDC while Kaputin was abroad, and this was soon followed by the resignation of Wingti in August 1994 after loss of a court case on the validity of his purported resignation and re-election by parliament in 1993. The new government quietly dropped the demand for extra equity in the Lihir project, and the project was approved in March 1995. The subsequent international share float of Lihir Gold Ltd provided an opportunity for the government to finance its share of the development costs from the proceeds of selling 40 per cent of its holding in the float — and its residual 17.6 per cent holding was in effect further privatized by assignment of half (6.8 per cent) to a trust on behalf of the Lihirian landowners.

Before Wingti was obliged to resign, his government had set in train what became the notorious purchase of the Cairns Conservatory, concluded in October 1994 under the direction of the next government, by the Public Officers Superannnuation Fund. The Ombudsman's Report (Ombudsman Commission

1999) on this money-laundering transaction provides a graphic account of the departure by ministers (led by Prime Minister Chan himself), and the most senior officials of the Department of Finance, from the high-minded principles that in the early years of independence they had advanced as justifications for public ownership.

Privatization in progress 1995–2005

Wingti's replacement as prime minister by his deputy Sir Julius Chan also led to the immediate departure (after being declared *persona non grata*) of the Holdings Corporation's expatriate managing director (Peter Steele) and to its winding-up before any of its planned privatizations had taken effect, but not before some K2 million of budget funding had been spent on its staff and board. However, independently of the Holdings Corporation, the Finance Department had sold the government's 70 per cent equity in PNG Forest Products (Pty) Ltd. to the 30 per cent shareholder and manager, Prime Group of Singapore.[6]

The Chan government remained interested in privatization, partly due to renewed pressure to that end from the World Bank, to which it had applied for new loans after being forced to devalue and then float the kina in October 1994. Additional impetus came from Chan's deputy and Finance minister, Chris Haiveta, who, however, hoped to avoid conformity with the World Bank's conditions — especially those relating to forestry — for its offered second structural adjustment loan in support of the 1995 budget, by borrowing against the government's share of oil exports from the Kutubu project. This borrowing (as proposed by merchant bankers Paribas Capital Markets and Salomon Brothers) would have involved a forward sale of the state's oil to these bankers at a fixed price of $US15 per barrel, granting them any excess of actual oil prices, with the state's net proceeds (after interest at around 15 per cent) used first to repay the state's liability to its joint venture partners and then to fund the 1995 budget deficit. A team of officials from the Bank of Papua New Guinea and the Department of Finance successfully persuaded the cabinet that this quasi-privatization was potentially very high cost and that a float of part of the state's 100 per cent equity in the Mineral Resources Development Company (MRDC)[7] would be more cost effective (State Negotiating Committee 1995, 3). This cabinet paper marked the first occasion privatization was seen as a means of raising fiscal resources.

Haiveta subsequently took a close personal interest in this proposal for a partial privatization of MRDC by means of an initial public offering (IPO). In August 1995 Haiveta replaced the MRDC board's chosen financial and legal advisers for the float (McIntosh Securities and Mallesons of Sydney) with his own appointees, Jardine Fleming of Hong Kong and Allens Arthur Robinson of Port Moresby, together with their Sydney partner firm (Allen, Allen and

Hemsley, Australia's largest law firm and leading specialist in mergers and acquisitions).

By 1995 the MRDC held on behalf of the government, landowners, and provincial governments, the state's initial equity in the Porgera Joint Venture (PJV) (10 per cent), Misima Mines (20 per cent), Kutubu Joint Venture (KJV) (22.5 per cent) and Lihir Gold (30 per cent). The additional 15 per cent state equity in Porgera that had been forcibly acquired by the Wingti government in 1993 was held separately.

MRDC's new advisers developed concepts whereby MRDC itself would remain wholly owned by the government, and would retain those portions of the state equity in mineral projects that had not been assigned to landowners and provincial governments, while the national government's own residual equity would be placed in a new entity, Orogen Minerals Ltd. Orogen was assured that it would have an option to purchase from MRDC up to 20 per cent of the state's usual 22.5 equity in future oil projects and 25 per cent of its 30 per cent in new mining projects. Orogen's initial holdings included 15.75 per cent in the KJV, 20.5 per cent in the Gobe Joint Venture, 15 per cent in Porgera, 6.81 per cent in Lihir Gold Ltd, and 20 per cent in Placer Dome's Misima Mine. Orogen would be floated both nationally and internationally, with the public able to take up 49.9 per cent, and with MRDC retaining 50.1 per cent on behalf of the government. Orogen was so constituted that MRDC would not have a majority on its board, and that the government's majority would not be voted at general meetings of the company except in regard to its name and place of registration (Port Moresby) (Orogen Minerals Ltd 1996, 23–32).

The float took place in October 1996 and was remarkably successful, with a substantial over-subscription. The total proceeds from the sale of 49.9 per cent of its shares amounted to K304 million (about $A288 million in 1995), of which 13 per cent was subscribed in Papua New Guinea by its institutions and some 6,400 resident individuals. This partial privatization was wholly transparent by virtue of the public flotation process, which included a prospectus containing independent technical experts' and accountants' reports on the various projects, and did not require a World Bank loan or any up-front charge on the national budget. Instead, the float contributed over K100 million to the budget, after clearing MRDC's debts, capitalizing Orogen, and meeting the float managers' fees, totaling some K16 million (see also Dorney 2000, 98–99).

The float also enabled some thousands of Papua New Guineans to subscribe for shares that yielded capital gains to those who sold in good time — its price rose from the discounted float price of K1.75 for Papua New Guineans (overseas investors paid $A2 per share) to over $A2.50 in 1997. Orogen's share price slumped to around $A1.00 during 2000–01, but recovered late in 2001 to $A1.90 when the Papua New Guinea government announced it was contemplating releasing its majority stake of 50.1 per cent, leading to Orogen's merger with Oil Search Ltd. Unlike the rest of Papua New Guinea's public enterprise sector during the 1990s, Orogen yielded dividends both to the government in its role as shareholder and to the public at home and abroad at levels above the average rate on Australian mining shares.

The other notable privatization by the Chan-Haiveta government was its sale of the government's 46 per cent holding in New Britain Palm Oil Ltd (NBPOL) to the Malaysian corporation Kulim in 1996. The British firm Harrison and Crosfield had established this very successful and profitable project near Kimbe in West New Britain in 1968 but had decided to divest its overseas operations in Papua New Guinea and elsewhere. The local management had persuaded Harrison and Crosfield to put its shares into a public international share offering, and the underwriters (McIntosh Securities) valued the firm at not more than K115 million (about $A110 million) of which the government would receive $A50 million for its shares. Chan and Haiveta were persuaded that a trade sale would realize more for the state's shares, and used the negotiating skills of Jakob Weiss, adviser to the Bank of Papua New Guinea, to devise an arrangement whereby the government first exercised its pre-emptive rights to buy out Harrison and Crosfield's 54 per cent at a price which valued the whole of NBPOL at K159 million (i.e. K1.59 million per 1 per cent), with funds provided by the ultimate purchaser, Kulim. The latter then bought the state's now 100 per cent holding (less 10 per cent retained in trust for landowners and the provincial government) at a price valuing NBPOL at K171 million (National Executive Council 1996). The outcome was that the state sold its shares at a price per 1 cent of K1.71 million, considerably more than the K1.15 million per 1 per cent that it was likely to have realized from the McIntosh public float's indicative pricing (where the price was heavily discounted because of the unfamiliarity of the Australian share market with tropical plantation businesses).

The government's net receipt from these transactions was K68.04 million. One of the conditions imposed by the government was that Kulim would in due course arrange a flotation of NBPOL into which it would place part of its holding, and this has since taken place on the Papua New Guinea Stock Exchange (National Executive Council 1996).

Despite these commercial successes, which also provided significant injections of foreign exchange into the reserves of the Bank of Papua New Guinea, the Chan-Haiveta government proved less adventurous in tackling privatization of genuine public enterprises — both Orogen and NBPOL concerned sale of state shares in privately managed concerns. The CSAs were badly affected by the nearly continuous depreciation of the kina after it was floated in 1994, a trend that was exacerbated by the rise and rise of the US dollar and the Japanese yen, the main currencies in which the external debts of the CSAs had been incurred.

Depreciation of the kina did not affect the external value of the debts, but raised the kina value, so at least equivalent increases in the CSAs' tariffs and charges became essential (since unlike Orogen and NBPOL they were not protected by export earnings denominated in dollars).[8] But the price controller when wearing his secretary for Finance hat was under constant pressure from his political masters to moderate the rate of inflation of the Consumer Prices Index (CPI) — and in this conflict of interest the CSAs' requests for approval of electricity tariff increases and the like were usually the losers.

A precondition for privatization would have been substantial liberation of the CSAs from price controls, which was unthinkable (because of ministers' concerns about aggravating the rising CPI) to both the Chan-Haiveta and the Skate governments (in 1998 the latter held out against allowing fare increases on domestic air routes to the point of the near-collapse of the private operators who were crippled by the rise in the kina cost of aviation fuel). Instead, these governments pursued a policy of 'corporatization' of the CSA sector, whereby they ceased to be statutory commercial authorities, each with its own act, but were registered as companies under the *Companies Act*. Ostensibly, this was to be a first step towards privatization, but no moves in that direction were discernible. Rather, the boards and management of the former CSAs used their new exemption from the provisions of the 1983 decision relating to terms and conditions of staffs to improve their personal positions. As companies, the former CSAs were also in effect freed from the 1983 NEC decision's rate of return targets and minimum dividend payments, though as they all declined deeper into bankruptcy this was immaterial.

The government of Bill Skate (1997–1999) followed the Chan-Haiveta government's example of milking the government-managed superannuation funds. The National Provident Fund as a result was by 1999 on the verge of liquidation (World Bank 1999, 187). Potentially even more serious was the spoliation of PNGBC by the Skate government's restructuring, which had the effect of subjecting it to direct government direction. By 1996 PNGBC was already carrying relatively high staff costs, but these increased rapidly in 1997–99, by 31 per cent alone in 1999, and the bank was by then alone among Papua New Guinea's banks with an average staff expense higher than the average operating profit per staff member. PNGBC's efficiency ratio was well over 60 per cent in 1997–99, compared with the common less than 50 per cent of its competitors.[9] By 1999 also, PNGBC was in breach of the central bank's minimum liquid asset ratio (MLAR), and it probably also barely met the Bank of Papua New Guinea's minimum 8 per cent capital adequacy ratio.

Iario Lasaro, the minister for Finance, instead of attending to his prudential supervision of the banking system, found time in his 1999 budget to announce privatization not of the remaining state entities (such as the now corporatized

CSAs and financial institutions), but of large areas of the traditional public sector, such as research institutes and training colleges, using the novel technique of instant cessation of their budget funding (see Curtin 2000a, 3). This 'sink or swim' approach was as short-lived as the government, which fell in July 1999.

The new government of Sir Mekere Morauta (July 1999–July 2002) reverted to the more institutionalized approach of the Wingti government of 1992–94 (of whose PDM party Sir Mekere had become the parliamentary leader). Wingti's Holdings Corporation was revived as the Independent Public Business Corporation (IPBC), complete with board, well paid executives (K450,000 a year for the executive chairman), teams of consultants, and access to a large loan from the World Bank (*Papua New Guinea Post-Courier* 28 February 2001; Weise 2000). In addition, like the Holdings Corporation, the Commission was not obliged to remit net privatization proceeds to the government's consolidated revenue (until its act was proposed to be amended in March 2002, see *The National* 28 March 2002).

But unlike all previous governments' privatization exercises, which had treated the CSAs and state-owned financial institutions as sacrosanct, the Morauta government committed itself to meeting the World Bank's requirement that at least major public enterprises should be 'brought to the point of sale' if not actually sold, during 2000, with PNGBC selected as the most feasible (see Curtin 2000b). This proved to be much easier said than achieved, given the need to bring PNGBC's loans portfolio into reasonable shape after the period of large increases in its unsecured lending during the Skate government. PNGBC had also been placed by the Skate government under the umbrella of a holding corporation, Pacific Finance, as part of an asset stripping exercise, and this also needed to be disentangled (Weise 2000).

The government eventually met the World Bank's extended deadline for bringing PNGBC to the point of sale in mid 2001, and then unexpectedly went one better by announcing on 29 November 2001 that a bidding process had been won by the smaller but nominally privately-owned Bank of South Pacific (BSP). Reportedly (*Papua New Guinea Post-Courier* 30 November 2001), the sale price valued PNGBC at K233 million, but with the government keeping a 25 per cent holding, proceeds would be K175 million, of which K22 million would be retained by the Privatization Commission (later IPBC), and the balance paid into the government's consolidated revenue. The government also indicated that part of its retained 25 per cent would be placed in the proposed Privatization Unit Trust (see below) to which the general public would be invited to subscribe in due course.

The 'trade sale' model adopted for privatization of PNGBC was similar to that employed for the state's shares in New Britain Palm Oil Ltd in 1996, and like that exercise suffered from some lack of transparency, in that the value of other bids was never disclosed. In the case of PNGBC, one of the other bidders was the ANZ Banking Group, already well established in Papua New Guinea. The prime minister's announcement of the sale to BSP said it was the government's 'preferred bidder' (*Papua New Guinea Post-Courier* 30 November 2001), implying that it was not necessarily the highest bid (it later emerged that all the other offers were nominally less than BSP's).[10]

In any event the government evidently preferred a domestic purchaser in which it already had large indirect interests (through the pension funds that have major shareholdings in BSP) to a foreign investor willing to pay in Australian dollars that would have boosted the frail kina's exchange rate. Moreover, it is not clear that the BSP tail now about to wag the PNGBC dog (the latter is much the bigger of the two banks) will indeed have a capital base adequate for the new venture. As of October 2001 the combined capital and reserves of the two banks amounted to 7.2 per cent of their combined but non-risk-weighted total assets. On the face of it, this ratio falls below the Basle Agreement's minimum capital adequacy rule of 8 per cent — but after risk weighting of its assets, the new bank just passed muster (cf. Rose 1999, 488). On the other hand, a take-over of PNGBC by a large if well-capitalized international bank like ANZ might well have reduced competition, with BSP reduced to minnow status by comparison.

Nevertheless, as the enlarged BSP's main shareholders included not only the government (25 per cent) but also government-controlled entities such as the Defence Force Retirement Benefits Fund, the National Provident Fund, the Public Officers Superannnuation Fund, and Motor Vehicles Insurance Ltd, there was some risk that the new bank would prove to be no more than a state-owned bank in disguise. However BSP's own track record has been one of independence from government interference despite its publicly-owned institutional shareholders, especially since it has listed its shares on the Port Moresby Stock Exchange, enabling the general public to subscribe and share in its outstanding profits performance since 2002, and it has become by far the biggest bank in Papua New Guinea, with well over 50 per cent of total deposits of the banking system.

The Morauta government's intention to set up a 'Peoples' Unit Trust' harked back to the Weiss proposal in 1991 and was just another version of the failed Investment Corporation of Papua New Guinea (ICPNG, which manages a form of unit trust holding shares mostly in unlisted domestic companies) unless it is itself privatized; some of the latter's assets disappeared during the Skate government's tenure, with its headquarters building being sold cheaply to its chief executive, and it has paid no dividends since 1997 (*Papua New Guinea Post-Courier* 29 October 2001, 10 August 2005). Unit Trusts in other countries typically invest in a broad range of equities at home and abroad. A Papua New Guinea Peoples' Trust, restricted perforce to holdings in at most one or two unlisted privatized companies could not offer local investors sufficient diversification to attract their support, as shown by the nil new investment in ICPNG since 1997.

The Somare government since 2002, like its predecessors, has been unduly concerned with the risks, first, that privatized 'natural' monopolies like Elcom and Telikom would be able to use their monopoly power to force up their prices or tariffs and earn 'excessive' profits, and, secondly, that when privatized the CSAs would fail to meet the so-called community service obligations that are ostensibly required of them by the constitution.

Successive governments have no doubt considered that if they addressed these issues it would at least in part head off the opposition to privatization by the unions, some students, and other members of the public. But that opposition will not be so easily fobbed off, and it is likely that the price controls still in place for future owners of Elcom (now PNG Power Ltd) and Telikom PNG will make it more difficult to complete the privatizations. Those putative owners will want to earn profits, the bigger the better from their point of view — and for the government and people of Papua New Guinea. Larger profits would deliver larger tax revenues, which the government could use to meet non-commercial community service obligations, in the form of subsidized power and communications. Moreover larger profits would in time attract new entrants to the industries in question, and end their so-called natural monopolies.

In that regard it should be noted that in reality there has been no evidence of the defining condition of falling marginal costs, not surprising given the small scale of the domestic market for power and telecommunications. These monopolies have always been protected in Papua New Guinea by legislation preventing new entrants (as, for example, in the cases of PNG Power and Telikom PNG, despite the nominal 'sunset clauses' opening access to them). In the event, the Somare government (2002–7) reneged on the Morauta government's almost completed sale of Telikom PNG to Fiji's privatized telecommunications corporation, and later refused to accept the larger offer by the African firm Econet (founded by a Zimbabwean but independent of the Mugabe regime in Zimbabwe). Evidently, like almost all previous governments, that of Sir Michael Somare was unwilling to forgo the ability to use state-owned enterprises as a means of rewarding its key supporters with directorships and executive posts even if this meant abysmal service standards. Far from Telikom PNG delivering the 'service obligations' that allegedly private sector management could not be trusted to fulfil, it has over thirty years increased the number of fixed lines only to 60,000, for a population of over 5.5 million, compared with Fiji's 100,000 for its population of only 800,000, while Fiji services more than double Telikom PNG's 50,000 mobile telephones. However, Telikom PNG eventually (2008) relinquished its monopoly control of the country's mobile and internet networks, which had resulted in one of the slowest and most costly services in the world (8 Mbps and K1.80 or $US0.60 per minute), according to a government minister (Sir Peter Barter, *Papua New Guinea Post-Courier* 17 May 2005).

Finally, the story of government equity in Papua New Guinea's mining and petroleum sector, that had begun with such acrimony when local communities in Bougainville objected to the start-up of the Panguna copper mine in 1970–72 and were not appeased when the government was offered equity of 20 per cent (see Denoon 2000), ended in April 2002 with the take-over of the government's 51 per cent owned Orogen Minerals by Oil Search Ltd. Apart from an enlarged — and *de jure* controlling — stake in Ok Tedi since 2002, and a minority (18 per cent) holding in Oil Search, the government's involvement in the mineral sector has ended, except for MRDC's role in administering the equity stakes of landowners and provincial governments in the Porgera, Lihir and Kutubu projects. The merger resulted in the government's receiving $A0.45 per share by way of return of capital from Orogen (i.e. $A73.7 million) plus 1.2 shares in Oil Search for each of its shares in Orogen, an implied price of $A1.97 per share, above Orogen's list price in Australia in 1996 of $A1.75 and well above its price of $A1.00 in October 2001 before the government disclosed it was reviewing its holding in Orogen. Time will tell whether the short-term gain offsets the government's abdication from the strategic role in the industry that it sought in the period from 1975 to 1995, but the cash benefits of that role were far from impressive, and disengagement relieves the government of the conflicts of interest that created so many difficulties at Panguna and Ok Tedi.

There remained a final twist in the story of government involvement at Ok Tedi. In 2001 BHP-Billiton decided to divest itself of its 52 per cent controlling interest in OTML in favour of a special purpose new entity, the PNG Sustainable Development Program Ltd (SDPL) in order to reduce its exposure to its environmentalist critics in Australia (the other shareholders are the national and provincial governments and landowners, and Inmet of Canada). The SDPL has no shareholders as a company limited by guarantee, but is nominally subject to control by its seven directors (namely Ross Garnaut, Jim Carlton, Don Manoe, Patricia Caswell, Jakob Weiss, Sir Ebia Olewale, and Lim How Teck) of whom three each were appointed by BHP Billiton and the government of Papua New Guinea and the last by the Board itself.[11] Thus SDPL could be seen as in part a *de facto* nationalization of the formerly private sector controlling ownership of OTML that had been exercised by BHP Billiton. SDPL is managed by its directors (of whom the chairman is Dr Ross Garnaut, who had been instrumental in bringing BHP into Ok Tedi on behalf of the Papua New Guinea government in 1975 — see Garnaut 2000) in accordance with the agreements by which it is charged with promoting sustainable development and the general welfare of the people of Papua New Guinea. SDPL derives most of its income from its 52 per cent share of dividends paid by its subsidiary, OTML, and its net income is placed in its long term and development funds, amounting to $US79.4 million and $US38 million respectively at the end of 2004. These funds have mostly been placed in offshore accounts earning less than 2 per cent in interest and other income in 2004. Time will tell whether the SDPL makes a genuine contribution to the development of Papua New Guinea relative to what might have been accomplished if OTML had itself assumed the BHP stake and become an independent Papua New Guinea mining company free to invest in probably more productive activities than those so far adopted by SDPL.[12]

Conclusion

One of the enduring strengths of Papua New Guinea is the pragmatism of both people and politicians, unfettered as they are by the fashions in ideologies that momentarily hold sway in other countries. Thus, just as in practice, despite the constitution, no governments have had overt ambitions for outright nationalization of the whole of the enterprise economy, tilts towards privatization have only been effective when the public sector has demonstrably failed to deliver, as has increasingly been the case since 1994. Even then, with the private sector's performance in Papua New Guinea less than stellar, having provided no net increase in the employment it offers since 1988 (Bank of Papua New Guinea 2003), it has hardly been a role model. Moreover external observers of the failures of Papua New Guinea's public sector need to remember the much more spectacular debacles engineered by private entrepreneurs in Australia (Bond Corporation in 1988, and in 2001 alone, HIH, OneTel, and Ansett) and most recently in the USA (Waste Management, Sunbeam, and Enron, the last a one-time major shareholder in Papua New Guinea's upcoming oil refinery). Enron's debts of K300 billion were 66 times larger than Papua New Guinea's total external debt in 2001. The World Bank's (1999) extolling of the benefits of privatization in terms of accountability and transparency also ring hollow when the world's fifth largest accountancy firm, Arthur Andersen, was directly involved in the frauds surrounding the bankruptcies of Bond, HIH, Waste Management, Sunbeam, and Enron (*The Australian* 17 January 2002). Even so, those bankruptcies demonstrate the condign punishment by the market of fraud and mismanagement, and in the last analysis it was only the protection of the explicit guarantees by government that protected Papua New Guinea's public enterprise sector from the same fate (including PNGBC and National Provident Fund in 1999).

Against that background one needs to preserve a degree of caution in recommending any particular ideology-based set of policies for or against public enterprise, and to revert to Jeremy Bentham's utilitarian calculus: what are the relative costs and benefits of alternative forms of enterprise management on a case by case basis? The promising performance of the CSAs in the later 1980s when their managements were not subject to political appointment is enough to suggest that under the right conditions, including, crucially, freedom from price controls and an appropriate non-government regulatory body, they might have been able to survive as public enterprises.

All the same, the Morauta government deserves considerable credit for being the first to follow through with implementation of its predecessors' supposed commitment to privatization of Papua New Guinea's state enterprise sector. Air Niugini, Telikom and Elcom were put on the market; PNGBC and Orogen Minerals had both been sold by April 2002. Prime Minister Morauta's own lead was impressive, given the context of two army mutinies (2001 and 2002) and student protests (June–July 2001). The Somare government also deserves credit for at least not reversing these privatizations since 2002, despite its electoral rhetoric, and in particular for preserving the independence from political direction of the Bank of Papua New Guinea that was Morauta's most signal achievement.

The main caveats emerging from the narrative in this chapter are, first, that while some trade sales may yield higher returns than floats, as with NBPOL but not perhaps PNGBC, the gains of floats, in terms of transparency and opening up to ownership by the public, are potentially very large, as demonstrated by the Orogen Minerals float in 1996. Secondly, whatever holding or privatization corporations and trusts are in place to manage the privatization process, success will finally depend on the kind of commitment to privatization of the managements of the individual enterprises that was evident at MRDC in 1996 and in PNGBC in 2001, but has yet to be seen anywhere else in Papua New Guinea's public enterprise sector (apart from the largely autonomous Bank of Papua New Guinea established by the new *Central Banking Act* 2000).

Finally, we have seen how small Papua New Guinea's public sector was in 1975, in both its administration and enterprise components; how the latter grew rapidly in the 1970s; and how the sale of PNGBC in 2001 was the first privatization of a wholly-owned public enterprise. The non-enterprise public sector by contrast has not grown at all, apart from education, despite enduring complaints, from the World Bank (in every one of its country reports since 1988) and other aid agencies, that the country suffers from an overblown and burgeoning public service. As demonstrated by Curtin (2000b), Papua New Guinea's public expenditure expressed as a ratio to its GDP at around 26 per cent is well below the norm in developed countries, and has consistently declined both in real financial terms per head of the population and, more pertinently, in numbers of public servants per head of the population (with, for example, not merely no increases in the ratios for police and defence but actual declines since 1975). This negative growth is perhaps a function of the very slow growth of per capita GDP since independence, and also of the failure of all Papua New Guinea's governments to address effectively the issue of reform of land tenure first proposed by the Faber Report (Overseas Development Group 1973, see also

Curtin 2003). Until conditions are created that enable both the public and the private sectors to grow, Papua New Guinea itself will not fulfil the ideals laid down in its constitution.

References

Administration of Papua New Guinea. 1974. *Administration of Papua New Guinea, July 1972 — June 1973*. Canberra: Australian Government Publishing Service.

Bank of Papua New Guinea. 2003. *Quarterly Economic Bulletin, December*. Port Moresby: Bank of Papua New Guinea.

Curtin, T. 1991. *The Economics of Public Investment in Education in Papua New Guinea*. Waigani: University of Papua New Guinea.

Curtin, T. 2000a. Public sector reform in Papua New Guinea and the 1999 budget. *Labour and Management in Development* (online) 1(4).

Curtin, T. 2000b. A new dawn for Papua New Guinea's economy? *Pacific Economic Bulletin* 15(2): 1–35.

Curtin, T. 2003. Scarcity amidst plenty. The economics of land tenure in Papua New Guinea. In *Land Registration in Papua New Guinea: Competing Perspectives*, ed. T. Curtin, H. Holzknecht and P. Larmour, 6–17. Canberra: Pandanus Press.

Denoon, D. 2000. *Getting Under the Skin. The Bougainville Copper Agreement and the Creation of the Panguna Mine*. Melbourne: Melbourne University Press.

Department of Finance and Planning. 1992. *Budget Documents, vol.1*. Port Moresby: Government Printer.

Dorney, S. 2000. *Papua New Guinea: People, Politics and History Since 1975*. Revised edition. Sydney: ABC Books.

Faber, M. L. O. and J. G. Potter. 1971. *Towards Economic Independence. Papers on the Nationalization of the Copper Industry in Zambia*. Cambridge: Cambridge University Press.

Floyd, R. H. 1979. *Selected Non-Financial Public Enterprises in Papua New Guinea*. Washington: International Monetary Fund.

Garnaut, R. 2000. The first 25 years of searching for development. *Pacific Economic Bulletin* 15(2) Supplement: 29–36.

Jackson R. n.d. *Ok Tedi: The Pot of Gold*. Waigani: University of Papua New Guinea.

May, R. 2001. *State and Society in Papua New Guinea: The First Twenty-Five Years*. Adelaide: Crawford House Publishing.

Millett, J. 1993. *Privatisation in Papua New Guinea: Limited Scope, Slow Progress*. Port Moresby: Institute of National Affairs.

Ministry for Finance. 1979. *The role of government in development*. Port Moresby (mimeo).

National Executive Council. 1982. *Government financial relations with Commercial Statutory Authorities*. Waigani: Papua New Government (unpublished).

National Executive Council. 1996. Share float and privatization of New Guinea Palm Oil Ltd. Waigani: Papua New Government (unpublished).

Ombudsman Commission of Papua New Guinea. 1999. *Investigation into the Purchase of the Conservatory, Cairns*. Port Moresby: Ombudsman Commission.

Orogen Minerals Ltd. 1996. *Prospectus*. Port Moresby: Orogen Minerals Ltd.

Overseas Development Group, University of East Anglia. 1973. *A Report on Development Strategies for Papua New Guinea* (Faber Report). Port Moresby: Office of the Chief Minister.

Rose, P. S. 1999. *Commercial Bank Management*. Boston: McGraw-Hill.

State Negotiating Committee. 1995. *Resource Based Financing. Report Prepared for the National Executive Council*. Waigani: Department of Finance.

Trebilcock, M. J. 1982. *Public Enterprises in Papua New Guinea*. Port Moresby: Institute of National Affairs.

Weise, D. 2000. *Impact of financial sector reform on business in PNG*. Port Moresby: Papua New Guinea Institute of Accountants (mimeo).

Whitworth, A. 1993. *Public Enterprise Policy: Independence to 1991*. Port Moresby: Institute of National Affairs.

World Bank. 1992. *Papua New Guinea. Competitiveness, Growth and Structural Adjustment*. Washington: International Bank for Reconstruction and Development.

World Bank. 1993. *Papua New Guinea. Jobs, Growth and International Competitiveness*. Washington: International Bank for Reconstruction and Development.

World Bank. 1999. *Papua New Guinea. Improving Governance and Performance*. Washington: International Bank for Reconstruction and Development.

Endnotes

[1] The author acknowledges the useful comments of Ronald Duncan, Chris Elstoft, Alan Robson, Anthony Siaguru, and Charles Yala, but remains responsible for any remaining errors and omissions.

[2] The subsequent expansion of copper output in Zambia without regard to profitability led ultimately to the government receiving far fewer social benefits, in the form of taxation, than it had received before nationalization. The instigator of that nationalization (Michael Faber) later led a team on behalf of the

World Bank to advise the chief minister of the soon-to-be independent government of Papua New Guinea on development priorities; the report recommended renegotiation of the Bougainville Agreement (Overseas Development Group 1973, 69,101), in addition to much increased involvement of the government in production and marketing activities.

[3] The consequence of falling marginal costs is that the competitive profit maximizing pricing rule of price equated to marginal cost necessarily creates losses that only a monopolist can avoid through its ability to maintain prices above marginal cost.

[4] The constitution's preamble provides for citizens and government bodies to have control of the bulk of economic enterprise and production, foreign investment, and major enterprises engaged in the exploitation of natural resources (see Chand and Yala, this volume).

[5] The government later raised its holding to 30 per cent when one of the private shareholders (Amoco) divested itself; in 1990 it offered 10 per cent equity in the mine to landowners and the provincial government; in 2001 BHP placed its 52 per cent in a trust company to create a fund to benefit the people of Western Province after mine closure. As of 2005 the mine is operated by Ok Tedi Mining Ltd on behalf of the remaining shareholders, namely the so-called PNG Sustainable Development Program Ltd that inherited BHP-Billiton's 52 per cent stake, the provincial government and the landowners (20 per cent), and one remaining external investor (Inmet of Canada, with 18 per cent).

[6] The Department also successfully negotiated sale of the state's shares in various other concerns, e.g. PNG Marine Products (1992), and the three Pacific Rim oil palm plantations in Oro, Milne Bay, and New Ireland to the respective non-government shareholders (1998).

[7] MRDC was the new name, after 1986, of the former Ok Tedi Development Company.

[8] For example, Elcom's debt had reached K400 million by 2001 (*Papua New Guinea Post-Courier* 8 October 2001).

[9] The efficiency ratio is the non-interest operating expense as a percentage of net operating income.

[10] In October 2001 ANZ paid $A100 million (about K200 million) for the operations of the Bank of Hawaii in Papua New Guinea (two branches), Vanuatu (two branches), and Fiji (three branches) — far fewer than PNGBC's more than thirty (*Papua New Guinea Post-Courier* 5 October 2001).

[11] Dr Jakob Weiss is the nominee of the Bank of Papua New Guinea.

[12] SDPL's biggest investments so far are in subsidiaries promoting 'sustainable energy' and 'micro-finance', neither of which has generated (nor is likely to generate) any returns. Ironically the rate of return on its offshore funds is well below the target rate for the CSAs described above.

Chapter 19

Policy Making on AIDS, to 2000

John Ballard and Clement Malau

Policy making on AIDS in Papua New Guinea has a number of features which set it apart from policy making on other subjects. Most obviously, AIDS presents a new subject for policy, unknown before the mid 1980s; the relevant inheritance from other sectors of policy is not limited to health, since AIDS affects all sectors concerned with development. Because AIDS has been a new issue, the process of its emergence on the policy agenda and the ways in which it has been defined as an issue must be examined; these are taken for granted in other sectors. Finally, because a major part of the strategy for dealing with AIDS concerns prevention through behaviour change, a range of cultural beliefs and practices concerning sensitive issues, particularly those of sexuality and gender relations, are brought to the fore in exceptional fashion; hence examining policy in isolation from practice is especially futile in relation to AIDS.[1]

Although overseas aid has played a significant role in the shaping of public policy in most sectors in Papua New Guinea, the international process of defining AIDS and of establishing a repertoire of policy responses has ensured that external precedents have been unusually forceful in shaping national AIDS policy. Thus it is impossible to discuss policy making on AIDS in Papua New Guinea without locating it within a global setting of policy making.

The international setting of AIDS policy

After the initial identification in the US of clusters of disease among immune-suppressed gay men in July 1981, other groups were found to be affected by what became known as the Acquired Immuno-Deficiency Syndrome (AIDS). In April 1984 discovery of the virus Human Immuno-Deficiency Virus (HIV) was announced and tests to identify those infected were rapidly developed. Although the World Health Organization was slow to mobilize a response to AIDS, it established in 1986 a Global Program on AIDS (GPA) which developed models, initially in Uganda, for short-term and medium-term HIV/AIDS programs for non-Western countries. GPA also convoked consultations among a growing band of AIDS specialists; these identified the principles of community-based health promotion adopted by Australia (Ballard 1998) and a few other Western countries as international best practice in the response to AIDS.

In July 1987, at the request of the Australian government, GPA turned its attention to Asia and the Pacific in a regional ministerial conference held in Sydney. GPA then organized week-long missions to most Southeast Asian and Pacific countries, including Papua New Guinea, to initiate planning for short-term programs. These followed the classical bio-medical template of responses: surveillance of sexually transmitted infection, information and education, and blood screening. From an early stage, GPA also brought together country AIDS managers for orientation and training. Up until the mid 1990s GPA provided substantial technical assistance as well as over K100,000 per year for research and projects, but little of this was actually spent.

GPA's successor UNAIDS, apart from regional conferences and training, gave low priority to the Pacific. In recent years technical assistance on AIDS has come from governments, notably Australia, while international non-government organizations, most of them faith-based, have been increasingly involved in financing, sponsoring and providing AIDS projects in Papua New Guinea, often in the context of wider health programs.

Papua New Guinea policy making on AIDS

Although no cases of HIV or AIDS had yet been identified in Papua New Guinea, in November 1986 the Department of Health established a National AIDS Surveillance Committee (NASC) to coordinate information, advise on prevention, and encourage research; later it became responsible for overseeing the activities prescribed in the Short-Term Plan for 1987–88. The first AIDS information pamphlets were prepared and distributed in a low-key exercise which sought to educate without raising fears. Letters appeared in the Papua New Guinea press, especially after the broadcast in Australia in April 1987 of the first major television campaign, *The Grim Reaper*. Much of the public discussion focused on the potential for AIDS imported by Australians, especially homosexual men, and members of the Surveillance Committee responded with factual information (Turner 1989). The death from AIDS of a PNG national in Australia was announced and a case of HIV in Papua New Guinea, that of an expatriate, was identified in June 1987, while the first clinical case of AIDS in Papua New Guinea was reported in March 1988. AIDS had made, at least in limited fashion, a public appearance.

From the start, a major issue in the Department of Health and in public discussion concerned the relative priority to be given to AIDS as against well-established health problems, notably malaria and tuberculosis. Dr Quentin Reilly, secretary for Health during the early period, was sceptical about the need for diverting resources to AIDS and he reflected the predominant view among doctors and politicians. In 1986 Clement Malau, a young doctor in the Papua New Guinea Defence Force (PNGDF), was assigned to the Department of Health as senior specialist medical officer for communicable diseases with AIDS as one of his responsibilities, working to the assistant secretary for disease control, Dr Timothy Pyakalyia. Over the next fifteen years Malau, Pyakalyia and a venereologist, Dr Tompkins Tabua, provided continuity as central actors in AIDS policy making, though Malau was absent for extended periods for AIDS training and positions overseas. They maintained most of Papua New Guinea's contacts with international AIDS organizations, representing Papua New Guinea at global and regional meetings on AIDS.

Some of the impetus for policy development derived from ministers of Health who took an interest in AIDS. A workshop on AIDS for members of parliament was organized in April 1988, at which a former Australian minister for Health, Dr Peter Baume, was keynote speaker. Following this, Tim Ward, the Papua New Guinea minister, won adoption by the National Executive Council of a *National Policy Document on AIDS Control in Papua New Guinea* (Department of Health 1988), prepared by the NASC, which was renamed the National AIDS Committee. The *Document* laid out broad policy directions in line with GPA's guidelines for policy making, ensuring confidentiality and non-discrimination, and it addressed directly the need for the churches to collaborate with departmental messages on condoms. The National Council of Churches had begun discussing AIDS issues, as had their counterparts in Australia during 1987, and the Council was given a seat on an enlarged NASC, along with international organizations and the Department of Anthropology and Sociology at the University of Papua New Guinea. Ward was shortly thereafter replaced as minister by Robert Suckling, owner of several bars in Port Moresby, who promoted a number of initiatives on condom education through mass media. Suckling also set up an *ad hoc* parliamentary group on AIDS to provide continuing orientation for MPs, but without secretariat support, it proved short lived.

During 1989–90 a *National Medium-Term Programme for the Prevention and Control of AIDS in Papua New Guinea 1989–1995* (Department of Health 1990) was drawn up under the auspices of the Disease Control Unit of the Department of Health. The central initiatives of the program fitted with GPA's standard biomedical top-down model for medium-term programs: an epidemiological sentinel survey, expansion of education and condom promotion campaigns, upgrading of STD clinics, and expansion of training in counselling and other skills. Negotiations were undertaken with prospective international donors to fund the program's proposed budget of $US6.321 million, one third of this devoted to STD clinics. However the government was unwilling to give AIDS a high funding priority. Some components of the program were funded, notably through staffing by WHO and the EEC of specialist positions in the AIDS/STD Unit and upgrading of the Goroka STD clinic. USAID initially funded a social marketing program for condoms and several research projects through the Papua New Guinea Institute for Medical Research, but later withdrew from AIDS and other health programs in the Pacific.

In November 1990 a national workshop on AIDS in the workplace was organized to persuade government and private sector employers of the need for educating their workforce; there it was apparent that only the Ok Tedi mining project and the PNGDF had undertaken serious prevention programs. During the early 1990s the international agenda on AIDS began to absorb the lessons of African experience, as the previous decade's development was undermined by the social and economic impact of the epidemic, particularly through the loss of trained manpower and the disruption of communities. The World Bank began to focus on AIDS and the UN Development Program established an HIV and Development Program under the direction of Elizabeth Reid, who had helped shape Australia's national strategy.

The AIDS/STD Unit sought to put this new dimension of AIDS on the Papua New Guinea agenda by organizing in February 1992 its most ambitious conference, a national seminar on the social and economic impact of AIDS, strongly supported by a new minister of Health, Galeva Kwarara. Kwarara had seen an Australian documentary video, *Susie's Story*, concerning a young wife and mother dying of AIDS after infection by a drug-using partner, and he was shocked by the implications of heterosexual transmission of the virus for a country where multiple sexual partnering was increasingly commonplace. Senior ministers were persuaded to attend the conference dinner and a drama on AIDS in the village, and a number of senior officials from across government departments were introduced to the issues. The conference also launched the PNGDF's new AIDS education program, designed by the director general of PNGDF Health Services and Malau and featuring the PNGDF's own *Gumi* brand of condoms.

At this point one hundred cases of HIV infection had been identified in Papua New Guinea, the great majority of them in Port Moresby, where most testing had taken place. Initial sero-surveillance showed very low levels of prevalence among populations at risk, highest among patients at STD clinics. The National AIDS Committee estimated that there were probably between five and ten thousand cases of infection, but the prospective nature of the threat to Papua New Guinea's economy and society was still too remote to win sustained government attention and resources.

Some initiatives were taken outside government. The Seventh Day Adventist Church and the Salvation Army took AIDS seriously on an international level, and both had AIDS education and care programs within Papua New Guinea from the early 1990s. Following the first regional conference on AIDS, held in Canberra in July 1990, Australian and Papua New Guinea NGOs were in occasional contact on AIDS, but the only sustained NGO activity of any kind in Papua New Guinea at this stage was that of environmental and forest groups. However, the Papua New Guinea Institute of Medical Research, based at Goroka, began to take a role in policy development, largely through the activities of a medical anthropologist, Dr Carol Jenkins. Jenkins organized the first major survey of sexuality in Papua New Guinea in 1991, training public servants and teachers as interviewers in their home areas during the Christmas leave period. Funded by USAID, the survey drew on 423 interviews in 40 language groups. When it was published (National Sex and Reproduction Research Team and Jenkins 1994) it was met with denial by some church groups, but it provided invaluable material for culturally sensitive education programs and served as a model for research elsewhere. With funding from a variety of sources, Jenkins also organized research interventions and peer education among provincial communicators, transport workers, sex workers, police, and security staff. She and Michael Alpers, director of the Institute of Medical Research, also organized the first explicitly AIDS-focused NGO, Action for Community Health, which, after long delays, was approved in 1996 before Jenkins left Papua New Guinea for AIDS work in Bangladesh.

Early in 1993 the Department of Health proposed that a National AIDS Council be established as a separate statutory authority with its own staff and power to coordinate a full multisectoral program. A second conference on the social and economic impact of AIDS was organized in July 1993, with a higher level of participation from senior officials, to promote the need for a council and for a national federation of non-government organizations working on AIDS. Jenkins, Malau and Barry Holloway, who directed an office of advanced planning under the Wingti government, attempted to sell the proposal for the council to government, but a cabinet committee chaired by Sir Julius Chan as deputy prime minister refused to grant space in the parliamentary agenda. When Peter Barter was named minister of Health under a new Chan government in 1994, Jenkins persuaded him to resurrect the proposal, but Chan himself rejected it, stating that AIDS needed no priority as against malaria and other diseases. However John Nilkare, as minister for Provincial Affairs, was sufficiently impressed to provide Jenkins with K100,000 for research and education programs.

Despite interest on the part of successive ministers for Health, the period from 1993 was one of reduced funding, reduced staff and no political commitment to AIDS. Jenkins described the situation as of 1995:

> [P]ositions in the STD/AIDS Unit supported by international donors were no longer filled. After mid-1994 the National AIDS Committee could no longer afford to hold its meetings, no further quarterly reports on STD and HIV/AIDS were compiled and other departments lost interest. The lack of funds has affected everything except salaries, e.g., no telephones, water, postage. Lack of funds, trained personnel, political support and leadership have had a seriously negative effect on AIDS prevention efforts (Jenkins and Passey 1998, 247).

The period also saw a sharp increase in the incidence of HIV: 351 new cases of HIV infection were reported in 1997, and 642 in 1998, despite lower levels of surveillance.

During this period of government inactivity, there were shifts in the international context of AIDS policy. The Global Program on AIDS, based in the World Health Organization, was replaced in 1996 by the Joint United Nations Program on AIDS (UNAIDS) after donor governments insisted on a unified UN focus for increasingly disparate activities. UNAIDS country program advisers were appointed to many countries and theme groups were established to coordinate all UN agencies' work on AIDS. Papua New Guinea was not provided with a country program adviser, but a theme group was formed under the leadership of the WHO representative.

The Medium-Term Plan 1998–2002 and the National AIDS Council

The arrival of a new government in 1997 produced a marked change in AIDS policy. The prime minister, Bill Skate, seeking to differentiate his policies from those of his predecessor, Julius Chan, took a direct interest in the issue, as did the secretary of Health, Dr Puka Temu, supported by his minister, Ludga Mond. Legislation to establish a National AIDS Council was fast-tracked, and the prime minister issued in August 1997 a directive calling on all departments, provincial governments, NGOs, churches, donors and the private sector to collaborate in the formulation of a national strategy on HIV/AIDS. Political support opened new possibilities for developing policy and programs.

The initial proposal for a new medium-term plan (MTP) was put forward by a team of UNAIDS/AusAID consultants. They anticipated the standard six-month arrangements for medium-term plans which had been drawn up under UNAIDS guidance in many countries. This preference was reinforced by a Papua New Guinea team that visited Uganda and returned to urge that Uganda's MTP be taken as a template for Papua New Guinea. What emerged was very different, for the process of consultation was taken seriously and led to a strategic document unusual, if not unique, in its genuinely multi-sectoral focus and its central concern with social, economic and ethical issues.

Although the Department of Health provided most resources, it agreed, in an exceptionally generous moment, that the Office of National Planning and Implementation (ONPI) should serve as lead agency. Thomas Lisenia of ONPI chaired both a multi-sectoral coordinating committee and a small secretariat, which served as interim secretariat for the National AIDS Council. A position as full-time coordinator, vital to the exercise, was funded by the UN Development Program and Katherine Lepani left the National Research Institute to take this post.

Six priority areas were defined and multi-sectoral working groups were established to focus on these:

- Education, Information and Media
- Counselling, Community Care and Support
- Legal and Ethical Issues
- Social and Economic Impact
- Monitoring, Surveillance, Evaluation and Research
- Medical and Laboratory

With over eighty people drawn from all sectors, in and out of government, the working groups met separately between September and December 1997 to produce draft strategy papers on their areas; several individual members drafted concept papers, and consultative workshops were organized. Lepani attended all meetings and pulled together the working party drafts into a draft MTP.

When the National AIDS Council legislation was passed by parliament in December 1997, Skate embraced a man living with AIDS, and a woman living with AIDS spoke movingly on national television, attempting to break the political and public silence on living with AIDS. The Council and its secretariat were in place by June 1998 when the *National HIV/AIDS Medium-Term Plan 1998–2002* (Papua New Guinea 1998) was launched. Puka Temu, then secretary for Health, argued at the launch that the process by which the plan had been developed was a suitable model not only for other policy areas in his own department, but throughout government. Acknowledgment was given in the plan to the vision and direction provided by Carol Jenkins.

As these developments materialized, AusAID, which had been slowly working its way towards support for AIDS programs in the region, announced a vast increase in AIDS funding for Papua New Guinea. When Australia had been asked for support of the first MTP, a feasibility study for a major Australian project was undertaken early in 1993 (Plummer 1993) and this was followed up the next year with another mission (Moodie *et al.* 1994). In 1996 a Sexual Health and HIV/AIDS Prevention and Care Project was established, with K3.5 million, to help the Department of Health; this was the largest AIDS project until then in Papua New Guinea. Under the direction of Dr Susan Crockett the project focused on upgrading sexual health clinics and training counsellors.

Up to this time, the Australian commitment to provide primarily budget, rather than project, aid to Papua New Guinea had meant that any major AIDS funding was dependent on Papua New Guinea government priorities. With the rise of political interest in AIDS within Papua New Guinea, the Australian government indicated that it would make available much more substantial funding, and was asked by the Papua New Guinea government to channel this through its new MTP. In March 2000 Australia announced that K100 million was being provided for a National HIV/AIDS Support Project (2000–5), initially directed by Crockett.

On replacing Bill Skate as prime minister in 1999, Sir Mekere Morauta made clear that he supported the AIDS policies of his predecessor, and Lady Roslyn Morauta became prominent in support of AIDS NGOs. A number of local AIDS organizations had sprung up. Perhaps best known were the work of Sister Rose Bernard, who had organized care and counselling for people living with AIDS in the Western Highlands for a decade, and the Friends Foundation, established for similar purposes by Tessie Soi, a social worker at Port Moresby General Hospital. However, NGOs received little financial support and were, as in other sectors, looked upon with suspicion and scepticism by government officials.

Meanwhile, the incidence of HIV climbed inexorably. By 1999 AIDS was reported as the leading cause of death at Port Moresby General Hospital (*Papua New Guinea Post-Courier* 7 December 1999). By mid 2001, 3900 cases of HIV infection had been reported, still on the basis of limited testing, with 65 per cent from the National Capital District, where most testing was conducted. An estimated HIV incidence of 10,000–15,000 cases was accepted by the National AIDS Council on the advice of an expert epidemiology workshop.

Retrospective from 2005

The collapse of the initial response to AIDS in the mid 1990s meant that the new National AIDS Council Secretariat, (NACS) headed by Malau, and its AusAID Support Project (NHASP), had to start from scratch in 2000. Their approach, with the MTP as their charter, was to address all sectors and all provinces, without establishing priorities. Despite the substantial funding available, it was clear from reviews during 2002–4 that, although there were achievements, there were major difficulties, particularly in mobilizing provincial AIDS committees, NGOs and other sectors, including the Department of Health. A *National Strategic Plan of HIV/AIDS* (2004–8) was drawn up, again without priorities, and in December 2004 the government accepted a longstanding proposal that the National AIDS Council be transferred to the Department of the Prime Minister and Cabinet.

In December 2004 a further epidemiology workshop estimated a national prevalence rate of 1.7 per cent, the highest in the Pacific region and amongst the highest in Asia. At the same time a survey by the Australian Strategic Policy Institute, advising the Australian government, found that Papua New Guinea's deteriorating services and infrastructure, high crime rates, economic stagnation and corruption were symptoms of a systemic lack of capacity to provide effective government. It warned that 'the institutions of governance in PNG have weakened to the point that they might collapse under the effects of … a full-blown AIDS crisis [that] will now be very hard to avoid' (ASPI 2004, 9). In

July 2005 the head of UNAIDS, Dr Peter Piot, labelled Papua New Guinea as at greatest risk in Asia and the Pacific of an African-type of generalized epidemic: 'That's the one county, I would say I think is really getting out of hand'.

Anthropologists have repeatedly found that local understanding of HIV in Papua New Guinea is contingent on cultural beliefs and practices and that generalized prevention messages are reinterpreted in these terms (Lepani 2005; Wardlow 2002). Accommodating Papua New Guinea's exceptional cultural diversity within viable public policy has been a substantial hurdle in all domains since the dawn of colonial rule and perhaps reaches an apogee in the development of policy on AIDS.

References

Australian Strategic Policy Institute (ASPI), 2004. *Strengthening Our Neighbour: Australia and the Future of Papua New Guinea*. Canberra: Australian Strategic Policy Institute.

Ballard, J. A. 1998. The constitution of AIDS in Australia: taking 'government at a distance' seriously. In *Governing Australia: Studies in Contemporary Rationalities of Government*, ed. M. Dean and B. Hindess, 125–138. Melbourne: Cambridge University Press.

Cullen, T. 2000. Repeating Mistakes: Press Coverage of HIV/AIDS in Papua New Guinea and the South Pacific. Unpublished PhD thesis, University of Queensland.

Department of Health, Papua New Guinea. 1988. *National Policy Document on AIDS Control in Papua New Guinea*. Port Moresby: Department of Health.

Department of Health, Papua New Guinea. 1990. *National Medium-Term Programme for the Prevention and Control of AIDS in Papua New Guinea 1989–1995*. Revised edition. Port Moresby: Department of Health.

Jenkins, C. and Passey, M. 1998. Papua New Guinea. In *Sexually Transmitted Diseases in Asia and the Pacific*, ed. T. Brown *et al.*, 230–254. Armidale: Venereology Publishing.

Lepani, K. 2005. *Still in the Process of Knowing: Making Sense of HIV and AIDS in the Trobriand Islands*. Paper presented to the AIDS in Oceania Working Session, Association for Social Anthropology in Oceania Annual Meeting, Lihu'e, Hawaii.

Malau, C. 1999. The evolving AIDS epidemic: challenges and responses in Papua New Guinea. *Development Bulletin* 50: 70–71.

Malau, C. *et al.* 1994. HIV/AIDS Prevention and Control in Papua New Guinea. *AIDS* 8: S117–S124, Supplement 2.

Moodie, Rob *et al.* 1994. Unpublished review for AIDAB.

National Sex and Reproduction Research Team and Jenkins, C. 1994. *Sexual and Reproductive Knowledge and Behaviour in Papua New Guinea*. Papua New Guinea Institute of Medical Research Monograph no. 10. Goroka: Papua New Guinea Institute of Medical Research.

Papua New Guinea. 1998. *Papua New Guinea National HIV/AIDS Medium Term Plan 1998–2002*. Port Moresby.

Plummer, D. 1993. The PNG HIV/AIDS Prevention and Care Project. Unpublished report to AIDAB.

Turner, D.M. 1989. Public Discussions and AIDS in Papua New Guinea. Unpublished paper.

Wardlow, H. 2002. Public health, personal beliefs: battling HIV in Papua New Guinea. *Cultural Survival Quarterly* 26(3).

Endnotes

[1] The term AIDS is used here in relation to policy, despite the common elision of HIV/AIDS to cover HIV as virus with AIDS as a syndrome of diseases produced by deterioration of the immune system.

Index

www.ingramcontent.com/pod-product-compliance
Lightning Source LLC
Chambersburg PA
CBHW061241270326

41928CB00041B/3348